1971

This book may be kept

# FOURTEEN DAYS

A fine will be charged for each day the book is kept overtime.

| | | | |
|---|---|---|---|
| | | | |
| | | | |
| | | | |
| | | | |
| | | | |
| | | | |
| | | | |
| | | | |
| | | | |
| | | | |
| | | | |
| | | | |
| | | | |
| | | | |
| | | | |
| | | | |
| | | | |

GAYLORD 142         PRINTED IN U.S.A.

# PURITY

## A MIDDLE ENGLISH POEM

EDITED WITH INTRODUCTION, NOTES, AND GLOSSARY

BY

ROBERT J. MENNER

ARCHON BOOKS
1970

[*Yale Studies in English, Vol. 61*]

SBN: 208 00914 0
Library of Congress Catalog Card Number: 78-91187
Printed in the United States of America

# PREFACE

The publication of this edition of *Purity*, which was presented as a doctoral dissertation in 1918, was delayed for a year because of my absence on military service. Meanwhile, the text of the poem had been discussed in two articles, first by Bateson (*Modern Language Review* 13. 377-86), and later by Gollancz (*ibid.* 14. 152-62). A third important article, by Emerson (*Publications of the Modern Language Association* 34. 494-522), appeared when this edition was ready for the press. Although I have taken note of what seemed to me the most significant of the many suggestions made in these articles, I was unable, at this late date, to discuss some of them as thoroughly as I should have liked. Professor Emerson proposed several emendations that I had already adopted in the text, the most important being *teme* for *tonne* of the manuscript (655); *nomon* (I change further to *nomen*) for *no mon* (1002); and *bolle* for *bolde* (1474). In these and other cases where he has anticipated me, and in most cases where my interpretation differs from his, I have thought it advisable to leave my notes as they stood, and simply to add a reference to his article.

I have adopted the title *Purity*, instead of *Cleanness* or *Clannesse*, for the reasons given by Osgood in the preface to his edition of *The Pearl*.

This edition was undertaken at the suggestion of Professor Albert Stanburrough Cook. I wish to express my thanks to him for his helpful advice throughout the preparation of it, though I feel that I owe him an even greater debt of gratitude for his direction and encouragement of my previous studies.

A portion of the expense of printing this thesis has been borne by the English Club of Yale University, from funds placed at its disposal by the generosity of the late Mr. George E. Dimock, a graduate of Yale in the Class of 1874.

Yale University,
May, 1920.

# CONTENTS

# INTRODUCTION

## I. THE MANUSCRIPT

A small quarto volume in the British Museum, Cotton MS. Nero A x + 4 (new numbering) contains, bound between two Latin manuscripts, the unique manuscript[1] of the four poems generally attributed to the author of *Sir Gawain and the Green Knight*. *Purity,* which occupies folios 61a-86a, follows *The Pearl,* and precedes *Patience* and *Gawain.* Several crude pictures illustrate episodes in the poems. Of the two which precede *Purity,* the first represents Noah and his family in the ark, and the second shows Daniel expounding the writing on the wall to Belshazzar and the queen.

The manuscript is written in a small, sharp handwriting, which varies considerably in size, of the late fourteenth century.[2] It is in many places very difficult to read, owing partly to the paleness of the ink, which has often faded so much that passages are hardly legible, and partly to the fact that certain lines have been blotted on the pages opposite them. Often the words have been so fully printed on the opposite page that one can read them plainly with the aid of a mirror. Dr. Knott pointed out the existence and value of these 'offsets,' as he calls them, in the text of *Gawain,* where they furnish in some cases the only

---

[1] The best description of the MS. is that by Sir Frederick Madden in his edition of *Sir Gawayne* (London, 1839), pp. xlvii-l. For the history of the MS. see also Gollancz's preface to his edition of *Patience* (London, 1915).

[2] Madden, p. 301, 'reign of Richard II'; Ward, *Catalogue of Romances in the British Museum* I. 387, 'end of the fourteenth century'; Gollancz, preface to *Patience,* 'end of fourteenth or early part of fifteenth century.'

evidence for the original reading.[1]  In *Purity,* in addition to the offsets of a few letters on folios 74b and 75b, unimportant because the text is here perfectly legible, almost all the initial words in the lines of fol. 64a, ll. 217-52, have been partly impressed on fol. 63b.  Since these words on 64a are often extremely faint and hardly decipherable, the offset is, in this last case, of some slight value in establishing and confirming the readings of the text, for instance, the initial *bot* of l. 226; but here too the offset is for the most part even less distinct that the original words.[2]

The offsets are less important for the text than the additions and corrections to the manuscript by a second hand, which sometimes obscure the original reading.  In his second edition Morris noted the fact that *sorewe* of l. 778 and *broþer* of l. 924 (see notes on both these lines) were written by a later hand over the original.  But there are traces of what is probably the hand of this same corrector in a great many other words and passages.  In some cases the original scribe's letters have been merely retraced; but in others the corrector's hand is more certainly betrayed by letters of a type that the original scribe never uses.  The following letters most strikingly distinguish the corrector's hand from that of the scribe: the corrector's *a* is like a modern printed *a,* whereas the scribe's is formed by two converging upright strokes and a cross-stroke; the corrector's *e* is a curved *e* made with one stroke and usually very flat, whereas the scribe's is made sharply with two strokes; the corrector's *d* has at the top a marked curl to the right, which the scribe's lacks; the corrector uses a

---

[1] *Mod. Lang. Notes* 30. 102-8.

[2] Offsets are very frequent in *The Pearl,* where every large initial letter is visible, some very distinctly, on the opposite page.  With a mirror considerable sections may be easily read off, e. g., on folios 47a and 48b (so at least in Osgood's photographs deposited in the Yale University Library), but they are of no value, as the original is also easily legible.

Greek *s* never used by the scribe. For the sake of convenience I give here a list of those words and passages in which the writing of the scribe has been tampered with.[1] The letters which cannot be the scribe's are italicized, and it is fairly certain that the words or passages in which they occur were corrected by the same man; but in other cases, though evidence of retracing is plain, it is possible that the attempts to make the faded parts of the manuscript more legible were not all due to this corrector: 108 sw(elt); 245-52 the ends of all these lines, and possibly more, on fol. 64a have been partly retraced; 245 tow*ch*ed; 247 þe vengi*au*nce (prob. written over vengaunce); 248 make h*ad* never; 249 forþrast al þat þryve schuld; 250 (m)ercyles (and) mawgre much scheued; 251 fylþe upon folde þat þe folk used; 252 wythouten any maysterz; 257 ?ffor (and possibly more at the top of fol. 64b); 322 boskez; 323 I sch*al* w*aken;* 324 alle þat; 431 ?(was)te*d*; 778 so*rewe* (see note); 918 (foo)schip; 922 (for)sake; 923 out of; 924 *bro*þer; 928 wore, and probably a few other letters on fol. 73b; 1015 þe*r* fau*r* (see note), i*s* (inserted above line)[2]; 1664 þat w*eldes*; 1669 on*e* (added to end of line, see note).

---

[1] According to Dr. Knott (*Mod. Lang. Notes* 30. 108), the words in the second hand, which appear in *Gaw.* 43, 81, etc., are written in a dark brown ink. This can naturally not be seen in my rotographs, and I have no means of determining whether the same corrector is at work in both poems. An examination of the manuscript would probably settle this, and would also, if the same difference in ink appears in *Purity,* lead to a more precise delimitation of retraced passages than I am able to give.

[2] Four other instances of insertions above the line occur, *on,* 432; *synne,* 520; *wont,* 739; the *el* of *Daniel,* 1756; but the writing is in each case so small that it is impossible to tell whether or not it is the scribe's. Omissions were undoubtedly made in each case, and I think that, with the exception of *synne,* 520, all these insertions are correct, whether by the scribe or not. Even *is* of 1015, which is almost certainly inserted by the second hand, because of the peculiar *s,* seems indispensable.

The scribe's own handwriting, even where there is no
question of revision, offers difficulties. In addition to frequent repetitions and omissions due to carelessness, it is
very hard to distinguish some of his letters: there is
usually no difference between *u* and *n;* a *t* whose cross-
stroke is careless frequently looks like a *c; bo,* because the
two letters are combined, cannot be distinguished from *lo;*
nor *ha* from *la* for the same reason, if the second stroke
of the *h* is not distinct below the line.

In printing the text, peculiarities of the manuscript in
the division of words and capitalization have been disregarded.[1] *I* and *j, u* and *v* have been normalized, and *ȝ,*
when it was written for *z,* so printed. The ordinary abbreviations for *and, with, þou, þat, n, -e,*[2] *-er, -es, -us, -(u)r,*[3]

----

[1] For the scribe's peculiarities in the division of words, see Osgood,
*The Pearl,* p. x, n. 1.

[2] It is difficult to determine when the strokes through long letters
are intended for abbreviations and when they are mere flourishes.
I have followed Morris in considering a stroke starting from the
first stroke of *h* and with a decided upward crook an abbreviation
for *e* in *bilooghe,* 116; *innoghe,* 297, 669, 1303; *loghe,* 366; also
*wyrle,* 475. But there is frequently a straight stroke from a long
letter which is certainly a mere flourish, since in some cases, e. g.,
*ho* 1126, an *e* would be out of the question. Only one of these, *kyth,*
912, is noted by Morris and expanded to *kythe,* but the stroke here
resembles that in the words below, and not at all the stroke with
the crook which I have considered an abbreviation. The following
words have this meaningless flourish: after *b* in *be,* 123, 173;
*brentest,* 379; *bryngeȝ,* 636; *biseged,* 1180; after *h* in *kyth,* 912;
*ho,* 1126; *heȝed,* 1584; after *l* in *leve,* 401, 1114; *whyl,* 1493.

[3] The curl above *o,* which previous editors of poems of this manuscript expanded consistently *ur,* was apparently used by the scribe
more generally to represent simply an *r* (cf. Cook, *Mod. Phil.*
6. 199 on the rhymes of *The Pearl*). I have regularly expanded the
abbreviation *r,* since such a word as *corte* never has *ur* when it
is actually written out (191, 1109, 1530, 1562, 1751) and *yor* (once
expanded *yor,* 715) is elsewhere consistently written *yõ* (94²,
618, 620, 801). The expansion to *r,* not *ur,* is further justified by
the occurrence of the abbreviation in such words as *for,* 756,

etc., have been expanded without italics, and, except for special cases, and for those words or letters which I have expanded differently from previous editors, without comment.

## II. THE WORKS OF THE AUTHOR OF PURITY

Scholars have generally agreed in attributing to the author of *Purity* the other three poems found in the same manuscript[1]: *Patience, The Pearl,* and *Sir Gawain and the Green Knight.* Attempts have been made to add several other poems to this group, and particularly to identify the author of *Gawain* with the author of the *Pistill of Susan,* the much-discussed Huchown of the Awle Ryale,[2] to whom, at one time or another, have been assigned almost all the anonymous poems of the Middle English alliterative school. At present there is no valuable evidence for the attribution to the Gawain-poet of any other poems than the four mentioned above, and possibly the saint's legend called *Erken-*

*forferde*, 560, *þor*, 1384, *worschyp*, 1127 (written out without *u* in 545, 651, 1120, 1592, 1616, 1802). In the following few cases, however, I have expanded *ur*, because other instances of the words written out with *ur* occurred: *bour*, 322, 1075, 1126 (written out *bour* 129), *fourre*, 1244 (written out *fowre*, 540), *tour*, 216, 1189 (written out *toures*, 1383).

[1] Morris, *Sir Gawayn and the Green Knight* (1864), title-page; Trautmann, *Über Verfasser und Entstehungszeit einiger Alliterierender Gedichte* (1876), pp. 25-33, and *Angl.* I. 118 ff.; Ten Brink, *Geschichte der Englischen Litteratur* (1877) I. 420 ff.; M. C. Thomas, *Sir Gawayne and the Green Knight* (1883), pp. 1-12; Knigge, *Die Sprache des Dichters von Sir Gawain and the Green Knight* (1885), pp. 1-14. Practically all those who have made special investigations of, or edited any of these poems, e. g., Fuhrmann, Gollancz, C. F. Brown, Osgood, Bateson, have accepted the opinion and arguments of the writers just mentioned.

[2] Neilson, *'Huchown of the Awle Ryale,' the Alliterative Poet.* Glasgow, 1902.

*wald*,[1] which was either written by the Gawain-poet or by some one who was closely imitating his style. The unjustified reliance of some of the earlier investigators on similarities of vocabulary and phraseology, together with the accumulation of evidence tending to disprove the common authorship of many alliterative poems once connected, has even aroused a certain amount of skepticism concerning the common authorship of the four traditionally assigned to the poet of *Purity*.[2] *Gawain*, in particular, has been singled out by Schofield[3] as unlikely to have been written by the poet of *Purity, Patience,* and *The Pearl*. The two homilies, *Purity* and *Patience,* based on the same text in Matthew, are so precisely similar in general development and in numerous details[4] that, in spite of their difference in length, they may naturally be regarded as sister-poems. *The Pearl* is linked to these homilies,[5] not only by its profound religious feeling and its moral earnestness, but by such striking relations of detail as the praise of the pearl (*Pur.* 1117-28), and the repeated mention of the Beatific Vision (see note on l. 25). That a poet of such religious fervor should have also written the best of the Middle English romances is indeed matter for comment.

Nevertheless the evidence that *Purity* and *Gawain* were

[1] Trautmann (*Angl. Anz.* 5. 23-5) and Knigge (pp. 4-8) tried to show that *Erkenwald* belonged to the Gawain-poet, because of similarities in vocabulary, phraseology, and style; C. F. Brown (*Publ. Mod. Lang. Ass.* 19. 126, n. 2) thinks that the abundance of legendary matter in *Erkenwald* is an objection to the theory of common authorship. The subject needs further investigation.

[2] Wells' statement (*Manual of the Writings in Middle English,* p. 578) that 'the evidence for authorship by one writer is very questionable,' is extreme.

[3] *Publ. Mod. Lang. Ass.* 24. 668, n. 1.

[4] These are given in their proper places in the Notes. Cf. Bateson, *Patience* (2d ed., Manchester, 1918), pp. xxi-ii.

[5] On the authorship of *The Pearl,* see especially Trautmann, *Angl.* I. 118-20.

written by one and the same man seems about as conclusive as any indirect evidence can be. The fact that some unreliable tests have been used in proof of the unity of authorship has had the unfortunate result of casting suspicion on the value of all the tests. In order to present as clearly as possible the arguments for common authorship that may still be considered valid in the light of our increased knowledge concerning all the alliterative poems, I shall sum up the most important evidence adduced by the earlier students of this group of poems, adding other evidence of common authorship which I believe should not be disregarded. This is all the more necessary since the next section, in which the relation of the poet to the rest of the alliterative group is discussed, will make plain the fallibility of some of the tests employed by Trautmann.

### 1. *Vocabulary.*

Trautmann (*Über Verfasser,* pp. 26-8) gave a list of 115 words common to *Gawain* and the other poems in the manuscript, and not found in *William of Palerne* or the *Alexander* fragments A and B. Kullnick[1] found that 30 words (15%) in *Gawain* occurred nowhere but in the other poems of this same manuscript. An examination of *NED.* reduces his list to about 20, although he has omitted a few others, for example, *tevel(yng)*, owing to the inexactness of the glossaries. As may be seen from the large number of words common to the Gawain-group and *The Wars of Alexander* (*Alex. C.*),[2] the test of vocabulary, though not altogether negligible, really indicates only a common dialect or proximity of dialectal provenience.

### 2. *Alliteration.*

Trautmann attached too much importance to his tests by

---

[1] *Studien über den Wortschatz in Sir Gawayne and the Grene Knyȝt* (Berlin, 1902), p. 53.
[2] Cf. p. xxiv.

means of alliteration,[1] since his investigations covered too
small a number of lines, and many characteristics which he
considered distinctive are found in other alliterative poems.
The most important peculiarity is the alliteration of *expoun*
with words beginning with *sp*.[2]  In addition, the consistent
agreement of the four poems in the manner of using alliteration is noteworthy, as Schumacher's study of all the poems
of the alliterative school shows.  One may note particularly
the practice of alliterating unstressed syllables,[3] and the
freedom from the tendency of the more pedantic poets to
rhyme only like vowels.[4]

### 3.  *Phraseology and Similar Passages.*

Trautmann's list of similar phrases in *Gawain* and the
other poems of the group is very meagre, and also misleading, since it includes a considerable number of phrases
which are mere alliterative commonplaces, such as 'busk
to bed,' 'draw adreȝ,' 'kever comfort.'  But there are
other parallels between *Purity* and *Gawain,* unnoticed by
Trautmann; these are so many in number, and often
so peculiar in kind, that they seem to me to constitute
indubitable proof of common authorship.  We do not
find, to be sure, phrases of any length occurring in exactly
the same form in the two poems, for it is characteristic of
the poet never to repeat himself exactly, even within the
limits of a single poem.  Unlike most of his fellow-craftsmen in alliterative poetry—for example, the author of *The
Destruction of Troy*—he is careful to change slightly any
peculiar alliterative combination which he repeats.  The

---

[1] See Miss Thomas' criticism, *Sir Gawayne,* pp. 6-7.
[2] Fischer, *Die Stabende Langzeile in den Werken des Gawaindichters* (Bonn, 1901), pp. 41-2; Schumacher, *Studien über den
Stabreim in der Mittelenglischen Alliterationsdichtung* (Bonn, 1914),
pp. 120-1.
[3] Schumacher, pp. 26-8.
[4] Schumacher, p. 56.

parallel passages vary in value as evidence: some are alliterative combinations which might have occurred to different poets, although I have tried to exclude all those which were actually used by other alliterative poets; some are valuable as indicative of a tendency to use the same unusual word, expression, or figure of speech, under similar circumstances; and some are inexplicable except as reminiscences of phraseology previously used (for examples of these last, see the section on Date, pp. xxxiii-vi). It is unnecessary to repeat here the many striking parallel passages that are given in the notes.[1] But it should be remembered that they include not only unusual alliterative combinations, such as *wonde wope* (*Pur.* 855; *Gaw.* 488), *troched toures* (*Pur.* 1383; *Gaw.* 795), and *taken in* (*þe*) *teche* (*Pur.* 943; *Gaw.* 2488), but also such a phrase as (*al*) *þat berez lyf* (*Pur.* 333; *Gaw.* 1229), which is found nowhere else in the alliterative poetry, and rarely elsewhere. I add the following parallels unrecorded in the notes:

|  | *Purity* |  | *Gawain* |
|---|---|---|---|
| 115 | þe derrest at þe hyӡe dese (cf. 1399). | 445 | þe derrest on þe dece (cf. 75). |
| 97 | laytez ӡet ferre (end of line). | 411 | layt no fyrre (end of line). |
| 544 | In devoydynge þe vylanye. | 634 | voyded of vche vylany. |
| 749 | And he hit gayn þynkez. | 1241 | gayn hit me þynkkeӡ. |
| 854 | And bowez forth fro þe bench. | 344 | Bid me boӡe fro þis benche. |
| 1089 | And ӡif clanly he þenne com, ful cortays þerafter. | 653 | His clannes & his cortaysye. |

[1] The following parallels are cited in the notes: *Pur.* 10, *Gaw.* 251; *Pur.* 43, *Gaw.* 2343; *Pur.* 114, *Gaw.* 73; *Pur.* 333, *Gaw.* 1229; *Pur.* 391, *Gaw.* 1152; *Pur.* 484, *Gaw.* 929; *Pur.* 521, *Gaw.* 1106, 1387; *Pur.* 599, *Gaw.* 1463; *Pur.* 706, *Gaw.* 1659; *Pur.* 735, *Gaw.* 1811; *Pur.* 805, *Gaw.* 1836; *Pur.* 832, *Gaw.* 1848; *Pur.* 855, *Gaw.* 488; *Pur.* 943, *Gaw.* 2488; *Pur.* 1376, *Gaw.* 58; *Pur.* 1383, *Gaw.* 795; *Pur.* 1408, *Gaw.* 802; *Pur.* 1459, *Gaw.* 790.

|          | *Purity*                         |       | *Gawain*                          |
|----------|----------------------------------|-------|-----------------------------------|
| 1118     | þaȝ hym not derrest be demed to dele for penies. | 78–9  | þe best gemmes, Þat myȝt be preued of prys wyth penyes to bye. |
| 1244     | þe welgest fourre.               | 2101  | þe best fowre.                    |
| 1420     | So faste þay weȝed to hym wyne.  Cf. 1508, and 1716 wale wyne. | 1403  | Wyȝeȝ þe wale wyn weȝed to hem oft. |

The following phrases pointed out by Trautmann (pp. 28-9) should be added:

|          |                                  |       |                                   |
|----------|----------------------------------|-------|-----------------------------------|
| 1065     | If þou wyl dele drwrye.           | 2449  | for ho hatȝ dalt drwry.           |
| 273      | Þose wern men meþelez.           | 2106  | For he is a mon methles.          |
| *Pat.* 489. | lansed (Gollancz, laused) a speche. | 2124  | & lance neuer tale.               |

### 4.  *Style.*

The test by means of stylistic mannerisms is more difficult to apply to the Gawain-poet, for the simple reason that he is too good an artist to clutter his lines with formal or meaningless tags. The frequent repetition of the same or similar second half-lines is so marked a characteristic of *William of Palerne, Morte Arthur,* and *The Destruction of Troy* that a comparison of the favorite formal phrases used in each makes diversity of authorship of such poems absolutely certain. The employment and the repetition of such conventional tags is so frequent in most poets of the alliterative school, that their very absence in the poems of the Gawain-group might be considered an indication of common authorship.

One stylistic trick of the Gawain-poet, however, is so peculiar that Knigge[1] rightly called attention to it as dis-

---

[1] *Die Sprache,* p. 6. Knigge uses it as an argument for considering *Erkenwald* one of the group, but his only example is the phrase 'þe prince þat paradis weldes' (195), and this may possibly have been taken over from the Gawain-poet by the author of *Erkenwald,* just as it was by the author of *Death and Life* (see p. xxvi, and

tinctive. It is the poet's habit of paraphrasing 'God' or 'Lord' by means of a relative clause, either with the pronoun 'he that . . .' or with some such common word for 'man' as *wyȝ, tolke,* as in *Pur.* 5, 'þe Wyȝ þat wroȝt alle þinges.' In the entire body of alliterative poetry no such expressions can be found outside the Gawain-poet, with the exception of two phrases which are plainly imitated from him.[1] The examples given below are divided into groups, in order to bring out the striking similarities of phraseology[2]; those noted by Trautmann are indicated by (T.) and those given by Knigge by (K.):

(a) *Pur.*   5   þe Wyȝ þat wroȝt alle þinges. (K.)
          280   þe Wyȝ þat al wroȝt.
     *Pat.*  111   þat Wyȝ þat al þe world planted. (K.)
          206   þat Wyȝe I worchyp, iwysse, þat wroȝt alle þynges.
     *Gaw.* 2441–2          þe Wyȝe hit yow ȝelde,
                    þat vp-haldeȝ þe heuen . . .
(b) *Pur.* 552   þe Soverayn þat syttez so hyȝe. (T., K.)
     *Pat.* 261   þat Syre þat syttes so hiȝe. (K.) Cf. *Pat.* 93.
     *Gaw.* 256   he þat on hyȝe syttes. (T., K.)
          2441–2   þe Wyȝe . . . þat vp-haldeȝ þe heuen, & on
                hyȝ sitteȝ.

196 n., where the slight variation of this phrase in *Winner and Waster* is also cited).

[1] Cf. p. xvi, n. 1 for the one phrase, and p. xxvi (*Alex. C.* 4518) for the other.

[2] Naturally the examples are more numerous in the Biblical paraphrases than in *Gawain*. References to God are, of course, common in all the alliterative romances, but though they employ commonly such simple expressions as 'bi him þat vs wrouȝt,' *Wm. of Palerne* 3133; 'he þat vs bouȝt,' *ibid.* 5004; 'Crist þat al weldes,' *ibid.* 3753, they nowhere employ such elaborate periphrases as these that are characteristic of the Gawain-poet. The closest parallels that I have been able to find (with the exception of those in *Alex. C.,* for which see p. 28) are such examples as 'his lufe, that heghe in heuen sittez,' *Morte Arthur* 1261, which slightly resembles the examples in (b), and a few other periphrases in *Morte Arthur* (ll. 1303, 2196, 2319), not important enough to quote here.

(c) *Pur.* 212 þat Lorde þat þe lyft made. (T.)
    1493 þe Lorde þat þe lyfte ȝemes. Cf. Lorde of þe
         lyfte, 435, 1356, 1448. (T.)
  *Gaw.* 1256 þat ilk Lorde þat þe lyfte haldeȝ.
(d) *Pur.* 510–1 to hym even þat al spedez and spyllez.
  *Gaw.* 1292 he þat spedeȝ vche spech.
(e) *Pur.* 31 he þat flemes uch fylþe fer fro his hert.
  " 1340 hym þat in heven wonies. Cf. 1807.
  " 1528 hym þat alle goudes gives. Cf. 1598, 1627.
  *Pat.* 176 he þat rules þe rak.
  *Gaw.* 2410 & he ȝelde hit ȝow ȝare, þat ȝarkkes al menskes.[1]

Under the heading of style may be added what is really a syntactical peculiarity hitherto unnoticed, and not found, I believe, outside the works of the Gawain-poet in any of the alliterative poems except the late *Death and Life*, whose author is in this as in other respects plainly imitating the poet of *Purity*. This is the use of an absolute construction attached to the sentence by means of *and*, somewhat as in modern Irish:

*Pur.* 1219 And he þe faynest freke þat he his fo hade. Cf. 1573.
*Gaw.* 53 & ho þe comlokest kyng þat þe court haldes.
*Gaw.* 1826 & ho sore þat he forsoke.

Finally, under this head may be included the argument brought forward by Miss Thomas,[2] based on the poet's mannerism of grouping similes in clusters of two or more. The validity of this test seems to me indisputable. In *The*

---

[1] For the sake of completeness I add a list of lines from *Pat.* and *Pur.* only, containing more similar expressions: *Pur.* 17, 195, 498, 644, 748; *Pat.* 129, 225. Cf. also such a phrase as 'welder of wyt' (*Pat.* 129) with 'worcher of þis worlde' (*Pur.* 1501), and the peculiar expression 'so gaynlych a God' (*Pur.* 728), which recurs in 'gaynlych God' (*Pat.* 83).

[2] *Sir Gawayne*, p. 12. Another point made by Miss Thomas (pp. 10–1) may be mentioned here, although it does not apply particularly to *Purity*: the fact that in *Patience, The Pearl*, and *Gawain*, is employed the device of closing the poem with approximately the same words with which it is begun.

*Pearl* 15 out of 35 comparisons occur in groups; in *Purity* 14 out of 24; in *Patience* 3 out of 7; in *Gawain* 6 out of 19.

Resemblances so minute and peculiarities so distinctive as these cannot be explained in any other way than by assuming that the author of *Purity, Patience,* and *The Pearl* also wrote *Sir Gawain and the Green Knight,* different in kind though it be. And it must be remembered that there is no good reason why this particular homilist should not have been at the same time a great writer of romance.[1] The preacher could not altogether hide himself in the romancer. Ten Brink says of *Gawain,*[2] 'all this art is in the service of moral ideas. It may be objected that our poet obtrudes the *Hæc fabula docet* altogether too plainly.' And conversely, the brilliance of coloring, the vivid descriptions of nature, and the picturesque and dramatic presentation of life, appear not only in the romance, but in the homilies. Jonah's adventurous voyage and the splendid scene of Belshazzar's banquet are related, to be sure, for the purpose of commending virtue, but seldom has a homilist enforced his moral by such excellent story-telling.

## III. THE ALLITERATIVE SCHOOL AND THE POET OF PURITY

The author of *Purity* is only one of many poets who are found writing alliterative verse in the latter half of the fourteenth century. The earliest poems of this new alliterative school,[3] the two shorter *Alexander* fragments, *Joseph of Arimathie,* and *William of Palerne,* appear in the

---

[1] Some of the ideas common to *Gawain* and *Purity* will be touched on in the sections of the Introduction entitled Date and Literary Art. Cf. also Bateson, *Patience,* pp. xxii-iii.

[2] *Early Engl. Lit.* I. 347.

[3] On Middle English works in long alliterative lines, see Wells' *Manual,* pp. 240-1, and *passim.*

West Midland about the year 1350, three hundred years after the last of the Old English alliterative poems. In spite of this blank of three centuries after the Norman Conquest, the alliterative poetry of the Middle English period can hardly be considered a revival of an obsolete form of verse, a deliberate attempt to imitate directly the alliterative line of Old English poetry.[1] For though the principles of the alliterative verse of the later school are still fundamentally the same as in Old English poetry, the differences in the employment of the various types of line and in the general structure[2] are too great to be explicable in any other way than by the assumption of the continued use of the long alliterative line, and its gradual transformation in that period from which no examples have come down to us. Alliteration itself, to be sure, was common in this period, not only in other forms of verse, such as that of Layamon and the lyrics of MS. Harley 2253 (c. 1310), but also in religious prose. Some slight evidence that the long alliterative line was employed, at least in popular verse, exists in two fragmentary prophecies, the text of which is very corrupt; these form the only connecting links in the long interregnum in the tradition of alliterative verse.[3]

The relations of the Middle English alliterative poems to one another, a matter obscure enough in itself, has been unnecessarily complicated and confused by the reckless assignment to a single poet of all those poems which have a number of alliterative phrases in common. Such an easy method, partly excusable in the early days when many of the alliterative poems had not been edited or investigated, is still persisted in by a few writers whose patriotism

[1] Cf. p. xlii.

[2] The best discussion of the development of the Middle English alliterative line from the Old English is Deutschbein's *Zur Entwicklung des Englischen Alliterationsverses*, Halle, 1902.

[3] Luick, in Paul's *Grundriss der Germanischen Philologie*, 2d ed., 2. 2. 160.

transcends their appreciation of facts. Similarities in the alliterative poems may be due (1) to the common use of a traditional stock of alliterative phrases, (2) to the imitation of one alliterative poet by another, a possibility that must be given particular attention, because the sudden renewal of interest in a form of verse too much neglected indicates the likelihood of a kind of literary contagion, and the rise of a 'school' of poets, and (3) to common authorship. The frequent disagreement of scholars and other writers about the authorship of many of the most important alliterative poems of the period gives rise to the mistaken impression that the alliterative poetry is a vast chaos of works so similar in style and conception that nothing definite can ever be decided about the composition or relations of any of them. This is not true. The gay but rather thin prettiness of *William of Palerne* is utterly different from the wealth of details chronicled in the smooth and even verse of *Morte Arthur,* and the style of neither of these poems is in any way comparable to the vigorous freshness of the lines of the Gawain-poet. And he, in turn, is as easily distinguished from the author (or must we say authors?) of *Piers Plowman* as Chaucer from Gower. But if there are striking differences in the style of the poets of the alliterative school, there are also striking resemblances in details which make it possible to distinguish within the group as a whole certain smaller groups in which the poems stand in more or less close relationship. It is important, then, to determine what little we can concerning the relations of the Gawain-poet to the other Middle English poets who used the same form of verse.

In the first place, there is no indication that the author of *Purity* was familiar with any of the three earliest alliterative poems in Middle English, the *Alexander* fragments A and B, *William of Palerne,* and *Joseph of Arimathie.* Beyond a few common alliterative phrases, there is nothing to show any connection between them and the works of the

Gawain-poet. With certain of the later poems *Purity* has more in common; some of the more striking resemblances to *Morte Arthur*,[1] *The Destruction of Troy*,[2] and *The Sege of Jerusalem*,[3] are mentioned in the notes. But, in general, these resemblances, too marked to be traceable to similar dialects or common poetic tradition, are insufficient actually to prove direct borrowing on either side, though one may strongly suspect it. That the relationship, whether direct or indirect, between these poems and *Purity* is closer than that between such a poem as *William of Palerne* and *Purity* is certain, but to define it further is difficult until the dates of all these poems shall have been more definitely determined. That all of them, *Gawain* included, were written by different authors has now been established beyond doubt.[4] Yet it is plain from the numerous parallels between *Morte Arthur* and *The Destruction of Troy* that there is some intimate connection between them, as is sufficiently evident from a comparison of the similar passages pointed out in Panton and Donaldson's edition of the latter poem.[5] Still

[1] See notes on ll. 838, 1411, 1452, 1689, and cf. *Pur.* 269-72 and *Morte Arthur* 2111.

[2] See notes on ll. 838, 1193, 1426, 1777, and cf. *Pur.* 1456, *Destr. Troy* 3169; *Pur.* 239, *Destr. Troy* 634, 11745.

[3] See notes on ll. 473, 867, 1456, and cf. *Pur.* 1413, *Sege* 849, 1174; and esp. *Pur.* 1423, *Sege* 854. It seems to me very likely that the author of the *Sege* was acquainted both with *Morte Arthur* and with the Gawain-poet.

[4] Trautmann, *Angl.* I. 120 ff.; Reicke, *Untersuchungen über den Stil der Mittelenglischen Alliterierenden Gedichte Morte Arthur, The Destruction of Troy, The Wars of Alexander, The Siege of Jerusalem, Sir Gawayn and the Green Knight* (Königsberg, 1906); and MacCracken's summary of the Huchown controversy, *Publ. Mod. Lang. Ass.* 25. 507-34.

[5] *EETS.* 39 and 56; cf. Neilson, *Huchown*, pp. 53-8. The resemblances between the two poems misled the editors (Preface, pp. xvii ff.) into believing that they were both by one poet. Brandes (*Engl. Stud.* 8. 410) also defended this view, in spite of Trautmann's refutation (*Angl.* I. 126-7), but this possibility was disposed

another intersecting group is formed by *Morte Arthur, The Awntyrs of Arthure,* and Huchown's *Pistell of Susan.* Since there are cogent reasons for refusing to attribute the first two of these poems to Huchown, the similarities should probably be explained as due to imitation or unconscious borrowing.[1] With *The Awntyrs of Arthure* the circle of relationship comes round once more to the Gawain-poet, since it is possible that the author of the *Awntyrs* was imitating *Gawain* in his hunting-scene.[2] Even more certain is some kind of relationship[3] between the Gawain-poet and the two poems, perhaps by the same author,[4] *The Parlement of the Three Ages* and *Winner and Waster,* but this is a matter which needs further investigation.

Of the longer poems of the alliterative school, it is *The Wars of Alexander (Alex. C.),* however, which bears the most marked resemblance in vocabulary and phraseology to the works of the Gawain-poet. Bradley was the first to take note of this connection, and suggested that it was to be explained by identity of authorship.[5] But this explanation was completely refuted by Henneman,[6] who showed that there were irreconcilable differences in the dialect, which is demonstrably more Northern in *The Wars,* since it

of beyond all doubt by Reicke's dissertation (see above) ; cf. also MacCracken, pp. 528-9.

[1] Cf. Lübke, *The Awntyrs of Arthur at the Tarn-Wathelan* (Berlin, 1883), pp. 30 ff.; Reicke, p. 6. MacCracken, who argues forcibly against Huchown's authorship, nevertheless dismisses altogether too summarily (p. 528) the resemblances pointed out by Amours (*Scottish Alliterative Poems: Scott. Text. Soc. 27.* lx-lxv).

[2] Amours, pp. 332 ff.

[3] Cf. Gollancz's preface to his separate edition of *The Parlement of the Three Ages* (London, 1915), and Neilson, *Huchown,* pp. 71-3.

[4] Gollancz, who edited both poems for the Roxburghe Club, 1897, believes so; but Bradley (*Athen.,* 1903, I. 658) thinks *The Parlement* may be imitative of *Winner and Waster.*

[5] *Academy,* Jan. 14, 1888.

[6] *Untersuchungen über das Mittelenglische Gedicht 'Wars of Alexander'* (Berlin, 1889), pp. 30-6.

contains many Northern words not used by the Gawain-
poet; in metrical usage, where the most obvious among
many differences is the practice of running the same alliteration through a number of lines in *The Wars;* and finally in
style[1] and general literary merit, not to mention the late
date generally assigned to *The Wars of Alexander.* The
fact that many very unusual words are common to the
Gawain-poet and *The Wars*[2] may well be explained by
assuming that the two poets wrote in neighboring dialects.
*The Wars,* it should be noted, has many words in common
with *Morte Arthur* and *The Destruction of Troy* which
are not used by the author of *Gawain,*[3] and its dialect is
therefore in all probability geographically intermediate
between that of *Morte Arthur* and *Gawain.*

But there are other similarities between *The Wars* and
the works of the Gawain-poet[4] which cannot, I think, be
explained either by common alliterative tradition or by
dialectal proximity. The most striking of these is the only
one mentioned by Bradley, whose comment I quote: 'In
the "Wars of Alexander," l. 1154, the reading of the
Ashmole MS. is—

þe pure populande hurle. passis it umbi.

In his note to the passage, the editor says that "Hurle is
shown by the alliteration to be an error, for *purle* or *perle*
(as in Dublin MS.)." He has apparently overlooked the
fact that the poem called "Patience" has the same peculiar
phrase, and in the form which he condemns as incorrect.
In l. 319 the poet makes the prophet Jonah say

þe pure poplande hourle playes on my heued.

The law of the alliterative verse does not require us to adopt
the reading of the Dublin MS., as three stave-rimes are a

[1] Cf. Reicke, pp. 32-3, 35, and *passim.*
[2] Kullnick, p. 53.
[3] Henneman, p. 31.
[4] Cf. Neilson, p. 73, for parallels between *Gaw.* and *The Wars.*

sufficient number for a line. There are often four, but this is not at all imperative. The line immediately preceding that quoted from the "Alexander" contains a non-alliterating substantive as the last word of the first hemistich:

> þe Wawis of þe Wild *see*. apon the wallis betis.

I therefore believe that *hurle* is the true reading, and that the *perle* of the Dublin MS. is a corruption due to the wish to complete the alliteration.'

The fact that such a singular and otherwise unexampled phrase occurs in these two poems, since it cannot be explained, as Bradley assumed, by common authorship, must be due to borrowing from one by the other. I mention here, besides the passages quoted in the notes,[1] some of which are very remarkable, a few other important similarities between *Purity* and *The Wars of Alexander,* which corroborate the assumption of imitation:

*Pur.* 952 þunder-þrast. *Alex.* 554 thonere thrastis.
(These are the only examples of this poetic expression cited by *NED.* s. v. *threst.*)

| | |
|---|---|
| *Pur.* 1046 As any dom my3t device of dayntyez oute. | *Alex.* 5297 It ware a daynte to deme for any duke oute. |
| *Pur.* 1135 Sulp no more þenne in synne þy saule þerafter (cf. 15, 550). | *Alex.* 4292 Þat is to say, all þe syn at solp may þe saule.[2] |
| *Pur.* 1322 As conqueror of uche a cost. | *Alex.* 1843 þe conquirour of ilka cost.[3] |
| *Pur.* 1455 For to compas and kest. | *Alex.* 415 How he my3t compas & kast. |
| *Pur.* 1626 Of sapyence þi sawle ful. | *Alex.* 3725 3oure saule sa ful of sapient. |

[1] See notes on ll. 1, 473, 665, 1209, 1402. *Alex.* 1393 must certainly be explained as a borrowing from *Pur.* 665.

[2] The resemblance here is the more striking if we compare the way in which the author of *Alex. B.* (335-6) paraphrased this same passage: 'alle manir þingus þat mihte vs soile wiþ sinne.'

[3] None of the alliterative combinations here given are to be found in Fuhrmann's study, nor have I included any that I could find elsewhere.

Finally, *Alex.* 4518, 'þat hathill at on hiȝe sittis,' is almost certainly imitated from the Gawain-poet, with whom, as we have seen, such periphrases for God are characteristic and distinctive. This is a plain indication that the author of *The Wars* is the borrower, a relationship that the late date[1] of *The Wars,* which there is no good reason for doubting, would in any case require.

The most obvious case of imitation of the Gawain-poet is that in *Death and Life.* Unmistakable evidences of the influence of *Piers Plowman* on *Death and Life,* especially in the treatment of the allegory, were long ago pointed out by Skeat.[2] That the poet of *Death and Life* was also familiar with *Purity,* and indebted to its author for a number of phrases, may be seen from the lines cited in the notes.[3] In addition to these proofs of borrowing from the Gawain-poet, the dependence of *Death and Life* is patent from the use of the peculiar absolute construction which was characteristic of the former.[4] This appears in the two lines:

86 & shee the most gracyous groome that on the ground longed
157 & shee the ffoulest ffreake that formed was euer.

This construction occurs nowhere, I believe, in the whole range of alliterative verse, except in these two poets.

It may be stated with certainty, then, that the works of the poet of *Purity,* though preserved to us in only one manuscript, were known and admired by his fellow-craftsmen in the composition of alliterative verse. And there is a satisfaction in realizing that the authors of *Death and*

[1] Wells (p. 103) says 'of date 1400-1450 or about 1450.'

[2] In the introduction to *Death and Life* in Hales and Furnivall, *Bishop Percy's Folio Manuscript* 3. 49-55. Cf. Hanford and Steadman, *Death and Life* (*North Carolina Studies in Philology* 15. 246-8).

[3] See notes on ll. 195, 223, 242, 521, 1267. *Pat.* 32 is reflected in *Death and Life* 107: 'Dame Mirth, & Dame Meekenes & Dame Mercy the hynd.'

[4] Cf. p. xvii.

*Life* and the pretentious *Wars of Alexander,* and probably others,[1] recognized in this poet, as we do to-day, a skilled artist in a difficult form of verse, and a master of poetic expression.

## IV. DATE

The works of the author of *Purity* are vaguely assigned to the last half, generally the last forty years, of the fourteenth century. Morris' final judgment placed the poems about 1360[2]; Trautmann thought that 1370 or 1380 would be more probable[3]; Ten Brink believed that the poet wrote in the sixties or seventies.[4] But apart from the evidences of the manuscript (c. 1400)[5] and the language,[6] little positive evidence has been adduced for the more precise dating of the poems within the period 1360-1400. The attempts to date *Gawain* by means of a possible connection with the Order of the Garter[7] are worthless, as this connection now

---

[1] For the probable influence of the Gawain-poet on *Piers Plowman,* see pp. xxix ff. Cf. Gollancz (*Camb. Hist.* I. 373): 'So far as we can judge from these extant poems, the most gifted poet of the school was the author of *Sir Gawayne and the Grene Knight:* he may well have been regarded as the master, and his influence on more northern poets, and on alliterative poetry generally, may explain in part, but not wholly, the parallel passages which link his work with that of other poets of the school, who used the same formulae, the same phrases and, at times, repeated whole lines, much in the same way as poets of the Chaucerian school spoke the language of their master.'

[2] *Specimens of Early English* (1867), p. 207.

[4] *Über Verf.,* p. 32.

[4] *Early Engl. Lit.* I. 336.

[5] Cf. p. vi.

[6] Fick, *Zum Mittelenglischen Gedicht von der Perle* (Kiel, 1885), p. 3.

[7] Gollancz (ed. *Pearl,* p. xlii) suggests 1360, certainly later than 1345, the probable date of foundation of the Order; cf. Schofield, *English Literature from the Norman Conquest to Chaucer* (1906), pp. 215, 217. Isaac Jackson (*Angl.* 37. 395-6) dates precisely 1362, when Lionel became Duke of Clarence.

appears extremely improbable.[1] If *The Pearl,* as seems
reasonably certain,[2] was influenced by one of Boccaccio's
eclogues of about 1360, *The Pearl* must have been written
at least several years after that date. The indubitable
dependence of *Purity* on the French version of Mandeville's
*Travels,* probably written in 1355 or 1356, although the
oldest (French) manuscript is dated 1371, led C. F. Brown[3]
to say that 'it is scarcely possible that the *Mandeville* was
known in England before this latter date.' But as there
is no reason why an earlier manuscript than the oldest one
extant might not have strayed over to England, the poet's
borrowing from Mandeville demonstrates only that *Purity*
was written after 1355-6.

Various attempts have been made to arrive at a more
definite date for *Purity* and *Patience* by establishing some
relationship between them and *Piers Plowman.* Trautmann's suggestion[4] that certain passages in the homiletic
poems were written under the influence of *Piers Plowman*
was elaborated by Miss Thomas.[5] Her arguments are such
as this: 'that the first six portions of Bible history treated
in Cleanness (*Purity*) . . . are all found as episodes in
*Piers Plowman.*' C. F. Brown, in discussing the incon-
clusiveness of Miss Thomas' evidence, points out[6] that
'when one considers that more than a score of Biblical
episodes might be reckoned up in the pages of *Piers Plowman,* it does not seem very significant that there should be

---

[1] Cf. Hulbert, *Mod. Phil.* 13. 710 ff.

[2] Schofield, *Publ. Mod. Lang. Ass.* 19. 203 ff.

[3] *Publ. Mod. Lang. Ass.* 19. 153.

[4] *Über Verf.,* p. 32.

[5] *Sir Gawayne,* pp. 27-32. The passages compared are: *Piers* B.
13. 384, *Pat.* 9; *Piers* B. 10. 342, 11. 310, 14. 191-2, 214-7, 259, 270-1,
274, *Pat.* 1-8, 35-53, 525-31; *Piers* B. 16. 97-126, *Pur.* 1085-1105;
*Piers* B. 15. 455-7, *Pur.* 55 ff.; *Piers* B. 1. 109-25, *Pur.* 205-24;
*Piers* B. 9. 129, *Pur.* 285; *Piers* B. 14. 39-44, *Pur.* 530-7.

[6] *Bubl. Mod. Lang. Ass.* 19. 123, n. 2. In this note Brown criticizes
other points in Miss Thomas' argument.

several episodes common to both poems.' The few verbal similarities which Miss Thomas was able to find are utterly worthless as indications either of borrowing or of reminiscence. Such an expression as *wylde worme(z)* (*Piers Plow.* B. 14. 41, *Pur.* 533) occurs also in *Awntyrs of Arthure* (Douce MS. 216), and in any case might as well be borrowed by the author of *Piers Plowman* as by the author of *Purity*. The evidence for dating *Purity* after 1377, the date of the B-version of *Piers Plowman,* is therefore entirely insufficient.

Recently, in his edition of *Patience,* Bateson, though he brought forward no new evidence, was inclined to accept the theory of some relationship between *Piers Plowman* and the Gawain-poet, but he disagreed with Miss Thomas in assuming that it was *Purity* and *Patience* that influenced the B-author of *Piers Plowman* (1377).[1] The only important evidence in these discussions of the possible relationship between the Gawain-poet and the author(s) of *Piers Plowman* is the connection between the virtues of Poverty and Patience which both poets emphasize. It is not unlikely that the persistent recurrence of this idea in the B-version of *Piers* may be due to the importance attached to it in *Patience*.[2] If this influence be admitted, *Patience* must be dated before 1377.

A verbal similarity more important than any hitherto

---

[1] Pp. xxiv-viii. Bateson's acceptance of Manly's theories regarding the separate authorship of *Piers Plowman* led him, in the appendix to his first edition of *Patience,* to propound some very bold and highly complicated arguments for the more accurate dating of the poems. In his second edition he has wisely abandoned these theories, and with his modified views of the relationship between the Gawain-poet and *Piers Plowman* I thoroughly agree.

[2] Cf. *Pat.* 35 ff. Note that the B-version says (10. 340-2) : 'And patriarkes and prophetes and *poetes* bothe . . . preyseden pouerte with pacience.' Bateson (pp. xxvii-viii) refers to the association of the two virtues by Augustine and the Franciscans.

pointed out is the line which occurs in the famous episode of the belling of the cat in *Piers Plowman:*

*Pur.* 1638 And þe byȝe of bryȝt golde abowte þyn nekke.
*Piers Plow.* C. 1. 178 Bere byȝes of bryȝt gold al aboute hure neckes,

where the B-version (Prolog. 161) has:

Beren biȝes ful briȝte abouten here nekkes.

This remarkable resemblance is the more noteworthy since the line in *Purity* is a literal translation of the Vulgate *torquem auream circa collum tuum* (Dan. 5. 16). It might be deduced from this that the C-version must have revised the B-version, and made it conform more exactly to the line in *Purity,* which must be the original, since the poet is here simply translating his source. But the present uncertainty about the manuscripts of *Piers Plowman* prevents the acceptance of the B-text at its face value. Whatever the exact nature of the relationship of the B and C versions may be, it seems plain that *Piers Plowman* is here imitating *Purity.*

More definite conclusions may be reached concerning the relative chronology of the four works of the Gawain-poet, although even on this point there has been flat disagreement among scholars. According to Ten Brink, the order of the poems was *Gawain, Pearl, Purity, Patience.*[1] But this arrangement was closely associated with, and is really dependent upon, the purely fictitious life of the poet that Ten Brink attempted to reconstruct. It is unnecessary, at this date, to show that *Patience* offers no ground for supposing its author 'an aging poet who has felt the pains of poverty and privation.'[2] We know nothing of the

---

[1] *Early Engl. Lit.* 1. 337 ff.
[2] *Ibid.* 1. 351. Gollancz still clings in his hypothetical biography of the poet to Ten Brink's order (*Camb. Hist.* 1. 369-70; *Encycl. Brit.,* 11th ed., under *Pearl;* Preface to ed. of *Patience*); but he states it cautiously and only as a probability. For criticism of

external life of the poet, though we may glean from his
works some knowledge of his opinions and position.[1]  And
hardly any one would now agree with Ten Brink's opinion
that *Purity* and *Patience* are the most mature products
of the poet's art, and the latter his masterpiece.[2]  Miss
Thomas followed Ten Brink in considering *Purity* and
*Patience* the poet's last works, but her discussion[3] of the
chronology of the poems is almost wholly taken up with
her attempt to prove that *The Pearl* came before *Gawain,*
and not after, as Ten Brink had maintained.  Her reasons
for considering *The Pearl* the earliest of the four poems
were vague and general: its isolation from the other three
in form and diction, and the much greater number of
comparisons.[4]  More definite reasons were advanced for
a close connection between *Purity* and *Gawain.*  Not only
similarities in phraseology, but also the enforcement of
the same moral in both poems, the extolling of the virtues
of loyalty (*trawþe*) and chastity, seemed to Miss Thomas
sufficient ground for refusing to separate these two poems
by *The Pearl.*  She therefore adopted the order *The Pearl,
Gawain, Purity, Patience.*[5]

Gollancz's attempt to reconstruct a biography, Schofield's articles
should be consulted. Bateson's hypothetical sketch of the poet's
life (pp. 55-63, 1st ed., abandoned in 2d ed.), and Osgood's less
fanciful deductions (pp. 1 ff.), show that an entirely different
chronology offers no difficulties for the imaginary reconstruction
of the poet's biography.

[1] See especially C. F. Brown, *The Author of the Pearl: Publ.
Mod. Lang. Ass.* 19. 115-48.

[2] *Early Engl. Lit.* 1. 350, 351.

[3] *Sir Gawayne,* pp. 12-25.

[4] *Ibid.,* pp. 22-5.

[5] Miss Thomas found no evidence in *Gawain* and *Purity* themselves for the priority of *Gawain,* except the fact that the author
would have been likely to introduce the knightly descriptions into
the Biblical setting of *Purity,* had he already employed them in
the romance, and again the fact that the lines in *Gawain* have

An entirely different order, *Purity* and *Patience, Pearl, Gawain,* was proposed by Osgood on the basis of the difference in the art and technique of the poems.[1] According to Osgood, the episodes in the homilies 'are more loosely articulated, both logically and in composition, and the moral element is clearly distinct from the sensuous.' Bateson agreed with Osgood in considering the homilies earlier, and attempted to fix more precisely their chronology and that of *Gawain.* He pointed out that the close relationship between *Purity* and *Gawain* on the one hand, and *Purity* and *Patience*[2] on the other, made it necessary to assume either the order, *Gawain, Purity, Patience,* or *Patience, Purity, Gawain,* and he thought the former impossible because of the dependence of *Purity* on *Patience.*[3]

The organic connection between *Purity* and *Patience* is so obvious that no one has ever proposed separating them. The many parallels between *Purity* and *Gawain* pointed out above,[4] and the paucity of parallels between *Patience* and *Gawain,* are sufficient, I believe, to justify Bateson's contention that *Purity* must come between *Patience* and *Gawain,* whether the order is *Gawain, Purity, Patience,* or *Patience, Purity, Gawain.*[5] But are there any more definite indica-

---

more of the freshness of an original. Neither of these points carries any weight, since the transference of the customs of chivalry to ancient settings is usual in poems of the kind, and the 'freshness' of the lines in *Gawain* may be due to the gradual perfecting of the poet's art. Cf. Bateson's criticism, *Patience,* p. xxii, n. 2.

[1] *Pearl,* pp. xlix ff. Schofield and Kittredge also believe that *Purity* and *Patience* are the poet's earliest works; see Schofield, *Publ. Mod. Lang. Ass.* 19. 165, and n. 2.

[2] *Patience,* p. xiii.

[3] I agree with Bateson's chronology, although the chief argument he advances (p. xxii) for the order *Purity, Patience,* is valueless unless one accepts the dependence of *Patience* on Tertullian's poem, which is more than doubtful; cf. p. xl.

[4] Pp. xv f. Cf. Bateson, p. xxi.

[5] *The Pearl* may be left out of consideration for the moment,

tions, other than these, and perhaps less liable to contradiction than the argument drawn from the poet's development
as an artist,[1] that any one of the three poems precedes
another? When the same or similar phrases and ideas are
used in more than one poem, it will be well to examine them
carefully for any evidence concerning which is the more
likely to have been suggested by the other. And although
this evidence is necessarily small in quantity, and involves
the consideration of fine points in the handling of words
and phrases, it is more tangible than general comparisons
of artistic merit.

Take first some phrases which are common to *Gawain*
and *Purity*. In *Purity* it is said of the angels who show
some unwillingness to accept Lot's offer of hospitality
(805-7):

> Þay nay þat þay nolde neȝ no howsez,
> Bot stylly þer in þe strete as þay stadde wern,
> Þay wolde lenge þe long naȝt and logge þeroute.[2]

Now the same phrase that occurs in this first line is found
again in *Gawain* 1836, in an entirely different context.
When Bernlak's wife beseeches the hero to accept a present
of her gold ring or girdle, the poet says:

> & he nay[ed] þat he nolde neghe in no wyse
> Nauther gold ne garysoun,

that is, he refused to *accept* either. *NED.* was able to find
no other instance of the verb *nigh* in this meaning 'take

since its difference in form prevents the same kind of comparison
with the other poems.

[1] I consider this argument of the artistic superiority of *Gawain*
a strong one for its being the last of the poems. Both the excellence
of narrative construction and the more skilful and easier handling
of the alliterative line (cf. p. 63) point to *Gawain's* being the most
finished product of the poet's art. But it is naturally difficult to
refute a man who declares the exact contrary to be the case.

[2] This paraphrases the last clause of Gen. 19. 2.

or accept.' How did the poet happen to use it in this strange sense? There can hardly be any other satisfactory explanation than that the convenient alliterative phrase 'nay þat he nolde neghe' recurred to him because he had already used it in expressing an act of refusal in another poem, in a case where the persons really refused to *approach* something. In other words, the unnatural use of the word in *Gawain* must follow the natural use of it in its ordinary meaning of 'approach' in *Purity*. The poet would never have used the verb in this extraordinary way unless it had been included in, and psychologically associated with, an alliterative phrase previously employed. One or two other phrases, which in *Purity* directly translate the Latin of the Vulgate, are used in *Gawain* in a less natural and more formal manner. So, for example, *Purity* 943, 'Lest ȝe be taken in þe teche of tyrauntez here' translates the Vulgate *ne et tu pariter pereas in scelere civitatis* (Gen. 19. 15); but in *Gawain* 2488, when the word *teche,* meaning 'sin,' is again used in the same phrase,[1] the expression becomes redundant, as though it were used formally: 'In tokenyng he watȝ *tane in tech of a faute.*'[2]

Another slightly different example is what seems to me a reminiscence in *Gawain* of a figure of speech elaborately developed in *Purity*. It is said of Christ, in *Purity* 1068,

---

[1] It should be remembered that the phrase 'taken in teche' is rare, and probably occurs only in these two instances.

[2] So the poet's translation of *ne irascaris* by 'tatz to non ille' (*Pur.* 735) he uses again at *Gaw.* 1811. Again it seems to me that the very bold construction at *Gaw.* 1805 'to dele yow for drurye,' with a personal pronoun the object of *dele,* could never have been used if the poet had not already used the natural construction 'dele drwrye' (*Pur.* 1065). So also when the poet says of the castle that Gawain approaches that its pinnacles were so thick 'þat pared out of papure purely hit semed' (802), it is easier to suppose that this strange comparison occurred to him because he had already described decorations actually 'pared out of paper' (*Pur.* 1408), than it is to assume the contrary.

that he 'ever is polyced als playn as þe perle selven.' And again in the long simile (1117-32) in which the pearl, whose dullness may be brightened by washing it in wine, is compared to the man whose vile sin may be washed away by penance, the poet says the sinner 'may polyce hym at þe prest by penaunce taken.' In *Gawain,* when the hero confesses his one act of disloyalty, Bernlak absolves him in the following manner (2391-4):

> Þou art confessed so clene, be-knowen of þy mysses,
> & hatz þe penaunce apert, of þe poynt of myn egge,
> I halde þe *polysed* of þat ply3t, & pured as clene,[1]
> As þou hade3 neuer forfeted.

*NED.* calls special attention to this instance as the only one in which the verb *polish* comes to mean 'cleanse, purify.' Surely the idea of using the word in this sense and in this passage would never have occurred to the poet if he had not in *Purity* spoken of the 'polishing of the soul by penance' in a comparison with the 'polishing of the pearl.' Such peculiar use of words and phrases as these can hardly be explained in any other way than as reminiscences of *Purity.*

The same test one might expect to apply with even greater ease to *Patience* and *Purity.* For, since both of these poems are paraphrases of different parts of the Vulgate, any poetic phrase translating the Biblical words in one poem, and appearing in the other without having any basis in the Biblical text in this second case, would offer strong presumption that the poem in which it directly translates the Biblical text was written first. But unfortunately most of the more important resemblances in phraseology between *Patience* and *Purity* occur in passages which in both poems are added by the poet to the Biblical story. Only two instances are of any importance, and these both appear to

---

[1] Cf. *Pur.* 1116: 'And pure þe with penaunce tyl þou a perle worþe.'

originate in *Patience* and to be transferred to *Purity*. When
the storm breaks on Jonah's ship, and the sailors take to
the oars to try to reach dry land, the Vulgate text says *et
non valebant,* which the poet translates 'Bot al watȝ nedles
note' (*Pat.* 220), a phrase which he repeats in *Purity* in
describing the vain attempt of the multitude to escape the
flood: 'Bot al watz nedlez her note' (*Pur.* 381).[1] A better,
and what seems to me a conclusive, instance is the phrase
'Goddes glam to hym glod' (*Pat.* 63); 'Godez glam to hem
glod' (*Pur.* 499). The Vulgate original for *Patience* is
*Et factum est verbum Domini ad Jonam* (Jonah 1. 1); for
*Purity, Locutus est autem Deus ad Noe, dicens* (Gen. 8. 15).
It is obvious that the poet has translated the Latin literally
in the phrase in *Patience,* and has then transferred it to
*Purity,* where the Latin has merely the usual expression
for 'he said.' The transference could work only one way.

A comparison of two longer passages in *Patience* and
*Purity,* those on the beatitudes, and those quoting Psalm
93. 8-9, makes the priority of *Patience* the more probable,
as Bateson has already suggested.[2] Even though one
should not assume that the passage on the beatitudes in
*Patience* (9 ff.) is directly modelled on Tertullian's poem,[3]
it seems more likely that the complete translation of them
in *Patience* was written first, and that the more casual and
less exact reference to one beatitude followed in *Purity*
(25 ff.). 'Me mynez on one amonge oþer, as Maþew
recordez,' the poet says in *Purity,* and it is easy to suppose
that the reason the poet deems it unnecessary to mention

---

[1] In this case the poet might, of course, have thought of the
phrase in his description of the flood, and later used it to translate
the Biblical clause, but it seems to me less likely, especially since
*note* is used in the line in *Pur.* in a slightly more strained sense:
'trouble, pains,' instead of merely 'work.'

[2] *Patience*, p. xxi.

[3] Cf. p. xl.

the others is because he had already done so in *Patience*.[1]
More important is the difference in the quotation from
Psalm 93. 8-9.[2] In *Patience* the quotation is not only
prefaced by the explicit statement that King David said it
in a psalm of the Psalter, but the four lines (121-4) are
an almost word for word, at least phrase for phrase, translation. The paraphrase in *Purity* (581 ff.), which is given
as though emanating from the poet himself, without any
suggestion of its being a reflection of the psalm, is much less
exact. The singular (*mon, þyself, þou*) is used for the
plural (Vulg. *insipientes, Pat. ffolez*); the sentences translated in one line in *Patience* (123, 124) are expanded into
two in *Purity* (583-4, 585-6); and finally, in *Purity,* the
clauses referring to God's all-hearing ear and all-seeing eye
are interchanged, whereas *Patience* preserves the order of
the original. The reader should examine these passages in
their context, and see for himself the improbability of the
poet's having written the vague impression first and the
exact translation afterward.

The few reasons that have hitherto been suggested for
believing that *Purity* was the first of the homilies are very
vague, and might as easily be made to prove exactly the
contrary. *Patience* is, to be sure, more concise than *Purity,*
but this is inevitable from the fact that it handles only one
incident, whereas *Purity* is of epic proportions, illustrating
the doom that awaits the impure by means of three long
narratives, which must be connected with one another by
transitional passages of exhortation and remonstrance. It
is easily conceivable that a poet who had written a short
homily on one of the virtues mentioned in the beatitudes
might desire to attempt a homily on another virtue, this

[1] Cf. the note on l. 51, in which the word *masse* is probably used
in a strained sense because the phrase is a reminiscence of
*Patience* 9-10.

[2] For the Vulgate text and the two passages paraphrasing it, see
note on l. 581.

time on a grander scale.[1]   If it is said that the style of
*Patience* is terser, and the lines more firmly knit together,
it may be replied that this impression is derived chiefly
from the sharper division[2] into stanzas of four lines, and
it may well be that the poet in his later and larger
work abandoned the confining limits into which he had
endeavored, somewhat unsuccessfully, to force his lines in
*Patience.*

Since the judgments of critics on the development of the
poet's art have not been unanimous, I have endeavored to
present some more convincing evidence for the chronology of his works.   This evidence, added to that already
adduced by others, is sufficient, I believe, to establish with
some degree of certainty the fact that *Purity* (and with
it *Patience*) precedes *Gawain,* and that *Patience* precedes
*Purity.*[3]   The place of *The Pearl* in the poet's works is
more difficult to determine, though artistic considerations[4]
would seem to require a position between the Biblical poems
and *Gawain.*   The order of the poet's works would then be
*Patience, Purity, (The Pearl?), Gawain.*

---

[1] This, in fact, seems to me more probable than that he should
have written the more pretentious work first and the shorter poem
afterward.

[2] On this division, see pp. xliii-iv.   Gollancz recognizes (*Camb. Hist.*
I. 361) that the division is less marked in *Purity.*   In general,
there does not seem to me to be much difference in the style or
handling of the line in the two poems.   There is the same abruptness
and tendency to anacoluthon in each.

[3] Osgood, p. xlix, is non-committal about the order of the two
poems, simply grouping them together—'*Purity* and *Patience.*'

[4] See Osgood, p. xlix; and Bateson, pp. xix ff.   It may be well
to mention that the lines on the pearl in *Purity* (1068, 1116 ff.)
cannot be considered in any way a reminiscence of *The Pearl,* since
the comparison in *Purity* is of an entirely different kind from the
symbolism in *The Pearl.*

## V.  SOURCES

The chief source of *Purity* is the Vulgate text of the Bible.   It would be impossible to enumerate exactly the lines of the poem which depend on the Latin text, since many passages, though based originally on the words of the Vulgate, are elaborated to such an extent that verbal reminiscences from the Bible appear only rarely in a rich mosaic of description.   So, for example, the marvelous ornamentation depicted in Mandeville's tale of Oriental splendor is superimposed on the Biblical description of the sacred vessels of the Temple (1439 ff.).   But it would be fair to say that about three-fifths of the lines of *Purity* have their ultimate source in the Latin of the Vulgate.   In the next section, which deals with the literary art of the poet, the manner in which he uses his main source will be discussed in greater detail.

The few apocryphal incidents which the poet adds to the Biblical stories he narrates can hardly be traced to any definite source.   The story of Lucifer[1] and the raven's treachery[2] were common tradition, and though Lot's wife's disobedience in serving salt to her guests,[3] and Christ's cutting of the bread,[4] are more unusual, no direct original has been discovered for either.   Holthausen[5] suggested that the poet may have been familiar with Peter Comestor's *Historia Scholastica,* but such parallels as he mentions—the raven's feeding on carrion, and the unnatural sin of the descendants of Adam—are not remarkable, since these interpretations were traditional, and the poet might have found them in many other commentators.   The only verbal

---

[1] See note on l. 211.
[2] See note on l. 459.
[3] See note on l. 819.
[4] See note on l. 1103.
[5] *Archiv* 106. 349.

similarity of importance[1] is insufficient to prove direct borrowing, especially when one remembers the frequency with
which mediæval commentators copied and recopied each
other's phrases.  It is noteworthy that the apocryphal material used by the poet, where it is not commonplace, consists
of homely anecdote.  This same characteristic of homely
simplicity may be seen in his whole attitude toward the
traditional commentaries.  In *Purity,* at least, he seems to
be less fettered than most homilists by theological doctrine
and conventional interpretations, even where these may have
been known to him.  He often shows himself remarkably
independent in his simple and direct application of Biblical
stories to spiritual truths,[2] and in such cases he is not at
all bound by the accumulated allegorizings of centuries of
scholastic exegesis.

The possible dependence[3] of *Patience* on the poem *De
Jona et Nineve,* once ascribed to Tertullian, has led to the
suggestion that another similar poem, *De Sodoma,* occurring
along with *De Jona* in the Latin poet's works, may have
been known to the Gawain-poet.[4]  But as Bateson, who
advanced this hypothesis, omits to mention it in his revised
edition of *Patience,* this point need not be considered.  Even
the dependence of *Patience* on Tertullian's *De Jona* now
appears more than doubtful.[5]

[1] See note on l. 660.
[2] Cf. note on l. 169, and the summary of the poem, pp. xlvi-vii.
[3] O. F. Emerson, *Publ. Mod. Lang. Ass.* 10. 242-8; Bateson,
*Patience,* pp. xli-vi.
[4] Bateson, 1st ed., Appendix I, pp. 64-7.
[5] See Liljegren's criticism (*Engl. Stud.* 48. 337-41) of Emerson
and Bateson; Gollancz, Preface to *Patience,* speaks of *De Jona*
only as 'an interesting and noteworthy parallel.'  A point not
mentioned by Liljegren may be noted here.  Emerson (pp. 246-7)
and Bateson (pp. xlv-vi) attempt to bolster up their arguments by
comparing Tertullian's treatment of the beatitudes in his homily
*De Patientia* with the opening of the poem *Patience.*  Tertullian's
purpose is to show that the virtue of patience is essential to the

Next to the Vulgate, Mandeville's *Travels,* in the original French, was the book most used by the poet in the composition of *Purity.* That the description of the Dead Sea (1022-48) is taken from the Old French version of Jean de Bourgoyne's (Mandeville's) famous work, was conclusively proved by C. F. Brown in 1904.[1] But the influence of Mandeville's book is to be found in other passages than this account of the marvels of the Dead Sea. For the splendor of Belshazzar's feast is heightened by the introduction of the wondrous artificial birds that flap their wings, and the gleaming jewels cut from precious gems, that Mandeville had seen at the court of the Great Chan and in the land of Prester John.[2]

The poet borrows from another Old French work in *Purity,* Jean (Clopinel) de Meun's part of the *Roman de la Rose.*[3] This, indeed, is the only source, besides the Bible, to which he refers in the whole range of his poetry, and here he mentions both the poet and his work (1057):

> For Clopyngnel in þe compas of his clene Rose.

attainment of bliss, and he therefore tries to prove that patience is recommended in at least four of the beatitudes: 'the poor in spirit' must be humble, and therefore patient: 'weepers and mourners' have to be patient; 'the gentle' cannot be impatient; 'the peacemakers' require patience. On the other hand, the reason why the Gawain-poet conjoins *Poverty* and *Patience* is simply that these qualities, the first and the last commended in the beatitudes, are the only two that have the same reward, the Kingdom of Heaven (*Pat.* 37-40)—and of this there is no hint in *De Patientia.* Any one writing on the theme of Patience would be likely to refer to the beatitudes, and the very different way in which Tertullian and the Gawain-poet make use of the beatitudes in this connection argues against any relation between the two.

[1] *Publ. Mod. Lang. Ass.* 19. 149-53.

[2] See note on l. 1464; Neilson (*Huchown,* p. 115, n. 1) remarked that 'Belshazzar's sacrilegious table jewellery' is described in terms borrowed from Mandeville.

[3] The passage is printed in the note on l. 1057.

The poet turns his quotation from Jean de Meun to rather unusual use. Chaucer, like many another poet, borrowed liberally from this author of the *Roman de la Rose;* but Chaucer, in addition, entered into the very spirit of his incisive satire. The author of *Purity* plainly understood the point of the passage he quotes from Reason's advice to the Lover to win a lady's favor by acting in accordance with her character, and doing whatever pleases her best. But it is unlikely that he would have turned this advice into a similar exhortation to win Christ's favor by conforming to the purity of his nature, if he had really comprehended the subtle cynicism of Jean de Meun's lines.

Though the poet obtained most of his material from Latin and Old French, he must surely have had native models, if not for his ideas, at least for the poetic form which he employed. It is unlikely that he imitated directly any of the few earlier poems of the Middle English alliterative school that have come down to us. And, though he shares with the other poets of the school a love of glittering splendor, and a fondness for nature in her wilder moods,[1] yet wherever direct dependence of one on the other seems probable, it is not the poet of *Purity* who is the borrower.[2] Nevertheless, it may be safely assumed that many a poet whose name and works have utterly disappeared, helped to teach him the difficult art of alliterative versification. It is often stated that the Old English poets were the masters of the Gawain-poet in literary art. The sea-pictures of Old English poetry, especially those of the Old English *Exodus,* it has been said,[3] have influenced the description of the storm in *Purity* 363-72. But not a jot of evidence has as yet been presented that either the Gawain-poet or any of his contemporaries was familiar with Old English poetry,

[1] Cf. Osgood, p. xx.

[2] Cf. pp. xxvi-vii.

[3] F. W. Moorman, *Interpretation of Nature in English Poetry: Quellen und Forschungen* 95. 105 (Strassburg, 1905).

or could even read a single line of it. For that reason, the vivid descriptions of sea and storm which are found in *Patience* and *Purity* must be considered simply the natural inheritance of a poetic tradition never entirely extinct, a tradition that from Beowulf to Swinburne has depicted the terror and grandeur of the sea.

## VI. LITERARY ART

A not uncommon tendency among the alliterative poets to divide poems into more or less distinct sections,[1] is particularly observable in the early work of the author of *Purity,* where the lines seem to be combined into groups of four. There is some basis in the manuscript for recognizing such a division,[2] for the same mark which in *The Pearl* occurs at the beginning of each strophe, is found at every fourth line (5, 9, etc.) in *Patience* and *Purity.* It has been said that this division into sections, which might almost be called stanzas, is consistently carried out in *Patience,* whereas in *Purity* it appears chiefly at the begining and end of the poem.[3] It would be more accurate to say that the more regular grouping of lines in *Patience* appears in various passages in *Purity,* especially at the beginning of the poem, but seems to have become less and less marked as the poem progresses. The first sixteen lines, for example, divide easily into four groups of four lines each, but in the passage following there is no reason for a

[1] Kaluza, *Strophische Gliederung in der Mittelenglischen rein Alliterirenden Dichtung: Engl. Stud.* 16. 169-80.

[2] The scribe's use of capitals corresponds with this division. Of the 110 lines which begin with capitals, only 7 are lines not immediately following a multiple of 4. But the scribe would naturally be more likely to capitalize wherever he had inserted a mark at the beginning of the line, and the capitalization is in any case somewhat erratic, since it often occurs where there is a less important division than where it is omitted.

[3] Gollancz, *Camb. Hist.* 1. 361.

pause after ll. 20, 36, 40, 44, 52, 56. But the twelve lines (61-72) which tell the excuses offered by the wedding guests are rather sharply divided into three sections of four lines each. At the end of the poem the tendency to groups of four is noticeable at ll. 1500-28, but thereafter the grouping is very irregular, except in Daniel's exposition of the writing on the wall (1725-40). It is, in fact, in such passages of dialogue that the grouping is most marked. Abraham's intercession for Lot and God's replies (729-64) exhibit this regularity of form, but it is not always limited to groups of four, since the dialogue of Lot and the angels (913-32) is grouped 6, 6, 4, 4. On the other hand, in the more important narrative passages, especially where an effect of rapidity is desired—the rising of the flood (361-424), the destruction of the evil cities (945-72), or the writing on the wall and its sequel (1529 ff.)—no definite arrangement can be traced. For this reason the poem can certainly not be said to be written in four-line stanzas. The division is not organic, but an indication of a desire on the part of the poet to give greater stability of form to his lines where that is needed.[1]

Just as in *The Pearl* the beginning of every fifth strophe is marked by a large illuminated letter, so *Purity* is divided by the same means into thirteen irregular sections.[2] Even

---

[1] I have retained Morris' numbering of the lines by fours, but I have not ventured to print the poem in four-line stanzas, as does Gollancz in editing *Patience,* since in many cases it would break up obviously connected parts, or at least retard the movement of the poem. Among the lines which, according to this arrangement, ought to end a stanza, are the following where there is hardly any or no pause (it must be remembered that a pause must be very marked to indicate a division, since enjambement is rare in the poem) : 200, 356, 472, 524, 612, 684, 784, 1272, 1420, 1444, 1456, 1544, 1556, 1564, 1572, 1580, 1696, 1772, 1780. Cf. Emerson, *Mod. Lang. Notes* 31. 2-4, for arguments against the adoption of the quatrain arrangement in *Patience.*

[2] The shortest is only 44 lines (557-600), while the longest is 456

though these divisions in *Purity* may not be the poet's,[1] they have been retained in the text as a convenient means of giving the modern reader an opportunity to pause in the perusal of this lengthy homily.

These convenient external divisions, however, must not give the impression that the poem is a mere jumble of Biblical incidents. The design of the whole is worked out with elaborate care. Purity is recommended by three long narratives from the Bible, which illustrate the vengeance that God takes on those who fail in this virtue: the Flood (249-544), the Destruction of Sodom and Gomorrah (557-1051), and the Downfall of Belshazzar (1157-1804). The inclusion of the last narrative, the longest of the three, is due to the wide application of the word *clannesse,* which comprises not only chastity, but purity in the sense of freedom from any defilement. It is thus that Belshazzar,[2] who defiles the sacred vessels of God at his impious feast, becomes a sinner against *clannesse* or purity.

The introduction to these illustrations of the poet's theme is also elaborate. The poet begins by declaring that one who undertakes to condemn purity need not lack material for his discourse (1-4). The man who worships God in uncleanness brings God's wrath upon him; we could, indeed, expect nothing else, since it would be strange if God, who

lines (1357-1812). In order to make the poem more easily readable, I have divided this last section, numbering ll. 1529-1640, XIIIa; ll. 1641-1740, XIIIb; ll. 1741-1812, XIIIc; and the eleventh and twelfth sections have been similarly divided, ll. 1049-1156 being numbered XIa, and ll. 1261-1356, XIIa. Kaluza's attempt (*Engl. Stud.* 16. 178) to divide *Purity* into sections of 60 lines each is unsuccessful.

[1] There is no apparent reason why there should be a division at 345, 485, or 689; but, on the other hand, the transitions are so carefully concealed that it would often be difficult to divide anywhere. That the scribe or illuminator may have made a mistake is plain from *Pearl* 961, where there is incorrect division.

[2] Cf. note on l. 1357.

is himself so pure, should not loathe evil (5-22). After this preamble comes the text of the homily, Christ's own statement in Matthew that only the pure in heart shall see God (23-8).[1] This, the poet now expounds, means that no one who is in any way defiled can approach God's pure presence (29-32) ; and to explain this concretely he narrates at length the parable of the Man without a Wedding Garment (51-168), repeating the spiritual significance of the parable at the end—that unclean deeds, like the foul clothes of the wedding-guest, exclude a man from the joy of the presence of the Lord. Of all sins by which a man may forfeit bliss (177-92), 'filth of the flesh' most displeases God, as may be seen from the fact that only in avenging this sin was his wrath really aroused (193-204).[2] He did not become angry when he overthrew Lucifer (205-33), nor when he drove Adam from Paradise (235-48), but only in the third place, when he brought the Flood upon the world for men's unchastity. Only after this complicated introduction does the poet narrate his three stories, the Flood, the destruction of Sodom, and Belshazzar's feast. In the brief conclusion (1805-12) he reminds the reader that he has shown the evils of uncleanness in three ways (1805), repeating his text at the end in true homiletic style, and closing with a prayer.

The stories from the Bible are naturally accompanied by passages of exhortation and admonition, which form subtle transitions from one narrative passage to another. After the poet has finished the story of the Flood, he urges his readers to avoid the sin which may prevent them from attaining to the sight of God (545-56). God kept his promise to Noah never again to destroy all flesh, but nevertheless he took wrathful vengeance on mankind once again for the same sin (557-80). Do not imagine that God

[1] Cf. note on l. 25.
[2] Cf. note on l. 204.

cannot perceive all the deeds of man and the thoughts of his heart. Those whom he finds pure he honors, but the others he scatters and slays in haste, as may be seen by his punishment of the wicked cities (581-600). After this story has been narrated, the poet introduces another and longer exhortation to purity, urging the sinner to strive to imitate Christ, whose pure birth and life the poet praises (1052-108). This he may do by means of penance, which will wash him of sin, as the pearl is brightened by wine (1109-32). But having once been shriven, let him beware of a return to sin. For God is especially angry that anything which was once his should become unclean, though it be only a basin or bowl consecrated to his service (1133-48). Thus, by carefully concealed art, the poet passes from his praise of purity to Belshazzar's desecration of the vessels of the Temple, his third and last narrative.

In addition to purity, one other virtue is commended, as a kind of second theme, throughout the poem—what the poet calls *trawþe*,[1] which includes not only faithfulness to men, but loyalty to God, or religious faith and belief. Besides the three instances of God's vengeance on men for sin against purity, four other incidents of punishments inflicted by Divine Justice are recorded, and each is because the sinner was lacking in *trawþe*. Lucifer is represented as a traitor (208 ff.); Adam is said specifically to have 'fayled in trawþe' (236); Lot's wife becomes a pillar of salt 'for two fautes þat þe fol was founde in mistrauþe' (996); Jerusalem fell because the people were found 'untrwe' (1161) in their faith. The importance of these two virtues, purity and loyalty, connect the poem closely with *Gawain,* where the hero is tested in both at once.

The finer points in the poet's workmanship may be seen in his use of the Vulgate. The parts of the Vulgate which form the basis of the illustrative stories in *Purity* are sub-

[1] Cf. Miss Thomas, *Sir Gawayne,* p. 20.

joined,[1] so that any one may examine in detail the different
methods of translation, paraphrase, and elaboration that
the poet employed.  It will not, therefore, be necessary here
to give more than a few illustrations of the poet's treatment of the Biblical narrative.  The most notable thing
about his translation is the frequency with which it is
absolutely literal.  Take, for instance, five lines of God's
speech to Noah (323-7), and compare it with the original
Latin (Gen. 6. 17-8):

> For I shal waken up a water to wasch alle þe worlde,
> And quelle alle þat is quik wyth quavende flodez.
> Alle þat glydez and gotz, and gost of lyf habbez,
> I schal wast with my wrath þat wons upon urþe;
> Bot my forward with þe I festen on þis wyse.

> Ecce adducam aquas diluvii super terram, ut interficiam
> omnem carnem in qua spiritus vitæ est subter cælum.
> Universa quæ in terra sunt, consumentur.  Ponamque
> fœdus meum tecum.

Often the construction is so changed as to take away all
semblance of Biblical style, and, although the translation
remains accurate, the naturalness of the alliterative phrase
completely conceals the Scriptural origin.  It would hardly
be suspected that Abraham's instruction to Sarah (625-6):

> Þre mettez of mele menge and ma kakez,
> Under aske ful hote happe hem bylive.

is an exact rendering of the Vulgate (Gen. 18. 6): *tria
sata similæ commisce et fac subcinericios panes.*  Even so
ordinary a line as (804)

> And in þe myry mornyng ȝe may your waye take

is a direct translation of *et mane proficiscemini in viam
vestram* (Gen. 19. 2).  In the following passage the first

[1] See Appendix.

line is translated with obvious literalness, but the second,
although it conveys the exact sense of the original, has no
verbal similitude (1669-70):

> Watz not þis ilke worde wonnen of his mowþe,
> Er þenne þe soverayn sa3e souned in his eres.

> Cumque sermo adhuc esset in ore regis, vox de
> cælo ruit (Dan. 4. 28).

The translation is generally most literal in the purely
narrative passages, and very much elaborated in such
descriptions as those of the Flood, of the destruction of
Sodom and Gomorrah, and of Belshazzar's feast. But the
fact that the narrative parts of Belshazzar's feast are greatly
expanded, as well as the story of the man without a wedding
garment, which contains no description, shows that this is
hardly the fundamental distinction between the use of literal
translation and elaborate paraphrase. It would, perhaps,
be truer and simpler to say that the poet elaborates whatever passages, narrative or descriptive, he wishes to emphasize. And since the Biblical stories he tells are important
for him only as illustrations of God's acts of vengeance
against sin, this would account for the great expansion of
the descriptions of the flood and the destruction of the
cities, since there God inflicts punishment by natural
agencies, and the poet must emphasize the terrible aspects
of nature; and it would likewise explain the space given
to the narrative of Belshazzar's downfall, since here God
metes out punishment by human agency, and the poet must
emphasize the terror of the king and the onslaught of his
enemies.[1]  A good example of the poet's method of elabora-

---

[1] It should, moreover, be remembered that the Biblical accounts
of Belshazzar's feast and the parable of the Wedding Garment are
comparatively short in the original, and need to be filled with more
details than the stories of Noah and Abraham and Lot; and also
that the poet is sometimes carried away with his story, and elaborates
a passage out of proportion to its importance; cf. p. lii.

tion is his description of the Flood, where many or most of the striking details of the picture are the poet's own invention, although he includes scattered through the passage (361-424) reminiscences or paraphrases of almost all the phrases in the brief Biblical account (361, cf. Gen. 7. 10; 363-4, cf. Gen. 7. 11; 369, cf. Gen. 7. 17; 385, cf. Gen. 7. 19; 405-6, cf. Gen. 7. 20; 408-9, cf. Gen. 7. 22-3; 413, cf. Gen. 7. 17; 415-6, cf. Gen. 7. 18).

The poet's thorough familiarity with the Bible, if it were not obvious from the ease with which he quotes and refers to it,[1] might be judged from the skill with which he harmonizes and combines different passages. This he exhibits not only in the fusion of the two accounts of the parable of the Wedding Feast,[2] and of the many passages concerning the siege of Jerusalem and the seizure of the vessels of the Temple,[3] but also in the interweaving of phrases and the combinations of details not consecutive in the original. Some cases where a Biblical phrase has been shifted from its original position or context may, of course, be due simply to faulty memory[4]; but others are plainly intentional. For instance, the poet omits Gen. 6. 5, since almost the same expression occurs later in Gen. 8. 21 (515-8), and for Gen. 6. 5 he substitutes a paraphrase of Gen. 6. 11, translating *cumque vidisset Deus terram esse corruptam* by 'when he knew uche contre coruppte in hitselven' (281), and combining the clause with a paraphrase of Gen. 6. 6 (283-4). Similarly in Daniel's account of Nebuchadnezzar's pride and exile, which in general follows Dan. 5. 18-21, are inserted the details of Dan. 4. 27-30—for example, Nebuchadnezzar's boastful speech (1663-8).

[1] Cf. Osgood, pp. xvii ff.
[2] Cf. note on l. 51.
[3] Cf. note on l. 1157.
[4] The closeness of the translation in many passages makes it improbable that the poet was composing entirely from memory.

Though the poet frequently rearranged his original, he omitted comparatively little in the Biblical passages which he followed.  Some omissions are made to avoid the repetition that is not uncommon in Scriptural style: for instance, the entrance of the animals into the ark (Gen. 7. 7-9, 14-6), where the phraseology is the same as in God's command to Noah (Gen. 6. 19-20).  So the sending out of the third dove is not mentioned, perhaps because the poet thought it would be an anticlimax after the second had brought back the green branch of olives.  To avoid an apparent inconsistency, the poet omits the passage in which Daniel says 'Let thy gifts be to thyself, and give thy rewards to another' (Dan. 5. 17), since Daniel later accepts the reward offered by Belshazzar.

Far more is added to the Biblical account than is taken away.  The apocryphal incidents attached to the Biblical stories were traditional, and therefore throw no light on the poet's invention or art.  Of the poet's own additions hardly any serves to modify or contribute to the characterization of the personages.  The only exceptions are the speech of Nebuchadnezzar (1663 ff.), where the poet has prefixed to the Biblical words the line (1623),

I am god of þe grounde, to gye as me lykes,

which may be an echo of the Herod of the mystery plays; and the behavior of Belshazzar, whose physical manifestations of terror (1542-3) and blustering rage (1583-5) are apparently emphasized in order to represent him as a typical 'boaster on bench.'  Again, the poet introduces some passages for the sake of making his story clearer or more coherent.  To Abraham's intercession for the faithful in the cities of the plain, he adds a special intercession for Lot (771-6), and in order to make the connection plainer, he makes the angels who appear to Lot refer to Abraham's prayer for him (924).

By far the largest part of the lines not dependent on the

Vulgate are elaboration of detail and ornamentation. It is significant that the poet does not modify or add to the narrative in order to enforce his moral, or call attention to the particular application of his story.[1]  To be sure, he tells us the significance and point of each narrative before he begins it; but once embarked on it, he depends for his moral effect solely on the vividness of his presentation of the doom of the wicked.  The brief outline of Belshazzar's story that he found in the fifth chapter of Daniel, he fills out with all the trappings of mediæval chivalry, the sound of trumpets and gay revelry, the lavish ornament of precious jewels, and all the splendor that God shatters in a single night.  Out of the few verses which relate the destruction of Sodom and Gomorrah, he forms a picture that in its terrible grandeur is unsurpassed by any poet of his time.

It is, in fact, the gorgeous color and swift movement of such passages of *Purity* that make the poem worthy to endure.  For, in spite of the fact that the outline is clear and carefully worked out, the poem is not well proportioned. The story of the destruction of the cities need hardly have had so long a preamble as that which includes the announcement of an heir to Abraham.  And the introduction to Belshazzar's Feast, which narrates the siege of Jerusalem and the seizure of the sacred vessels, both elaborated with much irrelevant detail, is also unnecessarily long.  The poet apparently found such excellent material for story-telling in the events recorded that he could not refrain from inserting it.  He becomes so engrossed in his narrative that he forgets that his stories are not being written for their own sake, but as illustrations of a particular theme.  Abraham's prayer for Lot illustrates another fault of the poet.  His

---

[1] The only instance I have noted is l. 302, which the poet adds in order to bring out his point that God was really wrathful; cf. note on l. 204.

remarkable resources of language, his scorn of repeating the same thought in the same words, is often a virtue, distinguishing him from many lesser poets who monotonously repeat the same alliterative phrase. But it becomes a fault when he attempts to find a different phrase for each of Abraham's questions and God's answers; and the whole passage, which is effective in the Bible because of its very simplicity and brevity, becomes in *Purity* a tedious *tour de force,* so obviously is the poet striving to avoid repetition.

It is also possible to discover faults in the poet's style; for the frequent abruptness and obscurity of his lines can hardly be ascribed to the defective state of the text. Anacoluthon and involved constructions are to be found in no small number in all his poems. But at his best this boldness in syntax and style results in extraordinary vigor and originality of expression. And with this virility of style is combined a sense of beauty that flashes out in brief simile, or unfolds itself in description of the wild aspects of nature, and the gorgeous pageantry of mediæval life in peace and in war. Yet the poet is capable also of tender feeling, such as is revealed in the strain of almost lyric sweetness in which he hymns the praise of the Virgin.[1] It is such qualities as these that enable us to recognize in *Purity,* in spite of its unevenness and lack of proportion, the author of the greater poems, *The Pearl* and *Sir Gawain and the Green Knight.*

## VII. METRE AND ALLITERATION

The poetry of the Middle English alliterative school is probably, as we have seen, not a learned revival of Old English alliterative poetry, but simply the continuation of a tradition of which the intermediate stages have been lost. In any case, it is certain that the long alliterative line of

[1] Ll. 1075 ff.

Old English poetry forms the basis for that used by the Middle English writers.  But though the essential principles are the same, Middle English alliterative verse differs strikingly from Old English in several respects.  The most important difference for the general movement of the verse is the tendency to make each line a rhythmic entity, and to avoid altogether the enjambement which is so marked a characteristic of Old English poetry.  The only means of defining the limits of the line in Old English was the alliteration, since it was usual to begin a sentence in the middle of one verse and to end it in the middle of another.[1] But as soon as the lines came to be all end-stopped, as in Middle English alliterative verse, the line was defined by the pause at the end, and the alliteration, since it was now no longer structurally indispensable, became much less strict.[2] The results of this decrease in the structural importance of alliteration will be seen below in the more detailed discussion of the use of alliteration in *Purity*.  The modification of the rhythm of the line was accompanied by many changes[3] in the types of half-line common in Old English, some of which were abandoned in Middle English, and others developed and modified.

Two entirely different theories are held concerning the form of the Middle English (and also Old English) alliterative line.  Without venturing into a discussion of the evidence for either one, the orthodox view may be given here, that each half-line contains two stresses.[4]  The first four lines of *Purity* would accordingly be read thus:

[1] Deutschbein, pp. 7 ff.

[2] Cf. J. Thomas, *Die Alliterierende Langzeile des Gawaindichters*, p. 9.

[3] For details, see Deutschbein's dissertation, and Luick in Paul's *Grundriss*, 2d ed., 2. 2. 162; for the form the types take in *Purity*, Thomas' dissertation should be consulted.

[4] This theory, which has the support of Sievers, Skeat, Schipper, and Luick, was followed by J. Thomas in his valuable dissertation

Clánnesse who so ḱýndly - cówþe coménde,
And rékken up alle þe résounz - þat ho by ríȝt áskez,
Fayre fórmez myȝt he t́ýnde - in fórþering his spéche,
And in þe cóntrare kárk - and cómbraunce húge.

As in most poems of the alliterative school, there was a strong tendency to avoid a masculine ending of the line, and the final syllable was generally a weak *e,* which was probably always pronounced.[1]

As in Old English, the alliteration is generally on the two stresses of the first half-line, and the first stress of the second half-line, but the presence of only one alliterating word in the first half-line, which is permissible in Old English, is rare in Middle English.[2] In general, however,

on the alliterative lines of the Gawain-poet. The dissertation of Fischer, a pupil of Trautmann, attempts to prove the existence of four stresses in the first half-line and three in the second (four in Old English). The great number of rash emendations that Fischer finds necessary in order to provide enough words for seven stresses to the line, inclines one to extreme distrust of his work and of the soundness of his theory—see, for example, the liberal besprinkling of *ful's* and *mony's,* p. 19 and *passim.* Kuhnke, whose dissertation is limited to *Gawain,* also follows the theory of four stresses for the half-line.

[1] Thomas (pp. 21 ff.) tries to show that all the lines of the original had weak ending, and those which do not he makes conform to the majority by adding *e*'s, organic and inorganic, and by several emendations. Though undoubtedly certain spellings, such as *ȝette* at the end of 867, lead to the suspicion that the original may have had *ȝette,* not *ȝet,* at 815, 1021, 1049 (Thomas notes only 815), and though it is naturally impossible to prove in most cases that there could *not* have been analogical and inorganic *e*'s, certain cases, such as *þerwyth* of 1501 and *hyȝt Cam* of 299, where Thomas is obliged to resort to unlikely emendations, show that the weak ending cannot be accepted as a rule without exception. For this reason, and because of the considerable number (8%) of masculine endings in the manuscript, I have not emended any of the final words of the line except for other than metrical reasons.

[2] The following lines of *Purity* contain only one alliterating word in the first half: 105, 175, 315, 427, 770, 779, 958, 993, 1073, 1518,

the principles of alliteration are much less strict than in Old English. Alliteration is becoming less of a structural necessity and more of an ornament. This may be seen, in the first place, in the fact that unstressed words and prefixes may bear the alliteration, as in the following lines:

63 On hade boȝt hym a borȝ, he sayde, by hys trawþe.
114 Ay þe best byfore and bryȝtest atyred. Cf. bifore, 918, 978.
127 And rehayte rekenly þe riche and þe poveren.
197 Bot never ȝet in no boke breved I herde.

Another indication that the alliteration is becoming mere ornament is the tendency to crowd as many alliterating words as possible in a single line. Lines with three alliterating words in the first half are very common, but many lines have even more. The author of *Purity* is especially fond of such superabundant alliteration, for example:

113 Wheþer þay wern worþy oþer wers, wel wern þay stowed.
661 Þenne sayde oure Syre þer he sete: 'Se, so Sare laȝes.'
1681 His hert heldet unhole, he hoped non oþer.

In *Purity,* as in most contemporary alliterative poems, double alliteration is not unusual. This is generally parallel—a a b b , as in

299 Sem soþly þat on, þat oþer hyȝt Cam.

Here, and in 345, 1304, 1573, 1622, it is essential in the structure of the verse, since these lines would otherwise have to be considered defective; but elsewhere it is added to the regular alliteration as additional ornamentation, as in

25 Me mynez on one amonge oþer, as Maþew recordez.
493 Myryly on a fayr morn, monyth þe fyrst.

Transverse alliteration—a b a b—appears in

515 For I se wel þat hit is sothe þat alle mannez wyttez,

1571, 1727, 1807. This list does not include those lines where double alliteration is possible. No alliteration appears in the second half-line of 28, and in MS. 520, 745 (emended in text).

and possibly in 228, 327, 1618. Inclusive alliteration—
a b b a—appears in

608 Hit is eþe to leve by þe last ende,

and perhaps in 67, 735.

Most of the peculiarities of the poet in the sounds and
combinations of sounds which are used for alliteration are
shared by his contemporaries.[1] Alliteration on the same
vowel, which is avoided in Old English poetry, is frequently
found in *Purity,* for example, 241, 277, 411, 713, 1006, 1035,
1301, 1470. Vowels alliterate freely with *h* before vowel,
whether it be of Germanic or Romance origin. Likewise,
no distinction is made between *w* and *wh— whyte,* for
example, alliterating with *wynnes* and *worschyp* (1120).
In general, *sk, sp, st,* as in Old English, do not alliterate
with *s;* and this is also the case with *sch* and *sm.*[2] Finally,
the poet exhibits a particular fondness for alliterating certain groups, such as *cl* (634, 839, 858, 965, 1400) and *str*
(307, 880, 1199, 1540). Sometimes two consecutive lines
have the same alliteration, but the practice of the author of
*Morte Arthur* of grouping from three to five lines together

---

[1] For the characteristics of the Gawain-poet in alliteration, see
Trautmann, *Über Verf.,* pp. 29-31; for further discussion of the
alliteration, see Fischer, pp. 38-48, Thomas, pp. 59-64, and especially
Schumacher's excellent dissertation on the alliteration of the whole
ME. school.

[2] *Sp* alliterates with itself without exception; *sk* 14 times with
itself, but once irregularly with *s* (523); *st* 35 times with itself,
and only once with *s* (999), since 995 may be considered double
alliteration (Schumacher, p. 110). The curious fact may be noted
here that in *excused,* 62, the *sk* alliterates, whereas in *excuse,* 70,
the alliteration is with *k; sp* is always the alliterative sound in
*expounde* (1058, 1492, 1565, 1606, 1729). *Sch* alliterates twice with
*s* (58, 566) and once with *sk* (600); *sm* alliterates only with itself
except at 566, and possibly 1019 (see note). Other peculiarities are
the alliteration of *z* with *s* (1169), cf. *Pat.* 470, *Gaw.* 517; and
*ch* with *k?* (464), but see Schumacher, p. 169.

by this means, is wholly unknown to the author of *Purity* and *Patience*.

## VIII.  DIALECT AND LANGUAGE[1]

It is difficult to determine precisely the dialect of this group of alliterative poems.  The criterion of rhyme is not altogether satisfactory because of the paucity of rhymes in *Gawain,* and the license in the use of rhyme required by the metre of *The Pearl*.[2]  The peculiarities of vocabulary, the large number of Scandinavian loan-words, for example, which have led some editors to place the poems in Lancashire or Cheshire,[3] are not sufficiently distinctive to fix the origin of the poem within such definite geographical limits. On the other hand, if these tests of the dialect of the original poem yield only vague results, it is certain that the dialectal traits of the manuscript as we now have it are overwhelmingly West Midland in character.

Among the characteristics that point to this dialect are

---

[1] A new investigation of the language of this group of poems is not attempted in this section.  The studies of the language of these poems by Morris, Schwahn, Fick, and Knigge (see Bibliography), though old, are still valuable, and should be consulted for details. Only the chief dialectal characteristics and a few other peculiarities of the language, knowledge of which may save the reader trouble, are mentioned.

[2] On the rhymes of *The Pearl,* see Fick, p. 8.

[3] Bateson (p. xxxii), following Morris, attributes the poems to Lancashire, but the evidence for this on the basis of the vocabulary of modern dialects is entirely insufficient.  Brunner (*Archiv* 132. 185) rightly criticizes this view, but he seems to me too skeptical in rejecting any conclusions about the original dialect of the poems. Wyld (*Engl. Stud.* 47. 47) objects to Lancashire on other grounds.

[4] These tests of dialect are based chiefly on the characteristics enumerated by Morsbach in his *Mittelenglische Grammatik* (Halle, 1896), pp. 15-7, esp. p. 15 n.; and Wyld in his *Short History of English* (London, 1914), pp. 122-3.  The only characteristic generally

(1) the frequent representation of OE. *eo* by *u*, as in *urþe*,
150; *brurdes*, 1474; (2) the frequent use of *o* before
nasals, as in *honde*, 174, 734 (as well as *hande*, 34, 155),
and *mon*, 124, 183, etc. (as well as *man*, 51, 180, etc.) ; (3)
the representation of OE. $\bar{y}$ by *u* (*ui*, *uy*),[1] as well as by *y*,
as in *fust*, 1535, beside *fyste*, 1723; *luþer*, 163, beside
*lyþerly*, 36; *huyde*, 915; *kuy*, 1259; (4) the participial
ending *-ande* as in the North, in contrast to the *-ende*
of East Midland; (5) the occurrence of the pronominal
form *þay* (from Old Norse), together with the native forms
*her, hem,* and the preservation of the feminine nom. *ho;*
(6) the use of the curious form *schyn*, 1435, 1810, as pres.
3 pl. of *schal*.[2]   The evidence of the manuscript, to be sure,
is not proof that the dialect of the original, as well as that
of the scribe, was West Midland, but there is every likelihood that they were not very different.   Morris declared[3]
that 'the uniformity and consistency of the grammatical
forms is so entire, that there is no internal evidence of
subsequent transcription into any other dialect than that
in which they were originally written.'   It would perhaps
be safer to say that most of the dialectal characteristics of
the manuscript are undoubtedly those of the poet himself.
The evidence of the manuscript, together with that of the
vocabulary and the rhymes of the other poems by the same
author, make it almost certain that *Purity* was actually
composed in the West Midland dialect.[4]

found in West Midland, and not usual in the poems of this group,
is the occurrence of *u* for *e* in such endings as *-us, -ud,* for *-es, -ed;*
but there are at least two examples of this—*flemus* (pres. 3 sg.),
*Pur.* 31, and *exorsismus* (pl.), 1579.

[1] That OE. *y* was often kept (written *u*, etc.) in West and Central
Midland, has been shown by Wyld, *Engl. Stud.* 47. 1-58. On the
basis of his investigation Wyld would assign the poems of this
group to Derbyshire rather than Lancashire (p. 47).

[2] Cf. Morris, *Early Engl. Allit. Poems,* p. xxvi.

[3] *Early Engl. Allit. Poems,* p. viii.

[4] It has been suggested by some students of the language, for

Certain Northern traits are generally assumed to be due to the fact that the poet was writing in the northern part of the West Midland area. Among Northern characteristics are (1) the ending of the pres. 2 and 3 sg. in *-s, -es* (*-ez*); (2) the occasional ending *-et* in the preterite of weak verbs, as in *bounet,* 1398; *tulket,* 1414 (Schwahn, p. 18); (3) the appearance of contract forms like *ma,* 625; *tatz,* 735; *bos,* 687; (4) the representation of OE. *hw* by *qu* (as well as by Southern *wh*), as in *quite,* 1440; *quo,* 1650; and (5) the representation of OE. *ā* by *a* (as well as by Southern *o*), as in *halde,* 652 (but *holde* once, 315).

Certain other peculiarities of the manuscript—phonological, orthographical, and morphological—may be noted here for the convenience of the reader.

I.   Phonological and Orthographical.

(a) Vowels. *ĕ* frequently becomes *i: kynned,* 915, 1072; *fyþer,* 530, 1026; *rydelles,* 969, but *redles,* 1197 (*e* here shortened from OE. *ǣ, ē*). Still more frequently *ĭ* appears as *e: wekked,* 855, beside *wykked,* 570; *þrevenest,* 1571, beside *þryvenest,* 1639; *þeder,* 64, 461, beside *þider,* 45, 61. The spelling *y* (for OE., ON. *ī*, OF. *i*) is much commoner than *i*. OE. *ūg, ōg,* and *āg* (final) are all spelled either *ow* or *o*, the last two frequently *ogh: bowe,* 45, 67, but *boȝ,* 1551, 1750; *innoghe,* 669, but *innoȝe,* 808; *wowes,*

instance Fick (p. 9), that the present form of the poems shows traces of being a copy by a Southern scribe. But it is no longer necessary to assume this, since most of these characteristics are now known not to be peculiar to the Southern dialect. Thus the representation of OE. *y* by *u* is now known to be West and Central Midland as well as Southern (see above, p. 72); the retention of *-i-* in the OE. weak verbs of the second class, as in *lyvyes, wonyes,* is not necessarily an indication of Southern dialect (see Schüddekopf's *Sprache u. Dialekt . . . William of Palerne,* Erlangen, 1886, p. 104, and Boerner's *Die Sprache Roberd Mannyngs of Brunne,* Halle, 1904, pp. 218-9); and the participles in *-ing* which occur in *The Pearl* and *Gawain* are at this late period Midland as well as Southern (Kaluza, *Engl. Gram.* 2. 191).

1403, but *woȝes*, 1424. *OE. ōw* appears both as *aw* (*au*) and *ow: stawed*, 360; *staued*, 352; *stowed*, 113.

(b) Consonants. Following a nasal, final *g* is often, and medial *g* is sometimes, written *k:*[1] *pink*, 1359 (for *þing*); *þinkez*, 916; *inspranc*, 408. Similarly after nasals, *g* frequently stands for *k: ring*, 592 (for *rink*); *stangez*, 439, plural of *stanc*, 1018 (OF. *estanc*). Final *s* is often written *z* (MS. *ȝ*), probably indicating the voicing of the consonant: *askez*, 2; *weldez*, 17; but *folȝes*, 6. The spelling *tz* (= *z*) occurs chiefly in unstressed forms like *hatz*, 1597; *watz*, 134. *W* sometimes occurs for *wh*, as in *wen*, 343 (cf. p. lvii on the alliteration of *wh* with *w*). Often *w* represents *v* in words of various origin: *þewes* (for *þeves*), 1142; *awayled*, 408; *wenge*, 201.

II. Inflection.[2]

(a) Nouns. The plural generally ends in -*es* (-*s*), -*ez*. Some plurals without ending occur: *syþe*, 1188, 1417; *myle*, 1387; *þink*, 1359; *ȝer*, 1192. Some remains of the OE. weak plural are to be found, for example, *yȝen*, 588, and the ending -(*e*)*n* has been added analogically to a few French words: *trumpen*, 1402, and perhaps *paune*, 1697 (see note). The adjectives *pover* and *sturn* have the plurals *poveren*, 127 and *sturnen*, 1402. The genitive case of nouns is frequently without ending in the singular: *kyte paune*, 1697; *ȝisterday steven*, 463 (here perhaps because of the initial *s*); especially in proper names, *Baltazar þewes*, 1436; *Israel Dryȝtyn*, 1314. In the plural the genitive case often ends in -*en* (OE. -*ena*): *blonkken bak*, 1412; *besten blod*, 1446; *chyldryn fader*, 684.

---

[1] That this confusion of *ng* with *nk* (which is one of Skeat's canons for Anglo-French spelling) is here not merely a scribal error, but due to the author himself, is shown by the rhyme in *Pearl: flonc* (for *flong*), 1165, with *ronk, bonc, wlonk*. On the unvoicing of final *d* see note on l. 473.

[2] The glossary should be consulted for the forms of the pronouns.

(b) Verbs. The infinitive ends in *-e,* sometimes in *-en.* The endings of the present indicative should be noted: sg. 1 *-e,* 2 and 3 *-es* (*-ez*); plur. *-e, -en,* sometimes *-es* (*-ez*). The present participle in *Purity* always ends in *-ande;* the past participle of strong verbs in *-en,* seldom in *-e.* The preterite 2 sg. sometimes ends in *-es* (*-ez*): *lantez,* 348; *moʒtez,* 655. The preterite and past participle of weak verbs sometimes omit the final *-d*[1]: *wyrle,* 475; *wer,* 69.

---

[1] Mabel Day (*Mod. Lang. Rev.* 14. 413) finds in the Gawain-poet 30 cases in which weak verbs ending in *l, n, r,* or a vowel, exhibit this irregularity before a vowel or unstressed *h,* or unstressed voiced *th.* Some of the cases here cited, e. g. *sware,* 1415, may be simply presents, since sudden change of tense is not uncommon in the poem.

# PURITY

## TEXT

# ABBREVIATIONS

M. = Morris, revised edition of 1869 (for full titles, see Bibliography).

M.¹ = Morris, 1864 } when differences between the editions are noted.
M.² = Morris, 1869

Sk. = Morris and Skeat, *Specimens,* 1884.

K. = Knigge.

Fi. = Fischer, pp. 61-3, unless otherwise stated.

Sch. = Schumacher, pp. 183-4, unless otherwise stated.

Th. = J. Thomas.

B. = Bateson, *Mod. Lang. Rev.* 13. 377-86.

G. = Gollancz, *ibid.* 14. 152-62.

E. = Emerson, *Publ. Mod. Lang. Ass.* 34. 494-522.

# PURITY

## I. Christ's Praise of Purity; The Wedding-Feast

Clannesse who so kyndly cowþe comende,     [61a]
And rekken up alle þe resounz þat ho by riȝt askez,
Fayre formez myȝt he fynde in for[þ]ering his speche,
And in þe contrare, kark and combraunce huge.     4
For wonder wroth is þe Wyȝ þat wroȝt alle þinges
Wyth þe freke þat in fylþe folȝes hym after—
As renkez of relygioun þat reden and syngen,
And aprochen to hys presens, and prestez arn called.     8
Thay teen unto his temmplé and temen to hymselven,
Reken wyth reverence þay r[ec]hen his auter,
Þay hondel þer his aune body and usen hit boþe:
If þay in clannes be clos, þay cleche gret mede;     12
Bot if þay conterfete crafte, and cortaysye wont,
As be honest utwyth, and inwith alle fylþez,
Þen ar þay synful hemself, and sulped altogeder,
Loþe God and his gere, and hym to greme cachen.     16
He is so clene in his corte, þe Kyng þat al weldez,
And honeste in his housholde and hagherlych served,
With angelez enorled in alle þat is clene,
Boþe wythinne and wythouten, in wedez ful bryȝt,     20
Nif he nere scoymus and skyg and non scaþe lovied,
Hit were a mervayl to much, hit moȝt not falle.

Kryst kydde hit hymself in a carp onez,

---

2 and *here, as generally, represented by* & *in* MS. — 3 MS., M.
forering; M. *note* forbering(?); Th. (*p. 44*), B. forþering. — 10
MS., wᵗ *which* M. *here, as always, expands* with, *I have expanded*
wyth, *since this is the spelling in over two-thirds of the cases where
the scribe writes it out:* MS. r..hen *with second and third letters
blurred, though* c *is partly legible.*—16 MS. (*but see Introd., p. x*);
M. boþe. — 17 corte, M. *here, as always, expands* courte (*but see
Introd., p. x, n. 3*).

Þer as he hevened aʒt happez, and hyʒt hem her
    medez. 24
Me mynez on one amonge oþer, as Maþew recordez,
Þat þus of clannesse unclosez a ful cler speche:
Þe haþel clene of his hert hapenez ful fayre,
For he schal loke on oure Lorde wyth a bone chere; 28
As so saytz, to þat syʒt seche ·schal he never
Þat any unclannesse hatz on, auwhere abowte;
For he þat flemus uch fylþe fer fro his hert
May not byde þat bur[n]e þat hit his body neʒen. 32
Forþy hyʒ not to heven in haterez totorne,
Ne in þe harlatez hod and handez unwaschen.
For what urþly haþel þat hyʒ honor haldez
Wolde lyke if a ladde com lyþerly attyred, 36
When he were sette solempnely in a sete ryche, [61b]
Abof dukez on dece, wyth dayntys served—
Þen þe harlot wyth haste helded to þe table
Wyth rent cokrez at þe kne, and his clutte traschez, 40
And his tabarde totorne, and his totez oute,
Oþer ani on of alle þyse, he schulde be halden utter,
With mony blame, ful bygge a boffet, peraunter,
Hurled to þe halle-dore and harde þeroute schowved, 44
And be forboden þat borʒe to bowe þider never,
On payne of enprysonment and puttyng in stokkez;
And þus schal he be schent for his schrowde feble,
Þaʒ never in talle ne in tuch he trespas more. 48
    And if unwelcum he were to a wor[d]lych prynce,

---

26 clannesse, *the scribe has corrected the first* s *from* ʒ.— 28 *MS.,
M.* bone; *Sch,* ?lovly.—30 *M.* anwhere (*MS. might be either* n
*or* u; *M. note* aywhere(?); *Fi.* awhere, *B.* anwhere: abowte, *the
last three letters are blurred and barely legible, like the last few
letters of most of ll. 26-36.* — 32 *M.* burne; *M.*² *is mistaken in
noting that MS. looks like* burre, *since the fourth letter resembles
rather the top of a* y. — 34 *MS.* harlateʒ, *though second* a *blurred;
M.* harloteʒ. — 38 *MS.* dukeʒ; *M.* dukes.— 40 *MS.* trascheʒ; *M.*
trasches.—49 *MS., M.* worþlych; *M.*² *note* worldlych(?).

Ȝet hym is þe hyȝe Kyng harder in [heven],
As Maþew melez in his masse of þat man ryche,
Þat made þe mukel mangerye to marie his here dere,                    52
And sende his sonde þen to say þat þay samne schulde,
And in comly quoyntis to com to his feste.
'For my boles and my borez arn bayted and slayne,
And my fedde foulez fatted wyth sclaȝt,                               56
My polyle þat is penne-fed and partrykez boþe,
Wyth scheldez of wylde swyn, swanez and cronez—
Al is roþeled and rosted ryȝt to þe sete;
Comez cof to my corte, er hit colde worþe.'                          60
    When þay knewen his cal þat þider com schulde,
Alle excused hem by þe skyly he scape by moȝt.
On hade boȝt hym a borȝ, he sayde, by hys trawþe,
'Now t[ur]ne I þeder als tyd, þe toun to byholde.'                   64
Anoþer nayed also, and nurned þis cawse:
'I haf ȝerned and ȝat ȝokkez of oxen,
And for my hyȝez hem boȝt; to bowe haf I mester,
To see hem pulle in þe plow aproche me byhovez.'                     68
'And I haf wedded a wyf,' so wer hym þe þryd,
'Excuse me at þe cort, I may not com þere.'
Þus þay droȝ hem adreȝ wyth daunger uch one,
Þat non passed to þe pla[c]e, þaȝ he prayed were.                    72
    Thenne þe ludych lorde lyked ful ille,                         [62a]
And hade dedayn of þat dede; ful dryȝly he carpez.
He saytz: 'Now for her owne sorȝe þay forsaken
    habbez,
More to wyte is her wrange þen any wylle gentyl.                     76
Þenne gotz forth, my gomez, to þe grete streetez,
And forsettez on uche a syde þe cete aboute;
Þe wayferande frekez, on fote and on hors,

---

50 *MS., M.* in her euen; *M.²* *note* her-in(?); *so Fi.*— 54 *B.*
to-com.— 57 *MS.* partrykeȝ; *M.* partrykes.— 62 *MS., M.* he; *Fi.*
þay.— 64 *MS.* tne; *M.* t[ur]ne.— 69 *MS., M.* sower; *M. note*
swer(?); *Fi.* (*p. 47*) *so* werp; *B.* so werned.— 72 *MS.* plate, as
*M. notes.*

Boþe burnez and burdez, þe better and þe wers,                      80
Laþez hem alle luflyly to lenge at my fest,
And bryngez hem blyþly to borӡe as barounez þay
  were,
So þat my palays plat ful be pyӡt al aboute;
Þise oþer wrechez iwysse worþy noӡt wern.'          84
   Þen þay cayred and com þat þe cost waked,
Broӡten bachlerez hem wyth þat þay by bonkez
  metten,
Swyerez þat swyftly swyed on blonkez,
And also fele upon fote, of fre and of bonde.          88
When þay com to þe corte, keppte wern þay fayre,
Styӡtled wyth þe stewarde, stad in þe halle,
Ful manerly wyth marchal mad for to sitte,
As he watz dere of degre dressed his seete.          92
Þenne seggez to þe soverayn sayden þerafter:
'Lo! lorde, wyth yor leve, at yor lege heste,
And at þi banne we haf broӡt, as þou beden habbez,
Mony renischche renkez, and ӡet is roum more.'          96
Sayde þe lorde to þo ledez, 'Laytez ӡet ferre,
Ferre out in þe felde, and fechez mo gestez,
Waytez gorstez and grevez, if ani gomez lyggez,
What-kyn folk so þer fare, fechez hem hider;          100
Be þay fers, be þay feble, forlotez none,
Be þay hol, be þay halt, be þay on-yӡed,
And þaӡ þay ben boþe blynde and balterande
  cruppelez,
Þat my hous may holly by halkez by fylled.          104
For, certez, þyse ilk renkez þat me renayed habbe
And denounced me noӡt now at þis tyme,
Schul never sitte in my sale my soper to fele,
Ne suppe on sope of my seue, þaӡ þay swelt schulde.'          108

---

86 metten, n *corrected by scribe from* ӡ.— 101 *MS., M.* forlotez;
*M. note* forletez(?).—104 may, *scribe apparently first wrote* ia
*and corrected to* m: *MS.* halkeӡ; *M.* halkes: *MS., M.* by; *Fi.* be.
— 108 *MS., M.*[1] þaӡ þaӡ; *M.*[2] þaӡ.

Thenne þe sergauntez, at þat sawe, swengen
 þeroute, [62b]
And diden þe dede þat [is] demed, as he devised hade,
And wyth peple of alle plytez þe palays þay fyllen—
Hit weren not alle on wyvez sunez, wonen wyth on
 fader. 112
Wheþer þay wern worþy oþer wers, wel wern þay
 stowed,
Ay þe best byfore and bryȝtest atyred,
Þe derrest at þe hyȝe dese þat dubbed wer fayrest;
And syþen on lenþe bilooghe ledez inogh, 116
And ay a segge soerly semed by her wedez.
So with marschal at her mete mensked þay were;
Clene men in compaynye forknowen wern lyte,
And ȝet þe symplest in þat sale watz served to þe fulle, 120
Boþe with menske and wyth mete and mynstrasy
 noble,
And alle þe laykez þat a lorde aȝt in londe schewe.
And þay bigonne to be glad þat god drink haden,
And uch mon wyth his mach made hym at ese. 124

## II. The Punishment of the Man in Foul Clothes

Now inmyddez þe mete þe mayster hym biþoȝt,
Þat he wolde se þe semble þat samned was þere,
And rehayte rekenly þe riche and þe poveren,
And cherisch hem alle wyth his cher, and chaufen
 her joye. 128
Þen he bowez fro his bour into þe brode halle,
And to þe best on þe bench, and bede hym be myry,
Solased hem wyth semblaunt and syled fyrre,

---

110 *MS.* þat demed; *M.* þat [is]; *Fi.* þat [he]. — 116 bilooghe,
*see Introd., p. x, n. 2.*—117 *MS., M.* soerly; *M. note* soberly(?);
*E.* serly. — 119 compaynye, *scribe corrected second y from i.* — 127
*MS.* povener, *i. e. scribe put curl for -er over wrong letter; cf.
Gaw. 124,* sylvener *for* sylveren.

Tron fro table to table and talkede ay myrþe.                    132
   Bot as he ferked over þe flor, he fande wyth his
     yȝe—
Hit watz not for a halyday honestly arayed—
A þral þryȝt in þe þrong unþryvandely cloþed,
Ne no festival frok, bot fyled with werkkez;                    136
Þe gome watz ungarnyst wyth god men to dele.
And gremed þerwyth þe grete lord, and greve hým
     he þoȝt.
'Say me, frende,' quod þe freke wyth a felle chere,
'Hou wan þou into þis won in wedez so fowle?                    140
Þe abyt þat þou hatz upon, no halyday hit menskez;
Þou, burne, for no brydale art busked in wedez!
How watz þou hardy þis hous for þyn unhap [to]
     neȝe,
In on so ratted a robe and rent at þe sydez?                    144
Þow art a gome ungoderly in þat goun febele;         [63a]
Þou praysed me and my place ful pover and ful
     [g]nede,
Þat watz so prest to aproche my presens hereinne.
Hopez þou I be a harlot þi erigaut to prayse?'                  148
Þat oþer burne watz abayst of his broþe wordez,
And hurkelez doun with his hede, þe urþe he biholdez;
He watz so scoumfit of his scylle, lest he skaþe hent,
Þat he ne wyst on worde what he warp schulde.                  152
Þen þe lorde wonder loude laled and cryed,
And talkez to his tormenttorez: 'Takez hym,' he
     biddez,
'Byndez byhynde, at his bak, boþe two his handez,
And felle fetterez to his fete festenez bylyve;               156
Stik hym stifly in stokez, and stekez hym þerafter
Depe in my doungoun þer doel ever dwellez,
Greving and gretyng and gryspyng harde

---

143 to *supplied by M.* — 146 *MS.* nede; *M.* [g]nede. — 148 *M.*
erigant.

Of teþe tenfully togeder, to teche hym be quoynt.' 160
  Thus comparisunez Kryst þe kyndom of heven
To þis frelych feste þat fele arn to called;
For alle arn laþed luflyly, þe luþer and þe better,
Þat ever wern fulȝed in font þat fest to have. 164
Bot war þe wel, if þou wylt, þy wedez ben clene,
And honest for þe halyday, lest þou harme lache,
For aproch þou to þat Prynce of parage noble—
He hates helle no more þen hem þat ar sowle. 168
Wich arn þenne þy wedez þou wrappez þe inne,
Þat schal schewe hem so schene schrowde of þe best?
Hit arn þy werkez, wyterly, þat þou wroȝt havez,
And lyved wyth þe lykyng þat lyȝe in þyn hert, 172
Þat þo be frely and fresch fonde in þy lyve,
And fetyse of a fayr forme, to fote and to honde,
And syþen alle þyn oþer lymez lapped ful clene;
Þenne may þou se þy Savior and his sete ryche, 176
  For fele fautez may a freke forfete his blysse,
Þat he þe Soverayn ne se—þen for slauþe one,
As for bobaunce and bost, and bolnande pryde,
Þroly into þe develez þrote man þryngez bylyve; 180
For covetyse, and colwarde and croked dedez,
For mon-sworne, and men-sclaȝt, and to much
    drynk, [63b]
For þefte, and for þrepyng, unþonk may mon have;
For roborrye, and riboudrye, and resounez untrwe, 184
And dysheriete and depryve dowrie of wydoez,
For marryng of maryagez, and mayntnaunce of
    schrewez,
For traysoun and trichcherye, and tyrauntyre boþe,
And for fals famacions and fayned lawez— 188
Man may mysse þe myrþe þat much is to prayse

161 *MS., M.* heveñ. — 168 *MS., M.* sowle; *M. note* fowle(?);
*Fi.* soudly. — 179 *MS., M.* pryyde, *but this is merely the scribe's
error in adding y after he had already made the abbreviation.* —
187 *M. suggests* loþe(?) *for* boþe.

For such unþewez as þise, and þole much payne,
And in þe Creatores cort com never more,
Ne never see hym with syȝt for such sour tornez.     192

### III.  God's Vengeance on Lucifer and on Adam

Bot I have herkned and herde of mony hyȝe clerkez,
And als in resounez of ryȝt red hit myselven,
Þat þat ilk proper Prynce þat paradys weldez
Is displesed at uch a poynt þat plyes to scaþe.     196
Bot never ȝet in no boke breved I herde
Þat ever he wrek so wyþerly on werk þat he made,
Ne venged for no vilte of vice ne synne,
Ne so hastyfly watz hot for hatel of his wylle,     200
Ne never so sodenly soȝt unsoundely to weng[e],
As for fylþe of þe flesch þat foles han used.
For, as I fynde, þer he forȝet alle his fre þewez,
And wex wod to þe wrache for wrath at his hert.     204
For þe fyrste felonye þe falce fende wroȝt,
Whyl he watz hyȝe in þe heven hoven upon lofte,
Of alle þyse aþel aungelez attled þe fayrest;
And he unkyndely as a karle kydde a reward.     208
He seȝ noȝt bot hymself how semly he were,
Bot his Soverayn he forsoke, and sade þyse wordez:
'I schal telde up my trone in þe tramountayne,
And by lyke to þat Lorde þat þe lyft made.'     212
With þis worde þat he warp, þe wrake on hym lyȝt,
Dryȝtyn wyth his dere dom hym drof to þe abyme,
In þe mesure of his mode, his metz never þe lasse;
Bot þer he tynt þe type dool of his tour ryche.     216
Þaȝ þe feloun were so fers for his fayre wedez     [64a]
And his glorious glem þat glent so bryȝt,
As sone as Dryȝtynez dome   drof to hymselven,

201 *MS., M.* weng. — 203 *MS.* þeweȝ; *M.* þewes. — 208 *MS., M.* areward; *NED.* a reward. — 211 *MS., M.*[1] tramountayne, *M.*[2] tra mountayne. — 215 *MS., M., G.* metȝ; *B.* meth (*see note*).

Þikke þowsandez þro þrwen þeroute,                        220
Fellen fro þe fyrmament fendez ful blake,
[S]weved at þe fyrst swap as þe snaw þikke,
Hurled into helle-hole as þe hyve swarmez.
Fy[lt]er fenden folk forty dayez lencþe,                  224
Er þat styngande storme stynt ne myȝt;
Bot as smylt mele under smal sive smokez forþikke,
So fro heven to helle þat hatel schor laste,
On uche syde of þe worlde aywhere ilyche.                228
Þis hit watz a brem brest and a byge wrache;
And ȝet wrathed not þe Wyȝ, ne þe wrech saȝtled,
Ne never wolde for wyl[fulnes] his worþy God
     knawe,
Ne pray hym for no pite, so proud watz his wylle.  232
Forþy þaȝ þe rape were rank, þe rawþe watz lyttel;
Þaȝ he be kest into kare, he kepes no better.

   Bot þat oþer wrake þat wex, on wyȝez hit lyȝt
Þurȝ þe faut of a freke þat fayled in trawþe,            236
Adam inobedyent, ordaynt to blysse,
Þer pryvely in paradys his place watz devised,
To lyve þer in lykyng þe lenþe of a terme,
And þenne enherite þat home þat aungelez forgart;  240

---

220 *M.*[1] Thikke; *M.*[2] [þi]kke, *but the* þ *and* i *are both distin-
guishable, the* i *very plainly in the offset; many of the words
beginning the lines of this fol. are hardly decipherable, and some are
partly 'offset' on the opposite page (see Introd., p. viii).*—222
*MS.* (?), *M.* weued; *M. note* wened (?); *Fi.* (*p.* 46) sweyed; *G.*
*reads* sweued, *saying that the first letter, though blurred, can still
be read. I cannot see this* s.—224 *MS.* fy..er; *M.*[1] fylter; *M.*[2]
fyltyr, *but* -er *fairly plain and confirmed by offset,* lt *very indistinct;*
*E.* fylter[ed].—225 er, r *blurred, but clear in offset.*—226 bot
*blurred, but confirmed by offset: MS.* smokeȝ; *M.* smokes.—228
*MS., M.* worlde; *Sch.* erþe *for allit.* (*but see note*).—229 *MS., M.*
þis, *upper part of* þ *indistinct in MS.; M. note* ȝis(?) *adopted by*
*Fi.*—230 *G. suggests* wroth.—231 *MS., M.* wylnesful; *Gollancz*
(*Athen. 1894. 2. 646*), *Fi.* wilfulnes.—233 *MS.* lyttlel—237 *MS.*
*M.* in obedyent; *M. note* obedience(?), *accepted by Fi.; but M.*
*in notes* in-obedyent(?), *so Sk.*

Bot þurȝ þe eggyng of Eve he ete of an apple
Þat enpoysened alle peplez þat parted fro hem boþe,
For a defence þat watz dyȝt of Dryȝtyn selven,
And a payne þeron put and pertly halden.          244
Þe defence watz þe fryt þat þe freke towched,
And þe dom is þe deþe þat drepez uus alle.
Al in mesure and meþe watz mad þe veng[a]unce,
And efte amended wyth a mayden þat make had never.   248

## IV.  GOD'S WARNING TO NOAH

Bot in þe þryd watz forþrast al þat þryve schuld:
Þer watz malys mercyles and mawgre much scheued,
Þat watz for fylþe upon folde þat þe folk used,
Þat þen wonyed in þe worlde wythouten any may-
          sterz.                                    252
Hit wern þe fayrest of forme and of face als,       [64b]
Þe most and þe myriest þat maked wern ever,
Þe styfest, þe stalworþest þat stod ever on fete,
And lengest lyf in hem lent of ledez alle oþer;     256
For hit was þe forme-foster þat þe folde bred,
Þe aþel aunceterez sunez þat Adam watz called,
To wham God hade geven alle þat gayn were,
Alle þe blysse boute blame þat bodi myȝt have,      260
And þose lykkest to þe lede þat lyved next after;

---

245 *MS.* towched *retraced like the rest of the last words in ll.*
*245-52 by second hand (see Introd., pp. viii-ix).*—247 *MS.* (*second*
*hand*), *M.* vengiaunce; *the crowding of the second stroke of* u
*before* c, *and the extension of the line over* u (*abbrev. for* n) *seem*
*to show that the corrector has made* iau *out of the scribe's original*
au, *cf. scribe's spelling in other instances, 744, 1013; Pat. 284.*—
248 *MS.* (*second hand*), *M*[1]. had; *M*[2]. hade.—252 *M.* [þ]at, *but* þ
*seems to me as legible as initial* þ *in two lines preceding, all extremely*
*faint.* — 257 *MS.* ffor, *the* r *resembles a modern* x, *and is unlike*
*either of the scribe's* r's (*cf.* broþer, *924, and see Introd., p. ix*);
*MS., M., Sk.* forme-foster; *M. note, Fi.* forme-fosterez. — 261
*MS., M., Sk.* lede; *M. in notes* ledes(?), *accepted by Fi.*

Forþy so semly to see syþen wern none.
Þer watz no law to hem layd bot loke to kynde,
And kepe to hit, and alle hit cors clanly fulfylle.        264
    And þenne founden þay fylþe in fleschlych dedez,
And controeved agayn kynde contrare werkez,
And used hem unþryftyly uch on on oþer,
And als with oþer, wylsfully, upon a wrange wyse.        268
So ferly fowled her flesch þat þe fende loked
How þe deȝter of þe douþe wern derelych fayre,
And fallen in felaȝschyp wyth hem on folken wyse,
And engendered on hem jeauntez wyth her japez ille.  272
Þose wern men meþelez and maȝty on urþe,
Þat for her lodlych laykez alosed þay were.
He watz famed for fre þat feȝt loved best,
And ay þe bigest in bale þe best watz halden.        276
    And þenne evelez on erþe ernestly grewen,
And multyplyed monyfolde inmongez mankynde;
For þat þe maȝty on molde so marre þise oþer,
Þat þe Wyȝe þat al wroȝt ful wroþly bygynnez.        280
When he knew uche contre coruppte in hitselven,
And uch freke forloyned fro þe ryȝt wayez,
Felle temptande tene towched his hert;
As wyȝe, wo hym withinne werp to hymselven:        284
'Me forþynkez ful much þat ever I mon made,
Bot I schal delyver and do away þat doten on þis
    molde,
And fleme out of þe folde al þat flesch werez,
Fro þe burne to þe best, fro bryddez to fyschez;        288
Al schal doun and be ded and dryven out of erþe  [65a]
Þat ever I sette saule inne, and sore hit me rwez
Þat ever I made hem myself; bot if I may herafter,
I schal wayte to be war her wrenchez to kepe.'        292
    Þenne in worlde watz a wyȝe wonyande on lyve,

269 *MS., M.* fende; *Sk., E.* fende[z]. — 275 *MS., M., Sk.* famed;
*M. note* fained(?). — 279 *MS., M.* marre; *Sk.* marre[d]. — 281 *MS.*
coruppte; *M., Sk.* corupte.

Ful redy and ful ryȝtwys, and rewled hym fayre;
In þe drede of Dryȝtyn his dayez he usez,
And ay glydande wyth his God his grace watz þe
    more.    296
Hym watz þe nome Noe, as is innoghe knawen;
He had þre þryven sunez, and þay þre wyvez,
Sem soþly þat on, þat oþer hyȝt Cam,
And þe jolef Japheth watz gendered þe þryd.    300
   Now God in nwy to Noe con speke
Wylde wrakful wordez in his wylle greved:
'Þe ende of alle-kynez flesch þat on urþe mevez,
Is fallen forþ wyth my face, and forþer hit I þenk.    304
Wyth her unworþelych werk me wlatez wythinne,
Þe gore þerof me hatz greved and þe glette nwyed;
I schal strenkle my distresse, and strye al togeder,
Boþe ledez and londe and alle þat lyf habbez.    308
Bot make to þe a mancioun, and þat is my wylle,
A cofer closed of tres, clanlych planed;
Wyrk wonez þerinne for wylde and for tame,
And þenne cleme hit wyth clay comly wythin[n]e.    312
And alle þe endentur dryven daube wythouten.
And þus of lenþe and of large þat lome þou make:
Þre hundred of cupydez þou holde to þe lenþe,
Of fyfty fayre overþwert forme þe brede;    316
And loke even þat þyn ark have of heȝþe þrette,
And a wyndow wyd upon, wroȝt upon lofte,
In þe compas of a cubit kyndely sware,
A wel dutande dor don on þe syde;    320
Haf hallez þerinne and halkez ful mony,
Boþe boskez and bourez and wel bounden penez.
For I schal waken up a water to wasch alle þe worlde,
And quelle alle þat is quik wyth quavende flodez;    324

---

312 *MS.* wᵗime.—322 *MS.* bourez (*see Introd., p. x, n. 3*).—322
*MS.* boþe, *but e peculiar, as though corrected from* o: boskez
*retraced by second hand, as also parts of ll. 324-5* (*see Introd., p. ix*).

Alle þat glydez and gotz and gost of lyf habbez,    [65b]
I schal wast with my wrath, þat wons upon urþe.
Bot my forwarde wyth þe I festen on þis wyse,
For þou in reysoun hatz rengned and ryȝtwys ben
    ever:                                                                       328
Þou schal enter þis ark wyth þyn aþel barnez
And þy wedded wyf; with þe þou take
Þe makez of þy myry sunez; þis meyny of aȝte
I schal save of monnez saulez, and swelt þose oþer.   332
Of uche best þat berez lyf busk þe a cupple;
Of uche clene comly kynde enclose seven makez,
Of uche horwed in ark halde bot a payre,
For to save me þe sede of alle ser kyndez;            336
And ay þou meng wyth þe malez þe mete ho-bestez,
Uche payre by payre to plese ayþer oþer;
Wyth alle þe fode þat may be founde, frette þy cofer,
For sustnaunce to yowself and also þose oþer.'        340
Ful grayþely gotz þis god man and dos Godez hestes,
In dryȝ dred and daunger, þat durst do non oþer.
Wen hit watz fettled and forged and to þe fulle
    grayþed,
Þenn con Dryȝttyn hym dele dryȝly þyse wordez.        344

## V. The Flood

'Now, Noe,' quod oure Lorde, 'art þou al redy?
Hatz þou closed þy kyst wyth clay alle aboute?'
'Ȝe, Lorde, wyth þy leve,' sayde þe lede þenne,
'Al is wroȝt at þi worde, as þou me wyt lantez.'      348
'Enter in, þenn,' quod he, 'and haf þi wyf wyth þe,
Þy þre sunez, wythouten þrep, and her þre wyvez;
Bestez, as I bedene have, bosk þerinne als,
And when ȝe arn staued styfly, stekez yow þerinne.    352
Fro seven dayez ben seyed I sende out bylyve
Such a rowtande ryge þat rayne schal swyþe,

324 *MS.* þat þat, *with a line drawn through second* þat; *M.*[1] þat
þat; *M.*[2] þat.

Þat schal wasch alle þe worlde of werkez of fylþe;
Schal no flesch upon folde by fonden on lyve,    356
Outtaken yow aȝt in þis ark staued,
And sed þat I wyl save of þyse ser bestez.'
[No]w Noe never sty[n]tez—þat [n]yȝ[t] he by-
    gynnez—
Er al wer stawed and stoken as þe steven wolde.    360
  Thenne sone com þe sevenþe day when samned wern
    alle,    [66a]
And alle woned in þe whichche, þe wylde and þe tame.
Þen bolned þe abyme, and bonkez con ryse,
Waltes out uch w[e]lle-heved in ful wode stremez,    364
Watz no brymme þat abod unbrosten bylyve;
Þe mukel lavande loghe to þe lyfte rered.
Mony clustered clowde clef alle in clowtez.
Torent uch a rayn-ryfte and rusched to þe urþe,    368
Fon never in forty dayez; and þen þe flod ryses,
Overwaltez uche a wod and þe wyde feldez.
For when þe water of þe welkyn wyth þe worlde
    mette,
Alle þat deth moȝt dryȝe drowned þerinne.    372
Þer watz moon for to make when meschef was
    cnowen,
Þat noȝt dowed bot þe deth in þe depe stremez.
Water wylger ay wax, wonez þat stryede,
Hurled into uch hous, hent þat þer dowelled.    376
Fyrst feng to þe flyȝt alle þat fle myȝt,
Uuche burde wyth her barne þe byggyng þay levez,
And bowed to þe hyȝ bonk þer brentest hit wer[e],
And heterly to þe hyȝe hyllez þay aled on faste.    380

359 *M.* now, *but I cannot distinguish first two letters, which are
very blurred: MS., M.* stystez, *M. note* styntez(?), *accepted by
Fi.: MS.* myȝ, *M., Sk.* niyȝ[t].—360 er al *very faint.*—365 *MS.,
M., Sk.* walle (*but cf.* 428).—376 *MS., M.* dowelled; *Sk.* dwelled.
—379 *MS., M.* wern; *Sk. emends to* were; *B. would read* bonkes.
380 *MS., M.*[1] aled; *M.*[2], *Sk.* [h]aled, *but consistency in this respect
would necessitate many more emendations.*

Bot al watz nedlez her note, for never cowþe stynt
Þe roȝe raynande ryg, þe raykande wawez,
Er uch boþom watz brurdful to þe bonkez eggez,
And uche a dale so depe þat demmed at þe brynkez.

    Þe moste mountaynez on mor þenne watz no more
      dryȝe,
And þeron flokked þe folke, for ferde of þe wrake.
Syþen þe wylde of þe wode on þe water flette;
Summe swymmed þeron þat save hemself trawed,    388
Summe styȝe to a stud and stared to þe heven,
Rwly wyth a loud rurd rored for drede.
Harez, herttez also, to þe hyȝe runnen,
Bukkez, bausenez, and bulez to þe bonkkez hyȝed;    392
And alle cryed for care to þe Kyng of heven,
Recoverer of þe Creator þay cryed uch one,
Þat amounted þe mase—his mercy watz passed,
And alle his pyte departed fro peple þat he hated.    396
Bi þat þe flod to her fete floȝed and waxed,    [66b]
Þen uche a segge seȝ wel þat synk hym byhoved;
Frendez fellen in fere and faþmed togeder,
To dryȝ her delful deystyne and dyȝen alle samen;    400
Luf lokez to luf and his leve takez,
For to ende alle at onez and for ever twynne.
By forty dayez wern faren, on folde no flesch styryed,
Þat þe flod nade al freten wyth feȝtande waȝez;    404
For hit clam uche a clyffe cubites fyftene,
Over þe hyȝest hylle þat hurkled on erþe.

    Þenne morkne in þe mudde most ful nede
Alle þat spyrakle inspranc, no sprawlyng awayled,    408
Save þe haþel under hach and his here straunge,
Noe þat ofte nevened þe name of oure Lorde,

---

382 *M. unnecessarily inserts* & *after* ryg; *if any word is omitted,
it would more probably be* ne. — 395 *MS., M.* þe masse þe mase;
*Sk.* þe mase. — 401 *MS.* to, *letters curiously combined,* o *perhaps
by another hand.* — 404 *MS., M., Sk.* waȝez, *M. note* wawez(?). —
408 *MS., M., Sk.* inspranc; *M. note* insprang(?).

Hym aȝtsum in þat ark as aþel God lyked,
Þer alle ledez in lome lenged druye.                                    412
Þe arc hoven watz on hyȝe wyth hurlande gotez,
Kest to kythez uncouþe þe clowdez ful nere.
Hit waltered on þe wylde flod, went as hit lyste,
Drof upon þe depe dam, in daunger hit semed,                          416
Withouten mast, oþer myke, oþer myry bawelyne,
Kable oþer capstan to clyppe to her ankrez,
Hurrok oþer hande-helme hasped on roþer,
Oþer any sweande sayl to seche after haven,                           420
Bot flote forthe wyth þe flyt of þe felle wyndez.
Whederwarde so þe water wafte, hit rebounde;
Ofte hit roled on rounde and rered on ende;
Nyf oure Lorde hade ben her lodezmon, hem had
     lumpen harde.                                                    424
  Of þe lenþe of Noe lyf to lay a lel date,
Þe sex hundreth of his age and none odde ȝerez,
Of secounde monyth, þe sevenþe day ryȝtez,
Towalten alle þyse welle-hedez and þe water flowed;   428
And þryez fyfty þe flod of folwande dayez,
Uche hille watz þer hidde wyth y[þ]ez ful graye.
Al watz wasted þat þer wonyed þe worlde wythinne,
Þer ever flote, oþer flwe, oþer on fote ȝede,                         432
That roȝly watz þe remnaunt þat þe rac dryvez,        [67a]
Þat alle gendrez so joyst wern joyned wythinne.
Bot quen þe Lorde of þe lyfte lyked hymselven
For to mynne on his mon his meth þat abydez,                          436
Þen he wakened a wynde on watterez to blowe;
Þenne lasned þe llak þat large watz are.
Þen he stac up þe stangez, stoped þe wellez,
Bed blynne of þe rayn, hit batede as fast;                            440

---

421 *MS., M., Sk.* flote, *E.* flote[d].—422 *MS., M., Sk.* rebounde;
*Fi.* rebounded.—430 *MS., M.* yreȝ; *M. note* yþez(?); *so Sk.,
Fi.*—431 wasted *perhaps partly retraced* (*see Introd., p. ix*).—432
on *inserted above line* (*see Introd., p. ix, n. 2*).—433 *at end of
precèding page* þat roȝly watz *as catchwords: Sk. note* rwly(?).

Þenne lasned þe loȝ lowkande togeder.

After harde dayez wern out on hundreth and fyfte,

As þat lyftande lome luged aboute

Where þe wynde and þe weder warpen hit wolde,　　444

Hit saȝtled on a softe day synkande to grounde;

On a rasse of a rok, hit rest at þe laste,

On þe mounte of Mararach of Armene hilles,

Þat oþerwayez on Ebru hit hat þe Thanes.　　448

Bot þaȝ þe kyste in þe cragez wer[e] closed to byde,

Ȝet fyned not þe flod, ne fel to þe boþemez;

Bot þe hyȝest of þe eggez unhuled wern a lyttel,

Þat þe burne bynne borde byhelde þe bare erþe.　　452

　Þenne wafte he upon his wyndowe, and wysed
　　þeroute

A message fro þat meyny hem moldez to seche:

Þat watz þe raven so ronk, þat rebel watz ever;

He watz colored as þe cole, corbyal untrwe.　　456

And he fongez to þe flyȝt and fannez on þe wyndez,

H[o]vez hyȝe upon hyȝt to herken typyngez.

He croukez for comfort when carayne he fyndez

Kast up on a clyffe þer costese lay drye;　　460

He hade þe smelle of þe smach and smoltes þeder sone,

Fallez on þe foule flesch and fyllez his wombe,

And sone ȝederly forȝete ȝisterday steven,

How þe chevetayn hym charged þat þe kyst ȝemed.　　464

Þe raven raykez hym forth, þat reches ful lyttel

How alle fodez þer fare, ellez he fynde mete;

---

449 *MS.,* wern; *Sk.* wer[e]; *Schwahn (p. 26)* wer enclosed, *but cf. 379.*—451 *MS., M.* wern; *Sk.* were.—452 *M.¹* lorde, *M.²* borde, *cf. 467.*—456 *MS., M., Sk.* corbyal; *G. and E. suggest* corby al.—458 *M., Sk.* hoveȝ, *but second letter blurred, perhaps second stroke of o omitted: MS.* typyngeȝ; *M.* typynges.—461 *MS., M.* smolteȝ; *Sk.* smolte, *following M.'s suggestion in Glossary.*—464 *MS., M., Sk.* kyst; *Fi. (p. 42) and Sch. (p. 169) would read* chyst *for alliteration, but elsewhere form always* kyst *(see Glossary and Introd., p. lvii, n. 2).*

Bot þe burne bynne borde þat bod to hys come,
Banned hym ful bytterly wyth bestes alle samen.        468
He sechez anoþer sondezmon and settez on þe
    dou[v]e,                                           [67b]
Bryngez þat bry3t upon borde blessed, and sayde:
'Wende, worþelych wy3t, uus wonez to seche,
Dryf over þis dymme water; if þou druye fyndez,        472
Bryng bodworde to bot blysse to uus alle;
Þa3 þat fowle be false, fre be þou ever.'
Ho wyrle out on þe weder on wyngez ful scharpe,
Dre3ly alle alonge day þat dorst never ly3t;           476
And when ho fyndez no folde her fote on to pyche,
Ho umbekestez þe coste and þe kyst sechez;
Ho hittez on þe eventyde and on þe ark sittez,
Noe nymmes hir anon and naytly hir stauez.             480
Noe on anoþer day nymmez efte þe do[wv]e,
And byddez hir bowe over þe borne efte bonkez to
    seche;
And ho skyrmez under skwe and skowtez aboute,
Tyl hit watz ny3e at þe na3t, and Noe þen sechez.      484

### VI. THE DEPARTURE FROM THE ARK

On ark on an eventyde hovez þe dowve,
On stamyn ho stod and stylle hym abydez.
What! ho bro3t in hir beke a bronch of olyve,
Gracyously umbegrouen al wyth grene levez;             488
Þat watz þe syngne of savyte þat sende hem oure
    Lorde,
And þe sa3tlyng of hymself wyth þo sely bestez.
Þen watz þer joy in þat gyn where jumpred er dry3ed,

---

467 *M*.[1] lorde; *M*.[2], *Sk.* borde, *noting that MS. reads* lorde;
*perhaps MS. intended for* lorde; *cf. 452 and Introd., p. x.—*469
*MS., M., Sk.* doune; *M. note* douue *or* douene(?); *Sk. note 'for*
douene'; *K.* (*p. 54*) douue; *cf. note on this line, and 481, 485.—*
481 *MS.* doveue *or* dovene; *M., Sk.* dovene, *cf. 469, 485. —* 485 *M.,*
*Sk.* downe; *K.* (*p. 54*) dowue.

And much comfort in þat cofer þat watz clay-daubed. 492
Myryly on a fayr morn, monyth þe fyrst,
Þat fallez formast in þe зer, and þe fyrst day,
Ledez loзen in þat lome, and loked þeroute
How þat watterez wern woned and þe worlde dryed. 496
Uch on loved oure Lorde, bot lenged ay stylle,
Tyl þay had typþyng fro þe Tolke þat tyned hem
        þerinne.
Þen Godez glam to hem glod þat gladed hem alle,
Bede hem drawe to þe dor, delyver hem he wolde. 500
Þen went þay to þe wykket, hit walt upon sone,
Boþe þe burne and his barnez bowed þeroute,
Her wyvez walkez hem wyth, and þe wylde after,
Þroly þrublande in þronge, þrowen ful þykke. 504
    Bot Noe of uche honest kynde nem out an odde, [68a]
And hevened up an auter and halзed hit fayre,
And sette a sakerfyse þeron of uch a ser kynde
Þat watz comly and clene—God kepez non oþer. 508
When bremly brened þose bestez, and þe breþe rysed,
Þe savor of his sacrafyse soзt to hym even
Þat al spedez and spyllez; he spekes wyth þat ilke
In comly comfort ful clos and cortays wordez : 512
'Now, Noe, no more nel I never wary
Alle þe mukel mayny [on] molde for no mannez
        synnez,
For I se wel þat hit is sothe, þat alle mannez wyttez
To unþryfte arn alle þrawen wyth þoзt of her herttez, 516
And ay hatz ben, and wyl be зet, fro her barnage ;
Al is þe mynde of þe man to malyce enclyned ;
Forþy schal I never schende so schortly at ones
As dysstrye al for manez [dedes], dayez of þis erþe. 520
Bot waxez now and wendez forth and worþez to
        monye,

Multyplyez on þis molde, and menske yow bytyde.
Sesounez schal yow never sese of sede ne of hervest,
Ne hete, ne no harde forst, umbre ne droȝþe,          524
Ne þe swetnesse of somer, ne þe sadde wynter,
Ne þe nyȝt, ne þe day, ne þe newe ȝerez,
Bot ever renne restlez—rengnez ȝe þerinne!'
Þerwyth he blessez uch a best, and bytaȝt hem þis
          erþe.          528
     Þen watz a skylly skyvalde, quen scaped alle þe
          wylde:
Uche fowle to þe flyȝt þat fyþerez myȝt serve,
Uche fysch to þe flod þat fynne couþe nayte,
Uche beste to þe bent þat bytes on erbez;          532
Wylde wormez to her won wryþez in þe erþe,
Þe fox and þe folmarde to þe fryth wyndez,
Herttes to hyȝe heþe, harez to gorstez,
And lyounez and lebardez to þe lake-ryftes;          536
Hernez and havekez to þe hyȝe rochez,
Þe hole-foted fowle to þe flod hyȝez,
And uche best at a brayde þer hym best lykez.
Þe fowre frekez of þe folde fongez þe empyre.          540
Lo! suche a wrakful wo for wlatsum dedez          [68b]
Parformed þe hyȝe Fader on folke þat he made;
Þat he chysly hade cherisched he chastysed ful hard[e],
In devoydynge þe vylanye þat venkquyst his þewez.          544
     Forþy war þe now, wyȝe þat worschyp desyres
In his comlych corte þat Kyng is of blysse,
In þe fylþe of þe flesch þat þou be founden never,
Tyl any water in þe worlde to wasche þe fayly.          548
For is no segge under sunne so seme of his craftez,
If he be sulped in synne, þat syttez unclene—
On spec of a spote may spede to mysse
Of þe syȝte of þe Soverayn þat syttez so hyȝe;          552

527 *MS.*, *M.*[1] rengneȝȝe; *M.*[2], *Sk.* rengneȝ ȝe. — 532 *MS.*, *M.*[1]
þat þat; *M.*[2], *Sk.* þat. — 543 *MS.*, *M.* hardee; *Sk.* harde. — 550
*M.*[2] *inserts* ne *after* þat.

For þat schewe me schale in þo schyre howsez,
As þe beryl bornyst byhovez be clene,
Þat is sounde on uche a syde and no sem habes,
Wythouten maskle oþer mote as margerye-perle.      556

## VII. A Warning of God's Wrath against Sinners

Syþen þe Soverayn in sete so sore forþoȝt
Þat ever he man upon molde merked to lyvy;
For he in fylþe watz fallen, felly he venged,
Quen forferde alle þe flesch þat he formed hade.      560
Hym rwed þat he hem uprerde and raȝt hem lyflode,
And efte þat he hem undyd, hard hit hym þoȝt;
For quen þe swemande sorȝe soȝt to his hert,
He knyt a covenaunde cortaysly wyth monkynde þere,    564
In þe mesure of his mode and meþe of his wylle,
Þat he schulde never, for no syt, smyte al at onez,
As to quelle alle quykez for qued þat myȝt falle,
Whyl of þe lenþe of þe londe lastez þe terme.      568
Þat ilke skyl for no scaþe ascaped hym never.
Wheder wonderly he wrak on wykked men after:
Ful felly for þat ilk faute forferde a kyth ryche,
In þe anger of his ire þat arȝed mony;      572
And al watz for þis ilk evel, þat unhappen glette,
Þe venym and þe vylanye and þe vycios fylþe
Þat bysulpez mannez saule in unsounde hert,
Þat he his Saveour ne see wyth syȝt of his yȝen,      576
Þat alle illez he hates as helle þat stynkkez;      [69a]
Bot non nuyez hym, on naȝt ne never upon dayez,
As harlottrye unhonest, heþyng of selven;
Þat schamez for no schrewedschyp schent mot he
      worþe!      580
    Bot sa[v]or, mon, in þyself, þaȝ þou a sotte lyvie,

553 *MS., M.* me; *Fi.* we. — 560 forferde *abbrev. in MS.* (*see Introd., p. x, n. 3*); *M.* fourferde, *note* forferde(?). —581 *MS.* sauyŏ; *M.* sauyour.

Þaȝ þou bere þyself babel, byþenk þe sumtyme
Wheþer he þat stykked uche a stare in uche steppe
   yȝe,
Ȝif hymself be bore blynde, hit is a brod wonder;    584
And he þat fetly in face fettled alle eres,
If he hatz losed þe lysten hit lyftez mervayle;
Traue þou never þat tale, untrwe þou hit fyndez.
Þer is no dede so derne þat dittez his yȝen;    588
Þer is no wyȝe in his werk so war ne so stylle
Þat hit ne þrawez to hym þro er he hit þoȝt have.
For he is þe gropande God, þe grounde of alle dedez,
Rypande of uche a ring þe reynyez and hert;    592
And þere he fyndez al fayre a freke wythinne,
Þat hert honest and hol, þat haþel he honorez,
Sendez hym a sad syȝt to se his auen face,
And harde honysez þise oþer, and of his erde flemez.    596
Bot of þe dome of þe douþe for dedez of schame—
He is so skoymos of þat skaþe, he scarrez bylyve;
He may not dryȝe to draw allyt, bot drepez in hast,
And þat watz schewed schortly by a scaþe onez.    600

### VIII. Abraham Entertains the Three Angels

Olde Abraham in erde onez he syttez
Even byfore his hous-dore, under an oke grene;
Bryȝt blykked þe bem of þe brode heven,
In þe hyȝe hete þerof Abraham bidez,    604
He watz schunt to þe schadow under schyre levez.
Þenne watz he war on þe waye of wlonk wyȝez
   þrynne;
If þay wer farande and fre and fayre to beholde,

584 *MS.* sele, *as M. notes.* — 586 *MS., M.*[1] he he; *M.*[2] he. — 590 *in*
þro, o *of MS. has apparently been altered to* e *by drawing a stroke
through it, but* o *nevertheless unmistakable; M., who prints MS.
as* þre, *suggests* þer(?), *which is accepted by Fi.* — 592 *MS., M.*
ring; *M. note* rink *or* renk(?). — 600 *MS., M.* scaþe; *Fi.* schaþe,
*cf. K. p. 65 (but see Introd., p. lvii, n. 2, and Glossary).*

Hit is eþe to leve by þe last ende. 608
For þe lede þat þer laye þe levez anunder,
When he hade of hem syȝt, he hyȝez bylyve,
And as to God þe good mon gos hem agaynez,
And haylsed hem in onhede, and sayde: 'Hende
 Lorde, 612 [69b]
Ȝif ever þy mon upon molde merit disserved,
Lenge a lyttel with þy lede, I loȝly biseche;
Passe never fro þi povere, ȝif I hit pray durst,
Er þou haf biden with þi burne and under boȝe
 restted; 616
And I schal wynne yow wyȝt of water a lyttel,
And fast aboute schal I fare yor fette wer waschene;
Resttez here on þis rote, and I schal rachche after
And brynge a morsel of bred to banne yor hertte.' 620
'Fare forthe,' quod þe frekez, 'and fech as þou
 seggez;
By bole of þis brode tre we byde þe here.'
 Þenne orppedly into his hous he hyȝed to Sare,
Comaunded hir to be cof and quyk at þis onez: 624
'Þre mettez of mele menge, and ma kakez,
Under askez ful hote happe hem bylive.
Quyl I fete sumquat fat, þou þe fyr bete,
Prestly at þis ilke poynte sum polment to make.' 628
He cached to his cou-hous and a calf bryngez
Þat watz tender and not toȝe; bed tyrve of þe hyde,
And sayde to his servaunt þat he hit seþe faste,
And he dervely at his dome dyȝt hit bylyve. 632
Þe burne to be bare-heved buskez hym þenne,
Clechez to a clene cloþe and kestez on þe grene,
Þrwe þryftyly þeron þo þre þerve kakez,

618 *MS., M.* wer waschene; *Fi.* forto waschen. — 629 *MS.* probably covho*us, though* v *is raised above* o *slightly, so that it very
much resembles a* b; *M.* cobhous, *but note* 'cov-hous= cow-
house (?).'

And bryngez butter wythal, and by þe bred settez;   636
Mete messez of mylke he merkkez bytwene,
Syþen potage and polment in plater honest.
As sewer in a god assyse he served hem fayre,
Wyth sadde semblaunt and swete, of such as he hade;  640
And God as a glad gest mad god chere,
Þat watz fayn of his frende, and his fest praysed.
Abraham, al hodlez, wyth armez upfolden,
Mynystred mete byfore þo men þat my3tes al weldez.  644
   Þenne þay sayden, as þay sete samen alle þrynne,
When þe mete watz remued, and þay of mensk speken.
'I schal efte here away, Abram,' þay sayden,
'3et er þy lyvez ly3t leþe upon erþe,   648
And þenne schal Sare consayve and a sun bere,   [70a]
Þat schal be Abrahamez ayre, and after hym wynne
Wyth wele and wyth worschyp þe worþely peple,
Þat schal halde in heritage þat I haf men 3ark[ed].'  652
Þenne þe burde byhynde þe dor for busmar la3ed,
And sayde sothly to hirself Sare þe madde:
'May þou traw for tykle þat þou t[em]e mo3tez,
And I so hy3e out of age, and also my lorde.'   656
For soþely, as says þe wryt, he wern of sadde elde,
Boþe þe wy3e and his wyf, such werk watz hem
    fayled;
Fro mony a brod day byfore ho barayn ay b[e]ne,
Þat selve Sare wythouten sede into þat same tyme.  660
Þenne sayde oure Syre þer he sete: 'Se! so Sare la3es,
Not trawande þe tale þat I þe to schewed.
Hopez ho o3t may be harde my hondez to work?
And 3et I avow verayly þe avaunt þat I made,   664
I schal 3eply a3ayn and 3elde þat I hy3t,

---

652 *MS.* 3ark; *Fi.* (*p. 9*) *reads* 'þat I hafe me(n) 3ark[ed].' —
654 *MS., M.* sothly; *M. note* softly *or* sotly(?); *Fi.* sotly.—655
*MS., M.* tonne; *E.* te[m]e.—659 *MS.* by ene (*perhaps=*eue), *M.*
byene, *M.² note* bycame(?)

And sothely sende to Sare a soun and an hayre.'
Þenne swenged forth Sare and swer, by hir trawþe,
Þat for lot þat þay lansed ho laȝed never.    668
'Now innoghe, hit is not so,' þenne nurned þe
    Dryȝtyn,
'For þou laȝed aloȝ, bot let we hit one.'
    With þat þay ros up radly, as þay rayke schulde,
And setten toward Sodamas her syȝt alle at onez;    672
For þat cite þerbysyde watz sette in a vale,
No mylez fro Mambre mo þen tweyne,
Where so wonyed þis ilke wyȝ þat wendez wyth oure
    Lorde,
For to tent hym wyth tale and teche hym þe gate.    676
Þen glydez forth God; þe god mon hym folȝez,
Abraham heldez hem wyth, hem to conveye
In towarde þe cety of Sodamas þat synned had þenne
In þe faute of þis fylþe. Þe Fader hem þretes,    680
And sayde þus to þe segg þat sued hym after:
'How myȝt I hyde myn hert fro Habraham þe trwe,
Þat I ne dyscovered to his corse my counsayl so dere?
Syþen he is chosen to be chef chyldryn fader,    684
Þat so folk schal falle fro, to flete alle þe worlde,    [70b]
And uche blod in þat burne blessed schal worþe,
Me bos telle to þat tolk þe tene of my wylle,
And alle myn atlyng to Abraham unhaspe bilyve.    688

## IX. ABRAHAM'S PLEA FOR LOT

    'The grete soun of Sodamas synkkez in myn erez,
And þe gult of Gomorre garez me to wrath.
I schal lyȝt into þat led and loke myselven
If þay haf don as þe dyne dryvez on lofte.    692

666 *M.*[1] soun, *M.*[2] soñ, *but cf. 1299, where M.*[2] *prints same abbrev.*
sone; *perhaps it should here be considered double* n *as in* heueñ,
*161.* — 667 *MS., M.*[1] by, *M.*[2] hy (*prob. misprint*). — 668 *M.* lansed,
*note laused*(?).—669 *MS.* ñned, *M.* nurned (*see Introd., p. x, n. 3*).
— 678 *Fi.* for to. — 692 *MS.* īf, *cf. Pearl, 1185, and* īs, *1524.*

Þay han lerned a lyst þat lykez me ille,
Þat þay han founden in her flesch of fautez þe werst:
Uch male matz his mach a man as hymselven,
And fylter folyly in fere on femmalez wyse.  696
I compast hem a kynde crafte and kende hit hem
    derne,
And amed hit in myn ordenaunce oddely dere,
And dy3t drwry þerinne, doole alþerswettest,
And þe play of paramorez I portrayed myselven;  700
And made þerto a maner myriest of oþer,
When two true togeder had ty3ed hemselven,
Bytwene a male and his make such merþe schulde
    co[m]e,
Wel ny3e pure paradys mo3t preve no better,  704
Ellez þay mo3t honestly ayþer oþer welde;
At a stylle stollen steven, unstered wyth sy3t,
Luf-lowe hem bytwene lasched so hote,
Þat alle þe meschefez on mold mo3t hit not sleke.  708
Now haf þay skyfted my skyl and scorned natwre,
And henttez hem in heþyng an usage unclene.
Hem to smyte for þat smod smartly I þenk,
Þat wy3ez schal be by hem war, worlde wythouten
    ende.'  712
    Þenne ar3ed Abraham, and alle his mod chaunge[d]
For hope of þe harde hate þat hy3t hatz oure Lorde.
Al sykande he sayde: 'Sir, wyth yor leve,
Schal synful and saklez suffer al on payne?  716
Weþer ever hit lyke my Lorde to lyfte such domez,
Þat þe wykked and þe worþy schal on wrake suffer,
And weye upon þe worre half þat wrathed þe never?
Þat watz never þy won þat wro3tez uus alle.  720

---

703 *MS., M.* conne; *M. note* come(?). — 713 *MS.* chaunge, *M.* chaunge[d].—715 sir *abbrev., as also at 900, 1622, M.*¹ *syre, M.*² sir; *apparently the only instance of expansion in the MS. is Gaw. 387, where Gollancz prints* Sir.

Now fyfty fyn frendez wer founde in ȝonde toune,  [71a]
In þe cety of Sodamas and also Gomorre,
Þat never lakked þy laue, bot loved ay trauþe,
And reȝtful wern, and resounable, and redy þe to serve  724
Schal þay falle in þe faute þat oþer frekez wroȝt,
And joyne to her juggement her juise to have?
Þat nas never þyn note, unnevened hit worþe,
Þat art so gaynly a God and of goste mylde!'  728
'Nay, for fyfty,' quod þe Fader, 'and þy fayre speche,
And þay be founden in þat folk of her fylþe clene,
I schal forgyve alle þe gylt þurȝ my grace one,
And let hem smolt al unsmyten smoþely at onez.'  732
'Aa! blessed be þow,' quod þe burne, 'so boner and
    þewed,
And al haldez in þy honde, þe heven and þe erþe;
Bot for I haf þis talke, tatz to non ille
Ȝif I mele a lyttel more þat mul am and askez.  736
What if fyve faylen of fyfty þe noumbre,
And þe remnaunt be reken, how restes þy wylle?'
'And fyve wont of fyfty,' quod God, 'I schal forȝete
    alle,
And wythhalde my honde for hortyng on lede.'  740
'And quat if faurty be fre, and fauty þyse oþer,
Schalt þow schortly al schende and schape non oþer?'
'Nay, þaȝ faurty forfete, ȝet fryst I a whyle
And voyde away my vengaunce, þaȝ me vyl þynk.'  744
Þen Abraham obeched hym and [hy]ȝly him þonkkez:
'Now sayned be þou, Savior, so symple in þy wrath!
I am bot erþe ful evel and usle so blake,
For to mele wyth such a Mayster as myȝtez hatz alle;  748

---

730 *MS., M.* &; *M. note* An(?), *and similarly, 864, 1346.*—739
wont *inserted above line (see Introd., p. ix, n. 2).*—745 *MS., M.* &
loȝly him þonkkeȝ; *Fi.* (*p. 47*) *reads* heȝly, *referring to Gaw. 773;*
*Sch. proposes* 'and boweȝ to him loȝly.'

Bot I have bygonnen wyth my God, and he hit gayn
　　þynkez,
Ȝif I, forloyne as a fol, þy fraunchyse may serve.
What if þretty þryvande be þrad in ȝon tounez,
What schal I leve [o]f my Lorde, if he hem leþe
　　wolde?'　　　　　　　　　　　　　　　　　752
Þenne þe godlych God gef hym onsware,
'Ȝet for þretty in þrong I schal my þro steke,
And spare spakly of spyt, in space of my þewez,
And my rankor refrayne for þy reken wordez.'　　756
'What for twenty,' quod þe tolke, 'untwynez þou hem
　　þenne?'　　　　　　　　　　　　　　　　[71b]
'Nay, ȝif þou ȝernez hit, ȝet ȝark I hem grace;
If þat twenty be trwe, I tene hem no more,
Bot relece alle þat regioun of her ronk werkkez.'　760
'Now, aþel lorde,' quod Abraham, 'onez a speche,
And I schal schape no more þo schalkkez to helpe.
If ten trysty in toune be tan in þi werkkez,
Wylt þou mese þy mode, and menddyng abyde?'　764
'I graunt,' quod þe grete God, 'graunt mercy,' þat
　　oþer,
And þenne arest þe renk, and raȝt no fyrre.

　　And Godde glydez his gate by þose grene wayez,
And he conveyen hym con wyth cast of his yȝe;　768
And as he loked along þere as oure Lorde passed,
Ȝet he cryed hym after wyth careful steven:
'Meke Mayster, on þy mon to mynne if þe lyked,
Loth lengez in ȝon leede þat is my lef broþer,　　772
He syttez þer in Sodomis, þy servaunt so povere,
Among þo mansed men þat han þe much greved.
Ȝif þou tynez þat toun, tempre þyn yre,
As þy mersy may malte þy meke to spare.'　　　776
Þen he wendez his way, wepande for care,

---

752 *MS., M.* if my; *M.*[1] *note* of (?), *which E. accepts.* — 769 *M.*
als, *but scribe has written* s *directly over* l. — 777 *MS., M.* wendeȝ
wendeȝ.

Towarde þe mere of Mambre, [morn]ande for
  so[rʒe],
And þere in longyng al nyʒt he lengez in wones,
Whyl þe Soverayn to Sodamas sende to spye.          780

## X.  Lot Entertains the Two Angels

His sondes into Sodamas watz sende in þat tyme,
In þat ilk eventyde, by aungels tweyne,
Mevande mekely togeder as myry men ʒonge,
As Loot in a loge-dor lened hym alone,              784
In a porche of þat place pyʒt to þe ʒates,
Þat watz ryal and ryche—so watz þe renkes selven.
As he stared into þe strete þer stout men played,
He syʒe þer swey in asent swete men tweyne;         788
Bolde burnez were þay boþe, wyth berdles chynnez,
Royl rollande fax, to raw sylk lyke,
Of ble as þe brere-flor where so þe bare schew[e]d;
Ful clene watz þe countenaunce of her cler yʒen;    792
Wlonk whit watz her wede and wel hit hem semed. [72a]
Of alle feturez ful fyn and fautlez boþe,
Watz non au[c]ly in ouþer, for aungels hit wern.
  And þat þe ʒep underʒede þat in þe ʒate syttez,   796
He ros up ful radly and ran hem to mete,
And loʒe he loutez hem to, Loth, to þe grounde,
And syþen soberly: 'Syrez, I yow byseche,
Þat ʒe wolde lyʒt at my loge and lenge þerinne;     800
Comez to yor knavez kote, I crave at þis onez;

---

778 *MS., M.* wepande; *Sch. suggests* mourninge: *M.*[1] sorewe,
*M.*[2] so[rʒe] *with note* 'sorewe *is written by a late hand over the
original word,' (see Introd., p. viii, and also note on this line*).—783
*M.S., M.* meuand, meuande.—785 *in place the second stroke of the*
p *covers an extra* l.—791 *MS., M.* scheweed.—795 *MS., M.* autly,
*G. reads MS.* aucly (*but see note*).—799 *M. inserts* satʒ (*form
would probably be* saytʒ) *after* soberly.—801 *MS.* knaueʒ kote;
*M.*[1] kuchieʒ-kote (*which MS. resembles because second stroke of* a
*is high*); *M.*[2] knaues kote.

I schal fette yow a fatte yor fette forto wasche.
I norne yow bot for on ny3t ne3e me to lenge,
And in þe myry mornyng 3e may yor waye take.'          804
And þay nay þat þay nolde ne3 no howsez,
Bot stylly þer in þe strete as þay stadde wern,
Þay wolde lenge þe long na3t and logge þeroute;
Hit watz hous inno3e to hem þe heven upon lofte.      808
Loth laþed so longe wyth luflych wordez
Þat pay hym graunted to go, and gru3t no lenger.
Þe bolde to his byggyng bryngez hem bylyve,
Þat [watz] ryally arayed, for he watz ryche ever.     812
        Þe wy3ez wern welcom as þe wyf couþe;
His two dere do3terez devoutly hem haylsed,
Þat wer maydenez ful meke, maryed not 3et,
And þay wer semly and swete, and swyþe wel arayed.    816
Loth þenne ful ly3tly lokez hym aboute,
And his men amonestes mete for to dy3t:
'Bot þenkkez on hit be þrefte, what þynk so 3e make,
For wyth no sour ne no salt servez hym never.'        820
Bot 3et I wene þat þe wyf hit wroth to dyspyt,
And sayde softely to hirself: 'Þis un[s]avere hyne
Lovez no salt in her sauce; 3et hit no skyl were
Þat oþer burne be boute, þa3 boþe be nyse.'           824
Þenne ho saverez wyth salt her seuez uch one,
Agayne þe bone of þe burne þat hit forboden hade,
And als ho scelt hem in scorne þat wel her skyl
    knewen.
Why watz ho, wrech, so wod?  Ho wrathed oure
    Lorde.                                            828
Þenne seten þay at þe soper, wern served bylyve,   [72b]
Þe gestes gay and ful glad, of glam debonere,
Welawynnely wlonk tyl þay waschen hade,

---

812 *MS.* þat ryally arayed; *M. inserts* watz *after* ryally. — 819
*MS., M.* þynk; *M. note* þyng(?). — 820 *MS. M., Fi.* so*u*r; *M. note*
savo*u*r(?). — 821 *MS., M.* wroth; *M. note* wro3t(?); *Fi.* wro3te.
— 822 *MS.* vnfav*er*e; *M. corrects to* vnsav*er*e.

Þe trestes tylt to þe woȝe and þe table boþe. 832
  Fro þe seggez haden souped and seten bot a whyle,
Er ever þay bosked to bedde, þe borȝ watz al up,
Alle þat weppen myȝt welde, þe wakker and þe
    stronger,
To umbelyȝe Lothez hous þe ledez to take. 836
In grete flokkez of folk þay fallen to his ȝatez;
As a scowte-wach scarred, so þe asscry rysed;
Wyth kene clobbez of þat clos þay clatz on þe wowez,
And wyth a schrylle scharp schout þay schewe þyse
    worde: 840
'If þou lovyez þy lyf, Loth, in þyse wones,
Ȝete uus out þose ȝong men þat ȝore-whyle here
    entred,
Þat we may lere hym of lof, as oure lyst biddez,
As is þe asyse of Sodomas to seggez þat passen.' 844
Whatt! þay sputen and speken of so spitous fylþe,
What! þay ȝeȝed and ȝolped of ȝestande sorȝe,
Þat ȝet þe wynd, and þe weder, and þe worlde stynkes
Of þe brych þat upbraydez þose broþelych wordez. 848
  Þe god man glyfte wyth þat glam and gloped for
    noyse;
So scharpe schame to hym schot, he schrank at þe hert,
For he knew þe costoum þat kyþed þose wrechez,
He doted never for no doel so depe in his mynde. 852
'Allas!' sayd hym þenne Loth, and lyȝtly he rysez,
And bowez forth fro þe bench into þe brode ȝates.
What! he wonded no woþe of wekked knavez,
Þat he ne passed þe port þe p[er]il to abide. 856
He went forthe at þe wyket and waft hit hym after,
Þat a clyket hit cleȝt clos hym byhynde.
Þenne he meled to þo men mesurable wordez,
For harlotez wyth his hendelayk he hoped to chast: 860

840 *MS.*, *M.* worde; *Fi.* wordeȝ. — 841 *MS.* wones; *M.* woneȝ.
— 843 *MS.*, *M.* hym; *M. note* hem(?), *which Fi. accepts.* — 856
*MS.* pil; *M.* peril.

'Oo, my frendez so fre, yor fare is to strange;
Dotz away yor derf dyn, and derez never my gestes.
Avoy! hit is yor vylaynye, ȝe vylen yorselven;
And ȝe ar jolyf gentylmen, yor japez ar ille.                    864
Bot I schal kenne yow by kynde a crafte þat is better: [73a]
I haf a tresor in my telde of tow my fayre deȝter,
Þat ar maydenez unmard for alle men ȝette,
In Sodamas, þaȝ I hit say, non semloker burdes;                 868
Hit arn ronk, hit arn rype, and redy to manne;
To samen wyth þo semly þe solace is better.
I schal biteche yow þo two þat tayt arn and quoynt,
And laykez wyth hem as yow lyst, and letez my gestes
            one.'                                               872
    Þenne þe rebaudez so ronk rerd such a noyse,
Þat aȝly hurled in his erez her harlotez speche:
'Wost þou not wel þat þou wonez here a wyȝe strange?
An outcomlyng, a carle, we kylle of þyn heved!                  876
Who joyned þe be jostyse oure japez to blame,
Þat com a boy to þis borȝ, þaȝ þou be burne ryche?'
Þus þay þrobled and þrong and þrwe umbe his erez,
And distresed hym wonder strayt wyth strenkþe in
            þe prece,                                           880
Bot þat þe ȝonge men, so ȝepe, ȝornen þeroute,
Wapped upon þe wyket and wonnen hem tylle,
And by þe hondez hym hent and horyed hym wythinne,
And steken þe ȝates ston-harde wyth stalworth barrez.           884
Þay blwe a boffet in blande þat banned peple,
Þat þay blustered as blynde as Bayard watz ever;
Þay lest of Lotez logging any lysoun to fynde,
Bot nyteled þer alle þe nyȝt for noȝt at þe last.               888
Þenne uch tolke tyȝt hem þat hade of tayt fayled,
And uch on roþeled to þe rest þat he reche moȝt.
Bot þay wern wakned al wrank þat þer in won lenged,
Of on þe uglokest unhap þat ever on erd suffred.               892

864 *MS.* iapeȝ; *M.* iapes. — 891 *MS., M.* wrank; *M. note* wrang(?).

## XI.  THE DESTRUCTION OF THE CITIES

Ruddon of þe day-rawe ros upon uȝten,
When merk of þe mydnyȝt moȝt no more last.
Ful erly þose aungelez þis haþel þay ruþen,
And glopnedly on Godez halve gart hym upryse;    896
Fast þe freke ferkez up ful ferd at his hert,
Þay comaunded hym cof to cach þat he hade,
'Wyth þy wyf and þy wyȝez and þy wlonc deȝtters,
For we laþe þe, Sir Loth, þat þou þy lyf have.    900
Cayre tid of þis kythe er combred þou worþe,    [73b]
With alle þi here upon haste, tyl þou a hil fynde;
Foundez faste on yor fete, bifore yor face lokes,
Bot bes never so bolde to blusch yow bihynde,    904
And loke ȝe stemme no stepe, bot strechez on faste,
Til ȝe reche to a reset, rest ȝe never.
For we schal tyne þis toun and trayþely disstrye,
Wyth alle þise wyȝez so wykke wyȝtly devoyde,    908
And alle þe londe wyth þise ledez we losen at onez;
Sodomas schal ful sodenly synk into grounde,
And þe grounde of Gomorre gorde into helle,
And uche a koste of þis kyth clater upon hepes.'    912
Þen laled Loth: 'Lorde, what is best?
If I me fele upon fote þat I fle moȝt,
Hou schulde I huyde me fro hem þat hatz his hate
     kynned,
In þe brath of his breth þat brennez alle þinkez,    916
To crepe fro my Creator, and know not wheder,
Ne wheþer his fooschip me folȝez bifore oþer bi-
     hynde?'
Þe freke sayde: 'No foschip oure Fader hatz þe
     schewed,

912 *M.*¹ kyth, *M.*² kythe (*but see Introd., p. x, n. 2, on the flourish
after* h).—913 *Fi. would insert* loȝly *after* þen.—916 *MS., M.*
þinkeȝ; *M. note* þingeȝ.—918 *last four letters of* fooschip *retraced,
as also* sake (922), (o)ut of (923), *etc.* (*see Introd., p. ix*).

Bot hiʒly hevened þi hele fro hem þat arn combred:  920
Nou wale þe a wonnyng þat þe warisch myʒt,
And he schal save hit for þy sake þat hatz uus sende
    hider,
For þou art oddely þyn one out of þis fylþe,
And als Abraham, þy[n em], hit at himself asked.'  924
'Lorde, loved he worþe,' quod Loth, 'upon erþe!
Þe[r] is a cite herbisyde þat Segor hit hatte,
Here utter on a rounde hil hit hovez hit one,
I wolde, if his wylle wore, to þat won scape.'  928
'Þenn fare forth,' quod þat fre, 'and fyne þou never,
Wyth þose ilk þat þow wylt þat þrenge þe after,
And ay goande on yor gate, wythouten agayntote,
For alle þis londe schal be lorne, longe er þe sonne
    rise.'  932
Þe wyʒe wakened his wyf and his wlonk deʒteres,
And oþer two myri men þo maydenez schulde wedde;
And þay token hit as t[a]yt, and tented hit lyttel,
Paʒ fast laþed hem Loth, þay leʒen ful stylle.  936
Þe aungelez hasted þise oþer, and aʒly hem þratten, [74a]
And enforsed alle fawre forth at þe ʒatez:
Þo wern Loth and his lef, his luflyche deʒter,
Þer soʒt no mo to savement of cities aþel fyve.  940
Þise aungelez hade hem by hande out at þe ʒatez,
Prechande hem þe perile, and beden hem passe fast:
'Lest ʒe be taken in þe teche of tyrauntez here,
Loke ʒe bowe now bi bot, bowez fast hence!'  944
And þay kayre ne con and kenely flowen;

---

921 *M.* walle, *but* e *of MS. written over second* 1. — 924 *MS.*
broþer *is written in a second hand, the* b *and* r *being unlike the
scribe's, over the* n *of* þyn *and what was apparently* em, *perhaps*
eme; *the first stroke of* n *is plainly visible just before the* b, *and
some other bits of the original handwriting may be distinguished.* —
926 *MS., M.* þen. — 928 wore *apparently retraced.* — 935 *MS., M.*
tyt. — 945 *MS., E.* kayre ne con; *M.* kayre-ne (*Glossary* kayrene);
*Fi. quotes and accepts Trautmann's emendation* encon (*see note*).

Erly, er any heven-glem, þay to a hil comen.
  Þe grete God in his greme bygynnez on lofte;
To wakan wederez so wylde þe wyndez he callez,    948
And þay wroþely upwafte and wrastled togeder,
Fro fawre half of þe folde flytande loude.
Clowdez clustered bytwene, kesten up torres,
Þat þe þik þunder-þrast þirled hem ofte.    952
Þe rayn rueled adoun, ridlande þikke,
Of felle flaunkes of fyr and flakes of soufre,
Al in smolderande smoke smachande ful ille,
Swe aboute Sodamas and hit sydez alle,    956
Gorde to Gomorra, þat þe grounde laused,
Abdama and Syboym, þise ceteis alle faure,
Al birolled wyth þe rayn, rostted and brenned,
And ferly flayed þat folk þat in þose fees lenged.    960
For when þat þe helle herde þe houndez of heven,
He watz ferlyly fayn, unfolded bylyve;
Þe grete barrez of þe abyme he barst up at onez,
Þat alle þe regioun torof in riftes ful grete,    964
And cloven alle in lyttel cloutes þe clyffez aywhere,
As lance levez of þe boke þat lepes in twynne.
Þe brethe of þe brynston bi þat hit blende were,
Al þo citees and her sydes sunkken to helle.    968
Rydelles wern þo grete rowtes of renkkes wythinne,
When þay wern war of þe wrake þat no wyȝe
    achaped;
Such a ȝomerly ȝarm of ȝellyng þer rysed,
Þerof clatered þe cloudes þat Kryst myȝt haf rawþe.  972
  Þe segge herde þat soun to Segor þat ȝede,    [74b]
And þe wenches hym wyth þat by þe way folȝed;
Ferly ferde watz her flesch þat flowen ay ilyche,
Trynande ay a hyȝe trot þat torne never dorsten.    976
Loth and þo luly-whit, his lefly two deȝter,

---

956 *MS., M.* swe; *M. note* sweyed(?) *accepted by Fi.; B.* swe[d]
or swe[led].

Ay folȝed here face, bifore her boþe yȝen;
Bot þe balleful burde þat never bode keped,
Blusched byhynden her bak, þat bale for to herkken.   980
Hit watz lusty Lothes wyf þat over he[r] lyfte
    schulder
Ones ho bluschet to þe burȝe, bot bod ho no lenger,
Þat ho nas stadde a stiffe ston, a stalworth image
Also salt as ani se, and so ho ȝet standez.            984
Þay slypped bi and syȝe hir not þat wern hir samen-
    feres,
Tyl þay in Segor wern sette, and sayned our Lorde;
Wyth lyȝt lovez uplyfte þay loved hym swyþe,
Þat so his servauntes wolde see and save of such woþe.  988
Al watz dampped and don and drowned by þenne;
Þe ledez of þat lyttel toun wern lopen out for drede
Into þat malscrande mere, marred bylyve,
Þat noȝt saved watz bot Segor þat sat on a lawe,       992
Þe þre ledez þerin, Loth and his deȝter.
For his make watz myst, þat on þe mount lenged
In a stonen statue þat salt savor habbes,
For two fautes þat þe fol watz founde in mistrauþe:    996
On, ho served at þe soper salt bifore Dryȝtyn,
And syþen, ho blusched hir bihynde, þaȝ hir forboden
    were;
For on ho standes a ston, and salt for þat oþer,
And alle lyst on hir lik þat arn on launde bestes.    1000
  Abraham ful erly watz up on þe morne,
Þat alle naȝt much niye hade nom[e]n in his hert,
Al in longing for Loth leyen in a wache,
Þer he lafte hade oure Lorde, he is on lofte wonnen;  1004
He sende toward Sodomas þe syȝt of his yȝen,
Þat ever hade ben an erde of erþe þe swettest,
As aparaunt to paradis þat plantted þe Dryȝtyn;

---

981 *MS.* he, *M.* he[r]. — 1002 *MS., M.* no mon, *M. inserting* [so]
*after* naȝt; *Fi. would omit* alle; *E. suggests* nomon (*see note*).

Nou is hit plunged in a pit like of pich fylled.                1008
Suche a roþun of a reche ros fro þe blake,                 [75a]
Askez upe in þe ayre and usellez þer flowen,
As a fornes ful of flot þat upon fyr boyles
When bryȝt brennande brondez ar bet þer anunder. 1012
  Þis watz a vengaunce violent þat voyded þise places,
Þat foundered hatz so fayr a folk, and þe folde
    sonkken.
Þer faure citees wern set, nou is a see called,
Þat ay is drovy and dym, and ded in hit kynde,          1016
Blo, blubrande, and blak, unblyþe to neȝe,
As a stynkande stanc þat stryed synne,
Þat ever of s[mell]e and of smach, smart is to fele.
Forþy þe derk Dede See hit is demed evermore,        1020
For hit dedez of deþe duren þere ȝet;
For hit is brod and boþemlez, and bitter as þe galle,
And noȝt may lenge in þat lake þat any lyf berez,
And alle þe costez of kynde hit combrez uch one.      1024
For lay þeron a lump of led, and hit on loft fletez,
And folde þeron a lyȝt fyþer, and hit to founs
    synkkez;
And þer water may walter to wete any erþe,
Schal never grene þeron growe, gresse ne wod nawþer. 1028
If any schalke to be schent wer schowved þerinne,
Paȝ he bode in þat boþem broþely a monyth,
He most ay lyve in þat loȝe in losyng evermore,
And never dryȝe no dethe to dayes of ende.              1032
And as hit is corsed of kynde, and hit coostez als,
Þe clay þat clenges þerby arn corsyes strong,

---

1015 þer faure *by second hand, the* r *of* þer *being unlike the
scribe's* (*cf. for* 257, broþer, 924) *and the* r *of* faur *having an
extraordinary flourish above it, apparently intended as abbrev. for*
e; *a faint stroke under* a *may indicate that the original had* fyve:
is, *inserted above line by second hand, which is betrayed by the
Greek* s.—1019 *MS., M., Sk.* synne.—1027 *Sk. inserts* þat *after*
þer. — 1028 *M.*[1] greue, *note* grene(?); *M.*[2] grene.

As alum and alkaran, þat angre arn boþe,
Soufre sour, and saundyver, and oþer such mony;     1036
And þer waltez of þat water, in waxlokes grete,
Þe spu[m]ande aspaltoun þat spyserez sellen;
And suche is alle þe soyle by þat se halves,
Þat fel fretes þe flesch and festre[s] bones.     1040
And þer ar tres by þat terne of traytores,
And þay borgounez and beres blomez ful fayre,
And þe fayrest fryt þat may on folde growe,
As orenge and oþer fryt and apple garnade,     1044
Also red and so ripe and rychely hwed     [75b]
As any dom myȝt device of dayntyez oute;
Bot quen hit is brused, oþer broken, oþer byten in
     twynne,
No worldez goud hit wythinne, bot wyndowande askes.  1048

### XIa.   Exhortation to Purity

Alle þyse ar teches and tokenes to trow upon ȝet,
And wittnesse of þat wykked werk, and þe wrake after
Þat oure Fader forferde for fylþe of þose ledes.
Þenne uch wyȝe may wel wyt þat he þe wlonk lovies;  1052
And if he lovyes clene layk þat is oure Lorde ryche,
And to be couþe in his corte þou coveytes þenne,
To se þat Semly in sete and his swete face,
Clerrer counseyl con I non, bot þat þou clene worþe.  1056
For Clopyngnel in þe compas of his clene Rose,
Þer he expounez a speche, to hym þat spede wolde,

1035 *MS., M., Sk.* alkaran; *M. note* alkatran(?). — 1037 *M., Sk.*
angre;  *M. note* augre = aigre(?). — 1038 *MS. has five strokes
between* sp *and* ande, *and the last of these strokes is an* i *as stroke
above shows; M., Sk.* spuniande; *M. note* spinnande(?); *Sk.
Glossary* spinnande *or* spumande, *latter adopted by NED.* — 1040
*MS., M., Sk.* festred; *M. note* festres(?). — 1041 *Sk. adds* kynde
*after* traytores. — 1048 *MS.* wyndowande; *M., Sk.* wydowande,
*noting MS. reading, but Sk. Glossary* 'or wyndowande.' — 1053 *E.*
clenelayk. — 1056 *MS., M.* counseyl counsayl.

Of a lady to be loved: 'Loke to hir sone,
Of wich beryng þat ho be, and wych ho best lovyes, 1060
And be ry3t such, in uch a bor3e, of body and of
　　dedes,
And fol3 þe fet of þat fere þat þou fre haldes;
And if þou wyrkkes on þis wyse, þa3 ho wyk were,
Hir schal lyke þat layk þat lyknes hir tylle.' 1064
If þou wyl dele drwrye wyth Dry3tyn, þenne,
And lelly lovy þy Lorde, and his leef worþe,
Þenne conforme þe to Kryst, and þe clene make,
Þat ever is polyced als playn as þe perle selven. 1068
　For loke fro fyrst þat he ly3t wythinne þe lel
　　Mayden,
By how comly a kest he watz clos þere,
When venkkyst watz no vergynyte, ne vyolence maked,
Bot much clener watz hir corse, God kynned þerinne. 1072
And efte when he borne watz in Beþelen þe ryche,
In wych puryte þay departed; þa3 þay pover were,
Watz never so blysful a bour as watz a bos þenne,
Ne no schroude-hous so schene as a schepon þare, 1076
Ne non so glad under God as ho þat grone schulde.
For þer watz seknesse al sounde þat sarrest is halden,
And þer watz rose reflayr where rote hatz ben ever,
And þer watz solace and songe wher sor3 hatz ay
　　cryed; 1080
For aungelles wyth instrumentes of organes and
　　pypes, [76a]
And rial ryngande rotes, and þe reken fyþel,
And alle hende þat honestly mo3t an hert glade,
Aboutte my Lady watz lent, quen ho delyver were. 1084
Þenne watz her blyþe barne burnyst so clene
Þat boþe þe ox and þe asse hym hered at ones:
Þay knewe hym by his clannes for Kyng of nature,

---

1071 *MS.* he *expunged, after* when. — 1075 *MS., M.* abos; *M.*
*note* abof(?); *Sk.* a bos.

For non so clene of such a clos com never er þenne.  1088
   And ȝif clanly he þenne com, ful cortays þerafter,
Þat alle þat longed to luþer ful lodly he hated;
By nobleye of his norture he nolde never towche
Oȝt þat watz ungoderly oþer ordure watz inne.  1092
Ȝet comen lodly to þat Lede, as lazares monye,
Summe lepre, summe lome, and lomerande blynde,
Poysened, and parlatyk, and pyned in fyres,
Drye folk, and ydropike, and dede, at þe laste—  1096
Alle called on þat Cortayse and claymed his grace.
He heled hem wyth hynde speche of þat þay ask after,
For what so he towched, also tyd torned to hele,
Wel clanner þen any crafte cowþe devyse.  1100
So clene watz his hondelyng uche ordure hit schonied,
And þe gropyng so goud of God and man boþe,
Þat for fetys of his fyngeres fonded he never
Nauþer to cout ne to kerve wyth knyf ne wyth egge;  1104
Forþy brek he þe bred blades wythouten,
For hit ferde freloker in fete in his fayre honde,
Displayed more pryvyly when he hit part schulde,
Þenne alle þe toles of Tolowse moȝt tyȝt hit to kerve.  1108
   Þus is he kyryous and clene þat þou his cort askes;
Hou schulde þou com to his kyth bot if þou clene
    were?
Nou ar we sore and synful and souly uch one,
How schulde we se, þen may we say, þat Syre upon
    throne?  1112
Ȝis, þat Mayster is mercyable, þaȝ þou be man fenny
And al tomarred in myre, whyl þou on molde lyvyes;
Þou may schyne þurȝ schryfte, þaȝ þou haf schome
    served,
And pure þe with penaunce tyl þou a perle worþe.  1116
Perle praysed is prys þer perre is schewed,  [76b]

---

1104 *MS., M.* cout; *M. note* cut(?).—1111 *MS.* sovly; *M.*
sov[er]ly; *Fi.* soudly *or* solwy.

Þaȝ hym not derrest be demed to dele for penies.
Quat may þe cause be called bot for hir clene hwes,
Þat wynnes worschyp abof alle whyte stones?　　1120
For ho schynes so schyr þat is of schap rounde,
Wythouten faut oþer fylþe, ȝif ho fyn were
And wax ever in þe worlde in weryng so olde,
Ȝet þe perle payres not whyle ho in pyese lasttes;　　1124
And if hit cheve þe chaunce uncheryst ho worþe,
Þat ho blyndes of ble in bour þer ho lygges,
No-bot wasch hir wyth worchyp in wyn, as ho askes,
Ho by kynde schal becom clerer þen are.　　1128
So if folk be defowled by unfre chaunce,
Þat he be sulped in sawle, seche to schryfte,
And he may polyce hym at þe prest, by penaunce taken,
Wel bryȝter þen þe beryl oþer browden perles.　　1132
　　Bot war þe wel, if þou be waschen wyth water of
　　　schryfte,
And polysed als playn as parchmen schaven,
Sulp no more þenne in synne þy saule þerafter,
For þenne þou Dryȝtyn dyspleses wyth dedes ful sore, 1136
And entyses hym to tene more trayþly þen ever,
And wel hatter to hate þen hade þou not waschen.
For when a sawele is saȝtled and sakred to Dryȝtyn,
He holly haldes hit his, and have hit he wolde;　　1140
Þenne efte lastes hit likkes, he loses hit ille,
As hit were rafte wyth unryȝt, and robbed wyth
　　þewes.
War þe þenne for þe wrake; his wrath is achaufed
For þat þat ones watz his schulde efte be unclene,　　1144
Þaȝ hit be bot a bassyn, a bolle, oþer a scole,
A dysche, oþer a dobler, þat Dryȝtyn onez served,
To defowle hit ever upon folde fast he forbedes,
So is he scoymus of scaþe þat scylful is ever.　　1148

　　1123 *Fi. adopts M.'s suggestion* (*in notes*) *of* wax ho euer.—1124
*MS., M.* pyese; *B.* pye[r]e.—1142 *MS., M.* þewes; *M. note*
þeues(?).

And þat watz bared in Babyloyn in Baltazar tyme,
Hou harde unhap þer hym hent and hastyly sone,
For he þe vesselles avyled þat vayled in þe temple
In servyse of þe Soverayn sumtyme byfore.                    1152
Ȝif ȝe wolde tyȝt me a tom, telle hit I wolde,              [77a]
Hou charged more watz his chaunce þat hem cherych
    nolde
Þen his fader forloyne þat feched hem wyth strenþe,
And robbed þe relygioun of relykes alle.                    1156

## XII. THE CAPTURE OF JERUSALEM

Danyel in his dialokez devysed sumtyme,
As ȝet is proved expresse in his profecies,
Hou þe gentryse of Juise and Jherusalem þe ryche
Watz disstryed wyth distres, and drawen to þe erþe. 1160
For þat folke in her fayth watz founden untrwe,
Þat haden hyȝt þe hyȝe God to halde of hym ever;
And he hem halȝed for his and help at her nede
In mukel meschefes mony, þat mervayl [is] to here; 1164
And þay forloyne her fayth and folȝed oþer goddes,
And þat wakned his wrath and wrast hit so hyȝe,
Þat he fylsened þe faythful in þe falce lawe
To forfare þe falce in þe faythe trwe.                      1168
    Hit watz sen in þat syþe þat Zede[c]hyas rengned
In Juda, þat justised þe Juyne kynges.
He sete on Salamones solie, on solemne wyse,
Bot of leaute he watz lat to his Lorde hende:              1172
He used abominaciones of idolatrye,
And lette lyȝt bi þe lawe þat he watz lege tylle.
Forþi oure Fader upon folde a foman hym wakned,
Nabigodenozar nuyed hym swyþe;                             1176
He pursued into Palastyn wyth proude men mony,

---

1155 *MS., M.* forloyne; *Fi., E.* forloyn[ed].—1159 *MS.* jhrlem,
*M.* Iherusalem.—1164 *M. inserts* [is].—1169 *MS.* ȝedethyas, *as
M. notes.*

And þer he wast wyth werre þe wones of þorpes.
He herȝed up alle Israel, and hent of þe beste,
And þe gentylest of Judee in Jerusalem biseged,          1180
Umbewalt alle þe walles wyth wyȝes ful stronge,
At uche a dor a doȝty duk, and dutte hem wythinne;
For þe borȝ watz so bygge b[a]tayled alofte,
And stoffed wythinne wyth stout men to stalle hem
          þeroute.          1184
Þenne watz þe sege sette þe cete aboute,
Skete skarmoch skelt, much skaþe lached;
At uch brugge a berfray on basteles wyse,
Þat seven syþe uch a day asayled þe ȝates;          [77b]
Trwe tulkkes in toures teveled wythinne,          1189
In bigge brutage of borde, bulde on þe walles;
Þay feȝt and þay fende of, and fylter togeder
Til two ȝer overtorned, ȝet tok þay hit never.          1192
At þe laste upon longe, þo ledes wythinne
Faste fayled hem þe fode, enfaminied monie;
Þe hote hunger wythinne hert hem wel sarre
Þen any dunt of þat douthe þat dowelled þeroute.          1196
Þenne wern þo rowtes redles in þo ryche wones;
Fro þat mete watz myst, megre þay wexen,
And þay stoken so strayt þat þay ne stray myȝt
A fote fro þat forselet to forray no goudes.          1200
Þenne þe kyng of þe kyth a counsayl hym takes,
Wyth þe best of his burnes a blench for to make:
Þay stel out on a stylle nyȝt er any steven rysed,
And harde hurles þurȝ þe oste, er enmies hit wyste.          1204
Bot er þay atwappe ne moȝt þe wach wythoute,
Hiȝe skelt watz þe askry þe skewes anunder;
Loude alarom upon launde lulted watz þenne;
Ryche, ruþed of her rest, ran to her wedes,          1208

1178 *MS.* wyth with. — 1179 *MS.* isrl, *with usual abbrev. for* e
*attached to* 1; *M.* Israel.—1180 *MS.* jrlem; *M.* Ierusalem (*so
also 1235, 1432*). — 1183 *MS., M.* baytayled. — 1189 *M.*[1] teneled, *M.*[2]
teueled. — 1189 *NED. prints* atwappene (*see note*).

Hard hattes þay hent and on hors lepes;
Cler claryoun crak cryed on lofte.
By þat, watz alle on a hepe hurlande swyþ[e],
Folȝande þat oþer flote, and fonde hem bilyve,     1212
Overtok hem as tyd, tult hem of sadeles,
Tyl uche prynce hade his per put to þe grounde.

   And þer watz þe kyng kaȝt wyth Calde prynces,
And alle hise gentyle forjusted on Jerico playnes,   1216
And presented wern as presoneres to þe prynce
   rychest,
Nabigodenozar, noble in his chayer;
And he þe faynest freke þat he his fo hade,
And speke spitously hem to, and spylt þerafter.    1220
Þe kynges sunnes in his syȝt he slow everuch one,
And holkked out his auen yȝen heterly boþe,
And bede þe burne to be broȝt to Babyloyn þe ryche,
And þere in doungoun be don to dreȝe þer his
   wyrdes.                          [78a]

   Now se, so þe Soveray[n] set hatz his wrake;   1225
Nas hit not for Nabugo ne his noble nauþer,
Þat oþer depryved watz of pryde with paynes stronge,
Bot for his beryng so badde agayn his blyþe Lorde; 1228
For hade þe Fader ben his frende þat hym bifore
   keped,
Ne never trespast to him in teche of mysseleve,
To C[a]lde wer alle calde, and kythes of Ynde—
Ȝet take Torkye hem wyth, her tene hade ben little.  1232

   Ȝet nolde never Nabugo þis ilke note leve,
Er he hade t[yrv]ed þis toun and torne hit to grounde.
He joyned unto Jerusalem a gentyle duc þenne,
His name watz Nabuzardan, to noye þe Jues;    1236
He watz mayster of his men and myȝty himselven,

---

1211 *MS.*, *M.* swyþee. — 1225 *MS.* soveray; *M.* soueray[n].—
1231 *MS.*, *M.* to Colde wer al Calde (*see note*); *Fi. suggests*
to-corven(!) *for* to Colde.—1234 *MS.*, *M.*, *E.* tuyred; *G.* tyrued:
*E.* torne[d].

Þe chef of his chevalrye his chekkes to make;
He brek þe bareres as bylyve, and þe burȝ after,
And enteres in ful ernestly, in yre of his hert.          1240
What! þe maysterry watz mene, þe men wern away,
Þe best boȝed wyth þe burne þat þe borȝ ȝemed;
And þo þat byden wer [s]o biten with þe bale hunger
Þat on wyf hade ben worþe þe welgest fourre.          1244
Nabizardan noȝt forþy nolde not spare,
Bot bede al to þe bronde under bare egge;
Þay slowen of swettest semlych burdes,
Baþed barnes in blod, and her brayn spylled,          1248
Prestes and prelates þay presed to deþe,
Wyves and wenches her wombes tocorven,
Þat her boweles outborst aboute þe diches,
And al watz carfully kylde þat þay cach myȝt.          1252
And alle [þat] swypped unswolȝed of þe sworde kene,
Þay wer cagged and kaȝt on capeles al bare,
Festned fettres to her fete under fole wombes,
And broþely broȝt to Babyloyn þer bale to suffer;          1256
So sytte in servage and syte þat sumtyme wer gentyle;
Now ar chaunged to chorles, and charged wyth
          werkkes,
Boþe to cayre at þe kart and þe kuy mylke,
Þat sumtyme sete in her sale syres and burdes.          [78b]

### XIIa. THE SEIZURE OF THE HOLY RELICS

And ȝet Nabuzardan nyl never stynt          1261
Er he to þe tempple tee wyth his tulkkes alle;
Betes on þe barers, brestes up þe ȝates,
Slouen alle at a slyp þat served þerinne,          1264
Pulden prestes bi þe polle, and plat of her hedes,
Diȝten dekenes to deþe, dungen doun clerkkes,

1243 *MS.* fo, *as M. notes.*—1253 *M. supplies* þat.—1257 *M.* to
(*with comma after* suffer *and semi-colon after* syte), *but MS.,
though very faint, seems to read* so.

And alle þe maydenes of þe munster maȝtyly h[e]
    kyllen
Wyth þe swayf of þe sworde þat swolȝed hem alle.   1268
Þenne ran þay to þe relykes as robbors wylde,
And pyled alle þe apparement þat pented to þe
    kyrke—
Þe pure pyleres [o]f bras portrayd in golde,
And þe chef chaundeler, charged with þe lyȝt,   1272
Þat ber þe lamp upon lofte þat lemed evermore
Bifore þ[e] Sancta Sanctorum, þer selcouth watz
    ofte.
Þay caȝt away þat condelstik, and þe crowne als,
Þat þe auter hade upon, of aþel golde ryche;   1276
Þe gredirne and þe goblotes garnyst of sylver,
Þe bases of þe bryȝt postes and bassynes so schyre,
Dere disches of golde and dubleres fayre,
Þe vyoles and þe vesselment of vertuous stones.   1280
Now hatz Nabuzardan nomen alle þyse noble þynges,
And pyled þat precious place, and pakked þose godes;
Þe golde of þe gazafylace to swyþe gret noumbre,
Wyth alle þe urnmentes of þat hous, he hamppred
    togeder.   1284
Alle he spoyled spitously in a sped whyle
Þat Salomon so mony a sadde ȝer soȝt to make,
Wyth alle þe coyntyse þat he cowþe, clene to wyrke,
Devised he þe vesselment, þe vestures clene;   1288
Wyth slyȝt of his ciences, his Soverayn to love,
Þe hous and þe anornementes he hyȝtled togedere.
Now hatz Nabuzardan num[men] hit al samen,
And syþen bet doun þe burȝ and brend hit in askes.   1292
    Þenne wyth legiounes of ledes over londes he rydes,
Herȝez of Israel þe hyrne aboute;

---

1267 *MS., M.* hokyllen, *E. suggests* hom kylled. — 1271 of, o
*blotted in MS.* — 1274 *MS.* þsancta, *M.* þ[e] sancta; *MS.* scor *with
abbrev. for um, M.* sanctorum.—1291 *MS.* nūnēd; *M.* numnend,
*but note* nummen(?).

Wyth charged chariotes þe cheftayn he fynde[z],
Bikennes þe catel to þe kyng, þat he caȝt hade,    [79a]
Presented him þe presoneres in pray þat þay token—  1297
Moni a worþly wyȝe whil her worlde laste,
Moni semly syre soun, and swyþe rych maydenes,
Þe pruddest of þe province, and prophetes childer,  1300
As Ananie, and Azarie, and als Mizael,
And dere Daniel also, þat watz devine noble,
With moni a modey moder chylde mo þen innoghe.
And Nabugodenozar makes much joye,  1304
Nou he þe kyng hatz conquest and þe kyth wunnen,
And dreped alle þe doȝtyest and derrest in armes,
And þe lederes of her lawe layd to þe grounde,
And þe pryce of þe profecie presoners maked;  1308
Bot þe joy of þe juelrye so gentyle and ryche,
When hit watz schewed hym so schene, scharp watz
    his wonder;
Of such vessel avayed þat vayled so huge,
Never ȝet nas Nabugodenozar er þenne.  1312
He sesed hem wyth solemnete, þe Soverayn he praysed
Þat watz aþel over alle, Israel Dryȝtyn;
Such god, such gomes, such gay vesselles,
Comen never out of kyth to Caldee reames.  1316
He trussed hem in his tresorye in a tryed place
Rekenly wyth reverens, as he ryȝt hade;
And þer he wroȝt as þe wyse, as ȝe may wyt hereafter,
For hade he let of hem lyȝt, hym moȝt haf lumpen
    worse.  1320
    Þat ryche in gret rialte rengned his lyve,
As conqueror of uche a cost he cayser watz hatte,
Emperor of alle þe erþe, and also þe saudan,

---

1295 *MS.* fynde, *M.* fynde[ȝ].— 1296 *Catchwords* Bikennes þe
catel *at bottom of preceding page.* — 1297 *M. expands the same*
*abbreviation above* p *differently,* presented, *but* prisoneres; *but cf.*
presoneres *written out in 1217.*— 1299 *M.*[1] soun; *M.*[2] sone, *cf. 666.*
— 1308 *M. expands* prisoners, *but cf. 1297.*

And als þe god of þe grounde watz graven his name, 1324
And al þurӡ dome of Daniel, fro he devised hade
Þat alle goudes com of God, and gef hit hym bi
    samples,
Þat he ful clanly bicnu his carp bi þe laste,
And ofte hit mekned his mynde, his maysterful
    werkkes. 1328
Bot al drawes to dyӡe wyth doel up[o]n ende;
Bi a haþel never so hyӡe, he heldes to grounde,
And so Nabugodenozar, as he nedes moste,
For alle his empire so hiӡe, in erþe is he graven.    [79b]
   Bot þenn þe bolde Baltazar, þat watz his barn
    aldest, 1333
He watz stalled in his stud, and stabled þe rengne;
In þe burӡ of Babiloyne þe biggest he trawed,
Þat nauþer in heven ne [on] erþe hade no pere;   1336
For he bigan in alle þe glori þat hym þe gome lafte,
Nabugodenozar, þat watz his noble fader;
So kene a kyng in Caldee com never er þenne.
Bot honored he not hym þat in heven wonies,   1340
Bot fals fantummes of fendes, formed with handes
Wyth tool out of harde tre, and telded on lofte,
And of stokkes and stones he stoute goddes callz
When þay are gilde al with golde and gered wyth
    sylver, 1344
And þere he kneles and callez, and clepes after help.
And þay reden him ryӡt, rewarde he hem hetes,
And if þay gruchen him his grace to gremen his hert,
He cleches to a gret klubbe and knokkes hem to peces. 1348
Þus in pryde and olipraunce his empyre he haldes,
In lust and in lecherye, and loþelych werkkes;
And hade a wyf for to welde, a worþelych quene,

---

1325 *MS., M.* fro, *M. note* for(?). — 1327 *M.*[1] bicuv*er which MS. resembles, M.*[2] bicnv. — 1329 *MS.* vpn. — 1330 *MS., M.* bi; *M. note* be(?), *accepted by Fi.* — 1336 *MS., M.* no erþe; *M. note* on(?).

And mony a lemman, never þe later, þat ladis wer
    called. 1352
In þe clernes of his concubines and curious wedez,
In notyng of nwe metes and of nice gettes,
Al watz þe mynde of þat man on misschapen þinges,
Til þe Lorde of þe lyfte liste hit abate. 1356

## XIII. Belshazzar's Feast

Thenne þis bolde Baltazar biþenkkes hym ones
To vouche on avayment of his vayneg[l]orie:
Hit is not innoghe to þe nice al noȝty þink use,
Bot if alle þe worlde wyt his wykked dedes. 1360
Baltazar þurȝ Babiloyn his banne gart crye,
And þurȝ þe cuntre of Caldee his callyng con spryng,
Þat alle þe grete upon grounde schulde geder hem
    samen,
And assemble at a set day at þe saudans fest. 1364
Such a mangerie to make þe man watz avised,
Þat uche a kythyn kyng schuld com þider;
Uche duk wyth his duthe and oþer dere lordes
Schulde com to his cort to kyþe hym for lege, [80a]
And to reche hym reverens, and his revel herkken, 1369
To loke on his lemanes and ladis hem calle.

To rose hym in his rialty rych men soȝtten,
And mony a baroun ful bolde, to Babyloyn þe noble. 1372
Þer bowed toward Babiloyn burnes so mony,
Kynges, cayseres ful kene, to þe cort wonnen,
Mony ludisch lordes þat ladies broȝten,
Þat to neven þe noumbre to much nye were. 1376
For þe borȝ watz so brod and so bigge alce,
Stalled in þe fayrest stud þe sterrez anunder,
Prudly on a plat playn, plek alþerfayrest,
Umbesweyed on uch a syde wyth seven grete wateres, 1380

1358 *MS.* vayne gorie; *M.* vayne g[l]orie. — 1359 *MS., M.* þink;
*M. note* þing(?).

Wyth a wonder wroȝt walle wruxeled ful hiȝe,
Wyth koynt carneles above, corven ful clene,
Troched toures bitwene, twenty spere lenþe,
And þiker þrowen umbeþor wyth overþwert palle.　1384
Þe place þat plyed þe pursaunt wythinne,
Watz longe and ful large and ever ilych sware,
And uch a syde upon soyle helde seven myle,
And þe saudans sete sette in þe myddes.　1388
Þat watz a palayce of pryde passande alle oþer,
Boþe of werk and of wunder and walle al aboute;
Heȝe houses wythinne þe halle to hit m[a]d,
So brod bilde in a bay þat blonkkes myȝt renne.　1392
　　When þe terme of þe tyde watz towched of [þe]
　　　feste,
Dere droȝen þerto, and upon des metten,
And Baltazar upon bench was busked to sete;
Stepe stayred stones of his stoute throne.　1396
Þenne watz alle þe halle-flor hiled wyth knyȝtes,
And barounes at þe sidebordes bounet a[y]where,
For non watz dressed upon dece bot þe dere selven,
And his clere concubynes in cloþes ful bryȝt.　1400
　　When alle segges were þer set, þen servyse
　　　bygynnes,
Sturnen trumpen strake steven in halle,
Aywhere by þe wowes wrasten krakkes,
And brode baneres þerbi blusnande of gold;　[80b]
Burnes berande þe bredes upon brode skeles,　1405
Þat were of sylveren syȝt, and s[e]rved þerwyth,

---

1385 _MS._ þõ wᵗ, _M._ þo*ur-with; M. note_ þore(?). — 1391 _MS., M._
to hit med; _Fi. proposes_ ful hyȝe(!). — 1393 _MS._ towched _quite
clearly; M._ to vsched; _Fi._ touched: _M. reads_ þe feste, _but in MS.
both words are written at the end of 1392 above a break, and though
some letters certainly precede_ feste, _I cannot distinguish them._ —
1398 _M._ aywhere, _but_ y _blurred in MS. and very much like_ o. —
1405 _MS._ þe þe. — 1406 _MS._ seved _with a flourish apparently over_
v, _M. reads MS._ severed, _and prints_ seerved.

Lyfte logges þerover and on lofte corven,
Pared out of paper and poynted of golde,　　　　1408
Broþe baboynes abof, besttes anunder,
Foles in foler flakerande bitwene,
And al in asure and ynde enaumayld ryche,
And al on blonkken bak bere hit on honde.　　　1412
And ay þe nakeryn noyse, notes of pipes,
Tymbres and tabornes, tulket among;
Symbales and sonetez sware þe noyse,
And bougounz busch batered so þikke.　　　　　1416
So watz served fele syþe þe sale alle aboute,
Wyth solace at þe sere course bifore þe self lorde,
Þer þe lede and alle his love lenged at þe table.
So faste þay weȝed to him wyne, hit warmed his hert, 1420
And breyþed uppe into his brayn and blemyst his
　　　mynde,
And al waykned his wyt, and wel neȝe he foles;
For he waytez on wyde, his wenches he byholdes,
And his bolde baronage aboute bi þe woȝes.　　1424
　　Þenne a dotage ful depe drof to his hert,
And a caytif counsayl he caȝt bi hymselven.
Maynly his marschal þe mayster upon calles,
And comaundes hym cofly coferes to lance,　　1428
And fech forþe vessel þat his fader broȝt,
Nabugodenozar, noble in his strenþe,
Conquerd with his knyȝtes, and of kyrk rafte,
In Jude, in Jerusalem in gentyle wyse:　　　　1432
'Bryng hem now to my borde, of beverage hem fylles,
Let þise ladyes of hem lape—I luf hem in hert!
Þat schal I cortaysly kyþe, and þay schin knawe sone
Þer is no bounte in burne lyk Baltazar þewes.'　1436
　　Þenne towchede to þe tresor þis tale watz sone,
And he wyth keyes uncloses kystes ful mony;

---

1408 *MS.* glolde. — 1414 *MS., M.* among; *Fi.* among[es]. — 1429
*MS., M.* forþe; *Fi.* for þe.

Mony burþen ful bryȝt watz broȝt into halle,
And covered mony a cupborde with cloþes ful quite.   [81a]
Þe jueles out of Jerusalem wyth gemmes ful bryȝt,      1441
Bi þe syde of þe sale were semely arayed;
Þe aþel auter of brasse watz hade into place;
Þe gay coroun of golde gered on lofte,                 1444
Þat hade ben blessed bifore wyth bischopes hondes,
And wyth besten blod busily anoynted,
In þe solempne sacrefyce þat goud savor hade,
Bifore þe Lorde of þe lyfte in lovyng hymselven,       1448
Now is sette for to serve Satanas þe blake,
Bifore þe bolde Baltazar wyth bost and wyth pryde.
Hoven upon þis auter watz aþel vessel,
Þat wyth so curious a crafte corven watz wyly.         1452
Salamon sete him s[eve]n ȝere and a syþe more,
Wyth alle þe syence þat hym sende þe soverayn Lorde,
For to compas and kest to haf hem clene wroȝt.
For þer wer bassynes ful bryȝt of brende golde clere, 1456
Enaumaylde wyth azer, and eweres of sute;
Covered cowpeȝ foul clene, as casteles arayed,
Enbaned under batelment wyth bantelles quoynt,
And fyled out of fygures of ferly[ch]e schappes.       1460
Þe coperounes of þe c[ov]acles þat on þe cuppe reres
Wer fetysely formed out in fylyoles longe,
Pinacles pyȝt þer apert þat profert bitwene,
And al bolled abof wyth braunches and leves,           1464
Pyes and papejayes purtrayed withinne,
As þay prudly hade piked of pomgarnades;
For alle þe blomes of þe boȝes wer blyknande perles,
And alle þe fruyt in þo formes of flaumbeande
       gemmes,                                          1468

---

1441 *MS.* jsrlem. — 1452 *MS. apparently* fo. — 1453 *MS.* s...n
*badly blurred, M.* s[eue]n. — 1458 *MS., M.* foul; *M. note* ful(?). —
1460 *MS., M.* ferlyle; *M. note* ferlyke(?); *Fi.* ferlyche. — 1461
*MS., M.* canacles. — 1465 papejayes, *second* p *ill-formed and perhaps not complete.*

Ande safyres, and sardiners, and semely topace,
Alabaund[a]rynes, and amaraunz, and amaffised
    stones,
Casydoynes, and crysolytes, and clere rubies,
Penitotes, and pynkardines, ay perles bitwene;     1472
So trayled and tryfled a-traverce wer alle,
Bi uche bekyr ande bol[l]e þe brurdes al umbe,
Þe gobelotes of golde graven aboute,
And fyoles fretted wyth flores and fleez of golde.     [81b]
    Upon þat auter watz al aliche dresset.     1477
Þe candelstik bi a cost watz cayred þider sone,
[U]pon þe pyleres apyked þat praysed hit mony,
Upon hit basez of brasse þat ber up þe werkes,     1480
Þe boȝes bryȝt þer abof, brayden of golde,
Braunches bredande þeron, and bryddes þer seten
Of mony [curious] kyndes, of fele-kyn hues,
As þay wyth wynge upon wynde hade waged her
    fyþeres.     1484
Inmong þe leves of þe [launces] lampes wer grayþed,
And oþer louflych lyȝt þat lemed ful fayre;
As mony morteres of wax merkked wythoute,
Wyth mony a borlych best al of brende golde.     1488
Hit watz not wonte in þat wone to wast no serges,
Bot in temple of þe trauþe trwly to stonde,
Bifore þe sancta sanctorum [þer] soþefast Dryȝtyn
Expouned his speche spyrytually to special prophetes. 1492
Leve þou wel þat þe Lorde þat þe lyfte ȝemes,

---

1469 *MS., M.* sardiners; *NED., B.* sardines. — 1470 *MS.* alabaũda-
rynes(?), *or* alabaũdarrynes(?), *the letter(s) after* d *are smudged
and perhaps retraced, a stroke preceding the* r *possibly indicating
an* i; *M.*[1] alabaunderrynes; *M.*[2] alabaunderynes *without remark.* —
1474 *MS., M.* bekyrande þe bolde; *B.* ande bole.—1479 *MS.* pon, *M.*
[V]pon. — 1483 *MS.* mony kyndes; *Bülbring (Sch., p. 185) proposed* mony curious kyndes; *B.* mony kyndes colored; *G.* mony
cler kyndes. — 1485 *Bülbring (Sch., p. 183) inserts* launces. — 1486
*M. corrects MS. to* louelych. — 1491 *MS.* sca scorum: *I insert* þer.
— 1492 *MS.* spũally; *M.*[1] specually; *M.*[2] spiritually.

Displesed much at þat play in þat plyt stronge,
Þat his jueles so gent wyth javeles wer fouled,
Þat presyous in his presens wer proved sumwhyle.  1496
Soberly in his sacrafyce summe wer anoynted,
Þurʒ þe somones of himselfe þat syttes so hyʒe;
Now a boster on benche bibbes þerof,
Tyl he be dronkken as þe devel, and dotes þer he
    syttes.                                                  1500
    So þe Worcher of þis worlde wlates þerwyth,
Þat in þe poynt of her play he porvayes a mynde;
Bot er harme hem he wolde in haste of his yre,
He wayned hem a warnyng þat wonder hem þoʒt.  1504
Nou is alle þis guere geten glotounes to serve,
Stad in a ryche stal and stared ful bryʒt[e];
Baltazar in a brayd bede [b]us þerof—
'Weʒe wyn in þis won—Wassayl!' he cryes.           1508
Swyfte swaynes ful swyþe swepen þertylle,
Kyppe kowpes in honde kyngez to serve;
In bryʒt bollez ful bayn birlen þise oþer,
And uche mon for his mayster machches alone.      [82a]
Þer watz rynging, on ryʒt, of ryche metalles,         1513
Quen renkkes in þat ryche rok rennen hit to cache,
Clatering of covaclez þat kesten þo burdes,
As sonet out of sau[t]eray songe als myry.             1516
Þen þe dotel on dece drank þat he myʒt;
And þenne [drinkez] arn dressed [to] dukez and
    prynces,
Concubines and knyʒtes, bi cause of þat merthe;
As uch on hade hym inhelde, he haled of þe cuppe. 1520
So long likked þise lordes þise lykores swete,
And gloryed on her falce goddes, and her grace calles,

1506 *MS.*, *M.* bryʒtʒ; *M. note* bryʒte(?).—1506 *MS.*, *M.* vus.—
1515 *M.* conacleʒ.—1516 *MS.* saueray; *M.* sau[t]eray.—1518
Bülbring (*Sch., p. 184*) *reads* Þenne [drinkes] arn dressed [for]
dukez and prynces; *B. would insert* dere *after* dressed; *G. reads*
þenne þat derrest arn dressed; *E.* þenne derely arn dressed.

Þat were of stokkes and stones, stille evermore—
Never steven hem astel, so stoken is hor tonge; 1524
Alle þe goude golden goddes þe gaulez ӡet nevenen,
Belfagor, and Belyal, and Belssabub als,
Heyred hem as hyӡly as heven wer þayres,
Bot hym þat alle goudes gives, þat God þay forӡeten. 1528

### XIIIa. The Writing on the Wall

For þer a ferly bifel þat fele folk seӡen—
Fyrst knew hit þe kyng, and alle þe cort after:
In þe palays pryncipale upon þe playn wowe,
In contrary of þe candelstik þat clerest hit schyned, 1532
Þer apered a paume, wyth poyntel in fyngres,
Þat watz grysly and gret, and grymly he wrytes;
Non oþer forme bot a fust faylande þe wryste,
Pared on þe parget, purtrayed lettres. 1536
When þat bolde Baltazar blusched to þat neve,
Such a dasande drede dusched to his hert,
Þat al falewed his face and fayled þe chere;
Þe stronge strok of þe stonde strayned his joyntes, 1540
His cnes cachches to close, and cluchches his hommes,
And he wyth plattyng his paumes displayes his lers,
And romyes as a rad ryth þat rorez for drede,
Ay biholdand þe honde til hit hade al graven, 1544
And rasped on þe roӡ woӡe runisch sauez.
When hit þe scrypture hade scraped wyth a s[c]rof
    penne,
As a coltor in clay cerves þo forӡes,
Þenne hit vanist verayly and voyded of syӡt; [82b]
Bot þe lettres bileved ful large upon plaster. 1549
Sone so þe kynge for his care carping myӡt wynne,
He bede his burnes boӡ to, þat wer bok-lered,
To wayte þe wryt þat hit wolde, and wyter hym to say, 1552

1524 *MS.* īs, *cf.* īf, *692.* — 1542 *MS.* le̅rs. — 1546 *MS.* strof, *as*
*M. notes.* — 1551 *M.* wer*e.*

'For al hit frayes my flesche, þe fyngres so grymme.'
Scoleres skelten þeratte þe skyl for to fynde,
Bot þer watz never on so wyse couþe on worde rede,
Ne what ledisch lore ne langage nauþer,                    1556
What typyng ne tale tokened þo draȝtes.
Þenne .þe bolde Baltazar bred ner wode,
And [b]ede þe cete to seche segges þurȝout
Þat wer wyse of wychecrafte, and warlaȝes oþer      1560
Þat con dele wyth demerlayk and devine lettres.
'Calle hem alle to my cort, þo Calde clerkkes,
Unfolde hem alle þis ferly þat is bifallen here,
And calle wyth a hiȝe cry: "He þat þe kyng wysses, 1564
In expounyng of speche þat spredes in þise lettres,
And make þe mater to malt my mynde wythinne,
Þat I may wyterly wyt what þat wryt menes,
He schal be gered ful gaye in gounes of porpre,       1568
And a coler of cler golde clos umbe his þrote;
He schal be prymate and prynce of pure clergye,
And of my þrevenest lordez þe þrydde he schal,
And of my reme þe rychest to ryde wyth myselven, 1572
Outtaken bare two, and þenne he þe þrydde." '
Þis cry watz upcaste, and þer comen mony
Clerkes out of Caldye þat kennest wer knauen,
As þe sage sathrapas þat sorsory couþe,                   1576
Wychez and walkyries wonnen to þat sale,
Devinores of demorlaykes þat dremes cowþe rede,
Sorsers, and exorsismus, and fele such clerkes;
And alle þat loked on þat letter as lewed þay were, 1580
As þay had loked in þe leþer of my lyft bote.
Þenne cryes þe kyng, and kerves his wedes.
What! he corsed his clerkes and calde hem chorles,
To henge þe harlotes he heȝed ful ofte;                 [83a]
So watz þe wyȝe wytles, he wed wel ner.              1585

1559 *MS.* ede; *M.* [b]ede.—1566 *MS., M.* make; *B. would read*
makes.—1583 *MS., M.* chorles; *Fi.* corles.

Ho herde hym chyde to þe chambre þat watz þe
    chef quene.
When ho watz wytered bi wyȝes what watz þe cause,
Suche a chaungande chaunce in þe chef halle,     1588
Þe lady to lauce þat los þat þe lorde hade,
Glydes doun by þe grece and gos to þe kyng;
Ho kneles on þe colde erþe, and carpes to hymselven
Wordes of worchyp wyth a wys speche.     1592
'Kene kyng,' quod þe quene, 'kayser of urþe,
Ever laste þy lyf in lenþe of dayes!
Why hatz þou rended þy robe, forredles hereinne,
Þaȝ þose ledes ben lewed lettres to rede,     1596
And hatz a haþel in þy holde, as I haf herde ofte,
Þat hatz þe gostes of God þat gyes alle soþes?
His sawle is ful of syence, saȝes to schawe,
To open uch a hide þyng of aunteres uncowþe.     1600
Þat is he þat ful ofte hatz hevened þy fader
Of mony anger ful hote wyth his holy speche.
When Nabugodenozar watz nyed in stoundes,
He devysed his dremes to þe dere trawþe,     1604
He kevered hym wyth his counsayl of caytyf wyrdes;
Alle þat he spured hym in space he expowned clene,
Þurȝ þe sped of þe spyryt þat sprad hym wythinne
Of þe godelest goddez þat gaynes aywhere.     1608
For his depe divinite and his dere sawes,
Þy bolde fader Baltazar bede by his name,
Þat now is demed Danyel of derne coninges,
Þat caȝt watz in þe captyvide in cuntre of Jues;     1612
Nabuzardan hym nome, and now is he here,
A prophete of þat province and pryce of þe worlde.
Sende into þe cete to seche hym bylyve,
And wynne hym wyth þe worchyp to wayne þe bote; 1616

1589 *M.* lauce; *M. note* lance(?); *Fi. suggests* layte(!). — 1595
*MS.* for redles; *M.*[1] for-redles; *M.*[2] for redles. — 1610 *MS., M.*
by; *M. note* be(?).

And þaʒ þe mater be merk þat merked is ʒender,
He schal declar hit also as hit on clay stande.'
   Þat gode counseyl at þe quene watz cached as swyþe;
Þe burne byfore Baltazar watz broʒt in a whyle.   [83b]
When he com bifore þe kyng and clanly had halsed,  1621
Baltazar umbebrayde hym, and 'Leve sir,' he sayde,
'Hit is tolde me bi tulkes þat þou trwe were
Profete of þat provynce þat prayed my fader,   1624
Ande þat þou hatz in þy hert holy connyng,
Of sapyence þi sawle ful, soþes to schawe;
Goddes gost is þe geven þat gyes alle þynges,
And þou unhyles uch hidde þat Hevenkyng myntes; 1628
And here is a ferly byfallen, and I fayn wolde
Wyt þe wytte of þe wryt þat on þe wowe clyves,
For alle Calde clerkes han cowwardely fayled.
If þou wyth quayntyse conquere hit, I quyte þe þy
     mede:                 1632
For if þou redes hit by ryʒt, and hit to resoun brynges,
Fyrst telle me þe tyxte of þe tede lettres,
And syþen þe mater of þe mode mene me þerafter,
And I schal halde þe þe hest þat I þe hyʒt have,  1636
Apyke þe in porpre cloþe, palle alþerfynest,
And þe byʒe of bryʒt golde abowte þyn nekke,
And þe þryd þryvenest þat þrynges me after
Þou schal be baroun upon benche, bede I þe no lasse.' 1640

## XIIIb. Daniel's Prophecy

   Derfly þenne Danyel deles þyse wordes:
'Ryche kyng of þis rengne, rede þe oure Lorde!
Hit is surely soth, þe Soverayn of heven
Fylsened ever þy fader and upon folde cheryched,  1644
Gart hym grattest to be of governores alle,
And alle þe worlde in his wylle welde as hym lykes.

---

1618 *MS., M.* stande; *Fi.* standez. — 1619 *MS., M.*[1] as as; *M.*[2] as.
— 1634 *MS., M.* tede; *M. Glossary, error for* tene (= ten?),
*accepted by Fi.* — 1646 *MS., M.* lykes, *E. suggests* lyked.

Who so wolde wel do, wel hym bityde,
And quos deth so he dezyre, he dreped als fast; 1648
Who so hym lyked to lyft, on lofte watz he sone,
And quo so hym lyked to lay, watz loȝed bylyve.
So watz noted þe note of Nabugodenozar,
Styfly stabled þe rengne bi þe stronge Dryȝtyn, 1652
For of þe Hyȝest he hade a hope in his hert,
Þat uche pouer past out of þat Prynce even;
And whyle þat watz cleȝt clos in his hert,
Þere watz no mon upon molde of myȝt as hymselven; 1656
Til hit bitide on a tyme, towched hym prydе [84a]
For his lordeschyp so large and his lyf ryche;
He hade so huge an insyȝt to his aune dedes,
Þat þe power of þe hyȝe Prynce he purely forȝetes. 1660
Þenne blynnes he not of blasfemy on to blame þe
     Dryȝtyn,
His myȝt mete to Goddes he made wyth his wordes:
"I am God of þe grounde, to gye as me lykes,
As he þat hyȝe is in heven his aungeles þat weldes. 1664
If he hatz formed þe folde and folk þerupone,
I haf bigged Babiloyne, burȝ alþerrychest,
Stabled þerinne uche a ston in strenkþe of myn armes;
Moȝt never myȝt bot myn make such anoþer." 1668
    'Watz not þis ilke worde wonnen of his mowþe,
Er þenne þe soverayn saȝe souned in his eres:
"Now Nabugodenozar innoȝe hatz spoken,
Now is alle þy pryncipalte past at ones, 1672

---

1648 *MS., M.* dezyre, *E. suggests* desyred. — 1654 *M.*[1] þat; *M.*[2]
[þ]at, *but* þ, *though very faint is still clear in MS.* — 1655 *Bülbring*
(*Sch., p. 184*) *suggests* connynge *or* counseyl *after* þat. — 1661 *MS.*
blasfemyon; *M.*[1] blasfemy on; *M.*[2] blasfemyon. — 1664 þᵗ weldes
*is written by second hand, and part of the original handwriting is
still visible under the small* ᵗ *of* þᵗ. — 1669 *M.* mowþe one, *but* one
*in MS. is written at the end of the line in a smaller and different
hand;* Fi. (*p. 48*) *perhaps* [þer] watz not þis ilke worde wonnen
of his mowþe. — 1672 *MS., M.* past; *Fi.* passed.

And þou, remued fro monnes sunes, on mor most
    abide,
And in wasturne walk, and wyth þe wylde dowelle,
As best, byte on þe bent of braken and erbes,
Wyth wroþe wolfes to won and wyth wylde asses."   1676
Inmydde þe poynt of his pryde departed he þere
Fro þe soly of his solempnete; his solace he leves,
And carfully is outkast to contre unknawen,
Fer into a fyr fryth þere frekes never comen.        1680
His hert heldet unhole, he hoped non oþer
Bot a best þat he be, a bol oþer an oxe.
He fares forth on alle faure, fogge watz his mete,
And ete ay as a horce when erbes were fallen;        1684
Þus he countes hym a kow þat watz a kyng ryche,
Quyle seven syþez were overseyed someres, I trawe.
   'By þat, mony þik thyȝe þryȝt umbe his lyre,
Þat alle watz dubbed and dyȝt in þe dew of heven;   1688
Faxe fyltered, and felt flosed hym umbe,
Þat schad fro his schulderes to his sch[e]re-wykes,
And twentyfolde twynande hit to his tos raȝt;
Þer mony clyvy, as clyde hit clyȝt togeder.          1692
His berde ibrad alle his brest to þe bare urþe,
His browes bresed as breres aboute his brode
    chekes;                                           [84b]
Holȝe were his yȝen and under campe hores,
And al watz gray as þe glede, wyth ful grymme
    clawres                                            1696
Þat were croked and kene as þe kyte paune;
Erne-hwed he watz, and al overbrawden;
Til he wyst ful wel who wroȝt alle myȝtes,
And cowþe uche kyndam tokerve and kever when hym
    lyked.                                             1700

1674 *M.*[1] *expands* wasterne; *M.*[2] wasturne, *latter probably cor-*
*rect.* — 1690 *MS., M.* schyre wykes. — 1696 *MS., M.* clawres; *Fi.*
clawes.—1697 *MS.* paune *or* panne; *M.* paune; *M. note* panne(?);
*Fi.* pawe; *B.* paume; *G. reads MS.* paune.

Þenne he wayned hym his wyt, þat hade wo soffered,
Þat he com to knawlach and kenned hymselven;
Þenne he l[o]ved þat Lorde and leved in trawþe
Hit watz non oþer þen he þat hade al in honde.      1704
Þenne sone watz he sende agayn, his sete restored,
His barounes boȝed hym to, blyþe of his come,
Haȝerly in his aune hwe his heved watz covered,
And so ȝeply watz ȝarked and ȝolden his state.      1708
  'Bot þou, Baltazar, his barne and his bolde ayre,
Seȝ þese syngnes wyth syȝt, and set hem at lyttel,
Bot ay hatz hofen þy hert agaynes þe hyȝe Dryȝt[y]n,
Wyth bobaunce and wyth blasfayme bost at hym kest, 1712
And now his vessayles avyled in vanyte unclene,
Þat in his hows hym to honor were hevened of fyrst;
Bifore þe barounz hatz hom broȝt, and byrled þerinne
Wale wyne to þy wenches in waryed stoundes.         1716
Bifore þy borde hatz þou broȝt beverage in þede
Þat blyþely were fyrst blest wyth bischopes hondes,
Lovande þeron lese goddez þat lyf haden never,
Made of stokkes and stonez þat never styry moȝt.    1720
And for þat froþande fylþe, þe Fader of heven
Hatz sende into þis sale þise syȝtes uncowþe,
Þe fyste wyth þe fyngeres þat flayed þi hert,
Þat rasped renyschly þe woȝe wyth þe roȝ penne.     1724
  'Þise ar þe wordes here wryten, wythoute werk
      more,
By uch fygure, as I fynde, as oure Fader lykes:
Mane, Techal, Phares, merked in þrynne;
Þat þretes þe of þyn unþryfte upon þre wyse.        1728
Now expowne þe þis speche spedly I þenk:
Mane menes als much as, maynful Gode              [85a]
Hatz counted þy kyndam bi a clene noumbre,

---

1703 *MS., M.* laued; *M. note* loued(?); *K. (p. 26)* loued. — 1711
*MS.* dryȝtn; *M.* dryȝt[y]n. — 1715 *M. reads* hom, *but MS. possibly
intended for* hem. — 1722 *MS., M.*¹ hatȝ sende hatȝ sende; *M.*²
hatȝ sende.

And fulfylled hit in fayth to þe fyrre ende. 1732
To teche þe of Techal, þat terme þus menes:
Þy wale rengne is walt in weȝtes to heng,
And is funde ful fewe of hit fayth-dedes.
And Phares folȝes for þose fawtes, to frayst þe
    trawþe; 1736
In Phares fynde I forsoþe þise felle saȝes:
Departed is þy pryncipalte, depryved þou worþes,
Þy rengne rafte is þe fro, and raȝt is þe Perses,
Þe Medes schal be maysteres here, and þou of menske
    schowved.' 1740

## XIIIc. Belshazzar's End

Þe kyng comaunded anon to cleþe þat wyse
In frokkes of fyn cloþ, as forward hit asked.
Þenne sone watz Danyel dubbed in ful dere porpor,
And a coler of cler golde kest umbe his swyre. 1744
Þen watz demed a decre bi þe duk selven:
Bolde Baltaza[r] bed þat hym bowe schulde
Þe comynes al of Calde þat to þe kyng longed,
As to þe prynce pryvyest preved þe þrydde, 1748
Heȝest of alle oþer, saf onelych tweyne,
To boȝ after Baltazar in borȝe and in felde.
Þys watz cryed and knawen in cort als fast,
And alle þe folk þerof fayn þat folȝed hym tylle. 1752
    Bot how so Danyel watz dyȝt, þat day overȝede,
Nyȝt neȝed ryȝt now wyth nyes fol mony,
For daȝed never anoþer day þat ilk derk after,
Er dalt were þat ilk dome þat Danyel devysed. 1756
Þe solace of þe solempnete in þat sale dured
Of þat farand fest, tyl fayled þe sunne;
Þenne blykned þe ble of þe bryȝt skwes,

1744 *MS.*, *M.*¹ cloler; *M.*² coler.—1746 *MS.* baltaȝa; *M.* Baltaȝa[r]. — 1747 *MS.*, *M.*¹ alof; *M.*¹ *note* aloft(?); *M.*² a lof; *Fi.*
al of. — 1759 *MS.*, *M.* blykned; *M. note* blaykned(?), *acceptèd by Fi.*

Morkenes þe mery weder, and þe myst dryves       1760
Porȝ þe lyst of þe lyfte, bi þe loȝ medoes.
Uche haþel to his home hyȝes ful fast,
Seten at her soper and songen þerafter;
Þen foundez uch a felaȝschyp fyrre at forþ naȝtes.   1764
Baltazar to his bedd with blysse watz caryed,
Reche þe rest as hym lyst, he ros never þerafter.    [85b]
    For his foes in þe felde in flokkes ful grete,
Þat longe hade layted þat lede, his londes to strye,   1768
Now ar þay sodenly assembled at þe self tyme,
Of hem wyst no wyȝe þat in þat won dowelled.
Hit watz þe dere Daryus, þe duk of þise Medes,
Þe prowde prynce of Perce and Porros of Ynde,      1772
Wyth mony a legioun ful large, wyth ledes of armes,
Þat now hatz spyed a space to spoyle Caldeez.
Þay þrongen þeder in þe þester on þrawen hepes,
Asscaped over þe skyre watteres, and sca[l]ed þe
        walles,                                     1776
Lyfte laddres ful longe and upon lofte wonen,
Stelen stylly þe toun er any steven rysed.
Wythinne an oure of þe [n]yȝt an entre þay hade,
Ȝet afrayed þay no freke; fyrre þay passen         1780
And to þe palays pryncipal þay aproched ful stylle.
Þenne ran þay in on a res, on rowtes ful grete;
Blastes out of bryȝt brasse brestes so hyȝe,
Ascry scarred on þe scue þat scomfyted mony.       1784
Segges slepande were slayne er þay slyppe myȝt,
Uche hous heyred watz wythinne a hondewhyle;
Baltazar in his bed watz beten to deþe,
Þat boþe his blod and his brayn blende on þe cloþes; 1788
The kyng in his cortyn watz kaȝt bi þe heles,
Feryed out bi þe fete, and fowle dispysed,
Þat watz so doȝty þat day and drank of þe vessayl;
Now is a dogge also dere þat in a dych lygges.     1792

1776 *MS., M.* scaþed, *B.* sca[l]ed.—1779 *MS.* myȝt.

For þe mayster of þyse Medes on þe morne ryses,
Dere Daryous þat day dyȝt upon trone,
Þat cete seses ful sounde, and saȝtlyng makes
Wyth alle þe barounz þeraboute, þat bowed hym after. 1796
And þus watz þat londe lost for þe lordes synne,
And þe fylþe of þe freke þat defowled hade
Þe ornementes of Goddez hous þat holy were naked.
He watz corsed for his unclannes, and cached þerinne, 1800
Done doun of his dyngnete for dedez unfayre,
And of þyse worldes worchyp wrast out for ever,      [86a]
And ȝet of lykynges on lofte letted, I trowe,
To loke on oure lofly Lorde late bitydes.                    1804
  Þus upon þrynne wyses I haf yow þro schewed,
Þat unclannes tocleves in corage dere
Of þat wynnelych Lorde þat wonyes in heven,
Entyses hym to be tene, tel[des] up his wrake;     1808
Ande clannes is his comfort, and coyntyse he lovyes,
And þose þat seme arn and swete schyn se his face.
Þat we gon gay in oure gere þat grace he uus sende,
Þat we may serve in his syȝt þer solace never blynnez.
                                                      Amen. 1812

1808 *MS.*, *M.* telled; *M. note* telles(?).

# NOTES

**1-4.** 'He who could fittingly commend Purity, and recount all the arguments (in her praise) that are justly due her, might find fair themes to aid his discourse, but in (undertaking) the contrary (i. e. the praise of Impurity) he would find great difficulty and trouble.' For 'rekken up alle þe resounz,' compare *Alex. C* 1280, where Arestes, reporting to Alexander, 'rekens hym þe resons,' i. e. 'gives him an account' of those that have been slain in battle.

**5.** þe **Wyȝ** þat **wroȝt alle** þinges. For similar periphrases in the poet's works, see Introd., pp. xvii ff.

**7-16.** This is the only passage in all the poet's works where he alludes to the vices of the clergy; and it should be observed that even here his condemnation of wicked priests is quite different from the violent denunciations of the author of *Piers Plowman*, since he is careful to contrast impartially the behavior and reward of righteous priests (12) with the sin of those who are vile and hypocritical.

**9.** Cf. *Pat.* 316: 'Efte to trede on þy temple, and teme to þy seluen,' and *Erken.* 15: 'He turnyd temples þat tyme þat temyd to þe deuelle.'

**10. reken wyth reverence.** Cf. 1318, and *Gaw.* 251: 'And rekenly hym reuerenced.'

**16. loþe.** M. read *boþe,* but this leaves *God and his gere* without any construction; a verb is obviously required, and the confusion of *bo* and *lo* elsewhere (e. g. *borde,* 452, 467) makes it certain that the scribe either intended *loþe* or mistook it for *boþe.* The vile priests 'hate God and all that pertains to him, and (consequently) drive him to wrath.'

**21. non scaþe lovied.** The combination of negatives in this line is puzzling; it may be paraphrased, 'If he were not scrupulous in his abhorrence (of evil), and (if it were not true that he) loved no sin, it would be very strange.'

**24.** Cf. *Pat.* 11: 'Aȝt happes he hem hyȝt, & vche on a mede.' With this whole passage (23-8) should be compared the lines on the beatitudes, *Pat.* 9-33.

**25 ff. as Maþew recordez.** Matt. 5. 8: 'Beati mundo corde, quoniam ipsi Deum videbunt.' After paraphrasing this verse (27-8), the text on which the whole poem is based, the poet states it conversely in 29-30, since he is to develop and illustrate his theme by contraries, and intends to set forth, not so much the joys that

await the pure in heart, as the terrible doom that falls upon those
who violate purity. For the doctrine of the Beatific Vision, implied
in these lines, see Osgood's note on *Pearl* 675. As Osgood notes,
the poet alludes to it again and again (reverting naturally in *Purity*
to his text) ; cf. *Pur.* 176, 178, 552, 576, 595, 1055, 1112, 1804-12;
*Pat.* 24.

    **32. May not byde þat bur[n]e þat hit his body neȝen.** A diffi-
cult line. M. in his second edition thought that *burre*, not *burne*, was
perhaps intended by the scribe, and paraphrased as follows: 'May
not abide (suffer) that man (?blow), that it (?he) should approach
his body.' The expression (*a*)*byde þe bur* occurs, it is true, *Pat.*
7, *Gaw.* 290 and 374, but it throws no light on the present passage.
M. found difficulty in reading *burne*, because he considered it the
antecedent of *hit*, and interpreted the second *þat* as a conjunction.
It is really a relative pronoun, which, combined with *his*, is the
usual means of expressing *whose* in ME., as in 1109: 'þus is he
kyryous and clene þat þou his cort askes' (for *þat . . . his* =
*whose*, see Mätzner, *Engl. Gram.*² 3. 549; Kellner, *Histor. Outlines
of Engl. Synt.*, p. 66). *Hit* does not refer to *burne*, but to *fylþe* of
the previous line. The difficulty of construing *neȝen* still remains,
and one must either supply an auxiliary verb, 'whose body it, i. e.
filth, (may) approach,' or emend to *neȝes* or *neȝe*. The whole
becomes clear in the light of the context. The poet has just
explained (29-30) that no one attains to the sight of our Lord
who has any taint of impurity. He now gives the reason for this
statement (31-32) : 'For he þat flemus uch fylþe fer fro his hert,'
etc., i. e. 'Christ, who banishes everything vile far from himself,
cannot endure the man whose body is stained with sin.' This idea
that no sinner can approach the presence of the Lord because he
is himself spotless in his purity is restated in 1109-12; cf. 17 ff.
for periphrases similar to 'he þat flemus,' etc., see Introd., pp. xvii ff.

    **33-48.** These lines lead to the introduction of the parable of the
Wedding Feast, and anticipate the situation of the man without a
wedding garment, recounted in due course in ll. 133-60.

    **40. traschez,** defined by Morris (and Stratmann) as 'trousers,'
was explained by Skeat in 1892 (*Notes on Engl. Etym.*, p. 305) as
the plural of *trash*, meaning simply 'rags.' *NED.* plausibly suggests, s. v. *trash*, that *trasches* may here mean 'old worn-out
shoes,' as in modern dialects, though no other instance of this
meaning has been found before 1746.

    **41. totez.** Skeat in 1892 (see *Notes*, p. 303) gave the following
explanation of this word: 'Dr. Morris says that *totez* is merely a
form of 'toes,' which I cannot accept. . . . The word is surely

the Low G. *tote,* a peak. Hexham has: *'een Tote,* a teat; *de Tote van een schoen,* the beak or lap of a shoe; *een Tote-pot,* a pot with eares,' &c. Cf. ME. *toten,* to peep out; *his ton toteden out,* his toes peeped out, Piers Pl. Crede, 425. I translate *tote* by extremity or end; the sense is, "the ends (probably of his toes) peeped out." ' I accept Skeat's explanation, though it seems to me as probable that the 'ends' are his elbows, and not his toes, since his 'tabarde totorne' is spoken of in the first half of the line. *NED.* quotes the suggestion 'that *totez* is a verb (viz. *tote,* toot v.), and that *toez* or *totz* 'toes' has been omitted before it, the reading being *his toez totez oute* "his toes peep out," ' and compares the phrase from *Piers Pl. Crede* quoted by Skeat (see above). This explanation is obviously impossible, since 'his totez oute' is one of four parallel descriptive phrases governed by *wyth* (40), as l. 42 shows.

**42. he schulde,** etc. An anacoluthon. The sentence begins at l. 35: 'What urþly haþel . . . wolde lyke if a ladde com,' etc., but by l. 42 the poet has forgotten that the *if*-clause which really ends only with *þyse* (42) is the object of 'wolde lyke,' and he uses it as the protasis of a condition of which 'he schulde be halden utter,' etc., is the apodosis.

**43. mony blame.** 'Many a rebuke'; cf. *mony anger,* 1602, where a particular exhibition of the general feeling is similarly expressed by the abstract noun. Such 'concretion' of abstracts is common in all periods of the language (see Einenkel, *Paul's Grundriss²* 1. 1137, § 181 κ), but *blame* and *anger* in this sense have become obsolete, though we still say 'he fell into a rage,' i. e. a 'fit of rage,' as *anger,* 1602, is a 'fit of anger.'

**a boffet, peraunter.** Cf. *Gaw.* 2343: 'ʒif I deliuer had bene, a boffet, paraunter.'

**48. in talle ne in tuch.** M. suggested emending *talle* to *tuly,* and glossed *tuch* as 'cloth' = Mod. Engl. *tuck.* Skeat's explanation is probably correct: 'I take this to mean: "though he should never again do wrong either in tale or in touch," i. e. by word or deed. I see no difficulty, especially when we notice the curious uses of *touch* in Sir Gawain and the Grene Knight [120, 1301, 1677] by the same author, and further note that, in that poem, the words *tale* and *touch* are alliterated, l. 1301.'—*Notes on Engl. Etym.,* p. 289.

**49. wor[d]lych.** I have adopted M.'s suggestion of 'worldly' here, since a contrast is certainly intended with the 'hyʒe kyng' in the next line (cf. 'urþly haþel,' 35); M.'s spelling, however, is unnecessary, as the dropping of the *l* is extremely common in ME.; see, e. g., *Piers Pl. Crede* 784, *Sege of Jer.* 1226, and glossary of *Alex. C.*

**50. in [heven].** This seems to me a less violent emendation than M.'s suggestion of *herin euen* for MS. *in her euen*, since any slight accidental mark might have been mistaken by the scribe for the abbreviation for *-er*, and so expanded. For the expression, cf. 1664; *Pat.* 257.

**51. as Maþew melez.** The story of the Parable of the Wedding Feast (51-162) is a combination of the versions given by Matthew 22. 1-14 and Luke 14. 16-24 (see Appendix for these passages). The excuses given by those invited (61-72), the lord's commanding his servants to gather in the wayfarers a second time (93 ff.), and the description of them (100 ff.), are given only in Luke; and the account of the maltreatment of the lord's messengers and his slaying of the guests first invited (Matt. 22. 6-7) is omitted, as in Luke. But several details, for example l. 84, and the whole passage (125-162) about the man without a wedding garment, are given only in Matthew.

**in his masse.** Cf. *Pearl* 497: 'As Mathew meleȝ in your messe.' This is a curious instance of the manner in which a word comes to be used in an extraordinary sense for the sake of alliteration. In *Pat.* 9-10, the poet wrote: 'I herde on a halyday at a hyȝe masse How Mathew melede'; but here, as in *The Pearl*, he uses *mass* of that portion of Matthew's gospel which he heard read at 'mass,' or simply as 'gospel.'

**59. ryȝt to þe sete.** This cannot be 'seat,' and is hardly likely to be an error for *fete*. It is possible that it is a noun corresponding to ME. *sete*, adj., meaning 'wholesome, appetizing' (cf. *Gaw.* 889: 'Sere sewes & sete, sesounde of þe best'); the phrase would then mean 'appetizingly.'

**66. ȝat.** This curious form, which has not been noticed because Schwahn overlooked it in his study of the verbs of these poems, is apparently intended as a past part. of *gete*—'I have desired and obtained yokes of oxen.' The only way I see of explaining it is to assume that it is by analogy to a pret. 3 sg. form *ȝat*, but even this form is unrecorded (see Bülbring, *Geschichte der Ablaute der Starken Zeitworter innerhalb des Südenglischen*, p. 67: *Quellen u. Forschungen* 63), though it occurs in the compounds, e. g. *forȝat, biȝat, underȝat* (Bülbring, p. 12, and *passim*). For such a transference of the pret. sg. form to the past part., *iwan* in Layamon might be compared (cited by Bülbring, p. 121). Formally it would be easier to associate *ȝat* with the ME. wk. verb *ȝate*, 'grant, assent,' from OE. *gēatan*, ON. *játta* (see Mätzner s. v. *ȝaten*); but the meaning of the words forbids. Since writing this note, I have found that Kölbing interprets a form *ȝat*, *Sir Tristram* 330, as pret. 3 sg. of *gete*. For the form *ȝete*, see note on 842.

**69. so wer hym.** M. printed *sower,* and suggested *swer,* but as this is plainly impossible because the alliteration is *w,* Fischer proposed *so werþ,* and Bateson *so werned,* 'refused,' though he also suggests *so weres.* There is no need of emendation, since *wer* occurs, *Pearl* 205, as pret. 3 sg., and makes excellent sense: 'thus the third defended, i. e. excused, himself.'

**71. droȝ hem adreȝ.** 'Drew back,' the line paraphrasing Matt. 22. 5: 'Illi autem neglexerunt et abierunt.' The phrase is very common in the alliterative poetry in the meanings 'draw back, withdraw'; 'delay': *Gaw.* 1031; *Morte Arth.* 3968, 4219; *Destr. Troy* 10043, 11647; *Awnt. Arth.* 513; York Play No. 35 (*Crucifixio Christi*), l. 2.

**76. wylle gentyl.** M. paraphrased: 'More to blame is their fault, than any forlorn gentile,' referring to *wylle of wone,* 'astray from human habitations,' etc., but, though ME. *wylle,* 'wandering, astray' (from ON. *villr*) is not unusual, this explanation seems far-fetched, since we should hardly expect the expression 'her wrange' to be contrasted in blameworthiness with a person. It is preferable to consider *wylle* the noun and *gentyl* the adjective, and paraphrase: 'their wrong is more to blame than any heathen rage.' For the meaning of *wylle,* cf. *Morte Arth.* 3836: 'And for wondson and will al his wit failede,' where Holthausen defines 'Wut' in glossary; for *gentyl,* adj., meaning 'heathen, pagan,' cf. 1432, and *NED.* The word-order, noun + adjective, is very common, e. g. *combraunce huge,* 4; *sete ryche,* 37; *schrowde feble,* 47; *man ryche,* 51; etc.

**85.** 'Then those who guarded the country went hither and thither,' literally, 'went and came'; *þay* is the antecedent of *þat;* the separation is common, cf. 61, 123, 889, 891, 985, and 1067-8.

**92.** See note on 114.

**101. forlotez.** This word is not recorded in the dictionaries, probably because M. suggested that it was a mistake for *forletez,* 'forsake.' Björkman (*Scand. Loan-Words* 1. 91) rightly included it among the ME. derivatives of OW. Scand. *lāta,* meaning here 'omit.'

**106.** M. placed the comma after *denounced me,* defining 'renounced me,' but this interpretation is unlikely for three reasons: (1) the pause comes in an unnatural place from the metrical point of view; (2) the lord would hardly limit his determination not to entertain the faithless guests so emphatically to 'noȝt now at þis tyme,' implying thus that he might entertain them at some other time; (3) *denounce* nowhere else has the meaning *renounce* (see *NED.* which, misled by M.'s punctuation, gives this single instance with a question). Thomas (*Alliterierende Langzeile des Gawayn-Dichters*, p. 9), because of the first objection, suggested placing the comma after *noȝt,* and defined *denounce* = 'sich für jemand erklären'; similarly Gollancz (*Mod. Lang. Rev.* 14. 152). Some such meaning must be assumed, since the word always means 'declare, announce, proclaim' in ME. (and OF.). The passage might be paraphrased: 'For certainly these men who have refused my invitation and made no proper announcement to me (Gollancz: have nowise proclaimed me) at this time, shall henceforth never sit in my hall to partake of my feast.' This makes *now* intelligible, and puts it in proper contrast with *never* of the next line, the invited guests by this one refusal forfeiting the lord's hospitality for ever. The phrase *now at þis time* is not uncommon; it occurs *Wm. of Palerne* 484; *Destr. Troy* 5615.

108. **suppe on sope.** 'Taste one sup.'

114. **ay þe best byfore.** The fact that the guests are here seated according to rank, leads Osgood to remark (*Pearl*, p. xl) that the orthodox view of the gradation of heavenly awards is here clearly' implied, and that the doctrine of the equality of reward, expounded so unmistakably in *Pearl* 421-719, must therefore be a later development in the poet's theological ideas. This conclusion is hardly justified, since there is no reason for thinking that the poet had any of the theological implications of the parable in mind in this purely narrative passage. When he comes to the interpretation of the parable (161-176), he makes nothing of this distinction of rank. We might expect such lines in the account of any elaborate feast where young knights and squires (86-7), as well as common people (101 ff.), were present. So in *Gawain,* at King Arthur's feast the guests seated themselves: 'Þe best burne ay abof, as hit best semed' (73). Cf. also *Pur.* 92: 'As he watz dere of degre dressed his seete' with *Gaw.* 1006: 'Bi vche grome at his degre grayþely watz serued.' Finally, even if one were tempted to extract the poet's theological conceptions from this passage, it would be as easy to deduce the poet's belief in the equality of heavenly rewards from 113: 'Wheþer þay wern worþy oþer wers, wel wern þay stowed,' and 120: 'And ȝet þe symplest in þat sale watz served to þe fulle,' as it would be to deduce his belief in their inequality from the other parts of the passage.

117. **soerly.** M. emends to *soberly,* which *NED.* does not give as an adjective; Emerson (*Publ. Mod. Lang. Ass.* 34. 496) suggested *serly,* 'severally, individually.' But the word is certainly the adjective from ON. *saurligr,* 'unclean,' corresponding to the ME. *sore, sorȝe,* meaning 'filth,' (*NED.* s. v. *sore,* sb.[3]), from ON. *saurr,*

possibly ON. *saurgan,* 'filth, mud'; emendation is unnecessary (unless perhaps to *soorly*). This adjective could very properly be used to describe the men who sat below, in contrast to those above that 'dubbed wer fayrest' (115); a few lines further on (119) the poet says there were few 'clene men in compaynye.' The word *sorȝe* and its derivatives occur elsewhere in the poems of this group. Gollancz adopts the suggestion of Ekwall (*Engl. Stud.* 44. 171) and Emerson (*Mod. Lang. Notes* 28. 176) that *sorȝe* means 'filth' in *Pat.* 275, where Jonah

> Stod vp in his stomak, þat stank as þe deuel;
> Þer in saym & in sorȝe þat sauoured as helle,

though Gollancz emends to *so[ur]*. He compares *sour turnes, Pur.* 192, perhaps rightly. In *Pur.* 846 *sorȝe* cannot have any other meaning than 'filth'; cf. 845, and *froþande fylþe,* 1721, which corresponds exactly to *ȝestande sorȝe.* Moreover, I think that the adjective itself (from ON. *saurligr*) occurs a second time in *Pearl* 226, where the poet, after speaking of the wondrous pearl on the maiden's breast, says:

> I hope no tong moȝt endure
> No sauerly saghe say of þat syȝt,
> So watȝ hit clene & cler & pure,
> Þat precios perle þer hit watȝ pyȝt.

Gollancz and Osgood interpret *sauerly* as 'savorly,' and Osgood glosses 'sweet.' G. translates:

> I trow no tongue might e'er avail
> To speak of that sight a fitting word,

and O., in his prose rendering, p. 27: 'No tongue, I think, could utter the sweet tale of that vision.' But this interpretation necessitates a violent wrenching of the meaning of *endure,* which means not 'avail' or 'be equal to a task' (Osgood's glossary), but 'suffer, bear' (see the various meanings in *NED.*). Even this unjustifiable definition of *endure* as 'avail' does not dispel the difficulties of the above interpretation, since the two lines would then have to be paraphrased: 'I think no tongue could avail to say (or be equal to the task of saying) a sweet (or pleasant) word of that sight.' As this would make no sense, G. is obliged to render *sauerly* by 'fitting.' O. avoids the difficulty in another way by translating *no sauerly saghe, 'the* sweet tale,' a translation which involves an apparently slight, but syntactically impossible change, since the redundant *no* can only be indefinite, and equivalent to the modern *any, a.* Translating, then, with due regard to syntax, and omitting for the moment the word *sauerly,* the passage would run: 'I think that no tongue could bear to say any . . . word of that sight—it was so clean and bright and pure.' We should expect some word contrasting with 'clean' and meaning 'base, vile,' and no word could be more suitable than that found in *Pur.* 117 as *soerly,* spelt here in *Pearl sauerly,* the *u* not standing for *v,* but being part of the diphthong *au.* Phonologically this representation of ON. *au* is regular, since it appears in ME. as *au, ou,* or *o* (Björkman, *Scand. Loan-Words* 1. 68 ff.; generally *au* or *ou* in these poems, Knigge, p. 84). Finally, it may be added that the ME. derivatives of ON. *saurr,* etc., may well have been confused with ME. *sore* (OE. *sār*), ME. *sour* (OE. *sūr*), and it is hard to say whether such a spelling as *sorȝe* is a mere scribal error or due to folk-etymological confusion with *sorȝe* (OE. *sorg*). The ME. *sory,* adj. (ON. *saurigr*), which the *Promptorium Parvulorum* defines 'soory, or defowlyd yn sowr or fylþe . . . , *cenosus cenulentus,*' (*NED.* gives only this example) could hardly help being confused with ME. *sorry* (OE. *sārig*), which often means 'vile, wretched' (see *NED.,* s. v. *sorry,* 5.).

**130. hym.** 'them.' I have not changed such forms, nor *by* to *be,* 212, etc.

**134. Hit watz,** etc. For similar clauses, cf. 257, 981.

**136. ne no festival frok.** We should expect a preposition, *with* or *in;* but perhaps we must supply something like 'did he have on.'

**144. on so ratted a robe.** A pleonastic construction, which is apparently a combination of two idioms: (1) one (a) + so + adj. — e. g. 'þu eært a swa hende gome,' *Layamon,* ed. Madden, 1. 162, l. 13; 'ane zuo greate emperur,' *Ayenbite of Inwyt,* ed. Morris, p. 100; and (2) the more usual order in Late ME., so + a + adj. — as in 'so gaynly a God,' *Pur.* 728. Mätzner (*Engl. Gram.*[2] 3. 197) quotes one example of this combination (one + so + a + adj.) : 'he yt wan of on so hey a kynge,' Robert of Gloucester's *Chronicle* 1166 (ed. Wright) ; but it is interesting that this construction appears in only two manuscripts, the other six having the more regular 'on so heie kynge.'

**145. ungoderly.** This word, which occurs again in l. 1092, is not recorded in Bradley-Stratmann, nor is *goderly* in any of the dictionaries. The intrusion of the *r* may perhaps be explained as a development from *godely* by analogy with such words as *hagherly* (18), and perhaps also with the form *goder,* which occurs in the ME. expression *goderhele,* from OE. (*tō*)*gōdre hǣle* (see *NED.,* s. v. *goderheal*) ; similarly Emerson, *Publ. Mod. Lang. Ass.* 34. 510.

**162. þat fele arn to called.** 'Multi enim sunt vocati.' But the poet does not mention the 'pauci electi,' since the whole point of the parable for him is the impossibility of the 'man without a wedding garment,' the man defiled with sin, approaching God's pure presence.

**164. fulȝed in font.** Cf. *Erken.* 299: 'fulloght in fonte'; *Awnt. Arth.* (Douce MS.) 225: 'folowed in fontestone.'

**167. for aproch þou.** If the text is correct, the sentence is very badly constructed: we should expect something like 'when you approach.' Perhaps the meaning is: 'See to it that your clothes are clean and fair for the holiday, lest you receive harm, for when you draw near that Prince of noble lineage (you will find that) he hates hell no more than those who are foul.' For l. 168, cf. 577.

**169.** The interpretations of the 'wedding garment' in the Middle Ages generally go back either to Augustine, who explained it as 'Caritas' (Migne, *Patr. Lat.* 38. 562), or to Jerome, whose explanation may be quoted entire: 'Vestis autem nuptialis præcepta sunt Domini, et opera quæ complentur ex lege et Evangelio, novique hominis efficiunt vestimentum. Si quis igitur in tempore judicii inventus fuerit sub nomine Christiano non habere vestam nuptialem, hoc est, vestam supercælestis hominis; sed vestem pollutam, id est, veteris hominis exuvias, hic statim corripitur.'—Migne, *Patr. Lat.* 26. 160. The interpretation given here in *Purity* bears some resemblance to Jerome's, but it is without the odor of theological doctrine implied in the 'garment of the new man,' and the comparison of a man's clothes with his deeds is more direct. Cf. note on 162, and Introd., p. xl.

**192. see hym with syȝt.** This is the only one of the common pleonasms of the kind, such as 'tell with tongue,' 'hear with ears,' that the poet permits himself, and this he uses frequently. 'See with sight (or eyes)' occurs in *Pur.* 576, 1710; *Pearl* 200, 296, 302, 985; *Gaw.* 197, 226, 1705. For other examples, see Fuhrmann, *Alliterierende Sprachformeln*, p. 15.

**sour tornez.** Probably 'evil devices'; see note on 117.

**195.** Cf. *Erken.* 161: 'Towarde þe prouidens of þe prince þat paradis weldes'; *Winner and Waster* 296: 'It es plesynge to the prynce þat paradyse wroghte'; and *Death and Life* 13: 'If thou haue pleased the prince that paradice weldeth.'

**201.** Bateson (*Mod. Lang. Rev.* 13. 378) proposed reading 'Ne never so sodenly soȝt un (= on), soundely to weng.' This is awkward and unnecessary, as Gollancz shows (*ibid.* 14. 153), the word meaning here 'fatally.' G. compares *unsoundyly*, *Gaw.* 1438, and *unsounde*, *Pat.* 58.

**204 ff.** After this line M. placed a comma, as though the fall of Lucifer were intended as an illustration of the Lord's wrath. But the poet's purpose was just the opposite, a fact which is extremely important in the structure of the poem, which has often been unjustly regarded as a series of Biblical incidents loosely strung together. After enumerating the various sins for which a man may forfeit the bliss of Heaven (177-192), the poet declares he has often heard it said that God never took such fierce and sudden vengeance on men as he did for fleshly sin (193-202); for only in avenging this sin did he abandon his customary demeanor and become really wrathful (203-4). The stories of Lucifer (205-34) and of the fall of Adam (235-48) are now introduced as illustrations of acts of vengeance in which God did *not* become angry. This is clearly emphasized at the end of the narrative of Lucifer's Fall, where the poet says 'And ʒet wrathed not þe Wyʒ' (cf. also 215). Similarly, after telling of the result of Adam's sin, he states expressly that this act of vengeance was carried out *in moderation,* and soon atoned for by means of a spotless maiden (247-8). But, in contradistinction to these two instances of God's vengeance, in the third instance, the destruction of the world by the Flood because of carnal sin, God showed merciless wrath (249-50). These last lines, then, continue the thought of ll. 192-204, and all that intervenes (204-48) is parenthetical or introductory, intended to make plain, by way of contrast, that God's most terrible vengeance is reserved for those who sin in the flesh.

**211. tramountayne.** 'North.' So Milton, *Par. Lost* 5. 755-7:

> At length came into the limits of the North
> They came, and Satan to his royal seat
> High on a hill, far-blazing.

The tradition that Lucifer had his seat in the north of heaven, and, in fact, the whole legend of the fall of Lucifer, was based on Isaiah 14. 12-3: 'Quomodo cecidisti de cælo, lucifer qui mane oriebaris? Corruisti in terram, qui vulnerabas gentes? Qui dicebas in corde tuo: In cælum conscendam, super astra Dei exaltabo solium meum, sedebo in monte testamenti in lateribus *aquilonis,* ascendam super altitudinem nubiam, similis ero Altissimo.' This, and other Biblical passages, such as Luke 10. 18, led to the early formation of the legend of the fall of the angels, the beginnings of which may be found in Jerome, Augustine, and Gregory. As Carleton Brown notes (*Publ. Mod. Lang. Ass.* 19. 124), these lines in *Purity* repeat directly some of the phrases of Isaiah. For references to Lucifer in Old and Middle English, see Skeat's excellent note on

*Piers Plowman* C. 2. 105; and for the development of the legend of Lucifer, see H. Ungemach, *Die Quellen der Fünf Ersten Chester Plays* (Erlangen, 1890), pp. 18 ff.

**215.** Gollancz (*Mod. Lang. Rev.* 14. 153) adopts M.'s explanation that *metz = mese* (G. *mes*), 'pity,' comparing the verb *mese,* 764, and *amesying, Pat.* 400. I have retained this reading in the text, though Bateson's suggestion (*ibid.* 13. 378) that *metz* is a scribal error for *meth,* had occurred to me also, and seems not unlikely in view of the other occurrences of *meth* (*meþe*) in 247, 436, 565.

**222.** **[s]weved.** Though I cannot distinguish the initial *s,* I adopt Gollancz's reading (*Mod. Lang. Rev.* 14. 153), since there is no instance of defective alliteration with *s* except at 958, where it is more easily explicable because of the proper names. G. compares *Pat.* 253, where the whale 'swayues to þe se-boþem'; cf. *NED.,* s. v. *swayve.*

**as þe snaw þikke.** Cf. *Fall and Passion* 25-8 (ed. Mätzner, *Sprachproben,* p. 125), where it is said of the false angels:

> Seue daies and seue niȝt,
> As ȝe seeþ þat falliþ snowe,
> Vte of heuen hi aliȝt
> And in to helle wer iþrow.

**223.** **helle-hole.** I have not been able to find any other instances of this word, which is not recorded by the dictionaries, except in *Erken.,* where it is used twice (291, 307), and in *Death and Life* (386), which shows other traces of imitation of *Purity* (see Introd., p. xxvi).

**as þe hyve swarmez.** So Milton, in an elaborate simile, compares the swarming of the devils to 'bees in spring-time,' *Par. Lost* 1. 768-75. The grouping of similes in clusters, as in these lines (222, 223, and also 226), is a characteristic trick of the poet, and is used by Miss Thomas (*Sir Gaw.,* p. 12) as a proof of the common authorship of *The Pearl, Gawain, Purity* and *Patience.* The other instances of this mannerism in *Pur.* occur at 554, 556; 790, 791; 1018, 1022; 1132, 1134; 1692, 1694, 1696, 1697.

**224.** **forty dayez.** The number is due to the alliteration. In the *Fall and Passion* (see quotation, 222 n.) the fiends fell seven days, and in *Piers Plowman* (B. 1. 119) and Milton (*Par. Lost* 6. 871) nine.

**225.** **er . . . ne.** This very unusual use of a redundant negative after *er* occurs again in 1205 'er þay atwappe ne moȝt,' which the *NED.* (s. v. *atwape*) emends to 'er þay atwappene moȝt.' That the negative particle cannot be disposed of in this manner is

plain from this line, where it could not be attached to the preceding
infinitive (*stynt*) as part of the ending. Einenkel discusses
pleonastic *ne* after verbs of fearing, etc. (*Anglia* 35. 222 ff.), as in
Chaucer's translation of Boethius 'he moot alwey ben adrad that
he ne lese that thing' (2. prose 4. l. 113, ed. Skeat); but students
of syntax, and the *NED.*, which does not even record the pleonastic
*ne* discussed by Einenkel, do not seem to have noted the construction after *er*. Though it is possible that this use of *ne* developed
independently in English, it is very likely that the poet borrowed
it from Old French, where, as in modern French, *avant que* . . .
*ne* was a common construction (see Tobler, *Vermischte Beiträge*
4. 45 f.). It should be noted that in each case the *ne* appears before
*myȝt* (*moȝt*). Cf. also the *ne* of *Pat.* 231: 'He watz no tytter out-
tulde þat tempest ne sessed.' Cf. Bateson, *Mod. Lang. Rev.* 13. 379,
who cites an instance from Caxton.

**226. smylt mele.** 'Strained meal.' I believe that *smylt* is the
past part. of an OE. **smyltan* (OM. **smeltan*) used here in the
sense of 'filter through.' The original meaning of the Germc.
stem **(s)melt* is 'disintegrate, dissolve' (Falk u. Torp., *Norweg.-
Dan. Etym. Wörterb.*, s. v. *smelte; cf. Kluge*, s. v. *schmelzen;*
Skeat, *Etym. Dict.*, s. v. *melt, smelt*). This sense of 'breaking
into pieces' may be traced in various ways in *melt*: Wright-
Wülcker, *Vocabularies* 235. 33, has 'Fatiscit, . . . dissolvitur, . . .
mylt'; cf. *Pur.* 1566, where *NED.* defines 'filter in' (see other
examples in *NED.*, s. v., *melt*, v., esp. 2 and 5). *NED.'s* earliest
example of *smelt*, except for the part. adj. *smelt* = 'enamelled,'
*Destr. Troy* 1667, is dated 1543, but this is in the specialized modern
meaning, which is certainly a late borrowing from Scandinavia
or the continent. *Smylt*, of which the *NED.* gives only this instance,
without etymology, defining '?fine,' is the native word (only the
derivative *smilting* in the specialized meaning 'amber' occurs in
OE.). It is possible that *smult*, for which the *NED.* quotes, without
definition, only 'With a smorther and a smoke smult through his
nase,' *Destr. Troy* 911, is the same word, here meaning 'break
through.' For the general meaning of the word the derivatives
of the Germc. **(s)mel* may be compared, e. g. Sw. *mula*, crumb;
Mod. Engl. dial. *in smill*, in pieces (see Wright's *English Dialect
Dict.*, s. v. *smuil*).

**228.** Schumacher's emendation of *worlde* to *erþe* is unnecessary,
as we may here have transverse alliteration; cf. Introd., p. lvii.

**230.** This line has offered great difficulty to the commentators.
M. translated *þe wrech saȝtled* 'appeased the vengeance,' as though
*wrech* = *wrache;* but the next line shows that *wrech* must refer

to Lucifer. Bateson (*Mod. Lang. Rev.* 13. 379) suggested that *wrathed* meant 'repented,' though such a meaning (or word) is unrecorded; Gollancz (*ibid.* 14. 154) would emend to *wroth,* and paraphrase 'and yet the creature (i. e. Satan) turned not,' but this stretching of the sense of 'writhe' would be unparalleled. The passage becomes clear without emendation if we take *wyȝ* as a reference not to Satan, but to God. God is called *wyȝ* also in 5, 280; cf. *Pat.* 111, 206. The lines may be paraphrased: 'And yet God did not become angry, nor did the wretch (Satan) ever become reconciled, nor would he ever acknowledge, because of wilfulness, his worthy God.' For a similar confusing change of subjects, cf. 1229-30 and note. On the significance of God's not being angry, the point which the commentators miss, see note on 204. Emerson (*Publ. Mod. Lang. Ass.* 34. 499) also explains *wyȝ* as God, and *þe wrech* as Satan, but he, too, misses the point of *wrathed.*

**233.** M. paraphrases: 'Wherefore, though the blow were smart, the sorrow was little.'

**235. þat oþer wrake:** 'the second vengeance,' for Adam's sin. Cf. the passage in *Pearl* 637-45:

> Inoȝe is knawen þat mankyn grete
> Fyrste watȝ wroȝt to blysse parfyt;
> Oure forme fader hit con forfete
> Þurȝ an apple þat he vpon con byte;
> Al wer we dampned for þat mete
> To dyȝe in doel out of delyt,
> And syþen wende to helle hete,
> Þerinne to won wythoute respyt.
> Bot þer oncom a bote as-tyt.

**241.** Cf. *Spec. Gy de Warewyke* 229-30:

> Ac þurw eging of þe fend and Eue
> He dede a sinne þat gan him greue,

And Chaucer, *Man of Law's Tale* 842-3:

> Sooth is that thurgh wommannes eggement
> Mankind was lorn and damned ay to dye.

**242. enpoysened alle peplez.** Cf. the strikingly similar phraseology of *Erken.* 294-6 (quoted by Knigge, p. 6, as proof of unity of authorship):

> Dwynande in þe derke dethe, þat dyȝt vs oure fader,
> Adam, oure alder, þat ete of þat appulle
> Þat mony a plyȝtles pepul has poysoned foreuer;

and also *Death and Life* 273:

> And plucked them of the plant and poysoned them both.

**248.** Cf. *Erken.* 298: 'Bot, mendyd w$^t$ a medecyne, ʒe are made for to lyuye.'

**251 ff.** The poet gives the usual explanation of the cause of the Flood—unchastity among mankind. In the light of other mediæval accounts, it is probable, according to Emerson (*Legends of Cain: Publ. Mod. Lang. Ass.* 21, 901), that the *fende* (269), originally the *filii Dei,* here represent the evil descendants of Seth, and the *deʒter of þe douþe* (270), the daughters of Cain (the *filias hominum* of the Bible). From their evil intercourse sprang the giants (272). The traditional interpretation is well stated by Peter Comestor: 'Moyses dicturus de diluvio præmisit causam ejus dicens, *Cumque cœpissent homines multiplicari super terram viderunt filii Dei,* id est Seth, religiosi, *filias hominum,* id est de stirpe Cain, *et* victi concupiscentia *acceperunt eas uxores,* et nati sunt inde gigantes. . . . Potuit etiam esse, ut incubi dæmones genuissent gigantes.'—*Historia Scholastica, De causa diluvii* (Migne, *Patr. Lat.* 198. 1081). For further details of the development of the legend, and for other accounts in Old and Middle English, Professor Emerson's interesting study, cited above, should be consulted.

**256. lengest lyf in hem lent.** A common alliterative formula; cf. *Pat.* 260, and Fuhrmann, pp. 54-5.

**257-61.** 'For they were the first progeny that the earth produced, the sons of the noble ancestor called Adam, to whom God had given every advantage and all the innocent bliss that a mortal might possess, and those who followed next after him (were) just like him (their ancestor); for that reason, none since that time have been so fair to look upon.' Cf. Gollancz, *Mod. Lang. Rev.* 14. 154.

**266-8.** Holthausen, in *Archiv* 106. 349, compared Comestor's 'exarserunt homines in alterutrum coeuntes' (Migne, *Patr. Lat.* 198. 1081), as the probable source of these lines. On Comestor as a possible source, cf. note on 660 and Introd., p. xxxix.

**280. bygynnez.** Cf. 947. On *begin* without a complement, see Kölbing's note on *Ipomadon* 15.

**284. as wyʒe.** It is perhaps noteworthy that the poet expressly states that God grieved as man, since such an implication of human feeling was generally explained away by the commentators. Alcuin says of this passage: 'Non Deum de facto suo pœnitet, nec dolet sicut homo' (*Interrog. in Gen.* 99: Migne, *Patr. Lat.* 100. 527). Augustine even declares that the better reading is *recogitavit,* not *pœnituit* (Migne, *Patr. Lat.* 34. 487).

**287. al þat flesch werez.** Vulg. 'omnem carnem,' Gen. 6. 17. Similarly 'omnem animam viventem,' Gen. 8. 21, is represented by 'al þat lyf habbez,' 308 (cf. 325), or 'al þat is quik,' 324. Cf. *Gaw.* 52: 'þat ever lyf haden.' Other phrases beginning with 'al þat' occur in the description of the Flood at 289-90, 303, 408, 431-2.

**299.** Parallel alliteration; for examples, see Introd., p. lvi.

**303.** A good example of the remarkable interweaving of the Biblical phrases. To *finis universæ carnis* (Gen. 6. 13) is added *omne quod movetur super terram* (Gen. 7. 14) which belongs to the description of the entrance of the animals into the ark, a passage omitted by the poet. For a similar line, cf. note on 307.

**304. Is fallen forþ wyth my face.** This translates Gen. 6. 13, 'venit coram me.' *Forþer* here means 'hasten.'

**307. strenkle my distresse.** The use of the word *strenkle,* 'scatter,' and the phrase 'boþe ledez and londe' of the next line, would seem to show that the poet has in mind 'ego dispersam eos cum terra,' Gen. 6. 13, though the last part of this line follows Gen. 6. 7. It may be that we should read *wyth* for *my,* which would make *strenkle* and *strye* parallel, and *al* the object of both; cf. 'watz disstryed wyth distres,' 1160, i. e. 'by force, with violence.' The abbreviation for *wyth* might easily be mistaken for *my,* especially as *me* occurs directly above the word. But it may be that the use of the word *strenkle* is a mere psychological reminiscence of the phraseology of Gen. 6. 13, and does not reflect the meaning of *disperdam eos,* etc. The text, as it stands, would then have to mean 'I shall dispel my grief, and destroy all,' etc.

**310. a cofer.** The ark is again so called at 339, 492. The word is also applied to the ark of God, and the ark in which Moses was laid (see *NED.*). Other remarkable names for Noah's ark are *kyste* (346, 449, 464, 478); *lome* (314, 412, 443, 495; cf. Jonah's boat, so called *Pat.* 160); *gyn* (491). The last name is applied to Noah's ark in the *Towneley Plays* (3. 128) and to Jonah's boat in *Patience* (146).

**311. for wylde and for tame.** Cf. 362. This is a formal phrase not based on the Biblical passage, and introduced to fill out the line, like 'and þat is my wylle,' 309. In general, the translation of God's directions for building the ark is, characteristically, almost word for word. Carleton Brown contrasts it with the brief account in *Genesis and Exodus,* and the curious reduction of the dimensions of the ark in *Cursor Mundi* (*Publ. Mod. Lang. Ass.* 19. 122-3).

**318. upon.** 'Open,' as in 453, 882.

**330. wedded wyf.** See Fuhrmann, p. 66. This phrase has come down to us in the marriage ceremony, which embodies many very ancient alliterative formulas, e. g. 'to have and to hold' (Fuhrmann, p. 28).

**333. þat berez lyf.** Cf. 1023, and *Gaw.* 1229: 'with alle þat lyf bere.' In 1023 the phrase translates Mandeville's 'q'ad en luy vie,' which the author of the Cotton MS. version of Mandeville renders in the same way, 'that berethe lif in him' (ed. Halliwell, p. 100), while the Northern translation (Egerton MS.) has 'na quikk thing' (ed. Warner, p. 50). Caxton uses the same phrase in his account of the Flood: 'Alle þat euer bare lyf' (*Golden Legend*, ed. Ellis, I. 114). The phrase *bear life,* which is not mentioned in *NED.,* does not occur in OE., nor is there apparently anything exactly corresponding in ON. or OF.

**348.** As E. Kock notes (*Angl.* 26. 368), 'as thou didst lend me wit' does not mean 'gavest me instruction, directest me,' as Skeat and Morris explain in their notes to the *Specimens of Early English,* but rather 'as far as thou hast given me power to understand,' 'as well as I could.'

**359. [n]yȝ[t].** MS. *myȝ;* M. printed *niyȝ[t],* but the *i* is not distinguished by the mark usually written above it when following *n* or *m,* and the scribe probably merely made an extra accidental stroke, as also in *Gaw.* 929, where Gollancz still prints *niyȝt.*

**363-434.** These lines are expanded from Gen. 7. 17-24, with much elaboration of the details, and several additions of the poet's own invention, such as the terror of those overtaken by the flood (373-404), and the picture of the ark at the mercy of the winds (415-24). The passage should be compared with the excellent storm-scene in *Pat.* 137-56, and those in *Destr. Troy* 1983-2020, 3688-714, 4625-36, 9636-43, 12495-518; *Sege of Jer.* 50-70; and the portents at Alexander's birth, *Alex. C.* 551-68. The passages in *Destr. Troy* are striking in detail, though somewhat repetitious; but no poet of the alliterative school has written anything comparable to the swift and sustained narration of the wild flight of those vainly endeavoring to escape the rising waters of the flood.

**364. wod stremez.** Cf. *Pat.* 162: 'And euer . . . wodder þe stremes.'

**367. clustered clowde.** Cf. 951.

**375. wylger.** Skeat, in the glossary to *Specimens of Early English,* says that the word is apparently an error for *wylder.* But this is unlikely, since the word occurs in the *Metrical Homilies,* ed. Small, p. 61, l. 7, which M. had quoted in his edition: 'And gert them the builders of the town of Babel thair wilgern werk.' The existence of the word therefore seems to be established, even though the other two manuscripts of the *Homilies* read *wyld* and *wilful* respectively.

**376. dowelled.** See glossary for other instances; also *Gaw.* 566. This intrusion of a vowel before *r* and *w* is common in this MS.; see Osgood's note on *Pearl* 11, and Knigge, p. 55.

**377. feng to þe fly3t.** Cf. 457.

**381.** Cf. *Pat.* 220: 'Bot al wat3 nedles note.'

**391. to þe hy3e runnen.** Cf. *Gaw.* 1152: 'Hi3ed to þe hy3e.'

**394. Recoverer of þe Creator.** The editors of the *Specimens* explain as 'recoverer (saviour) of þe creature' (!), a note that must have been written by Skeat, since M. in his glossary had defined *recoverer* correctly as 'recovery' (see *NED.* for examples). The word is not a vocative, but the object of *cryed.* 'They besought rescue from the Creator.'

**395. þe mase.** MS. *þe masse þe mase.* The manuscript reading is certainly a dittograph, since it makes the line too long; but the meaning remains doubtful. If *masse* could be interpreted as 'mountain,' it would be possible to explain *þat* as a relative conj., and translate 'each one that ascended the mountain.' But it seems more reasonable to interpret *þat* as 'so that,' and accept *mase* as the correct reading, following the suggestion of Professor Child (quoted by Morris). We should then paraphrase 'so that the state of confusion increased.' In either case the transition to *his mercy watz passed* is extremely abrupt, as we should expect some adversative conjunction, such as 'but.'

**408. alle þat spyrakle inspranc.** This translates Gen. 7. 22: 'Cuncta, in quibus spiraculum vitæ est.'

**425-8.** The date of the Flood, which is given at the beginning of the Biblical account (Gen. 7. 10-11), is transferred by the poet to the end, and connected with the statement of the duration of the Flood in 429 (Gen. 7. 24).

**433-4.** Two difficult lines, of which four explanations have been offered. (1) Skeat paraphrased: 'that the remnant that the rack drives were glad that all kinds of animals, so well lodged, were safely kept inside.' This makes good sense, but his explanation of *ro3ly* as 'peaceful, comforted, merry, glad' is forced, even if the word could be connected with Swed. *rolig,* 'pleasant, calm,' OE. *rōw,* 'sweet,' as he suggests. (2) Bateson paraphrases: 'So that the relic (from the flood) that the rack drives about, within which all kinds thus lodged were assembled together, was in dire straits.' According to Bateson, *ro3ly* = 'rough' (cf. *roghlych. Pat.* 64), but with this interpretation, the lines follow the preceding less naturally as a result, since 431-2 refer simply to the drowning of all living creatures, and not to the fury of the storm. (3) Gollancz paraphrases: 'That was rough for the remnant that the rack drives, so that all the species, thus lodged, were mixed up pell-mell within.' The construction which makes *þe remnaunt* dative would be unusual, and Emerson (*Publ. Mod. Lang. Ass.* 34. 502) rightly asks 'why should it be "rough for the remnant" because of the loss of life mentioned in the preceding lines?' (4) Emerson explains *joyst* as a past participle of ME. *joissen* (cf. *rejoissen*), 'rejoiced, glad,' and paraphrases the second line 'within which all species so happy were joined together.' He remarks that this 'would seem to require in *roȝly* some such idea as Morris suggested by conjecturing *rwly,* "sorrowful," or Skeat who proposed "pleasant, glad," as the meaning.' (4) would seem to me the most natural interpretation, but I think it would be unwise to emend, because the existence of *roghlych,* adj., *Pat.* 64, is a presumption in favor of *roȝly,* adj., here, however difficult it may be to fit the meaning to the context.

**436. meth.** Apparently dependent on *mynne,* just as though the verb were not already followed by *on his mon.*

**446. rasse.** The same word occurs at *Gaw.* 1570, and apparently means 'top, height,' but it can hardly be connected with mod. dial. *raise,* 'cairn' (ON. *hreysi*), as Kullnick thinks (*Studien über den Wortschatz in Sir Gaw.,* p. 16).

**447-8.** 'Et la delez y ad vn autre montaigne qad a noun Ararach, mes ly Iuys lappellent Thanez, ou larche Noe se arresta.'—Mandeville, ed. Warner, p. 74. Brown points out that the form *Mararach* probably resulted from the poet's following some scribe who had carelessly run together Mandeville's *noun Ararach;* the passage also explains the reference to the name *Thanes.*

**449. in þe cragez wer[e] closed.** Cf. *Ancient Scott. Prophecy* I. *EETS.* 42. 22, l. 139: 'Scho has closede him in A cragge of cornwales coste.'

**452. bynne borde.** Cf. *Morte Arthur* 804: 'bynne þe schippeburde'; *Hegge Play of Noah* 209, ed. Manly, in *Specimens of Pre-Shak. Drama:* 'with-in my shypp-borde.' The expression 'within board,' which is still used, was due to the fact that 'board' had the meaning 'side(s) of a ship,' the technical sense of 'on board' still being 'close alongside a ship' (see *NED.*). But in *upon borde,* 470, 'board' is used for 'ship,' as in *Elene* 238.

**453. wafte he upon his wyndowe.** A common phrase: 'Wayueȝ vp a wyndow,' *Gaw.* 1743; 'weued vp a window,' *Wm. of Palerne* 2978; 'wayfez vp a wyndow,' *Alex. C.* 945 (Dublin MS.); 'wayuet [printed waynet] up a window,' *Destr. Troy* 676; cf. 'wayue vp the wiket,' *Piers Plow.* B. 5. 611.

**459. carayne he fyndez.** This had become the customary explanation of the failure of the raven to return to the ark. The raven is said to have stopped to feast on a carcass, in both Jewish and Arabic tradition, and in the latter Noah cursed the raven for this reason (Ginzberg, *Legends of the Jews* 1. 164; *Jewish Encycl.* 9. 323). Chrysostom gave this explanation (Migne, *Patr. Græc.* 53. 234), but I have not been able to find it in Latin writers until Avitus of Vienne (fl. 500), who interprets the raven's feasting on carrion allegorically in his *De Diluvio Mundi*, ll. 563-73 (ed. Peiper, *Monumenta Germ. Hist., Auct. Antiquissimi* 6, pt. 2, p. 251). The tradition became popular through Isidore, who knew Avitus, and may have obtained from the *De Diluvio* the second of the two explanations given in the *Quæst. in Vet. Test.* 26 (*Patr. Lat.* 83. 233): 'Corvus non est reversus, aut aquis utique interceptus, aut aliquo supernatante cadavere illectus.' The later commentators generally follow Isidore, though often giving only the second of his alternative explanations, e. g. Alcuin (*Patr. Lat.* 100. 530), Rabanus Maurus (*ibid.* 107. 522), Peter Comestor (*ibid.* 198. 1085). Thus the legend of the raven's finding carrion came to be almost an essential part of the Biblical story; references to it appear e. g. in Herman of Valenciennes, *Histoire de la Bible* (see F. Mehne's summary in his *Inhalt u. Quellen des Bible d. H. de V.,* Halle, 1900, pp. 15-6); in English, in the earlier *Genesis* 1447-8; *Cursor Mundi* 1875-94; Mirk's *Festial, EETS. Ext. Ser.* 96, p. 73; and especially in the mystery plays: *Hegge Noah* 246; *Towneley Noah* (No. 3) 499-504; *York Noah* (No. 9) 225-32. The cursing of the raven (*Pur.* 468) is not mentioned in any of the Latin or English works just cited, with the single exception of the *York Noah Play* 231-2:

> Then be he for his werkis wrange
> Euermore weried with-owten ende.

The *Cursor Mundi* adds to its account the comment (1889-92) that messengers who delay long on their journey are called 'raven's messengers' because of the raven's treachery to Noah. The author of the Old English *Adrian and Ritheus* (ed. Kemble, *Salomon and Saturn,* p. 202) makes the raven's failure to return to the ark the cause of its color being changed from white to black. This explanation of the raven's color is obviously a Christian adaptation of the classical story told by Chaucer in the *Manciple's Tale,* and Gower in the *Confessio Amantis* (3. 782 ff.), of the raven's (in Chaucer the crow's) white feathers becoming black because it told of the infidelity of Phœbus' wife. It should be noted that Chaucer makes much of the treachery of the bird (271 ff.), a characteristic emphasized by the author of *Purity* (455-6), because of its faithlessness to Noah.

**469. douve.** MS. doune. M. assumed the existence of a feminine word *dovene,* on the analogy of such feminine forms as *vixen;* OE. *wylfen,* ME. *wulvene.* But since there is no trace of such a word elsewhere, it is better to assume that the scribe merely mistook a *u* for an *n,* and that *doveue*(?) in 481 is either miswritten for *dowue,* the form that occurs in 485, or due to the repetition of the final *ve.*

**473. to bot.** Morris and Skeat explained as 'to boot,' i. e. 'for our good,' but if this interpretation were accepted, *blysse to uus alle* would have to be construed in apposition to *bodworde.* That is impossible, since the apposition of an abstract with a concrete noun, though not uncommon in Old English poetry, would be altogether anomalous here. I think *bot* is simply another instance of the unvoicing of the final *d* which occurs so frequently in this manuscript (see Introd., p. lxi, and Knigge, p. 56); i. e., *bot* stands for *bod(e),* exactly as *dyt* for *dyd(e), Pearl* 681. The line would then mean: 'Bring a message to announce (foretell) bliss to us all.' For similar lines, cf. *Alex. C.* 1489: '"I bringe þe bodword of blis, ser bischop," he said'; *Sege of Jer.* 965: 'Now is me bodeword of blys broȝt froward rome'; *Gol. and Gaw.* 171: 'And broght to the bauld king boidword of blis.'

**484. hit watz nyȝe at þe naȝt.** Trautmann (*Über. Verf.,* p. 28) quotes this and *Gaw.* 929, 'hit watz neȝ at þe niyȝt,' as evidence of common authorship, since the construction is different in the other alliterative poems; cf. 'it neiȝed niȝt,' *Wm. of Palerne* 770, 2599; 'it nied þe night,' *Alex. A.* 817; 'it neght to þe night,' *Destr. Troy* 672, 1075.

**488.** Cf. the 'grene graciouse leues' of Jonah's woodbine, *Pat.* 453.

**499.** Cf. *Pat.* 63: 'Goddes glam to hym glod þat hym vnglad made.' On the importance of this parallel, see Introd., p. xxxvi.

**504. þrublande in þronge.** Cf. 879: 'þus þay þrobled and þrong.' The word *þroble* is not recorded by *NED.,* though Bradley-Stratmann gives these instances (s. v. *þrublen*). It is apparently a variant of the verb *thrumble,* 'crowd together,' of which *NED.* gives no earlier example than 1589, from Bruce's *Sermons,* although the simple verb *thrum,* meaning 'compressed,' is found in *Layamon,* ed. Madden, l. 3, l. 18.

**þrowen.** This past part. means 'crowded,' as does the part. adj. *þrawen,* 1775, which M. rightly defined 'close, thick.' This meaning, which is not noted in *NED.,* may have arisen from such a use of *throw* as that in 879, where it is coupled with 'þrobled and þrong.' The semantic development would then be 'rush' (as in 220, 590), 'rush together,' 'crowd.' In the alliterative poetry, *kast* is the commoner word for most transitive senses of 'throw,' while the word *throw* itself is used in a great variety of intransitive senses (see Glossary, and cf. *Pearl* 875; *Pat.* 267).

**514.** Emerson (*Publ. Mod. Lang. Ass.* 34. 504) would preserve MS. reading, taking *mayny* as an adjective, meaning 'great, powerful.'

**520. [dedes].** MS. *synne,* inserted above the line. The alliteration makes it very improbable that the original word was *synne,* which was probably inserted by a second hand on the analogy of *for no mannez synnez* in 514. It cannot be assumed that the line is an instance of introverted alliteration: 'as disstrye al for manez synne dayez of þis erþe,' since *s* only once alliterates with *st* elsewhere in the poem (see Introd., p. lvii, n. 2). I do not think that it is necessary to supply *in* before *dayez,* as does M.; if anything else is missing it would be more likely to be *al þe,* corresponding to 'cunctis diebus,' Gen. 8. 22.

**521.** This line is imitated in *Death and Life* 248: 'Waxe fforth in the word & worth vnto manye.'

**worþez to monye.** Vulg. *multiplicamini.* Trautmann (*Über Verf.,* p. 28) compares the unusual phrase 'worþeȝ to youreȝ,' *Gaw.* 1106, 1387; but 'to noȝt worþe,' *Pat.* 360, which he also adduces, is common, occurring, for example, *Ormulum* 10960; *Ywain and Gaw.* 1642. The construction is OE. (see Einenkel's *Streifzüge durch die Mittelenglische Syntax,* p. 211).

**524. umbre.** This word, which M. derived from Lat. *imber,* is very probably from AN. *umbre,* OF. *ombre* (from Lat. *umbra*); 'shade' makes a good contrast to 'drought.' The phrase *umbre ne droȝþe* happens to be the poet's own addition to the series of contrasted words in Gen. 8. 22 which he is here paraphrasing.

**529. skylly skyvalde.** Three explanations have been proposed of this obscure phrase: (1) M. paraphrased: 'Then was a design (purpose) manifested (ordered)'; (2) Skeat paraphrased: 'Then was a separative (i. e. general) dispersion, when escaped all the wild animals,' comparing Icel. *skilja,* to separate, for the meaning of *skylly,* and suggesting that *skyvalde* was connected with Icel. *skīfa,* to cut in twain; (3) M. quotes in his glossary Professor Child's suggestion that *skyvalde* may be connected with Somerset *scaffle,* to scuffle. M.'s explanation is to be preferred to either (2) or (3). (3) may be disregarded, since the *EDD.* gives no such meaning for *scaffle,* and there would hardly be any possibility of connecting the words phonologically. If the meaning 'scramble,' which Professor Child apparently had in mind, fitted the context, it might be referred to ON. *skȳfa,* 'shove, push,' but such a meaning is unlikely because (a) *skylly* would make no sense (see below), (b) 'shoving' or 'scrambling' would hardly be used of the birds, which are mentioned first (529). Skeat's proposal (2) is very unlikely, because ON. *skīfa* really means 'to splice,' and the definition of *skylly* as 'separative, i. e. general,' is far-fetched. The use of *skyly* as a noun in 62 (not noted in *NED.*) makes it quite certain that it is also a noun here, and, since *skyl* is used in this poem (569, 709) in the sense of 'ordinance, decree,' Morris' paraphrase (1) is very plausible, though it is possible that *skylly* means 'separation': 'then was a separation devised,' etc. The derivation of *skyvalde* still remains obscure, though ultimate connection with ME. *skift,* 'ordain, devise' (ON. *skipta;* cf. OFris. *skiffa*) seems probable. In any case, it is clear that *skylly* must be a noun (*NED.* gives no adjective form before 1768), and *skyvalde* a verb.

**533. wylde wormez.** See Introd., p. xxix.

**537. hernez.** M. is probably right in defining 'eagles' (OE. *earn,* ME. *ern, arn*), though *NED.* arbitrarily puts all such forms with initial *h* under *heron, hern.* The spelling of OE. *earn* with *h* occurs as early as Layamon's *Brut,* where MS. B has *hearnes* for MS. A's *arnes* (2. 489, l. 25). Moreover the first example which *NED.* gives for the contracted spelling *herne* from *heron* is probably *herne,* 'eagle.' The line is 'The pauylyon with the golden herne [two MSS. have erne],' *Rich. Coer. de Lion* 2284, ed. Brunner; but this is surely 'golden eagle,' like the one which adorned the pavilion of Lanval's fairy mistress: 'Un aigle d'or ot desus mis' (*Lanval* 87, *Die Lais der Marie de France,* ed. Warnke).

**549-51.** The difficulty of these lines arises from the fact that *so seme* needs completion. M. attempted to solve the problem by inserting *ne* after *þat* (550): 'there is no one so goodly in his deeds, that is not impure (in God's sight) if he is soiled by sin.' Bateson (*Mod. Lang. Rev.* 13. 381) connected 549 with the preceding lines, and translated *so seme,* 'so scrupulous (as God),' making 549 the protasis of the lines which follow it. Gollancz (*ibid.* 14. 155) paraphrases:

> For no man under the sun is goodly enough in works,
> If he be soiled by sin that fits him uncleanly.

But this avoids the difficulty; *so seme* surely cannot be made to mean 'goodly enough.' If we accept the text as it stands, my own opinion is that this is another instance of anacoluthon. The poet says: 'For there is no man under the sun so goodly in his deeds, if he is soiled by unclean sin'—and intended to continue 'that can attain the kingdom of heaven'; but, he breaks off, as he wishes to emphasize the fact that a very little may keep a man from the bliss of heaven, and declares 'a speck of a spot may cause [such a man] to miss the sight of our Lord.'

**552. þat syttez so hyȝe.** Cf. 1498.

**553-4.** 'In order that I may appear in those bright dwellings, I must be clean as a burnished beryl.' The omission of the subject in 553, and of an object for the impersonal *byhovez*, are peculiar. Bateson (*Mod. Lang. Rev.* 13. 381) refers *þat* to 'speck of a spot,' and paraphrases 'For that (spot) shall expose me in those bright mansions,' connecting this line with the preceding; cf. Emerson, *Publ. Mod. Lang. Ass.* 34. 504.

**556. Wythouten maskle oþer mote.** Cf. *Pearl* 726, 'wythouten mote oþer mascle,' and *Pearl* 843.

**557-600.** These lines are a transition to the narration of God's next act of vengeance for the same sin.

**564 ff.** These lines repeat the idea of 519-20, and partly reflect Gen. 9. 11: 'Statuam pactum meum vobiscum, et nequaquam ultra interficietur omnis caro aquis diluvii, neque erit deinceps diluvium dissipans terram.'

**569-70.** 'This promise (that God would never again destroy *all* flesh) never escaped him, i. e. he never forgot, because of any wickedness (however great). Nevertheless he did take terrible vengeance on wicked men afterwards.'

**574. þe venym and þe vylanye.** Similarly in *Pat.* 71, God wishes to avenge himself on the 'vilanye & venym' of the people of Nineveh.

**579. heþyng of selven.** Not 'contempt of God's self,' as M. explained, but 'scorning (i. e. violating the purity) of one's body,' as is clear from 709-10.

**581. savor.** MS. sauyor. 'Savior' is an impossible reading, and the Latin of the psalm here quoted shows that *savor* must have been the original word, translating 'intelligite' or 'sapite' (see quotation below). Curiously enough, Hampole uses the very same word to translate the same verse: 'The vnwis, withouten kunynge, and fulis, withouten puruyaunce of the tother warld, that ere in noumbire of cristen men, vndirstandis and *sauyrs* this' (cited in *NED.*, s. v. savour, v., 12, where other examples of the meaning 'perceive, apprehend,' are given). It should also be noted that in *Pat.* 121 (quoted below) the poet uses the word *feel* in translating the same passage. The scribe's mistake was an easy one to make, since he had just written *saveour* five lines before. I add the Vulgate version of the verses on which ll. 581-6 depend, and also the passage in *Patience* where they are again paraphrased:- 'Intelligite, insipientes in populo; et stulti, aliquando sapite. Qui plantavit aurem, non audiet? aut qui finxit oculum, non considerat?' (Ps. 93. 8-9).

> O Foleȝ in folk, feleȝ oþer whyle,
> & vnderstondes vmbe-stounde, þaȝ [ȝ]e be stape fole!
> Hope ȝe þat he heres not þat eres alle made?
> Hit may not be þat he is blynde þat bigged vche yȝe.
> —*Pat.* 121-4.

**582. babel.** 'þaȝ þou bere þyself babel,' corresponds to the Vulgate *stulti*, as 'þaȝ þou a sotte lyvie' corresponds to *insipientes*. *Babel* as an adjective is unusual, and not recorded in the dictionaries. It must be ultimately connected with Lat. *babulus,* 'fool,' though there is apparently no corresponding word in OF. Whether this *babel* has any connection with ME. *babel,* Mod. Engl. *bauble,* is difficult to determine, because the origin of OF. *ba(u)bel* is itself obscure.

**589-90.** These lines evidently reflect the first clause of Ps. 93. 11: 'Dominus scit cogitationes hominum, quoniam vanæ sunt.' The thought may be paraphrased: 'However cautiously and secretly a man may work, his thoughts fly swiftly to God even before he has conceived them.' *þro* is undoubtedly the right word in 590 (see notes on text), as it is a favorite with the poet, and the more usual meaning 'eager,' easily develops into 'quick, swift,' as, for example, in *Gaw.* 1021.

**591. grounde of alle dedez.** Cf. *York Creation* (No. 1) 74: 'þu gloryus god þat es grunde of all grace.'

**592 ff.** Rev. 2. 23: 'Ego sum scrutans renes et corda, et dabo unicuique vestrum secundum opera sua.'

**ring.** See Introd., p. xli.

**597 ff.** Anacoluthon. 'But (to speak) of (God's) judgment on men for shameful deeds—he abhors that sin so much that he swiftly scatters (the sinners); he may not delay, but slays in haste.'

**598. scarrez.** The meaning is certainly 'scatters' (as also in 838, 1784); cf. such passages as Ps. 58. 12; 88. 11, where the Psalmist speaks of the Lord 'scattering' his enemies (Vulgate *dispergere*). *NED.* quotes this line s. v. *scare,* v., as its first instance of the meaning 'to take fright, to be scared (at),' a definition that is obviously impossible here, as the reference is to

God. *NED.* does recognize a verb *skair*, Orm's *skeʒʒredd*, 'to scatter' ('of obscure origin'), citing under this word a passage already cited under *scare*, but this meaning cannot be limited to a verb with the form *skair*. Cf. note on 838.

**599. draw allyt.** Not 'to draw back a little,' as M. explained, but to 'delay'; *allyt* is not here equivalent to *a lyte*, a little, but to *on lyte*, 'with delay,' or at least the expression has been confused with *lyte*, 'delay' (see *NED.*, s. v. *lite*) ; cf. *on-lyte droʒen*, 'hesitated,' *Gaw.* 1463, and *on lyte lette*, *Gaw.* 2303.

**611. as to God.** In this passage (611 ff.), where the angels are identified with God, and the number suddenly shifted from plural to singular, most strikingly in 647, the poet is but following the language of the Bible. Abraham addresses the three men as *Domine* (Gen. 18. 3) ; when the angels first speak, the plural is used, *dixerunt* (Gen. 18. 5, 9), but later we have *Dixit autem Dominus* (Gen. 18. 13). Of this same passage, the *Cursor Mundi* says (2707-8) :

> Toward him com childir thre
> Liknes o god in trinité,

and the author of *Piers Plowman* uses this instance 'where god cam goynge a-thre' (C. 19. 243) as proof of the existence of the Trinity. The application of this and other similar Biblical passages to the doctrine of the Trinity has been expounded by the fathers, e. g. Ambrose, *Patr. Lat.* 14. 435 (cf. *Cath. Encycl.* 15. 49a, s. Trinity).

**618. yor fette wer waschene.** Fischer proposed substituting for this unusual expression the equivalent phrase found in 802, 'yor fette forto wasche.' But the poet happens, in this case, to be following and translating in a curiously literal manner, a variant of the Latin text of Gen. 18. 4 which read 'et laventur pedes vestri,' instead of the usual 'et lavate pedes vestros' (the Greek has νιψάτωσαν, variant νιψάτω, 'let them (him) wash your feet'). The Latin reading used by our poet was the one known to Bede (*Patr. Lat.* 93. 312), and was adopted in the Sistine edition of the Vulgate (1590) ; for other instances, see Vercellone, *Variæ Lectiones Vulgatæ Latinæ Bibliorum* (Rome, 1860) 1. 61a. Both the earlier and the later Wycliffite versions also follow this reading 'et laventur,' etc.: 'But I schal bringe to a litil mesure of water, and ʒoure fete be wayshid.'

**620. to banne yor hertte.** 'Et confortate cor vestrum,' Gen. 18. 5. M. connected *banne* with Scotch *bawne*, 'fortification,' and Gollancz would read *baune*, 'fortify' (see *Athen.* 1894, 2. 646). The word may be an aphetic form of *enbaned*, 1459; cf. note on that line.

**637. mete.** M. put a semicolon after this word, thinking it the object of *settez* of the preceding line. But this marked enjambement would be such an anomaly that Thomas proposed putting *mete* at the end of the line above (*Die Alliterierende Langzeile des Gawaindichters,* p. 8). This is unnecessary, as *mete* is most naturally interpreted as an adj., 'meet, fitting,' modifying *messez.* This interpretation, it should be noted, deprives *NED.* of its earliest instance of *meat* in the specific modern sense; the next example given is dated 1460.

**644.** Cf. 748, 1699, and 'God, þat al þis myhtes may,' the opening line of a well-known hymn (Patterson, *Middle Engl. Penitential Lyric,* p. 64).

**647. here away.** 'Hither,' as the Latin, 'revertens veniam ad te,' shows. *NED.*'s first example is 1400, Wright-Wülcker, *Vocabularies,* 590. 41. The expressions *here away, there away* are very common in modern dialects (see *EDD.*). Cf. Barbour's *Bruce* 10. 32 (MS. E.):

> For gif the king held thar away,
> He thoucht he suld soyn vencust be.

For the omission of the verb, cf. 665, and Kellner, *Synt.,* p. 45.

**652. ȝarked.** MS. ȝark. 'That shall hold in heritage that which I have prepared for men.' Since M. took *ȝark* to be an adj., defining 'select,' he must have interpreted, 'in order that I may have chosen men.' Though *yark,* adj., occurs in modern dialects, the single example in OE. is very doubtful (see Bosworth-Toller, *Supplem.* s. v. *gearc*). In any case, *halde in heritage* seems to require an object, which could only be the second *þat* = 'that which.'

**656. t[em]e.** Emerson (*Publ. Mod. Lang. Ass.* 34. 506) also suggests *teme* for *tonne.*

**659. bene.** MS. by ene (eue?). M. suggested *bycame,* because 'the sense would require *hade* before *byene,* if *byene = ben.*' But perhaps the idea of the pret. auxiliary may be carried over from the previous line 'watz hem fayled,' and *bycame* certainly does not fit the preceding *ay,* which seems to require a pluperfect sense. The poet could not have said Sarah 'ever *became* barren.'

**660.** This line closely resembles Peter Comestor's comment: 'Ad hæc, etiam, ipsa sterilis erat' (Migne, *Patr. Lat.* 198. 1099). It is the only passage where I have discovered any noteworthy verbal similiarity between Comestor and the poet; cf. Introd., p. xxxix.

**661. Se! so Sare laȝes.** For this use of *so* after *see!* cf. 1225.

**665.** Cf. *Gaw.* 1981: '& þay ȝelden hym aȝayn ȝeply þat ilk.'

In *Alex. C.* 1393 (Ashmole MS.), just as in this line in *Purity*, the verb is omitted after ʒapely: 'And þai ʒapely aʒayne and ʒildis þam swythe,' though the Dublin MS. has 'and þai ʒopely ayayn ʒeldyn þaim swythe.' On the forms *aʒain* and *again* in the alliterative poetry, see Schumacher, pp. 198 ff.

**668.** 'That she did not laugh on account of any words they uttered.'

**671.** **ros up radly.** Cf. 797; *Pat.* 378; *Gaw.* 367. The phraseology is strikingly similar, though it must be remembered that *rise radly* is a common phrase (cf. Fuhrmann, p. 52).

**683.** **his corse.** 'Him.' The use of ME. *corse* as equivalent to the personal pronoun is borrowed from the similar use of OF. *cors* (Einenkel, *Grundr.*² I. 1126, § 173 εε; for the OF. see Tobler, *Verm. Beitr.* I. 30-6). Cf. *Destr. Troy* 1865-6:

Syn he no knowlage, ne Acoyntaunse of my cors has,
Ne I hardely herde of hym hade in my lyue.

The use of *body* in the same sense is frequent in ME.; cf. Mätzner's *Wörterbuch*, and Campion-Holthausen's note on *Perceval* 150.

**689.** For the expression, compare Dunbar's *Tua Mariit Wemen and the Wedo* 115: 'Quhen that the sound of his saw sinkis in my eris.'

**693-712.** The poet's own elaboration.

**706.** **stylle stollen steven.** Cf. 1778, and *Gaw.* 1659: 'Wyth stille stollen countenaunce.'

**708.** **meschefez on mold.** Cf. *Piers Plow.* B. Prol. 67, C. 13. 178; *Rich. Redeless* 3. 9.

**724.** Knigge (p. 5) compares *Erken.* 245: 'For I was ryʒtwis and rekene and redy of the laghe.'

**727.** **þyn note.** *þyn* again occurs before initial *n*, 1638. Before *h*, *þyn* occurs once, 876, elsewhere *þy* (*þi*), 920, 1625; also *þi erigaut*, 148.

**735.** **tatz to non ille.** Cf. *Gaw.* 1811: 'Tas to non ille.'

**740.** **for hortyng.** Here practically equivalent to 'from hurting,' though the peculiar sense of *for* of course arose from the meaning 'to prevent, against' (see *NED.*, s. v. *for* 23. d, esp. quotation from *Alex.*).

**743.** **forfete.** Two explanations of this line are possible: (1) we may consider *forfete* elliptical, and equivalent to 'be fre' of 741, paraphrasing 'though only forty be without (sin), yet I shall delay for a time'; or (2) we may consider *forfete* a noun, the object of *fryst,* and paraphrase 'though (the number be only) forty, I shall delay the punishment.' The meaning given to *forfete* in (2) is possible, since Mätzner gives the definition 'Busse für Vergeben, überhaupt Busse, Strafe' (though *NED*. gives nothing exactly equivalent), but the construction would be decidedly awkward. (1) seems therefore preferable, in spite of the fact that this meaning of the verb is unexampled.

**744.** Cf. 1013, and esp. *Pat*. 284.

**747.** The idea is repeated from 736, where it corresponds regularly to Gen. 18. 27.

**748.** Cf. *Pat*. 329.

**768-76.** This special intercession for Lot is inserted by the poet, Lot not even being mentioned in the Biblical account. Cf. Introd., p. li.

**772. my lef broþer.** Cf. note on 924.

**775.** Cf. 907.

**778. [morn]ande for so[rȝe].** MS. *wepande for sorewe,* but the last word rewritten by a second hand. It seems to me very probable that the last three words of the line were copied by the scribe from the line above *wepande for care,* and that the second hand, recognizing the dittograph, boldly changed *care* to *sorewe*. The scribe was quite evidently nodding at this passage; cf. 775 *wendeȝ wendeȝ,* 783 *mevand mevande.*

**781.** On *was* and *is* as plurals, see Kellner, *Synt.,* p. 48; Mätzner, *Gram.*[2] 2. 151.

**795. au[c]ly, MS. autly.** Gollancz is mistaken in declaring that *aucly* is the reading of the MS. (*Mod. Lang. Rev.* 14. 156), since the letter is plainly *t* in this case. But the scribe may easily have written *t* for *c* as he did in *plate* for *place*, 72, especially as he had just written *autl* in *fautleȝ* of the preceding line. I adopt Gollancz's suggestion that the word is that recorded in *NED.* s. v. *awkly,* adj., 'untoward, perverse,' found in the *Lindisfarne Gospels* as *afulic* (ONth. *afu(h)*, ON. *afugr*), and in Archbishop Parker as *awkly*. The adjective *awk* is more common. Gollancz paraphrases: 'There was nothing amiss in either for they were angels.' Before Gollancz's explanation came to my notice, I had thought the word might be *autly*, as it stands in the text, a variant of *authly*, *Alex. C.* 3234 (Ashmole MS.), which Skeat defines 'sadly,' but which might better be defined 'dreadful, horrible'; cf. the peculiar noun *aut*, 'dread,' *Laud Troy Book* 10096 (*EETS.* 121). But there are obvious difficulties with the etymology of this word (Skeat suggested ON. *auðr*, 'desolate'), and the meaning 'dreadful' is here less apt than 'amiss, awry.'

**796. underȝede.** This form is explained by Zupitza in his note on *Guy of Warwick* (*EETS. Ext. Ser.* 25, 26) 8231, which I quote entire: 'vnduryode = understood, learnt. Cf. l. 10804:

And hys moonyng *vndurʒode.*

The word is wanting in Stratmann, but Halliwell (Diction., 901) quotes from our MS.:

> The hors sone *unduryede*
> That Befyse was not on hys rygge.

Cf. besides Alliterative Poems, ed. Morris, b. 796:

> And þat þe ʒep *underʒede,* þat in þe ʒate syttez.

Morris, in his note to this passage and in the glossary, takes *underʒede = underʒete,* but this is certainly wrong. The word in question is not OE. *undergeat* (= vnderʒate, l. 10430), but *\*undergeeode = undereode.* As to the signification, cf. *understand.'*

**798. Loth.** The unusual position of the word is due to the requirements of the alliteration. The vocative *Loth* in 841, occupying the same position in the line, halts the rhythm in the same peculiar way; cf. *Gaw.* 2469.

**805.** Cf. *Gaw.* 1836: 'And he nayed þat he nolde neghe in no wyse.'

**812.** For the word-order compare the similar line, *Destr. Troy* 750: 'Þat was rially arayed with a riche bede.'

**819. þrefte.** In a paper read before the Philological Society, according to a brief summary in the *Athen.* 1894. 2. 646, Gollancz explained that *'threfte* is for *therfte,* unleavened.' *NED.* gives neither form, although it has duly recorded the related word *tharf,* which is not uncommon, and appears at 635 in its regular ME. form *þerve.* Gollancz was certainly right in explaining *þrefte* as 'unleavened,' since this form *threft,* with metathesis, is given by the *EDD.* as a variant of *tharf.* The word is not included in M.'s glossary.

**819-28.** The incident of Lot's wife putting salt into the food of her visitors, contrary to Lot's express command, is purely apocryphal, as is likewise the statement (996-1000) that this was one of the reasons why she was turned into a pillar of salt. O. F. Emerson, in *Mod. Lang. Rev.* 10. 373-5, points out that this interesting legend has its ultimate origin in Hebrew tradition, according to which Lot and his wife quarreled about giving salt to the strangers, Lot's wife being turned into a pillar of salt because of her disobedience. Lot's command that 'no sour ne no salt' should be served is due, as Emerson explains, to the fact that the unleavened bread must contain neither yeast nor salt. As this legend does not appear in any of the well-known mediæval accounts, Emerson suggests that the poet may have been directly acquainted with the Hebrew commentaries on the Bible.

It may be well to call attention, in this connection, to another element in the Hebrew legend of Lot that seems to have been familiar to the poet of *Purity:* Lot's great wealth, which is emphasized at 786, 812, 878, though there is no hint of it in the Biblical passages paraphrased. The only indication of Lot's wealth in the Bible occurs in Gen. 13. 6, where it is said of Abraham and Lot 'for their substance was great, so that they could not dwell together.' But in Rabbinical literature Lot's reputation in this respect has been greatly developed. The *Jewish Encycl.* says: 'He was besides very greedy of wealth; and at Sodom he practised usury (Genesis Rabbah li. 8). His hesitation to leave the city (comp. Gen. 19. 16) was due to this regret for his great wealth which he was obliged to abandon (Gen. R. l. 17).'

**821. wroth.** Emendation to *wroȝt,* as M. suggests, is not absolutely necessary, since the form ending in *-th* occurs elsewhere, e. g. *wrouthe, Alex.* and *Dind.* 88. 775.

**822 ff.** Lot's wife says: 'These disagreeable fellows don't like any salt in their sauce; yet there is no reason why other people should go without, even though the two be (so) fastidious.'

**831. tyl þay waschen hade.** Washing after, as well as before, meals was the custom in the Middle Ages, and is mentioned constantly in the romances (cf. Schultz, *Das Höfische Leben* 1. 415 ff., 432).

**832.** Cf. *Gaw.* 1648: 'Þenne þay teldet tableȝ· [on] trestes alofte.'

**838.** Cf. *Morte Arth.* 2468: 'Skayres þaire skottefers and theire skowtte-waches'; and *Destr. Troy* 1089: 'Skairen out skoute-wacche for skeltyng of harme'; and see also 598 n.

**842. ȝete.** This is an indisputable occurrence of *get* with initial *ȝ* (OE. *gietan*), since the word alliterates with *ȝong* and *ȝorewhyle,* and the meaning forbids derivation from OE. *gēatan* (cf. *NED.* s. v. *get* 64, on *get out* used transitively). Schumacher (pp. 209, 211) gives two other examples—*ȝet, Sege of Jer.* 971, and *ȝeten, Alex. C.* 1107. These instances of forms with the initial continuant are sufficient to dispose of *NED.*'s assertion that the 'solitary example in ME. of *ȝeten* without prefix . . . may be referred to the influence of *biȝeten.*'

**846. sorȝe.** See note on 117.

**848.** The idea is: 'of the sin about which they raised a cry with those fearful words,' but *þose broþelych wordeȝ* is made the subject. Gollancz interprets 'the spew which those wild words cast up' (*Mod. Lang. Rev.* 14. 157).

**855-6.** The meaning is: 'He feared no harm from the wicked men which should prevent him from going out of the gate to meet the danger.'

**855. wonded no woþe.** Cf. *Gaw.* 488: 'For woþe þat þou ne wonde.'

**867.** Cf. *Sege of Jer.* 99: '& 30 a mayde vnmarred þat neuer man touched.'

**882. wapped upon.** 'Flung open.' Cf. *Gol. and Gaw.* 127: 'The yettis wappit war wyde.'

**886. blynde as Bayard.** Originally *bayard* meant simply a bay-colored horse, particularly the magic horse given by Charlemagne to Renaud, but, as *NED.* explains, it was 'alluded to in many phrases and proverbial sayings, the origin of which was in later times forgotten, and "Bayard" taken as the type of blindness or blind recklessness.'

**890. roþeled.** If this were the only occurrence of the word, one might suggest that it is based on ON. *hroða*, 'to huddle up' (see Cleasby-Vigfusson); but this derivation would hardly explain the use of the word in 59, where it is difficult to ascertain the exact meaning. *NED.* cites both passages without attempting to derive or define the words. The difficulty is increased by the line in the *Parlement of the Three Ages* (261): 'Then this renke alle in rosett *rothelede* thies wordes,' where the word seems to mean simply 'uttered'; but it is possible that this is a different word, to be referred to ME. *roþe,* ON. *rāða* (cf. *rothe* v.[1] and v.[2] in *NED.*).

**891-2.** 'But those who dwelt in the house were suddenly (?) roused (and rescued) from one of the most terrible calamities that ever happened.'

**918.** This line reflects Gen. 19. 19: 'ne forte apprehendat me malum.'

**923. oddely þyn one.** 'Peculiarly or entirely alone.' The original construction with the personal pronoun *him one* (= 'alone'), *thee one,* passed into *his one, thine one,* just as *thee self* became *thyself* (see Einenkel, *Grundr.,* 2d ed., I. 1086, 174 β). Cf. Scotch *his lane,* and the expression *by his lonesome.*

**924. Abraham þy[n em].** The corrector who wrote *broþer* over *em* was probably thinking of 772, where Abraham speaks of Lot as 'my lef broþer' (Vulgate *frater*). This Hebraism, *brother* for *kinsman,* occurs with reference to Lot and Abraham at Gen. 13. 8, 11; 14. 14, 16, where the Vulgate has *frater.*

**931.** Cf. 767.

**933.** In the Biblical account, Lot's attempts to arouse the household (Gen. 19. 14) precede his conversation with the angels (Gen. 19. 15-22), paraphrased by 893-932. The poet transposed the order of events, apparently in order not to delay by this conversation his rapid narrative of the flight of Lot and his family.

**935. token hit as t[a]yt.** 'They took it as a joke' translating Gen. 19. 14: 'Et visus est eis quasi ludens loqui.' The scribe, thinking of the common phrase *as tyt*, 'at once' (see Glossary, s. v. *tid*), wrote *tyt* for *tayt*, 'play, sport, game.' That *tayt* (ON. *teiti*, 'joy, gladsomeness') had such a meaning in ME. (given in Bradley-Stratmann, but not in *NED.*) is plain from *Alex. C.* 3979, where Skeat defines 'play, game' (cf. also ON. *leik ok teiti*). One may compare the very similar paraphrase in the *Cursor Mundi* (2815-6):

> Bot al þat loth to þaim can sai
> Þam thoght it was not bot in plai.

Bateson and Gollancz would leave the word *tyt*. Gollancz interprets *as tyt*, 'as mere tittle-tattle,' and assumes a word *tit*, of which *tittle* is the frequentative and *tattle* a variant. This is possible, but there is no record of such a word elsewhere. The word can hardly be *tit*, 'small' (cf. Icel. *tittr*, 'small bird'), as Gollancz points out (*Mod. Lang. Rev.* 14. 157).

**943.** Cf. *Gaw.* 2488: 'In tokenyng he watȝ tane in tech of a faute.'

**945. kayre ne con.** Fischer says (p. 62): '*-ne* als negation gefasst, stört den sinn; M. hält *-n(e)* für die endung des inf., dann aber ist der vers zu kurz. Mit Prof. Trautmann möchte ich *en-con* lesen und dieses *en-* für das alte *on-* halten. Noch Orm 2801 sagt *onginnen*. Also *encon* nordengl. für *engon*. Der sinn ist dann: "sie machten sich auf dem weg." ' M.'s explanation that the *-n(e)* is the infinitive ending is less rash than emendation to a word otherwise unknown; and even though it were necessary to drop the final *e*, this does not, as Fischer asserts, make the verse too short, since we have 'and þy wedded wyf' (330) and 'and wyth besten blod' (1446), of exactly the same metrical type. But Emerson's explanation (*Publ. Mod. Lang. Ass.* 34. 508) is preferable.

**956. swe.** Fischer would read *sweyed*, as M. suggested; Bateson, *swed;* but compare *sweȝe*, pret. 3 sg., *Gaw.* 1796, and *swey*, *Pat.* 429.

**958.** Cf. note on 222.

**961. houndez of heven.** For the application of the term 'hound' to a heavenly power, one may compare the famous passage in Dante, *Purg.* I. 101, 'infin che il Veltro verra,' which early commentators often considered a reference to Christ (see Toynbee's *Dante Dictionary*, s. v. *Veltro*). The resemblance to the title of Francis Thompson's poem, *The Hound of Heaven,* is striking, and his application of the term to Christ may go back to this interpretation of Dante's 'Hound,' though it should be remembered that the alliterative phrase was used by Shelley in *Prometheus Unbound* I. 34, 'Heaven's winged hound . . . tears up my heart,' where the reference is to the eagle which Æschylus calls Διὸς πτηνὸς κύων (*Prom.* 1022). ˌThat mediæval writers saw no objection to this association of hounds with angels and ministers of grace, may be seen from the fanciful interpretation current in the Middle Ages of *Dominicani,* as *Domini cani.* The context of this line in *Purity* reminds one of the descriptions of the Harrowing of Hell, and it is possible that the idea of the 'houndez of heven' here, and perhaps also that of the commentators on Dante's *Veltro,* go back to some obscure legendary conception. The use of the phrase here was probably also influenced by the contrasting idea of the 'hound(s) of Hell,' which was common: 'þarinne is mony on hungri hund' (*Eleven Pains of Hell* 244, in Morris's *Old Engl. Miscellany, EETS.* 49).

**972. clatered þe cloudes.** The phrase is common; cf. *Destr. Troy* 4626, 5787, 12501; *Alex. C.* 555; *Sege of Jer.* 54.

**976.** Cf. *Pist. of Susan* 225: 'But ʒit we trinet a trot, þat traytour to take.'

**983. þat ho nas.** 'without becoming'; i. e. she became a statue at once.

**1002. nom[e]n.** MS. no mon. M.'s attempt to make sense of this line by inserting *so* before *much*—'þat alle naʒt [so] much nuye had no mon in his hert'—solves only half the difficulty, as two subjects (*þat* and *no mon*) remain for the relative clause. Even Fischer's further change, the omission of *alle,* which makes the line parenthetical, does not dispose of the awkwardness of the following line. The syntactical difficulties disappear and the whole passage reads smoothly, if one assumes that the scribe made the simple mistake of writing *no mon* for *nomen* (this form occurs l. 1281); *þat,* referring back to Abraham, would be the subject of the relative clause, and *leyen* would be parallel to *nomen,* the *hade* which precedes *nomen* being understood for *leyen:* 'Abraham, . . . who had had (felt) anxiety all night and lain awake on Lot's account.' The fact that the verb *nym* is here used of continued rather than momentary action is unusual, but such straining of meaning is not uncommon in this and other alliterative poems; cf. the use of the word in OE., where it means 'hold, have' as well as 'take' (see definitions in Bosworth-Toller, *niman* II). It may be noted that *nummen* alliterates with *nyes* in *Pat.* 76. Emerson (*Publ. Mod. Lang. Ass.* 34. 509) has recently suggested this emendation independently.

**1013.** Cf. *Pat.* 370: 'Þe verray vengaunce of God schal voyde þis place.'

**1015. faure citees.** In discussing the poet's indebtedness to Mandeville (see 1022 n.), C. F. Brown points out that the mention of four cities instead of five is the only important variation from Mandeville's account. 'The number four,' he writes, 'is found only in John of Würtzburg (Tobler, *Descrip. Ter. Sanct.*, p. 178) and in the *De Situ*, an itinerary of the middle of the 12th century (Marquis de Vogué, *Les Eglises de la Terre Sainte*, p. 416). But there are no other similarities between these accounts and the passage in *Cleanness*, and it is extremely improbable that our author was acquainted with them. Moreover, we may account for our author's change in the number of cities, without supposing any such dependence. The fifth city in the Mandeville list is Segor (Zoar), though it is stated that it was not destroyed at the time that the others were, but, through the intercession of Lot, was saved for a long time. It is very likely that our author felt that to include Segor among the destroyed cities was a contradiction of God's promise to Lot that it should be spared (Gen. 19: 21-22), and therefore corrected the number to four. If this explanation be accepted, it furnishes another instance of our author's careful observance of the Biblical text' (*Publ. Mod. Lang. Ass.* 19, 152). There would be nothing improbable in this suggestion, especially since the poet states plainly that Segor (Zoar) was saved (992). But in the manuscript *per faure* has undoubtedly been partly written by a second hand (see Introd., p. ix, for other instances). The *r* of *faure* and the flourish after it (expanded *e* in the text) are altogether unlike the scribe's handwriting, and a thin line below the *a* may indicate that this letter has been written over a *y*. I suspect, therefore, that the original reading may have been *fyue,* which was changed to *faure* by a later hand for the sake of consistency with 992. If this were true, we should have the same kind of correction that was made in 924 (see note), where *em* was changed to *broþer* because *broþer* had been used in 772. It is possible, then, that the poet was following Mandeville after all, and gave the number of cities destroyed as five.

**1019. smelle.** MS., M. *synne.* The scribe probably miswrote *synne* because he had just written it in the line before. The poet elsewhere usually alliterates *sm* only with itself, and not with simple *s* (*Pur.* 226, 461, 771, 732, 955; *Gaw.* 407, 1763, 1789). Cf. 461.

**1022-48.** These lines are based on Mandeville's *Voyage d' Outre Mer* (ed. Warner, p. 50): 'Entour celle mer croist mult dalum et dalketran. . . . Leawe de cel mere est mult amere et salee; et si la terre estoit moillie de celle eawe, elle naporteroit point de fruit. Et la terre de luy change souent sa colour. Et iette fors

del eawe vne chose qe homme appelle aspalt, auxi grosses pieces
come vne chival, touz les iours et a toutes cousteez. . . . Et
est dit Mer Mort pur ceo qelle ne court point; ne homme ne beste
qad en luy vie ne purroit morir en cel meer. Et ceo ad estee proue
mointefoitz qe homme gettoit dedeinz gentz qi auoient deseruy
mort, et demorroient iii. iours ou iiii., mes ils ne poaient morir. . . .
Et qi metteroit fer dedeins, il noeroit par dessure; et qi mitteroit
vne plume dedeins, elle irroit au founz. . . . Et si croissent
arbres delez qi portent pommes tres beles et de bele colour a
regarder et toutes maners a semblant, mes qi les brusera ou trenchera
parmy, il ne trouera dedeins qe cendres.'

**1026. to founs.** Mandeville's *au founz;* cf. Osgood's note on
*Pearl* 111.

**1048. wyndowande askes.** Cf. Mandeville's *Travels* (Cotton
MS., ed. Halliwell, p. 107): 'And there let Julianus Apostata dyggen
him up, and let brennen his Bones, . . . and let *wyndwe the
Askes* in the Wynd.'

**1057-66.** The passage here paraphrased consists of ll. 8021 ff.
(ed. Marteau) of the *Roman de la Rose,* this part being written,
as the poet rightly states, by Jean Clopinel, better known as Jean
de Meun. It is part of Reason's advice to the Lover about the
manner in which he should undertake to set free the imprisoned
Bel Acueil, son of Courtesy; and the point of the passage, as
our poet sees, is that favor is to be won by observing the character
of the lady beloved, and doing that which pleases her best. I
quote the more relevant parts of this long discourse:

> De Bel-Acuel vous prenés garde
> Par quel semblant il vous regarde,
> Comment que soit, ne de quel chiere;
> Conformés-vous à sa maniere:
> S'ele est ancienne et méure,
> Vous metrés toute vostre cure
> En vous tenir méurement;
> Et s'il se contient nicement,
> Nicement vous recontenés.
> De li ensivre vous penés:
> S'il est liés, faites chiere lie,
> S'il est correciés, corrocie;
> S'il rit, riés; plorés s'il plore,
> Ainsinc vous tenés chacune hore
> Ce qu'il blasmera, si blasmés,
> Et loés quanqu'il loera;

Moult plus en vous sen fiera.
Cuidiés que dame a cuer vaillant
Aint ung garcon fol et saillant? . . .     (8021-4)

Et s'uns sages d'amors parole
A une damoisele fole,
S'il li fait semblant d'estre sages,
Ja là ne torra ses corages. . . .     (8051-4)

Briément faites en toute place
Quanque vous pensés qui li place.
S'ainsinc le faites, n'en doutés,
Jà n'en serés arrier boutés,
Ains vendrés à vostre propos,
Tout ausinc cum ge le propos.     (8091-6)

**1065 ff.** This application of Jean de Meun's advice is of course
entirely the poet's own; cf. Introd., p. xlii.

**1067.** The word *conforme* is borrowed from *Roman de la Rose*
8024 (see above).

**1068. as þe perle selven.** This comparison of Christ with the
pearl reflects the common interpretation of the pearl of great price
(Matt. 13. 45, 46) as a symbol of Christ. Among the commentators
who gave this explanation were Origen (Migne, *Patr. Græc.* 13.
856); Ephraem Syrus (*Select Works*, p. 84, ed. Morris); Augustine,
who gives other possible interpretations (*Patr. Lat.* 35. 1371);
Maximus of Turin (*Patr. Lat.* 57. 528); Bede (*Patr. Lat.* 92. 69);
Walafrid Strabo (*Patr. Lat.* 114. 133); Radbertus (*Patr. Lat.*
120. 505). For other interpretations, see Osgood's note on *Pearl* 735.

**1075-80.** The poet frequently renders homage to the Virgin (cf.
*Pearl* 423 ff., 453 ff.; *Gaw.* 647 ff.); but nowhere has he written
fairer lines in her praise than this series of contrasts describing
her joy in the birth of Christ. The belief in the Virgin's painless
delivery arose early (cf. Livius, *The Blessed Virgin in the Fathers
of the First Six Centuries,* London, 1893, pp. 204-7); and this is
reflected in the innumerable hymns on the Five Joys of the Virgin,
which regularly include the birth of Christ as one of the five joys.
With l. 1077 may be compared *Birth of Jesus* 599-60 (in Horstmann's
*Altengl. Legenden,* 1875):

Heo bar a betere burþone þan wymmen now do,
Heo hedde elles igroned sore and nouȝt ascaped so.

So in the Nativity Plays, the miraculous delivery of Mary excites
the wonder of the midwives (Chester 528-66; Coventry 203 ff., ed.
Hemingway).

**1078. seknesse al sounde.** Cf. *Roman de la Rose* 4441-2:

> C'est langor toute santéive
> C'est santé toute maladive.

**1084. were.** This use of the subjunctive to express an unconditional occurrence is noteworthy; we should expect *watz;* cf. also 209 and *Gaw.* 143, though in the latter instance *were* may possibly be an ind. plural due to attraction. Kellner (*Engl. Stud.* 18. 290) calls attention to a subjunctive in rhyme in *Ipomadon* (1596), where we should expect the indicative:

> A messyngere, it semyd, he were,
> For be his syde a box he bare,

and explains this instance and a similar use of *were* in *Guy of Warwick* (2798) as due to the necessities of rhyme. It is noteworthy that the two instances in *Purity* occur at the end of the line, where the weak metrical ending is usual.

**1086.** The adoration of the ox and the ass, like the singing of the angels (1080 ff.), had become traditional. Both are found in the *Pseudo-Matthew,* Chap. 14 (Cowper, *Apocryphal Gospels,* p. 53).

**1103-8.** Christ's clean cutting of the bread is mentioned in the Towneley Play (No. 28) *Thomas of India* 264-5:

> Ihesu, goddis son of heuen at sopere satt betweyn;
> Ther bred he brake as euen as it cutt had beyn.

These lines are spoken by Peter in order to convince the doubting Thomas of Christ's resurrection, and the reference is to the supper at Emmaus, where, according to Luke 24. 35, the disciples recognized Christ *in fractione panis.* The passage in *Purity* and that in the Towneley Play probably go back to a common source based on Luke's words.

**1109. kyryous and clene.** The lines on Christ's cutting the bread have, of course, little to do with Christ's purity, and the passage is introduced only by means of a kind of play on words. *Clene* means at once 'pure,' and, with reference to cutting, 'smooth, sharp, without ragged edges.' So *kyryous* in this line = 'skilful' as far as the cutting of the bread is concerned, but = 'particular' in connection with Christ's abhorrence of everything vile.

**1118. hym.** This use of the dative (accus.) for the nominative is extraordinary. Einenkel quotes examples of various cases where the dative pronoun was substituted for the nominative (*Grundr.,* 2d ed., 1. 1085, § 141 *a;* 1093, § 144 *δ*), but none is quite like this instance. It may be that we have a case of attraction, the pronoun,

which should be the subject of *be demed,* being somehow thought
of as the object of *to dele.*

**1123.** 'For "*& wax euer,*" etc., the sense seems to require that
we should read "*& wax ho euer,*" etc.'—M. Perhaps the idea of
the condition is carried over from the previous clause, and the
repetition of the pronoun is therefore unnecessary.

**1124. in pyese.** Gollancz (*Mod. Lang. Rev.* 14. 158) explains
as a variant of ME. *o pece,* often found in *Generydes* as a mere
emphasis of 'still, yet.' But it is unlikely that '*in pyese* probably =
OF. *en paix* (*NED.* places *o pece* under *peace* and *piece*),' as he
suggests, since the spelling *pyece* would point to *piece* (see ME.
variants of the two words in *NED.*), and, on the other hand, the
ordinary meaning of *o pece* (*NED.,* s. v. *piece,* 14b), 'continuously,
constantly,' seems too colorless for the context. Bateson suggested
*in pyere* '[in use] among precious stones,' but this meaning can
hardly be obtained from the emendation. Some contrast is evidently intended with the *uncheryst* of the following line, and it
may be that the word was originally *pryse.* The phrase *in price*
meaning 'esteemed, valued' is not uncommon (see *NED.,* s. v.
*price,* sb. 8). The lines would then mean: 'The pearl does not dull
while it is held in esteem, but if it happens to become neglected,' etc.

**1127.** Schofield (*Publ. Mod. Lang. Ass.* 24. 600, n. 1) refers
to Pliny's *Natural History* 9. 56, where it is said of the pearl:
'Usu atteri non dubium est coloremque indiligentia mutare.'

**1131.** For the figure of polishing the heart and making it 'shyne
þurʒ schryfte' (1115), compare Richard Rolle of Hampole's *Twelve
Profits of Tribulation* (ed. Horstmann 2. 50): 'Forþy ne pleyne
þe not þof god furblisshe þi hert þat hit shyne & be made clene;
for in no oþer maner þou may not se god; as saies seynt *Matheu:*
"Blessid be þo clene of hert: for þai shal se god." '

**1157. Danyel in his dialokez.** The account of the siege and
destruction of Jerusalem is taken, not from the brief summary in
the first chapter of Daniel, but from the longer narrative in Jere-
miah 52. 1-26 (practically the same in 2 Kings 24. 18—25. 17).
See Appendix for the passages of the Vulgate here paraphrased by
the poet. Details obtained from other parts of the Bible will be
mentioned below as they occur.

**1172-4.** This reference to Zedekiah's idolatry is based on 2 Chron.
36. 12-4.

**1189. teveled.** M. printed *teneled,* but Miss E. M. Wright (*Engl.
Stud.* 36. 223-4) connected it with *teuelyng, Gaw.* 1514 (M. *tenelyng;*
but Gollancz, rev. ed. of 1912, *teuelyng*), and related the word to
dialectal *tevel,* 'to confuse,' and perhaps to *tave,* 'to strive, toil,

labour.' In the sense of 'strive, struggle,' the only instances in ME. are the two in *Purity* and *Gawain* (see further *NED.*, s. v. *tevel, tavel*).

**1193. upon longe.** 'At length, finally.' *NED.* does not record *up(on) long* in a temporal sense, but it occurs at *Erken.* 175, *upone longe.* Cf. *upon laste, Pat.* 194; *(up)on first, Gaw.* 9, 491, 528, 2019; *opon late, Alex. C.* 2331.

**1193-4.** The famine in the Greek camp is similarly described in *Destr. Troy* 9376-7:

> Þat hom failed the fode, and defaute hade:
> Hongur full hote harmyt hom þen.

**1205. ne.** Cf. note on 225.

**1209.** Cf. *Alex. C.* 2981: 'With hard hattis on þaire hedis hied to þaire horsis,' and *Winner and Waster* 51: 'Harde hattes appon hedes and helmys with crestys.'

**1226. Nabugo.** This curious abbreviation of Nebuchadnezzar's name, which occurs again at 1233, is due to the French manner of dividing the name—*Nabugo de Nozar* (so always in MS.). Gower twice uses the form *Nabugod* (*Mirour de L'Omme* 1887, 10338).

**1229-32.** M. placed a period after 1230, but this punctuation is obviously wrong, since it leaves without an apodosis the condition whose protasis consists of 1229-30. The poet has just declared (1226-8) that Zedekiah was brought low, not because of Nebuchadnezzar (who was only God's instrument), but because of his wickedness in the sight of the Lord. He proceeds to explain that if the Lord had not become angry with Zedekiah, Nebuchadnezzar would have been sent elsewhere; cf. Jer. 38. 17-8. The passage may be paraphrased: 'For if the Father, who had previously guided him, had (still) been his friend, and if (Zedekiah) had never sinned against him (the Lord) by his apostasy, all (Nebuchadnezzar's hosts) would have been called away to Chaldea and the countries of India—and they would have had little trouble in taking Turkey by the way.' The reasons for the obscurity of the lines are (1) the subject of *trespast* (1230) is omitted, even though it is different from the subject of the preceding clause; (2) the scribe apparently misunderstood the lines, and wrote, with incorrect capitalization: 'To Colde wer alle Calde'; (3) the last line (1232) has little connection with the general idea, and was apparently added as an afterthought.

**1267.** Cf. *Death and Life* 205: 'Merry maydens on the mold shee mightilye killethe.'

**1291. nummen.** MS. *nunnend;* cf. the similar mistake, *Pat.* 3, *aswagend* for *aswagen.*

**1294.** Cf. *Pat.* 178: 'Her3ed out of vche hyrne to hent þat falles.'

**1317-20.** The poet is careful to explain that Nebuchadnezzar remained unpunished for his seizure of the holy vessels because he reverently stored them in his treasury, whereas Belshazzar 'let of hem ly3t,' and thereby aroused God's wrath; cf. also 1151-6. This was also the explanation given by Jerome in his *Commentarium in Danielem:* 'Quamdiu vasa fuerunt in idolio Babylonis non est iratus Dominus: videbantur enim rem Dei secundum pravam quidem opinionem, tamen divino cultui consecrasse: postquam autem humanis usibus divina contaminant, statim pœna sequitur post sacrilegium' (Migne, *Patr. Lat.* 25. 519).

**1324.** god of þe grounde. Cf. 1663.

**1327.** bi þe laste. 'At last, finally.' *NED.* records the phrase (s. v. *last*) only in the meaning 'by the latest,' but it is frequently a mere variant of the commoner *at þe laste* (four times in *Purity,* see Glossary), as in *Destr. Troy* 3188-90:

> At þe last, when the lede hade left of his speche,
> ffele of þe folke febull it thughten;
> But yche lede *by the last* aliet þerto.

It may be noted that in the instance just quoted, as in this line in *Purity,* there is another word in the line beginning with *b*.

**1329-56.** This transition is the poet's own, the mention of Belshazzar's worshiping false gods (1340 ff.) anticipating 1522 ff.

**1357 ff.** Belshazzar's feast is frequently cited in illustration of the sin of sacrifice, for example, in Robert of Brunne's *Handlyng Synne* 9347-434, and Gower's *Confessio Amantis* 5. 7012-31, where Nebuzaradan, Nebuchadnezzar, and Belshazzar are all three deemed guilty of sacrilege, and in the *Mirour de L'Omme* 7177-88, where Gower mentions only Nebuzaradan and Belshazzar.

**1376.** Cf. *Gaw.* 58: 'Hit were now gret nye to neuen.'

**1383.** troched toures. As Skeat explained in 1892 (see *Notes on Engl. Etym.,* p. 306), *troched* was originally applied to a stag's horn, meaning 'tufted at the tip with small tines' (cf. OF. *troche* in this sense). This term of the chase was then used figuratively as a term of architecture, a *troched tour* being one 'adorned with small pointed pinnacles.' The only other instance of this poetical application of the word occurs at *Gaw.* 795: 'Towre[s] telded bytwene, trochet ful þik.'

**1385.** 'The palace that covered the ground enclosed within.' The word *pursaunt* is again used in *Pearl* 1035: 'So twelue in poursent I con asspye.' *NED.,* following Morris, is surely right in including this instance from the *Pearl* s. v. *purcinct,* although Bradley-

Stratmann, Gollancz, and Osgood printed *pourseut,* 'succession,' a meaning of *pursuit* that *NED.* does not find before Lord Bacon.

**1391. þe halle to hit m[a]d.** Emerson (*Publ. Mod. Lang. Ass.* 34. 513) interprets *to hit med* as 'in their middle or midst.'

**1401 ff.** Cf. the similar description of the beginning of the banquet in *Gawain* (114-24):

> Þise were diȝt on þe des, and derworþly serued,
> & siþen mony siker segge at þe sidbordeȝ.
> Þen þe first cors come with crakkyng of trumpes,
> Wyth mony baner ful bryȝt, þat þer-bi henged,
> Nwe nakeryn noyse with þe noble pipes,
> Wylde werbles & wyȝt wakned lote,
> Þat mony hert ful hiȝe hef at her towches;
> Dayntes dryuen þer-wyth, of ful dere metes,
> Foysoun of þe fresche, and on so fele disches,
> Þat pine to fynde þe place þe peple bi-forne
> For to sette þe sylueren, þat sere sewes halden.

**1402.** Cf. *Alex. C.* (Dublin MS.) 1386: 'Sterne stevyn vpon stroke straked trompettes.' The blare of trumpets generally announced the beginning of elaborate banquets (cf. Schultz, *Das Höfische Leben* I. 423).

**1407-12.** In these lines, as M. notes, 'we have evidently an allusion to the "table subtleties" of the fourteenth century.'

**1408. pared out of paper.** Cf. *Gaw.* 802: 'Pared out of papure.'

**1410. foler.** Gollancz, in a paper read before the Philological Society, suggested that this word, not defined by Morris, and not found in the dictionaries, meant 'foliation' (see the summary of Gollancz's paper, *Athen.* 1894. 2. 646). It would be possible to derive such a word from an AN. *\*foler,* OF. *\*folier,* representing a Lat. *\*folarium.* Godefroy gives an OF. noun *fuellier,* but this would either be a formation on *fuel* or at least influenced by the stem-stressed form. The line means 'birds fluttering among the foliage.' Cf. further Gollancz's note, *Mod. Lang. Rev.* 14. 199.

**1411.** Cf. 1457, and *Morte Arth.* 3355: 'Enamelde with azoure.'

**1414. tulket.** *NED.* cites this line both under *tulk* (the only instance), where it is derived from ON. *tūlka,* and also under *tuck,* v.,[2] where it emends to *tukket,* as it does also the *tulkid* of *Alex. C.* 2427, following Skeat's suggestion in his edition of *Alex.,* in spite of the fact that the word occurs with *l* in both MSS. of the poem. Skeat declared in his Glossary, s. v. *tulkid,* that 'we often find *kk* written more like *lk,* the double letter being denoted only by doubling the down stroke,' and compared *tuke up, Alex.* 773 and

3610, used of the blowing of trumpets. But in *Purity,* at least, *kk*
is always written out distinctly, and the occurrence of the form *tulk*
both here and in *Alex.* can hardly be attributed to a mere scribal
trick or error, even though the connection with ON. *tūlka* may be
doubtful.

**1416. bougounz busch.** Brett, in *Mod. Lang. Rev.* 10. 188-9,
defines *bougounz* as 'drumsticks,' since OF. *bougon* has various
meanings, 'many denoting some instrument with a rounded, swollen
extremity, or one with such a rounded swelling in some part of
its length.' He translates the line: 'And drumsticks' noise (striking, strokes) clattered (rattled) so thick (fast).'

**1426.** Cf. 1619, and *Destr. Troy* 3192: 'When counsell was kaght
of knightes & oþer.'

**1445.** Cf. 1718.

**1452.** Cf. *Morte Arth.* 211: 'Crafty & curious, coruen full
faire.'

**1456.** Cf. *Sege of Jer.* 1261: 'Bassynes of brend gold & oþer bry3t
ger.'

**1459. enbaned . . . bantelles.** In the *Transactions of the
Philological Society* for 1903 (6. 365), Skeat discusses these difficult words at length, and since he not only gives the probable
etymologies but explains this line in particular, I quote a considerable part of his note, which is under the heading *Bantel:* 'This
word occurs in the poem called Cleanness, 1459, where a castle is
described as, "Enbaned vnder batelment with *bantelles* quoynt":
in the *Pearl,* 992, where the new Jerusalem has *"banteles* twelve on
basyng boun"; and in the Pearl, 1017, "The wal abof the bantels
bent." The word belongs rather to Northern than to Provençal
French. Godefroy has merely *bane,* with the sense of 'horn.' But
Mistral has mod. Prov. *bano,* a horn, with a number of phrases
in which it is used; also *baneto,* a little horn; the F. *bantel* represents a mod. Prov. form *bantello or O.F. *banetel,* a double
diminutive. The difficulty in the present case is to find out in
what secondary sense the word 'horn' has to be taken. For this
purpose we have to consider the curious word *enbaned,* which
also occurs in these poems, and is likewise a derivative of the
O.F. *bane,* a horn. It occurs twice; once in the line already quoted:
"Enbaned vnder batelment with bantelles quoynt," the subject
being "castles arayed"; and in Gawain, 790, where a castle-wall
is described as being "Enbaned vnder the abataylment in the best
lawe," i. e. in the best way. Thus in both cases the word *enbaned*
is a term used in fortification. But the mod. Prov. *enbaner* is
similarly used, and is explained by "garnir ou munir de cornes,"

and *enbanamen,* sb., is distinctly said to be "terme de fortification, ouvrage a cornes." This "ouvrage a cornes" is described in Littré as a term in fortification, exactly like what in English is termed a 'horn-work'; see N.E.D. Moreover, the mod. F. *corne* is used, architecturally, with the sense of a 'salient angle.' We may conclude that an *embanamen* was made with a kind of horn-work, an outwork with angles, including a space like three sides of a square beyond the main-wall; and such a horn-work may well have been called a *bantel.* The phrase *under batelment* suggests that these outworks were battlemented like the main wall itself; and the phrase *on basyng boun* means that they were prepared on a good foundation. They would require a firm basis because of their superior height. I would, therefore, explain "Enbaned vnder batelment with bantelles quoynt" by "provided, beneath battle-ments, with fair outworks." . . . The pictures in Knight's Old England of such castles as Rochester (fig. 375) or Cardiff (fig. 390) probably show what is meant. Thus Rochester keep-tower has a three-angled projection or 'horn' at each of its four corners, and the battlements on these projections are higher and more conspicuous than the rest. The most conspicuous part of the Tower of London has similar *bantels* at each corner.'

**1461.** c[ov]acles. MS., M. canacles. Cf. 1515 'clatering of covacles (M. conacles).' Bödtker pointed out (*Mod. Lang. Notes* 26. 127) that the word should be *covacle,* as in *Partonope of Blois* 1768: 'þe covacle of Rube redde.' The scribe undoubtedly thought the word was *conacle (canacle),* mistaking *ou* for *on,* and he would naturally write *con-* or *can-* indifferently, since he made no distinction between *on* and *an* (see Knigge, p. 16). Although there are French variants of OF. *couvercle* without the *r,* such as *couve(s)cle* (see Godefroy's *Complément*), Bödtker thinks the 'English form rather represents an independent change from *covarcle* to *covacle,* due to analogy of the frequent nouns in -*acle.'* The usual form *couvercle* is used by Chaucer, *Hous of Fame* 2. 284.

**1464 ff.** The poet is here adorning his description of Belshazzar's feast with details which he had read in Mandeville's account of the wonders of the Great Chan's palace and the land of Prester John. The 'richly enameled birds' (1410-1), and those which seem to be waving their feathers on the ornamental boughs of the candlestick (1484-6), as well as the 'fruit of flaming gems' (1468 ff.) are all found in Mandeville: 'Et deuant la table del emperour as grantz festes lem porte grant tables dor, ou il y a paouns dor et molt dautres maners oiseaulx toutz dor et enameles et molt noble-ment ouerez. Et les fait homme dauncer et bauler en batant lez

paumes ["pennes" interlined in MS. R; both Cotton and Egerton
MSS. translate *wings*] et en fait homme des grantz museries. . . .
Par dessure vne partie de la sale y ad vne vigne faite de fyn or,
qui est entendue tout par dessur; et y a plusours treches de reisins
des blanches, iaunes, rouges, viertz et noirs, toutz de pierres
preciouses. Ly blanc sount de cristall et de bericle et de yris; les
iaunes sount de toupaces; les rouges des rubiis, des grenaz et des
alabaundines; les vertz sont des emeraudes, des peridoz et des
crisolites; et li noyrs sount des oniches et des geracites. Et sount
toutz si proprement faitz qils roient touz proprement reysins' (ed.
Warner, p. 107, ll. 31-42). To these passages from the account
of the splendor of the Great Chan's court, may be added a similar
description of artificial birds in the land of Prester John: 'Et
auoit fait faire molt de diverse chose et de diuerses museries des
histoires et de diuerses bestes et des oiseaux, qi chanteroient et
tourneient par engine come ils fussent toutz vifs' (p. 137, l. 35).
The names of the two rarely mentioned jewels *penitotes* (1472)
and *alabaundarynes* (1470) the poet almost certainly borrowed
from the passage from Mandeville quoted above. All the poets
of the alliterative school delight in ornamenting their descriptions
with lists of precious stones (cf. *Piers Plow.* B. 2. 8-14; *Rich.
Redeless* 1. 35-48; *Alex. C.* 3329 ff., 3660 ff., 5259-80; *Sege of Jer.*
1245-64; *Parl. Three Ages* 117-29; *Howlat* 339-45; *Awnt. Arth.*
391-6). But it should be noted that *alabandine* occurs in none of these
lists, and the *peridot* only in *Awnt. Arth.* 396 in the forms *pelicocus,
pelidoddes* (see Amour's note), and *Sege of Jer.* 1247: 'with perles
& peritotes.' The list of jewels which corresponds most exactly
with this given in *Purity* is that of *Pearl* 1002 ff. The description
most similar in other details is that of the hall of an Indian palace
in *Alex. C.* (1660 ff.), where there are golden vines with grapes
fashioned from various precious gems, and marvelously painted
birds which are made to sing. But these descriptions are commonplace in mediæval romance; cf. *Eneas,* ed. Salverda de Grave, pp.
389-90; *Huon de Bordeaux* 4921 ff.

**1472. pynkardines.** This is the only occurrence of the word,
which must be corrupted, though it is difficult to say from what.
M. in his glossary has '?*perre carnadine,* carnelian stone (Marsh).'
The word *pintadine* is given by Littré, and defined 'genre de mol-
lusques (*meleagrina*) dont une des espèces fournit les perles
orientales et la nacre de perle,' and it is also found in Mistral's
dictionary of Provençal. It has come into English, according to
the *Century Dict., Supplement,* from Span.-Amer. *pintadina.* If
the word could be shown to be old, *pynkardine* might easily be
considered a corruption from it.

**1473. a-traverse.** *NED.*'s earliest example of this word bears the date 1430.

**tryfled.** Amours is probably right in considering *tryfled* of this line a variant form of *trefoiled* (see his long note on *Awnt. Arth.* 354). This occurrence would be older than any example (noun or adj.) cited by *NED*.

**1474. bekyr ande bolle.** MS. *bekyrande þe bolde.* M. interpreted *bekyrande* as 'bickering, fighting'; but a warrior can hardly be thrust so suddenly into a description of the ornamentation of cups and goblets, even if we were to overlook the extreme awkwardness of the construction 'each warrior (fighting-man), the bold.' As emended, lines 1473-4 mean: 'thus all the edges of each beaker and bowl were decorated crosswise.' Another case of the conjunction *ande* being mistaken for a participial ending probably occurs in *glaymande glette, Pat.* 269, and perhaps also *ramelande myre, Pat.* 279, where both *NED.* (s. v. *gleiming* and *ramelande*) and Emerson (*Engl. Stud.* 47. 129-30) would read *glaym ande glette, ramel ande myre. NED.* gives the following ME. forms for *beaker: biker, becure, byker, biker,* so that the form *bekyr* is unexceptionable. Miss Weston's translation (*Romance, Vision and Satire,* p. 157) indicates that she recognized some corruption in the text:

> So, twined and twisted, doth the fair design
> Bold, on the border of each beaker shine.

This emendation has also occurred to Professor Emerson (*Publ. Mod. Lang. Ass.* 34. 515).

**1476.** Ekwall (*Engl. Stud.* 49. 484) explains *fleez* as plural of *fly* (OE. *flēoʒe*), but his objection to 'golden fleece' as ornamentation seems to me groundless; cf. Emerson, *Publ. Mod. Lang. Ass.* 34. 516.

**1485. [launces].** I adopt Bülbring's ingenious suggestion of inserting this word before *lampes,* since it does away with the difficulty of having to make 1485 refer back to the *bryddes* (1482), and at the same time makes *lampes* and *oþer lovelych lyʒt* the parallel subjects of the new sentence. The poet is plainly introducing a new detail in 1485-92, a fact which is obscured and confused by the scribe's omission of *launces,* an easy mistake to make when the next word also began with *la.* The word occurs again at *Pearl* 978.

**1491.** This emendation also occurred to Emerson (*Publ. Mod. Lang. Ass.* 34. 516).

**1513-6.** M.'s marginal gloss, 'Music of all kinds is heard in the hall,' is altogether misleading, since the poet is not speaking of musical instruments, which have been mentioned in their proper place at 1413-6, but merely of the merry clattering of cups and covers which sounded *like* music. The general meaning is well brought out in Miss Weston's translation (though the meaning of *rok* (see 1514 n.) is misunderstood) :

> The bowls so bright, with wine they swiftly fill,
> Rich metal, touching metal, rang full loud
> As men to catch the cups together crowd,
> Clashing, the maids the covers cast away,
> As song from psaltery ring the sounds so gay.

*Hit* must refer to the wine (1508); the 'renkkes (1514) are the 'swyfte swaynes' (1509) who quickly seize the cups and run to catch the wine which is being poured.

**1514. rok.** M. defined 'crowd, throng,' and connected with Scot. *rok* (see *NED.*, s. v. *ruck*). Bateson and Gollancz both accept this meaning, but though the latter finds a possible parallel for the figurative use of *rok* in *Destr. Troy* 7149, his explanation of *þat ryche rok* as 'the rich crowd of liveried servants' seems far-fetched. It is more probable that the word is ME. *rok(ke) (roche)*, OF. *roque (roche)*, here used in the figurative sense of 'castle.' *NED.* does not record this sense in English, but it is frequent in OF. Godefroy, s. v. *roche* (under which he includes the forms *roque, roke*) defines 'château fort bâti sur une roche,' and La Curne de Ste.-Palaye gives a definition 'château, forteresse,' s. v. *roche* 2, citing an example from the *Roman d'Alexandre* (c. 1177). Another sufficiently early OF. example (quoted by Du Cange, s. v. *rocca*) is to be found in Philippe Mousket's *Chronique Rimée* (ed. Reiffenberg, 1836-8, in *Collect. des Chroniques Belges*) 17037-9:

> S'en ot Buiémont de Sésile.
> Et cil fu au prendre Andioce,
> U il a mainte forte roce.

The meaning 'fortress, castle,' is extremely common in mediæval Lat. (see Du Cange's *Glossarium*, s. v. *rocca, roccha*), and is used in Italian by both Dante and Boccaccio. Tommaso's *Dizion.* cites Francesco de Buti, who, in commenting on Dante's 'sicura quasi rocca in alto monte' (*Purg.* 32. 148), says 'Rocca si chiama la fortezza ben fornita.' The alliterative phrase *rich rock(s)*, *rock* being employed in its literal sense, occurs at *Pearl* 68: 'Where rych rokkeȝ wer to dyscreuen,' and *Gol. and Gaw.* 238: 'Reirdit on ane riche roche, beside ane riveir.' In *Purity* the form with *k* and that with *ch* are used indifferently: *rok*, 446; *roches*, 537; cf. *roche*, *Gaw.* 2199; *rokkeȝ*, *Pearl* 68, *Pat.* 254.

**1518. [drynkez] arn dressed [to].** The line is obviously too short, and three ways of correcting it have been suggested (see textual notes). Bateson's insertion of *dere* is simple, but *arn dressed* would then have to mean 'arose,' and this gives little point to the line. Gollancz's general interpretation of the passage (*Mod. Lang. Rev.* 14. 161) is plausible, but his emendation, 'þat derrest [arn dressed], dukez and prynces,' is awkward. Bülbring's proposal '[drinkes] arn dressed [for] dukez and prynces,' i. e. 'prepared for,' is unlikely, because such a statement would not follow the account of the servants hurrying for the drinks in ll. 1508 ff. I suggest '[drynkez] arn dressed [to] dukez,' etc., i. e. 'portioned out to, divided among'; cf. defin. 2 c in *NED.* 'to arrange amongst; to divide,' and examples.

**1520. hade hym inhelde.** 'Had poured in for himself,' as was first correctly explained by Emerson, *Mod. Lang. Notes* 30. 9. *NED.*'s only example of the cpd. *inhelde* is from Chaucer's invocation to Venus, *Troilus* 3. 44:

> Ye in my naked herte sentement
> Inhelde, and do me shewe of thi swetnesse.

The simple verb (*NED. hield*) is common in the sense of 'pour out.' *NED.* followed M., who glossed *in helde,* 'in mind, in purpose, disposed,' inserts under the noun *hield,* defining 'inclination,' but this is the only example given of this particular figurative meaning.

**1543. romyes.** 'Roars'; a common word in ME. *NED.* says: 'Of obscure origin. The synonymous Scottish form *rummis(h)* may indicate an OF. form *\*rumir, \*romir,* with lengthened stem *\*rumiss-.*' But we do not have to reconstruct a word from which to derive *romy.* A form *rumier,* from Lat. *rumigare,* is given both in Körting's *Latein.-Roman. Wörterbuch* and in Meyer-Lübke's *Roman. Etymolog. Wörterbuch,* as a variant of *rungier,* which is the regular development in OF. Meyer-Lübke says that the form *rumier* is Old Lotharingian. The word appears in Provençal and Portuguese in the form *romiar.* Now though Godefroy does not give the form *rumier,* he gives as one of his definitions of *rongier* (*rungier*) 'rugir,' with two examples. OF. *rumier,* variant (dialectal?) of *rungier,* would naturally be borrowed into English in the form *rumy, romy* (both occur in *NED.*), just as OF. *chastier* > ME. *chasty.* We need not concern ourselves with how the meaning 'roar' developed in OF. But it may be pointed out that the Latin *ruminare,* which has exactly the same meaning as *rumigare,* has come to mean 'snore' in one of the examples given by Du Cange: '*fortiter dormientem et ruminantem,* hoc est, stertentem, ronchissantem.'

**1584. he3ed.** Gollancz (*Mod. Lang. Rev.* 14. 161) says '*he3ed* = shouted, called aloud,' not 'hied' (i. e. hastened); but where does he find this verb, ME. *he3e*, 'shout'? Bateson's objection to the forms *he3ed*, for *hi3ed*, is unwarranted; cf. Knigge, p. 44.

**1594. in len þe of dayes.** The expression occurs again at *Pearl* 416, translating, as Osgood notes, the Biblical 'in longitudinem dierum,' Ps. 22. 6; 92. 5 (Vulg.).

**1598.** Cf. 1608 and 1627. The Vulg. has *spiritum deorum sanctorum* (Dan. 5. 11) and *spiritum deorum* (Dan. 5. 14).

**1602. mony anger.** Cf. 43 n.

**1616. wayne.** The verb *wayne*, which Skeat (*Trans. Phil. Soc.* 1885. 7. 365) considered a 'ghost-word,' a mere miswriting or misreading of *wayue*, certainly existed in ME., as it occurs in *Pearl* (131, 249) in rhyme. It is used in a variety of senses, the exact meaning being difficult to determine in particular instances, and has been derived from ON. *vegna*, 'proceed,' OF. (Northern) *waignier* (*gaaignier*, the Central F. form borrowed later as *gain*), 'gain, acquire,' and finally from OE. *\*wægnan*, found only in the cpd. *bewægnan*, *Beowulf* 1193, where it means 'offer.' From the apparent meaning of the word in this line (*Pur.* 1616) and 1701, it would seem that in some cases, at least, the word may be borrowed from OF. *waignier* (see Godefroy, s. v. *gaaignier*), an etymology which M. proposed in his glossary, but which Mätzner (*Sprachproben*) rejected with reference to *Gaw.* 264, in favor of *\*wægnan*. The latter derivation seems to fit some of the instances in *Gaw.* better; but it is possible that two original independent words have coalesced in ME. *wayne*. As *wayne* in the poems of this group, at least, is always transitive (*Gaw.* 264, 984, 1032, 2456, 2459; *Pearl* 131, 249; *Pat.* 467), there is no good reason for appealing to ON. *vegna*. The easy confusion with *wayue* increases the difficulty of determining the exact meaning of the word.

**1634. tede lettres.** M. suggested that *tede* was an error for *tene* (= *ten*), but Gollancz explained *tede* as 'tied' (see report of paper read before the Philological Society in *Athen.* 1894. 2. 646). This is probably the correct explanation, as the lines paraphrase the Vulgate '*ligita* dissolvere' (Dan. 5. 16), just as 'unhyles uch hidde' of 1628 paraphrases 'obscura interpretari' of the same verse. Cf. also the expression in *Gaw.* 35: 'With lel letteres loken.'

**1638.** Cf. *Piers Plow.* C. 1. 178: 'Bere by3es of bry3t gold al aboute hure neckes'; cf. further, Introd., p. xxx.

**1642.** Cf. Introd., p. 61, for the omission of Dan. 5. 17.

**1647-8.** The Vulg. (Dan. 5. 19) makes no contrast here: 'Quos volebat, interficiebat; et quos volebat, percutiebat.' The Authorized and Revised Versions translate: 'Whom he would he slew; and whom he would he *kept alive*,' where the Wycliffite versions had 'smote.' The two renderings depend on the double meaning of the original Hebrew. The poet probably introduced the contrast of his own accord, since the parallel clauses of the Vulgate immediately following make it plain that a contrast is intended: 'Et quos volebat, exaltabat; et quos volebat, humiliabat' (translated, 1649-50).

**1661. blasfemy on to blame.** M.'s first reading *blasfemy on* is preferable to his second *blasfemyon*. For the position of *on* before the infin., compare 'on to pyche,' 477; 'on to sene,' *Pearl* 45.

**1664-70.** This reflects Dan. 4. 27-8.

**1675.** Cf. *Pat.* 392: 'Ne best bite on no brom, ne no bent nauþer.'

**1687.** A puzzling line. M. glosses 'His thighs grew thick,' and Miss Weston translates:

His thighs beneath his trunk waxed thick enow.

This makes a modicum of sense, but I do not see how this meaning can be got out of the line as it stands. Accepting *thyȝe* as 'thighs,' the line runs literally: 'By that time many thick thighs crowded about his flesh.' But how can Nebuchadnezzar have *many* thick thighs? And if he did, how could they possibly 'þryȝt umbe his lyre'? I believe that *thyȝe* is not a noun at all, but the verb, the pret. 3 pl. of ME. *the,* OE. *þēon,* 'to grow, increase' (see *NED.,* s. v. *thee,* v.¹) reflecting here the *crescerent* of Dan. 4. 30 which is being paraphrased in this passage (see Appendix for the Vulg. version); *þryȝt* would then be a past participle used as an adjective or adverb (cf. the use of *þryȝt* in 135). The bold use of *mony þik* without a noun, meaning 'many thick hairs or tufts of hair' (glossing Vulg. *capilli*), would at first sight seem a valid objection to this interpretation. But one may compare the equally bold absolute use of *mony* in 1692, where *þer mony clyvy* must mean 'where many (hairs) cling together.' The substantive use of adjectives is remarkable in *Gawain* (see Schmittbetz's *Das Adjectiv in Syr Gaw., Engl. Stud.* 32. 359-69). Among the examples cited by Schmittbetz may be noted particularly: *ȝeþ mony,* 284; *mony ioyleȝ,* 542; also *þe sylueren,* 124, for 'the silver dishes'; *þe scharp,* 424, 1593, 1902, 2313, 2332, for 'the sharp weapon'; *þe fresche,* 122, for 'the fresh meat.' This construction accepted, the line would mean: 'By that time many thick (tufts of hair) were growing about his flesh.'

**1689.** M. compares *Morte Arth.* 1078: 'His fax and his foretoppe was filterede togeders.'

**1690. sch[e]re-wykes.** M., accepting the MS. *schyre,* defined 'bare,' a meaning which the word never has in the alliterative poems or elsewhere in ME. We should expect Nebuchadnezzar's hair to fall from his shoulders to the middle of his body. Now ME. *schare, schere* (OE. *scearu*) is the regular word for the groin, or private parts; ME. *wyke,* 'corner, angle' (ON. *vík,* OE. *wīc*), is generally used with some qualifying word, referring to a part of the body; Bradley-Stratmann cites *wike of þe eghe, Catholicon Anglicum,* p. 417, and *wykez, Gaw.* 1572, where the word refers to the corners of the mouth (cf. ON. *munnvik,* and *wick* of modern English dialects). I assume, therefore, that the original word here was a compound *schere-wykes,* meaning 'pubic corners' or 'groin.'

**1694. His browes bresed.** *Bresed,* 'bristled,' is here the pret. of the verb, as is plain from the context. *NED.* assumed that it was a part. adj., as in *Gaw.* 305, where the Green Knight 'bende his bresed broȝeȝ.' *NED.*, which cites only these two examples, makes the word unnecessarily mysterious; it suggests no derivation nor etymologically connected word, and defines 'Perhaps: Bristly, shaggy, rough.' That *brese* is really a verb meaning 'bristle' can hardly be doubted, since the corresponding noun *bresse,* 'bristle,' occurs in the alliterative *Thomas à Becket,* where it is said that the Boar will 'nocht ster bresse for all þare sterne werdis' (128); the form *brisse* occurs in the same poem in l. 105, and Jamieson cites *bress* from Dunbar (Mätzner, s. v. *bresed,* compares Scot. *bress*). *NED.* gives one form with metathesis: *brust,* s. v. *birse,* sb.,[1] OE. *byrst;* but it should also have given these forms *bresse, brisse* from *Thomas à Becket* (c. 1360). None of the *birs(e)* forms (i e. forms without final *-t*) cited by *NED.* are earlier than the 16th century.

**1695. campe hores.** Chaucer uses the same expression in describing Lycurgus in the *Knight's Tale* 1276:

> And lyk a griffon loked he aboute,
> With kempe heres on hise browes stoute.

**1697. paune.** Gollancz would read *pauue* (see textual notes), but the plural seems to be required by the context, and the spelling *uu* for *w* would be anomalous. The form *paune* is not impossible; cf. the analogical *-en* in *trumpen,* 1402.

**1703. l[o]ved.** Knigge, p. 26, says: 'Ein interessanter Schreibfehler ist B 1703: *laued* für *loued* (*lofjan*). Der Schreiber sah *ou = ov* für den Diphth. *ou* an, und dafür schrieb er *au*. M. setzt unnötigerweise ein ? hinter sein mit Recht vermutetes *loued*.'

**1772. Porros of Ynde.** Porus of India does not, of course, appear in the Bible, but his association with Darius was familiar

through the Alexander legend; compare, for example, *Alex. C.*
3182-3:

> How þat ser Dary with his dukis eft drissis him to fiȝt,
> Had prayd eftir powere to Porrus of ynde.

**1776. sca[l]ed.** MS. *scaped.* This emendation, which is surely
necessary, gives an earlier instance of *scale* than *NED.*, whose first
example is from *Morte Arth.* 3034: 'Skyftis his skotiferis and
skaylis the wallis.'

**1777.** Neilson compares *Destr. Troy* 4751: 'Layn ladders alengt
& oloft wonnen.'

**1805. upon þrynne wyses.** Cf. Introd., p. xlv.

## PREFATORY NOTE TO THE GLOSSARY

The glossary aims to record, with the exception of the articles, not only every word, but in all but the commonest words, every instance of each form of a word. No omission has been made unless the numbers are followed by 'etc.' When the designations of mood and tense are omitted, supply pres. ind.; when the mood only, supply ind. When the preterite forms of weak verbs are not given, they end regularly in -(*e*)*d*. To save space, many verbal and nominal forms have been condensed by means of the hyphen. This division is merely a mechanical device, and does not mark the morphological ending. The dash always represents the form in black-face type, and never refers to the form immediately preceding, e. g. '**abyde** . . . inf. 764; abide 856; 3 sg. -z, 436,' simply means that the form in l. 436 is *abydez*.

In order not to multiply cross-references unnecessarily, forms spelled with *i* are recorded under *y* without being listed under *i*. *þ* follows *t*; initial *ʒ* follows *y*, but medial *ʒ* follows *g*. It has not seemed advisable in the etymologies to attempt to define in each case the exact relationship of the Middle English word to the one from which it is derived or to which it is related; when the relationship is indirect, the etymon is preceded by 'Cf.' Thus the unnecessarily elaborate statement that **aʒly,** adv., is from a ME. adj., *aʒly,* which is formed from a ME. n., *aʒe,* which in turn is derived from ON. *agi,* is condensed into 'Cf. ON. *agi.*' No etymology is given for a word obviously derived from the one preceding or following, if the derivative is found only in Middle English. Similarly no etymology is given for a compound if it is found only in Middle English, and the simple word(s) occur in the text. Since most of the words derived from Old English come from Mercian forms, the Mercian form is generally given after the West Saxon, though it is only specially so marked in exceptional cases. The asterisk indicates a form differing from that of the manuscript. The definitions of words are of necessity sometimes purely contextual, since the alliterative verse frequently requires a considerable extension or modification of the original meaning of a word. The following abbreviations are used:

| | |
|---|---|
| AN. | Anglo-Norman. |
| Flem. | Flemish. |
| Fris. | Frisian. |
| LOE. | Late Old English. |
| MDu. | Middle Dutch. |
| MHG. | Middle High German. |
| MLG. | Middle Low German. |
| NF. | Norman French. |
| Norw. | Norwegian. |
| OF. | Old French (Central). |
| OHG. | Old High German. |
| OM. | Mercian dialect of Old English. |
| ON. | Old Norse (Icelandic). |
| ONth. | Northumbrian dialect of Old English. |
| OS. | Old Saxon. |
| OSw. | Old Swedish. |

# GLOSSARY

## A.

**Aa,** interj., *O,* 733.

**abate,** v. tr., *put an end to:* inf. 1356. OF. abatre.

**abayst,** pp., *abashed, confounded,* 149. OF. abaïss–, from abaïr.

**Abdama,** prop. n., *Admah,* 958 (Gen. 10. 19). Lat. Adama.

**abof,** adv., *above,* 1409, 1464, 1481: above, 1382. OE. ābufan.

**abof,** prep., *above,* 38, 1120. OE. ābufan.

**abominacion,** n., *abomination:* pl. -es, 1173. OF. abomination.

**aboute,** adv., *around, round about,* 83, 346, 443, 483, 618, 1390, 1424, 1475: abowte, 30. OE. ābūtan.

**aboute,** prep., *round about,* 78, 817, 956, 1185, 1294, 1417, 1694; *near, in,* 1251: aboutte, 1084; abowte, 1638. OE. ābūtan.

**Abraham,** prop. n., 601, 604, 643, 678, 688, 713, 745, 761, 924, 1001: Abram, 647; Habraham, 682; gen. sg. Abrahamez, 650. Lat. Abraham.

**abyde,** v. intr., *abide, remain,* 365, 436, 1673; tr. *await,* 486, 764, 856: inf. 764; abide, 856, 1673; 3 sg. -z, 436, 486; pret. 3 sg. abod, 365. OE. ābīdan.

**abyme,** n., *abyss,* 214, 363, 963. OF. abi(s)me.

**abyt,** n., *clothing,* 141. OF. (h)abit.

**achape,** v. tr., *escape:* pret. 3 sg. 970. OF. eschaper, achaper.

**achaufe,** v. tr., *kindle, arouse:* pp. 1143. OF. eschaufer.

**Adam,** prop. n., 237, 258. Lat. Adam.

**adoun,** adv., *down,* 953. OE. ādūne<of dūne.

**adrez,** adv., *away, off,* 71. See **drȝ,** adj.

**afraye,** v. tr., *disturb, arouse:* pret. 3 pl. 1780. OF. effreier.

**after,** adv., *afterward,* 261, 570, 1050, 1239, 1530; *behind,* 503. OE. æfter.

**after,** conj., 442.

**after,** prep., 6, 420, 681, 770, 857, 930, 1639, 1750, 1796; *for,* 619, 1098, 1345; temporal, 650, 1755. OE. æfter.

**agayn,** adv., *again,* 1705: aȝayn, 665. OE. ongēan, -gegn; infl. by ON. ī gegn.

**agayn,** prep., *against,* 1228; *contrary to,* 266, 826; agayne, 826.

**agaynes,** prep., *against,* 1711; *contrary to,* 611: agaynez, 611.

**agayntote,** n., *looking back,* 931. Cf. OE. tōtian, v.

**age,** n., 426, 656. OF. age.

**aȝly,** adv., *fearfully, dreadfully,* 874, 937. Cf. ON. agi, n.

**aȝt,** adj., *eight,* 24, 357; as pron., aȝte, 331. OE. eahta, æhta.

**aȝt,** v., see oȝe.

**aȝtsum,** adj., *one of eight,* 411.

**al,** adj., *all,* 2, 5, 260, 339, etc.; *the whole,* 264, 313, 323, 355, etc.; as pron., *everything,* 17, 19, 259, 308, etc.; *everybody,* 62, 163, 393, 1231; referring to both men and animals, 360, 361, 362: sg. al,

17, 59, 249, 779, etc., alle, 260,
339, 396, etc.; pl. alle, 2, 5, 42,
111, etc.; gen. pl. in cpds. alþer-
(q. v.). OE. eall, all. See also
alle-kynez.

al, adv., *wholly, quite, completely,*
247, 345, 381, 488, 643, 834, 891,
1003, 1114, 1254; *very much,*
*greatly,* 715, 1553; al aboute, 83,
346: alle, 14, 346, 367, 965. OE.
eall, all.

*\* alabaundaryne, n., *a precious*
*stone of a red or violet color,*
*now called 'almandine':* pl. -s,
1470. Lat. alabandina, OF. ala-
baundine.

alarom, n., *alarm,* 1207. OF.
alarme.

aldest, see olde.

aled, see hale.

aliche, see iliche.

alkaran, n. (properly alkatran),
*mineral pitch,* 1035. OF. alkatran, Arab. al-qatrān.

allas, interj., *alas,* 853. OF.
(h)alas.

alle-kynez, adj., *of every kind,* 303.
Originally gen. alles cynnes.
OE. eall + cynn.

allyt, 599 (see note).

alofte, adv., *aloft,* 1183. LOE. on
lofte, ON. ā lopti. See also
lofte.

aloȝ, adv., *in a low voice, softly,*
670. See loȝ.

alone, adv., 784, 1512. OE. eall +
ān.

along, adv., 769; as adj. in phrase
'alle alonge day,' *all through*
*the day,* 476. OE. andlang.

alose, v. tr., pp., *famed,* 274. OF.
aloser.

als, also, see as.

also, adv., 65, 88, 340, 391, 656, 722,
1302, 1323: als, 194, 253, 268,
351, 827, 924, 1033, 1275, 1301,
1526; alce, 1377. OE. eall +
swā.

altogeder, *entirely, wholly,* 15. OE.
eall + tōgædere.

alþerfayrest, superl. adj., *fairest of*
*all,* 1379. OE. ealra + fægerost.

alþerfynest, superl. adj., *finest of*
*all,* 1637. OE. ealra, OF. fin.

alþerrychest, superl. adj., *richest*
*of all,* 1666. OE. ealra + rīcost.

alþerswettest, superl. adj., *sweetest*
*of all,* 699. OE. ealra + swētost.

alum, n., 1035. OF. alum.

amaffised, perhaps for amattised,
*amethystine,* 1470.

amaraunt, n., *emerald:* pl. amaraunz, 1470. OF. esmeraude, w.
intrusive *n,* and perhaps confused with 'amaranthe.'

ame, v. tr., *esteem, consider:* pret.
1 sg. 698. OF. esmer, Picard
amer.

amen, n., 1812. Lat. amen.

amende, v. tr., *rectify, remedy:*
pp. 248. OF. amender.

amonest, *admonish, warn:* 3 sg.
-es, 818. OF. amonester.

among, prep., *among,* 774: amonge,
25. Adv. *at intervals,* 1414. OE.
on gemong.

amount, v. intr., *arise:* pret. 3 sg.
395. AN. amunter, OF. amonter.

Ananie, prop. n., Hananiah, 1301
(Dan. 1. 6). OF. Ananie.

and, conj., 2, 4, 7, 8, etc.; in adversative sense, often = *but,* 208,
265, 805, 935, 1165; *if,* 730, 739,
864, 1346: ande, 1469, 1474, 1625,
1809. OE. and.

angel, see aungel.

anger, n., *anger, rage,* 572; *fit of anger,* 1602. ON. angr.

angre, adj., *sharp, bitter,* 1035.

ankre, n., *anchor:* pl. -z, 418. OE. ancor.

anon, adv., *at once, forthwith,* 480, 1741. OE. on ān(e).

anornement, n., *ornamentation, decoration:* pl. -es, 1290. Cf. ME. ano(u)rn, v. (adapted from OF. ao(u)rner).

anoþer, adj., *another, a second,* 469, 481, 1755; as pron. 65, 1668. OE. ān ōþer.

anoynt, v. tr., *anoint:* pp. 1446, 1497. OF. enoynt, pp.

anunder, prep., *under, beneath,* 609, 1206, 1378, 1409. Adv. þer anunder, *underneath,* 1012. OE. on + under.

any, adj., 30, 76, 420, 548, etc.; pl. 252; ani on, 42: ani, 42, 99, 984. OE. ǣnig.

aparaunt, n., *dependency,* 1007. OF. aparant.

apere, v. intr., *appear:* pret. 3 sg. 1533. OF. aper–, from aparoir.

apert, adv., *plainly, openly,* 1463. OF. apert.

apparement, n., *ornaments,* 1270. OF. aparement.

apple, n., 241; apple garnade, *pomegranate,* 1044. OE. æppel.

aproche, v. intr., *approach:* inf. 68, 147 (tr.); 3 pl. -n, 8; ?pres. subj. 2 sg. aproch, 167; pret. 3 pl. 1781. OF. aprocher.

apyke, v. tr., *adorn, array,* 1637: pp. 1479. Etym. obscure.

araye, v. tr., *dress, attire,* 134, 812, 816; *set in order,* 1442; *adorn,* 1458: pp. (all cases). OF. areier.

arc, see ark.

are, adv., *before,* 438, 1128. ON. ār.

arest, v. intr., *stop:* pret. 3 sg. arest, 766. OF. arester.

arȝe, v. intr., *be afraid, disheartened,* 713; tr., *frighten,* 572: pret. 3 sg. 572, 713. OE. eargian.

ark, n., 317, 329, 335, 357, 411, 479, 485: arc, 413. OE. earc.

arm, n., pl.: -ez, 643; -es, 1667. OE. earm.

Armene, adj., *Armenian,* 447. OF. Armenie, n.

armes, (pl. only) n., *arms, weapons,* 1306; ledes of armes, 1773. OF. armes.

as, adv., *like, as,* 208, 222, 284, 456, 554, 556, 577, 639, 641, 695, 750, 783, 838, 1011, 1018, 1022, 1269, 1319, 1656, 1675; after neg. *so much as,* 579; *such as, for example,* 7, 14, 179, 1035, 1044, 1093, 1301, 1576; introd. inf., 520, 567; introd. noun in apposition, 1007, 1217, 1324, 1748; in phrases: als(o) tyd, 64, 935, 1099, 1213; als (as) fast, 440, 1648, 1751; as bylyve, 1239; as swyþe, 1619; correl. with 'so,' 'such,' 190, 202, 640, 748, 1046, 1075, 1076; correl. with 'as,' 'als,' 'also,' 886, 984, 1046, 1134, 1516, 1527: als, 64, 1068, 1134, 1324, 1648, 1730, 1751; also, 984, 1045, 1099, 1792. OE. eall + swā.

as, conj., *as, just* as, 25, 29, 51, 95, 110, 203, 223, 226, 297, 348, 351, 360, 411, etc.; *according as,* 92; *while,* 133, 443, 645, 769, 784, 787, 1520; *as if, as though,* 82, 611, 671, 1142, 1466, 1484, 1527, 1581; also as, *just as,* 1618; as sone

as, 219; als much as, 1730;
þer(e) as, *where, when,* 24, 769.
OE. eall + swā.

**asayl,** v. tr., *assail:* pret. 3 sg. 1188.
OF. asaillir.

**ascape,** v. intr., *escape;* tr. 569:
pret. 3 sg. 569; 3 pl. asscaped,
1776. NF. escaper, ascaper.

**ascry,** n., *outcry, alarm, clamor,*
1784: askry, 1206; asscry, 838.
OF. escrie.

**asent,** n., *accord,* in phrase 'in
asent,' *together,* 788. OF. assent.

**ask,** v. tr., *ask,* 924, 1098; *require,*
2, 1127, 1742; *seek,* 1109: **2 sg.**
-es, 1109; 3 sg. -ez, 2; -es, 1127;
3 pl. ask, 1098; pret. 3 sg. 924,
1742. OE. āscian.

**askez,** n., in pl., *ashes,* 626, 736,
1010: askes, 1048, 1292. OE.
asce, sg.

**aspaltoun,** n., *asphalt,* 1038. OF.
asphaltoun.

**asse,** n., *ass,* 1086: pl. -s, 1676. OE.
assa.

**assemble,** v. intr., 1364: tr. 1769;
pp. 1769. OF. assembler.

**assyse,** n., *manner, fashion,* 639:
asyse, 844. OF. assise.

**asure,** n., *lapis lazuli,* 1411: azer,
1457. OF. asur, azur.

**astele,** v., *escape from, slip from*
(w. dat.): pret. 3 sg. astel, 1524.
OE. æt + stelan.

**at,** prep., 40, 70, 94, 95, etc.; *of,*
924; *from,* 1619; *according to,*
348; with both casual and temporal meaning, 632, 1163; in
idiomatic phrases: at a brayde,
539; at ese, 124; at þe last(e),
446, 888, 1096, 1193; at lyttel,
1710; at onez, 402, 519, 566, 672,

732, 909, 963, 1086, 1672; at þis
onez, 624, 801; at a slyp, 1264.
OE. æt.

**atlyng,** vbl. n., *purpose, intention,*
688. See **attle.**

**a-traverce,** adv., *crosswise,* 1473.
OF. a travers.

**attle,** v. tr., *ordain:* pp. 207. ON.
ǣtla.

**attyre,** v. tr., *attire:* pp. 36; atyred,
114. OF. atirer.

**atwappe,** v. tr., *escape:* inf. 1205.
See **wappe.**

**aþel,** adj., *noble, illustrious, excellent, fine;* 207, 258, 329, 411, 761,
940, 1276, 1314, 1443, 1451. OE.
æðele.

**\*aucly,** adj., *awry, amiss,* 795 (see
note).

**aunceter,** n., *forefather:* gen. sg.
-ez, 258. OF. ancestre.

**aune,** adj., *own,* 11, 1659, 1707:
auen, 595, 1222; owne, 75. OE.
āgen.

**aungel,** n., *angel:* pl. -ez, 207, 240,
895, 937, 941; -es, 1664; -s,
782, 795; aungelles, 1081; angelez, 19. OF. angele.

**aunter,** n., *marvel:* pl. -es, 1600.
OF. aventure.

**auter,** n., *altar,* 10, 506, 1276, 1443,
1451, 1477. OF. auter.

**auwhere,** adv., *anywhere,* 30. OE.
ā + hwǣr.

**avaunt,** n., *promise,* 664. Cf. OF.
ava(u)nter, *boast.*

**avay,** v. tr., *inform:* pp. 1311. OF.
avei-, from avier.

**avayment,** n., *exhibition,* 1358.
OF. aveiement.

**avised,** part. adj., *determined,* 1365.
OF. aviser.

avow, v. tr., *vow, promise:* 1 sg.
664. OF. avouer.

avoy, exclam., *fie,* 863. OF. avoi.

avyl, v. tr., *defile:* pret. 3 sg. 1151;
pp. 1713. OF. aviler.

away, adv., 286, 744, 862, 1275;
*gone, absent,* 1241; here away,
*hither,* 647 (see note). OE. on
weg.

awayl, v. intr., *avail:* pret. 3 sg.
408. See vayle.

ay, adv., *ever,* 114, 132, 276, 296, 337,
375, 497, 517, 659, 723, 931, 975,
976, 978, 1016, 1031, 1080, 1413,
1472, 1544, 1684, 1711; ay a,
*every,* 117. ON. ei.

ayre, n., *air,* 1010. OF. air.

ayre, n., *heir;* 650, 1709: hayre,
666; here, 52. OF. (h)eir.

ayþer, adj., ayþer oþer, *each other,*
338, 705. OE. æghwæðer,
ægðer.

aywhere, adv., *everywhere,* 228,
965, *1398, 1403, 1608. OE.
æghwær.

Azarie, prop. n., *Azariah,* 1301
(Dan. 1. 6). OF. Azarie.

azer, see asure.


B.

babel, adj., *foolish,* 582 (see note).

baboyn, n., *baboon:* pl. -es, 1409.
OF. babuin.

Babyloyn, prop. n., *Babylon,* 1149,
1223, 1256, 1372; Babiloyn, 1361,
1373; Babiloyne, 1335, 1666.
OF. Babiloine.

bachler, n., *young knight:* pl. -ez,
86. OF. bacheler.

badde, adj., *wicked,* 1228. ?Short-
ened form of OE. bæddel.

bak, n., *back,* 155, 980, 1412. OE.
bæc.

bale¹, n., *conflagration,* 980. ON.
bāl; cf. OE. bǣl.

bale², n., *evil, harm, woe,* 276, 1256.
OE. bealu.

bale, adj., *dire, tormenting,* 1243.
OE. bealu.

balleful, adj., *wretched,* 979. OE.
bealofull.

Baltazar, prop. n., *Belshazzar,* 1333,
1357, 1361, 1395, 1450, 1507, 1537,
1558, 1620, 1622, 1709, *1746,
1750, 1765, 1787; gen. Baltazar,
1149, 1436. Lat. Baltassar, OF.
Baltazar.

Baltazar, pron. n., *Belteshazzar*
(Vulg. Baltassar), name given
to Daniel (see Dan. 1. 7), 1610.

balterande, part. adj., *stumbling,
hobbling,* 103. Cf. Dan. baltre,
Norw. dial. baltre; Yorkshire
dial. balter.

baner, n., *banner:* pl. -es, 1404.
OF. banere.

banne, n., *proclamation, order,* 95,
1361. Cf. OE. gebann.

banne¹, v. tr., *curse,* 468; *bring a
curse upon,* 885: pret. 3 sg. 468,
885. OE. bannan.

banne², v. tr., *?fortify, ?strengthen:*
inf. 620 (see note).

bantel, n.: pl. bantelles, *outworks,*
1459 (see note).

barayn, adj., *barren,* 659. OF.
baraine, fem.

bare, adj., 452, 1246, 1254, 1693; as
noun, *bare skin,* 791; quasi-adv.,
*only,* 1573. OE. bær.

bare, v. tr., *show, disclose:* pp.
1149. Cf. OE. ābarian.

bare-heved, adj., *bare-headed,* 633.

barer, n., *barrier:* pl. -es, 1239; -s,

1263. AN. barrere, OF. barriere.

**barnage,** n., *childhood,* 517.

**barne,** n., *child,* 378, 1085, 1709: barn, 1333; pl. -z, 329, 502; -s, 1248. OE. bearn.

**baronage,** n., *baronage,* 1424. OF. baronage.

**baroun,** n., *baron,* 1372, 1640: pl. -es, 1398, 1706; -ez, 82; -z, 1715, 1796. AN. barun, OF. baron.

**barre,** n., *bar,* 884; *barrier,* 963: pl. -z, 884, 963. OF. barre.

**barst,** see **berst.**

**base,** n.: pl. -s, 1278; -z, 1480. OF. base.

**bassyn,** n., *basin, vessel,* 1145: pl. -es, 1278, 1456. OF. bacin.

**bastele,** n., *tower on wheels:* gen. sg. -s, 1187. OF. bastille.

\* **batayled,** part. adj., *fortified with battlements,* 1183. OF. bataillier.

**bate,** v. intr., *abate, cease:* pret. 3 sg. batede, 440. Cf. OF. abatre.

**batelment,** n., *battlement,* 1459. OF. \*bataillement.

**bater,** v. intr., *beat:* pret. 3 sg. 1416. bat– (cf. OF. battre) + freq. suffix -er.

**baþe,** v. tr., *bathe:* pret. 3 pl. 1248. OE. baðian.

**bausen,** n., *badger:* pl. -ez, 392. OF. bausen.

**bawelyne,** n., *bowline,* 417. Cf. ON. bōglīna, Sw. boglina.

**bay,** n., *space between columns, recess,* 1392. OF. ba(i)ee.

**Bayard,** n., 886 (see note). OF. baiard.

**bayn,** adv., *readily, willingly,* 1511. Cf. ON. beinn, *straight, direct.*

**bayt,** v. tr., *bait, feed:* pp. (= *fattened*), 55. ON. beita.

**be,** v. intr.: inf., 43, 45, 47, etc.; by, 212, 356, 1610; 1 sg. am, 736, 747, 1663; 2 sg. art, 142, 145, 345, 728, 923; 3 sg. is, 5, 17, 19, etc.; 1 pl. ar, 1111; 2 pl. ar, 864; arn, 352; 3 pl. ar. 15, 168, 864, etc. (11 times); arn, 8, 55, 162, etc. (14 times); pres. subj. 1 sg. be, 148; 2 sg., 173, 547, 878, 1113, 1133; 3 sg., 83, 234, 474, etc.; by, 104; bi, 1330; 2 pl. be, 943; 3 pl., 12, 101, 102, etc.; ben, 103, 165, 353, etc.; pret. ind. 2 sg. watz, 143; were, 1623; 3 s. watȝ, 92, 120, 134, etc. (781 used as plural); was, 126, 257, 373, 1395; 3 pl. wern, 84, 89, 119, etc.; wer, 115, 721, 789, 815, 1551; were, 118, 274, 1401, etc.; weren, 112; pret. subj. 2 sg. were, 1110; 3 sg. were 22, 37, 49, 72 (see note on 1084); wer, 1029, 1527; wore, 928; 3 pl. were, 82, 1074; wer, 360, 607, 618; wern, 113; imper. sg. be, 474, 733, 746, 1061; bes, 904; pp. ben, 328, 424, 517, etc.; \*bene, 659 (see note); nas (= ne was), 727, 983, 1226, 1312; nere (= ne were), 21. OE. bēon.

**becom,** v. intr., *become:* inf. 1128. OE. becuman.

**bed,** n., *bed,* 1787: bedd, 1765; bedde, 834. OE. bedd.

**bede,** v. tr., *offer,* 1640; *bid, command* (often by confusion w. bidde, q. v.), 130, 440, 500, 630, 1223, 1246, 1507, 1551, \*1559, 1610, 1746: 1 sg. 1640; pret. 3 sg. bede, 130, 500, 1223, 1246,

1507, 1551, 1559, 1610; bed, 440, 630, 1746. OE. bēodan.

beden, see bidde.

beke, n., *beak,* 487. OF. bec.

bekyr, n., *beaker, goblet,* 1474. ON. bikarr.

Belfagor, prop. n., *Baalpeor,* 1526 (Num. 25. 3, etc.). Lat. Beelphagor.

Belssabub, prop. n., *Beelzebub,* 1526 (2 Kings 1. 2, etc.). Lat. Beelzebub.

Belyal, prop. n., *Belial,* 1526 (Deut. 13. 13, etc.). Lat. Belial.

bem, n., *beam, ray,* 603. OE. bēam.

bench, n., 130, 854, 1395; benche, 1499, 1640. OE. benc.

bent, n., *field, heath,* 1675. OE. Beonet– in place-names.

berde, n., *beard,* 1693. OE. beard.

berdles, adj., *beardless,* 789. OE. beardlēas.

bere, v. tr., *carry,* 1405, 1412; *bring forth, produce,* 584, 649, 1042, 1073; *support, hold,* 1273, 1480; *possess,* in phrase 'bere lyf,' 333, 1023; refl. *behave,* 582: inf. 649; 3 sg., -z, 333, 1023; 3 pl. -s, 1042; pres. subj. 2 sg. bere, 582; pret. 3 sg. ber, 1273; 3 pl. bere, 1412; ber, 1480; pres. part. berande, 1405; pp. bore, 584; borne, 1073. OE. beran.

berfray, n., *a movable tower used to besiege a castle,* 1187. OF. berfrai.

berst, v. tr., *burst, break,* 963, 1263; intr. 1783: 3 sg. brestes, 1263; 3 pl. brestes, 1783; pret. 3 sg. barst, 963. OE. berstan, ON. bresta.

beryl, n., 554, 1132. OF. beril, Lat. beryllus.

beryng, vbl. n., *bearing, behavior,* 1060, 1228.

best, n., *beast,* 288, 333, 528, 539, 1488, 1675, 1682: beste, 532; pl. -ez, 351, 358, 490, 509; -es, 468, 1000; besttes, 1409; gen. pl. -en, 1446. OF. beste.

best, see god.

bete¹, v. tr., *beat:* 3 sg. -s, 1263; pret. 3 sg. bet, 1292; pp. beten, 1787. OE. bēatan.

bete², v. tr., *replenish, kindle:* imper. sg. bete, 627; pp. bet, 1012. OE. bētan.

better, see god, well.

Beþelen, prop. n., *Bethlehem,* 1073. Lat. Bethlehem.

beverage, n., 1433, 1717. OF. beverage.

bi, adv., *by,* 985. See by, prep.

bibbe, v. intr., *bib, drink:* 3 sg. -s, 1499. Probably Lat. bibere.

bicnowe, v. tr., *acknowledge (as true):* pret. 3 sg. bicnu, 1327. OE. becnāwan.

bidde, v. tr., *bid, command, request* (often confused w. bede, q. v.): 3 sg. biddez, 154, 843; byddez, 482; pret. 3 pl. beden, 942; pp. beden, 95; bedene, 351. OE. biddan.

biden, see byde.

bifalle, v. intr. *happen:* pret. 3 sg. bifel, 1529; pp. bifallen, 1563; byfallen, 1629. OE. befeallan, -fallan.

bifore, adv., of place, 114, 918; of time, 659, 1152, 1229, 1445: byfore, 114, 659, 1152. OE. beforan.

bifore, prep., of place, 903, 978, 997, 1418, etc.: byfore, 602, 644. OE. beforan.

**bigge,** adj., *big, great, large:* 1190,
1377; bygge, 43, 1183; byge,
229; superl. bigest, 276; biggest,
1335. Etym. uncertain.

**bigge¹,** v. tr., *buy:* pp. bo3t, 63, 67.
OE. bycgan.

**bigge²,** v. tr., *build:* pp. 1666. ON.
byggya.

**bikenne,** v. tr., *deliver:* 3 sg. -s,
1296. Cf. OE. cennan; OHG.
bichennan.

**bilde,** part. adj., *built:* 1392; bulde,
1190. OE. byldan.

**bileve,** v. intr., *remain:* pret. 3 pl.
1549. OE. belǣfan.

**bilooghe,** adv., *below,* 116. See
lo3.

**birle,** v. tr., *pour drink,* 1715; abs.,
1511: 3 pl. -n, 1511; pp. byrled,
1715. OE. byrelian.

**birolle,** v. tr., *drench:* pret. 3 sg.
959. See role.

**bischop,** n., *bishop:* gen. pl. -es,
1445, 1718. OE. bisceop.

**bisege,** v. tr., *besiege:* pret. 3 sg.
1180. Cf. OF. sege, *siege.*

**biteche,** v. tr., *deliver, commit:* inf.
871; pret. 3 sg. byta3t, 528. OE.
betǣc(e)an.

**bitter,** adj., 1022. OE. biter.

**bityde,** v. intr. and impers., *happen,
befall:* 3 sg. -s, 1804; pres.
subj. 3 sg. bytyde, 522; pret.
3 sg. bitide, 1657; bityde, 1647.
OE. betīdan.

**blade,** n., *blade (of a knife):* pl.
-s, 1105. OE. blæd.

**blake,** adj., *black,* 221, 747, 1449; as
noun, 1009: blak, 1017. OE.
blæc.

**blame,** n., *blame,* 260; *rebuke,* 43.
OF. bla(s)me.

**blame,** v. tr.: inf. 887, 1661. OF.
bla(s)mer.

**blande,** n., in phrase 'in bland,'
*together,* 885. Cf. ON. ī bland.

**blasfemy,** n., *blasphemy,* 1661:
blasfamye, 1712. OF. blasfemie.

**blast,** n., *blast (of trumpet):* pl.
-es, 1783. OE. blǣst.

**ble,** n., *color, complexion,* 791, 1126,
1759. OE. blēo.

**blemyss,** v. tr., *dull:* pret. 3 sg.
blemyst, 1421. OF. blemiss–,
from blemir.

**blench,** n., *trick, strategem,* 1202.
Cf. OE. blencan, *deceive.*

**blend,** v. tr., *mingle:* pret. 3 pl.
blende, 1788. ON. blanda
(blend, blendr in pres. sg.).

**blende,** see blynne.

**blesse,** v. tr., *bless:* 3 sg. -z, 528;
pp. blessed, 1445; blest, 1718.
OE. blēdsian, blētsian.

**blessed,** part. adj., 470, 686, 733.

**blo,** adj., *livid,* 1017. ON. blār.

**blod,** n., *blood,* 1248, 1446, 1788;
*child,* 686. OE. blōd.

**blom,** n., *flower, blossom:* pl. -ez,
1042; -es, 1467. ON. blōm.

**blonk,** n., *horse:* pl. -ez, 87;
blonkkes, 1392; gen. pl. blonkken, 1412. OE. blonca.

**blowe,** v. intr., *blow,* 437; tr. 885:
inf. 437; pret. 3 pl. blwe, 885.
OE. blāwan.

**blubrande,** pres. part., *boiling,
surging,* 1017. Imitative; cf.
Germ. dial. blubbern.

**blusch,** v. intr., *glance, look:* inf.
904; pret. 3 sg. 980, 998, 1537;
bluschet, 982. OE. blyscan; cf.
MLG. bloschen.

**blusnande,** pres. part., *gleaming,*

shining, 1404. Based on Gmc.
*blus (cf. OE. āblysian).

bluster, *stray about:* pret. 3 pl. 886.
Cf. LG. blustern.

blyken, v. intr., *become pale,* 1759;
*shine, gleam,* 1467: pret. 3 sg.
blykned, 1759; pres. part. as adj.
blyknande, 1467. ON. blikna.

blykke, v. intr., *shine:* pret. 3 sg.
603. OE. blīcan.

blynde, adj., *blind,* 103, 584, 886;
as noun, 1094. OE. blind.

blynde, v. intr., *become dim:* 3 sg.
-s, 1126. Cf. OE. āblindian.

blynne, v. intr., *cease,* 440: pres.
3 sg. -s, 1661; -z, 1812; pp.
blende, 967. OE. blinnan.

blysful, adj., *joyful,* 1075.

blysse, n., *bliss, joy,* 237, 260, 473,
1765; especially *the joy of
Paradise,* 177, 546. OE. bliss<
blīþs.

blyþe, adj., *gentle, kind,* 1085, 1228;
*joyful,* 1706. OE. blīðe.

blyþely, adv., *gladly, kindly,* 1718:
blyþly, 82. OE. blīðlice.

bobaunce, n., *boasting, pride,* 179,
1712. OF. bobance.

bode, n., *command,* 979. OE. bod.

bod(e), see byde.

bodworde, n., *message,* 473.

body, n., 32, 1061; w. reference to
the Eucharist, 11; *any one, a
person,* 260: bodi, 260. OE.
bodig.

boffet, n., *blow,* 43; figurative, 885.
OF. buffet.

boȝe, n., *bough,* 616: pl. -s, 1467,
1481. OE. bōg.

boȝ(ed), see bowe.

boȝt, see bigge.²

boke, n., *book,* 197, 966. OE. bōc.

bok-lered, part. adj., *learned in
books,* 1551. OE. bōc + lǣred.

bol, n., *bull,* 1682: pl. boles, 55;
bulez, 392. ?ON. boli; perhaps
OE. *bulla (cf. bulluc).

bolde, adj., *bold, daring, brave,* 904,
1372; as epithet with attenuated
meaning, *noble, fine,* 789, 1333,
1357, 1424, 1450, 1537, 1558, 1610,
1709, 1746; absol. 811. OE.
beald, bāld.

bole, n., *bole (of tree), trunk,* 622.
ON. bolr.

bolle, n., *bowl,* 1145, *1474: pl. -z,
1511. OE. bolla.

bolled, part. adj., *embossed,* 1464.
ME. bolle, variant of bolne
(q. v.).

bolne, v. intr., *swell:* pret. 3 sg.
363; pres. part. as adj. bolnande,
179. ON. bōlgna.

bonde, n., *bondman, serf,* 88. OE.
bonda<ON. bōndi.

bone¹, n., *command,* 826. ON. bōn.

bone², n., *bone:* pl. -s, 1040. OE.
bān.

bone, adj., *good,* in phrase 'bone
chere,' 28. OF. bon.

boner, adj., *kind, compassionate,*
733. OF. bonnaire.

bonk, n., *hill, ridge,* 379, 392, 482;
*bank,* 86, 363, 383: pl. -ez, 86,
363, 383, 482; bonkkez, 392.
OScand. *banke, ON. ᶠbakki.

bor, n., *boar:* pl. -ez, 55. OE. bār.

borde, n., *board,* 1190; *table,* 1433,
1717; *ship, side of a ship,* in
phrases: upon borde, 470;
bynne borde, *within board,* 452,
467. OE. bord.

borgoun, v. intr., *bud:* 3 pl. -ez,
1042. OF. borjoner.

borȝ, n., *city,* 45, 82, etc.; *estate,*
63: borȝ, 63, 834, 878, 1183, 1242,
1377; burȝ, 1239, 1292, 1335,

1666; borȝe, 45, 82, 1061, 1750;
burȝe, 982. OE. burh.

borlych, adj., *noble*, 1488. ?OE.
*būrlic (see Skeat, *Academy*,
Mar. 24, 1894).

borne, n., *water, flood*, 482. OE.
burna.

borne, see bere.

bornyst, see burnyst.

bos, n., *cow-stall*, 1075. ON. bāss;
cf. ONth. bōsig.

bos, see byhove.

bosk, n., *bush*: pl. -ez, 322. Cf.
Sw. buske, Dan. busk.

bosk(ed), see busk.

bost, n., *boast, boasting*, 179, 1450,
1712. Etym. obscure.

boster, n., *boaster*, 1499.

bot, n., *remedy, help*, 1616; bi bot,
*to advantage*, 944: bote, 1616.
OE. bōt.

bot, v. tr., *announce, proclaim*: inf.
473 (see note). OE. bodian.

bot, adv., *only, merely*, 335, 747,
803, 833, 1145.

bot, conj., 13, 133, 136, 165 etc.; bot
if, *unless*, 1110, 1360; bot þat,
*were it not that*, 881. OE. būtan.

bot, prep., *except*, 209, 374, 992,
1056, 1119, 1399, 1535, 1668. OE.
būtan.

bote, n., *shoe*, 1581. OF. bote.

boþe, adj., 242, 789, 978, 1035, 1222;
absol, as pron., 824; boþe two,
155. ON. bāþir.

boþe, conj. correl.: boþe . . .
and, 20, 80, 103, 121, 308, 322, 502,
658, 1086, 1259, 1390, 1788; and
. . . boþe, 11, 57, 187, 794, 832,
1102.

boþem, n., *bottom*, 1030; valley,
383, 450: boþom, 383; pl. -ez,
450. Cf. OE. botm.

boþemlez, adj., *bottomless*, 1022.

bougoun, n., *a beating instrument*:
gen. pl. -z, 1416 (see note). OF.
boujon.

bounden, part. adj., *fastened, built*,
322. OE. bunden, pp. of bindan.

bounet, v. intr., *betake oneself to,
go*: pret. 3 pl. bounet, 1398. Cf.
ON. būinn, pp. of būa, *to get
ready*.

bounte, n., *munificence*, 1436. AN.
bunte, OF. bonte.

bour, n., *bower, lady's chamber,
private room*, 129, 1075, 1126;
*stall*, 322: pl. -ez, 322. OE. būr.

boute, prep., *without*, 260; obj. un-
expressed, 824. OE. būtan.

bowe, v. intr., *betake oneself, go,
walk, flee*, 45, etc.; *bow, be
obedient*, 1746: inf. 45, 67, 482,
944, 1746; boȝ, 1551, 1750; 3 sg.
-z, 129, 854; pret. 3 pl. 379, 502,
1373, 1796; boȝed, 1242, 1706;
imper. pl. -z, 944. OE. būgan.

boweles, n., in pl., *bowels*, 1250.
OF. bo(u)el, sg.

boy, n., 878. Cf. E. Fris. boi.

boyle, v. intr., *boil*: 3 sg. -s, 1011.
OF. boillir.

braken, n., *bracken, fern*, 1675. Cf.
Sw. bräken.

brasse, n., *brass*, 1443, 1480; as
noun, *brass trumpets*, 1783: bras,
1271. OE. bræs.

brath, n., *violence, fierceness*, 916.
Cf. ON. brāðr, adj.

braunches, see bronch.

brayd, n., *sudden movement;* in
phrase 'in a brayd,' *suddenly, at
once*, 1507; at a brayde, 539.
Cf. OE. gebregd, and ON.
bragð.

brayden, see browden.

brayn, n., *brain, brains*, 1248, 1421,
1788. OE. bræg(e)n.

**bred,** n., *bread,* 620, 636, 1105. OE. brēad.

**brede,** n., *breadth, width,* 316. OE. brǣdu.

**brede,** n., *roast meat:* pl. -s, 1405. OE. brǣde, brēde.

**brede,** v. tr., *beget,* 257; intr., *grow,* 1482; *become,* 1558: pret. 3 sg. bred, 257, 1558; pres. part. bredande, 1482. OE. brēdan.

**breke,** v. tr., *break:* pret. 3 sg. brek, 1105, 1239; pp. broken, 1047. OE. brecan.

**brem,** adj., *fierce, raging,* 229. ?OE. brēme.

**bremly,** *fiercely,* 509.

**brende,** part. adj., *refined by fire, burnished,* 1456, 1488. See **brenne.**

**brenne,** v. tr., *burn,* 916, 959, 1292; intr., 509, 1012: 3 sg. -z, 916; pret. 3 sg. 959; brend, 1292; 3 pl. brened, 509; pres. part. brennande, 1012. ON. brenna.

**brent,** adj., *steep, high:* superl. brentest, 379. OE. brant; cf. Mod. Sc. brent.

**brere,** n., *briar:* pl. -s, 1694. OE. brēr.

**brere-flour,** n., *briar-rose,* 791.

**brese,** v. intr., *bristle:* pret. 3 pl. 1694 (see note).

**brest,** n., *breast,* 1693. OE. brēost.

**brest,** n., *disruption, destruction,* 229. ON. brestr.

**brestes,** see **berst.**

**breth,** n., *breath,* 916; *savor, smell,* 509, 967: brethe, 967; breþe, 509. OE. brǣð.

**breve,** v. tr., *write down, tell:* pp. breved, 197. ON. brēfa.

**breyþe,** v. intr., *rush:* pret. 3 sg. 1421. ON. bregða.

**brode,** adj., *broad, wide,* 129, etc.; of time, *long,* 659; *great,* 584: brode, 129, 603, 622, 854, 1404, 1405, 1694; brod, 584, 659, 1022, 1377, 1392. OE. brād.

**bronch,** n., *branch,* 487: pl. braunches, 1464, 1482. OF. branche.

**bronde,** n., *brand,* 1012; *sword,* 1246: pl. -z, 1012. OE. brond.

**broþe,** adj., *angry, wrathful,* 149, 1409. ON. brāðr.

**broþely,** adj., *vile, bad,* 848, 1030: broþelych, 848.

**broþely,** adv., *basely,* 1256.

**broþer,** n., *brother,* 772. OE. brōðor.

**brow,** n., *eye brow:* pl. -es, 1694. OE. brū.

**browden,** part. adj., *woven, intertwined,* 1132; brayden, 1481. OE. bregdan, pp. brogden.

**brugge,** n., *bridge, drawbridge,* 1187. OE. brycg.

**brurd,** n., *edge, border:* pl. -es, 1474. OE. brerd, breord.

**brurdful,** adv., *brimful,* 383. OE. brerdful.

**bruse,** v. tr., *bruise:* pp. 1047. OE. brȳsan.

**brutage,** n., *temporary parapet,* 1190. AN. brutesche, OF. bretesche.

**brych,** n., *transgression, sin,* 848. OE. bryce.

**bryd,** n., *bird:* pl. bryddez, 288; bryddes, 1482. OE. brid.

**brydale,** n., *wedding-feast,* 142. OE. brȳdealo.

**bryȝt,** adj., *bright,* 20, 1278, 1400, 1439, 1441, 1456, 1481, 1511, 1638, 1759, 1783; as noun, 470: comp. bryȝter, 1132. OE. beorht, berht, breht.

bry3t, adv., *brightly,* 218, 603, 1012:
*bry3te, 1506; superl. bry3test,
114. OE. beorhte.

brymme, n., *bank (bordering
water),* 365. Cf. Sw. bräm,
MHG. brem.

brynge, v. tr., *bring,* 82, etc.; bryng
to resoun, *show the meaning of,
explain,* 1633: inf. 620; 2 sg.
-s, 1633; 3 sg. -z, 470, 629, 636,
811; pret. 3 sg. bro3t, 487, 1429;
3 pl. bro3ten, 86, 1375; imper.
sg. bryng, 473, 1433; pl. -z, 82;
pp. bro3t, 95, 1223, 1256, 1439,
1620, 1715, 1717. OE. bringan.

brynk, n., *brink, edge:* pl. -ez, 384.
Cf. ON. brekka, MLG. brinc.

brynston, n., *brimstone,* 967. Cf.
ON. brennistein.

bukke, n., *buck:* pl. -z, 392. OE.
bucca.

bulde, see bilde.

bule, see bol.

burde, n., *woman, lady,* 378, 653,
979: pl. -s, 868, 1247, 1260, 1515;
-z, 80. Etym. uncertain.

bur3(e), see bor3.

burne, n., *man,* *32, 142, 149, 288,
452, 467, 502, 633, 686, 733, 826,
878, 1223, 1242, 1436, 1620; *person,* 824; *servant,* 616: pl. -z,
80, 789; -s, 1202, 1373, 1405,
1551. OE. beorn.

burnyst, part. adj., *burnished,* 1085:
bornyst, 554. OF. burniss–,
from burnir.

burþen, n., *burden,* 1439. OE.
byrðen.

*bus (MS. vus), v. intr., *drink:*
inf. 1507. Cf. MDu. buizen,
ModE. booze.

busch, n., *?beating, striking,* 1416.
Cf. OF. buschier, v.

busily, adv., *carefully,* 1446. Cf.
OE. bysig, *busy.*

busk, v. tr., *make ready, prepare,*
333, 351; *dress,* 142; *conduct,*
1395; refl., *betake oneself, go,*
633; intr., 834: 3 sg. -ez, 633;
pret. 3 pl. bosked, 834; imper.
sg. busk, 333; bosk, 351; pp.
busked, 142, 1395. ON. bûa-sk,
*prepare oneself.*

busmar, n., *scorn, mockery,* 653.
OE. bismer.

butter, n., *butter,* 636. OE. butere.

by, prep., *by, near, along,* 86, 622,
636, 767, 974, 1039, 1041, 1403,
1424, 1442, 1590, 1761; expressing means, agent, cause, manner,
62, 104, 117, 600, 608, 712, etc.;
with distributive meaning, payre
by payre, 338; in phrases: bi
bot, 944; bi cause of, 1519; by
kynde, 865, 1128; bi þe laste,
1327; by ry3t, 2, 1633; by his
trawþe, 63, 667; by þat, as conj.
and adv., 397, 967, 1211, 1687;
by, elliptically, as conj., *by the
time that,* 403; bi, 985, 1327, etc.
(19 times). OE. be, bi.

byddez, see bidde.

byde, v. intr., *abide, wait, remain,*
449, etc.; tr., *await,* 622; *endure,*
32: inf. 32, 449; 3 sg. bidez,
604; 1 pl. byde, 622; pret. 3 sg.
bod, 467, 982; 3 pl. byden, 1243;
pret. subj. 3 sg. bode, 1030; pp.
biden, 616. OE. bīdan.

byfallen, see bifalle.

byfore, see bifore.

bygge, see bigge, adj.

byggyng, n., *dwelling, home,* 378,
811. ON. bygging.

bygynne, v. intr., *begin:* 3 sg. -z,
280, 359, 947; -s, 1401; pret.

3 sg. bigan, 1337; 3 pl. bigonne,
123; pp. bygonnen, 749. OE.
beginnan.

by3e, n., *necklace, ring,* 1638. OE.
bēah.

byholde, v. tr., *behold, look at:* inf.
64; beholde, 607; 3 sg. -s, 1423;
biholdez, 150; pret. 3 sg., byhelde, 452; pres. part. biholdand,
1544. OE. behaldan, -hāldan.

byhove, v. impers., *behoves, is
necessary:* 3 sg. -z, 68, 554; bos
(contracted form), 687; pret.
3 sg. 398. OE. behōfian.

byhynde, adv., *behind,* 155: bihynde, 904, 918. OE. behindan.

byhynde, prep., *behind,* 653, 858:
bihynde, 998; byhynden, 980.
OE. behindan.

bylyve, adv., *quickly, at once,* 156,
etc.; *soon,* 365; as bylyve, *as
soon as possible, immediately,*
1239: bylyve, 156, 180, 353, 365,
598, 610, 632, 811, 829, 962, 991,
1239, 1615, 1650; bylive, 626;
bilyve, 688, 1212. OE. be līfe.

bynde, v. tr., *bind, tie:* imper. pl.
-z, 155. OE. bindan.

bynne, prep., *within,* only in phrase
'bynne borde,' 452, 467. OE.
binna(n).

byrled, see birle.

byseche, v. tr., *beseech:* 1 sg. 799;
biseche, 614. OE. besēcean.

bysulp, v. tr., *defile, befoul:* 3 sg.
-ez, 575. See sulp.

bysyde, adv., *hard by, near,* after
her, þer: 673; bisyde, 926. OE.
be sīdan.

byta3t, see biteche.

byte, v. tr., *bite,* 1047; *cause a
sharp pain,* 1243: intr. with 'on,'

532, 1675: inf. 1675; 3 sg. -s,
532; pp. byten, 1047, biten, 1243.
OE. bītan.

bytterly, adv., *bitterly,* 468. OE.
biterlīce.

bytwene, adv., *here and there,* 637,
951: bitwene, 1383, 1410, 1463,
1472. OE. betwēonan.

bytwene, prep., *between,* 703, 707.
OE. betwēonan.

bytyde, see bityde.

byþenk, v. refl., *consider, reflect,*
582; *take into one's head, resolve,* 125, 1357: 3 sg. biþenkkes,
1357; pret. 3 sg. biþo3t, 125;
imper. sg. byþenk, 582. OE. bi-
þencan.

## C.

cache, v. tr., *catch, capture, seize,
take,* 898, 1215, 1252, 1296, 1514,
1612, 1789, 1800; with 'away,'
*snatch,* 1275; *conceive,* 1426;
*receive,* 1619; *drive,* 16; *?fasten,*
1254; intr., *run, hasten,* 629;
*?knock, strike,* 1541: inf. 1514;
cach, 898, 1252; 3 pl. -n, 16;
cachches, 1541; pret. 3 sg. ca3t,
1426; cached, 629; 3 pl. 1275;
pp. ka3t, 1215, 1254, 1789; ca3t,
1296, 1612; cached, 1619, 1800.
NF. cachier.

cagge, v. tr., *fasten, bind:* pp. 1254.
Etym. uncertain.

cal, n., *invitation,* 61.

Caldee, prop. n., *Chaldea:* Caldee,
1339, 1362; Caldye, 1575; Calde,
*1231, 1747. Lat. Chaldæa, OF.
Caldee.

Caldee, prop. n., *Chaldean:* pl.
Caldeez, 1774; as adj. 1316;
Calde, 1215, 1562, 1631.

**calf**, n., 629. OE. cealf, cælf.

**calle**, v. tr., *proclaim,* 1564; *summon, call away,* 162, 948, 1231, 1562; *name, call, address as,* 8, 258, 1352, 1370, 1583; w. weakened meaning, *be called,* almost = *be,* 1015, 1119; *ask (for),* 1522; w. after 1345; *invoke,* 1343; w. on, 1097; w. upon, *address,* 1427: inf. 1370; 3 sg. -z, 948, 1345; -s, 1427; callz, 1343; 3 pl. -s, 1522; pret. 3 sg. calde, 1583; 3 pl. called, 1097; imper. sg. calle, 1562, 1564; pp. called, 8, 162, 258, 1015, 1119, 1352; calde, 1231. ON. kalla.

**callyng**, n., *proclamation,* 1362.

**Cam**, prop. n., *Ham,* 299. Lat. Cham; OE., OF. C(h)am.

**campe**, adj., *shaggy, like whiskers,* 1695. ON. kampr, *beard.*

**candelstik**, n., *candlestick, chandelier,* 1478, 1532: condelstik, 1275. OE. candelsticca.

**capel**, n., *horse:* pl. -es, 1254. ON. kapall.

**capstan**, n., *capstan,* 418. Cf. Prov. cabestan.

**captyvide**, n., *captivity (of Jews),* 1612. OF. *captivite.

**carayne**, n., *carrion,* 459. NF. caroine.

**care**, n., *sorrow, affliction,* 234, 393, 777, *terror,* 1550: kare, 234. OE. cearu, caru.

**careful**, adj., *sorrowful,* 770. OE. cearful.

**carfully**, adv., *sorrowfully,* 1252, 1679.

**carle**, see **karle**.

**carnel**, n., *battlement, embrasure:* pl. -es, 1382. OF. carnel, var. of crenel.

**carp**, v. intr., *speak, talk:* 3 sg. -ez, 74; -es, 1591. ON. karpa.

**carp**, n., *discourse, speech,* 23, 1327.

**carping**, vbl. n., *speech,* 1550.

**carye**, v. tr., *carry:* pp. 1765. NF. carier.

**cast**, see **kest**, n.

**castel**, n., *castle:* pl. -es, 1458. NF. castel.

**casydoyne**, n., *chalcedony:* pl. -s, 1471. OF. cassidoine.

**catel**, n., *property,* 1296. NF. catel.

**cause**, n., *cause, reason,* 65, 1119, 1587; bi cause of, 1519: cawse, 65. OF. cause.

**cayre**, v. intr., *go,* 85, 901; *return,* 945; *pull,* 1259; tr. *pull, drag* (perhaps confused w. carie), 1478: inf. 945, 1259; pret. 3 pl. 85; imper. sg. cayre, 901; pp. 1478. ON. keyra.

**cayser**, n., *emperor,* 1322: kayser, 1593; pl. -es, 1374. ON. keisari.

**caytif**, adj., *base, wicked, wretched,* 1426: caytyf, 1605. NF. caitif.

**certez**, adv., *certainly,* 105. OF. certes.

**cerve**, see **kerve**.

**cete, cety**, see **cite**.

**chambre**, n., *chamber,* 1586. OF. chambre.

**charge**, v. tr., *load,* 1295; *charge,* 464, 1258; pp. *heavy, hard,* 1154; charged with, *laden with, bearing,* 1272: pret. 3 sg. 464; pp. 1154, 1258, 1272, 1295. OF. chargier.

**chariot**, n., *cart, wagon:* pl. -es, 1295. OF. chariot.

chast, v. tr., *restrain:* inf. 860. OF. chastier.

chastyse, v. tr., *punish:* pret. 3 sg. 543. ?OF. *chastiser.

chaufen, v. tr., *warm, increase:* inf. 128. OF. chaufer.

chaunce, n., *chance, fortune,* 1125, 1129, 1154, 1588. OF. cheance.

chaundeler, n., *stand or support for a candlestick,* 1272. AN. chandeler, OF. -ier.

chaunge, v. tr., *change,* 1258; intr., 713; chaungande, *varying, rapidly shifting,* 1588: pret. 3 sg. *713; pp. 1258. OF. changer.

chayer, n., *throne,* 1218. OF. chaere.

chef, adj., *chief, main,* 1272, 1586, 1588; *first,* in phrase 'chef fader,' 684.

chef, n., *head, commander,* 1238. OF. chef.

cheftayn, n., *ruler,* 1295: chevetayn, 464. OF. chevetaine.

cheke, n., *cheek:* pl. -s, 1694. OE. cēace.

chekke, n., *attack:* pl. -s, 1238. OF. eschec.

chere, n., *countenance, appearance,* 139, 1539; *entertainment,* 128; with a bone chere, *joyfully,* 28; make god chere, *make merry, be cheerful,* 641: cher, 128. OF. ch(i)ere.

cherisch, v. tr., *hold dear, take care of,* 543, 1154, 1644; *entertain,* 128: inf. 128; cherych, 1154; pret. 3 sg. cheryched, 1644; pp. cherisched, 543. OF. cheriss–, from cherir.

chese, v. tr., *choose:* pp. chosen, 684. OE. cēosan.

chevalrye, coll. n., *knights,* 1238. OF. chevalerie.

cheve, v. intr., *happen:* pres. subj. 3 sg. cheve, 1125. OF. chever.

chorl, n., *serf,* 1258; as term of contempt, *villain,* 1583: pl. -es, 1258, 1583. OE. ceorl.

chosen, see chese.

chyde, v. intr., *rail, scold:* inf. 1586. OE. cīdan.

chylde, n., *child,* 1303; *descendant,* 684; in phrase 'moder chylde,' 1303: pl. childer, 1300; gen. pl. chyldryn, 684. OE. cild.

chyn, n., *chin:* pl. chynnez, 789. OE. cinn.

chysly, adv., *carefully,* 543. Cf. OE. cīs, *fastidious.*

cience, see syence.

cite, n., *city:* cite, 673, 926; cete, 78, 1185, 1559, 1615, 1795; cety, 679, 722; pl. citees, 968, 1015; cities, 940; ceteis, 958. OF. cite.

clam, see climme.

clanly, adv., *purely, chastely,* 264, 1089; *neatly,* 310; *courteously,* 1621; *wholly,* 1327: clanlych, 310. OE. clǣnlic.

clannes, n., *purity,* 12, 1087, 1809: clannesse, 1, 26. OE. clǣnness.

claryoun, n., *clarion,* 1210. Late Lat. clariōnem, perhaps OF. *clarion (regularly clairon).

clat, v. intr., *beat:* 3 pl. clatz, 839. Cf. clatter, and Mod. Dial. clat.

clater, v. intr., *rattle, echo,* 972; *crash, be shattered,* 912: inf. 912; pret. 3 pl. 972. OE. clatrian.

clatering, vbl. n., *clattering,* 1515.

clawre, n., *claw:* pl. -s, 1696. Cf. OE. clawu.

clay, n., 312, 346, 1034, 1547; *clay wall*, 1618. OE. clæg.

clay-daubed, part. adj., *plastered with clay*, 492.

clayme, v. tr., *call for, beg:* pret. 3 pl. 1097. OF. claim–, from clamer.

cleche, v. intr., w. to, *seize on, grasp*, 634, 1348; tr. *obtain*, 12: 3 sg. -z, 634; -s, 1348; 3 pl. cleche, 12. ?OE. *clǣcean.

clef, see cleve.

cle3t, see clicche.

cleme, v. tr., *plaster:* imper. sg. cleme, 312. OE. clǣman.

clene, adj., *clean, pure, chaste*, 17, 19, 27, 119, 165, 554, 634, 730, 1053, 1056, 1067, 1072, 1085, 1088, 1101, 1109, 1110, 1288; of beasts, 334, 508; *exact*, 1731; w. weakened meaning, *fair, bright*, 792, 1119, 1458: comp. clener, 1072. OE. clǣne.

clene, adv., *in a clean manner*, 175, 1100; *fairly, skilfully*, 1287, 1382, 1455; *clearly*, 1606: comp. clanner, 1100. OE. clǣne.

cleng, v. intr., *cling:* 3 sg. -s, 1034. OE. clingan.

clepe, v. intr., *call:* 3 sg. -s, 1345. OE. cleopian.

cler, adj., *clear, bright*, 792, 1128, 1456, 1471, 1532, 1569, 1744; *fair*, 1400; of sound, 1210; *plain, easily understood*, 26, 1056: clere, 1400, 1456, 1471; comp. clerer, 1128; clerrer, 1056; superl. clerest, 1532. OF. cler.

clergye, n., *clergy*, 1570. OF. clergie.

clerk, n., *scholar, learned man*, 193, 1562, 1575, 1579, 1583, 1631; *priest*, 1266: pl. -es, 1575, 1579, 1583, 1631; -ez, 193; clerkkes, 1266, 1562. OE. and OF. clerc.

clernes, n., *splendor*, 1353.

clepe, v. tr., *clothe, dress:* inf. 1741. OE. clǣðan.

cleve, v. intr., *cleave, split:* pret. 3 sg. clef, 367; 3 pl. cloven, 965. OE. cleofan.

clicche, v. tr., *hold*, 1655; intr. *fasten*, 858; *stick*, 1692: pret. 3 sg. cle3t, 858, cly3t, 1692; pp. cle3t, 1655. (The form 'cle3t' may belong to 'cleche.') OE. clyccean.

climme, v. tr., *climb, ascend:* pret. 3 sg. clam, 405. OE. climban.

clobbe, see klubbe.

Clopyngnel, prop. n., *Clopinel*, 1057 (see note).

clos, n., *enclosure*, 1088; *house*, 839. OF. clos.

clos, pp. as adv., *fast*, 858, 1655; *?secretly*, 512. OF. clos, pp.

close, v. tr., *close, shut*, 310, 346; *enclose*, 12, 1070; *fasten*, 1569; intr., 1541: inf. 1541; pp. clos, 12, 1070, 1569; closed, 310, 346. OF. clos–, from clore.

cloþe, n., *cloth*, 634, 1637, 1742; pl. *clothes, garments*, 1440; *bed-clothes*, 1788: cloþ, 1742; pl. -s, 1400, 1440, 1788. OE. clǣð.

cloþe, v. tr., *dress:* pp. 135. OE. clǣðian.

cloven, see cleve.

clowde, n., *cloud:* pl. -ez, 414, 951; cloudes, 972; clowde, 367. OE. clūd.

clowt, n., *piece, shred:* pl. -ez, 367; cloutes, 965. OE. clūt.

cluchche, v. intr., *bend:* 3 sg. -s, 1541. Var. of ME. clicche (q.v.).

cluster, v. intr.: pp. 367, 951. Cf.
OE. cluster, n.

clutte, part. adj., *patched,* 40. Cf.
OE. geclūtod, pp.

clyde, n., *plaster,* 1692. OE. cliða.

clyffe, n., *cliff,* 405, 460: pl. -z, 965.
OE. clif.

cly3t, see clicche.

clyket, n., *latch,* 858. OF. cliquet.

clyppe, v. tr., *fasten:* inf. 418. OE.
clyppan.

clyve, v. intr., *stick, cling,* 1630;
*cling together,* 1692: 3 sg. -s,
1630; 3 pl. clyvy, 1692. OE.
clifian.

cne, see kne.

cnowen, see knawe.

cof, adj., *quick,* 624. OE. cāf.

cof, adv., *quickly,* 60, 898.

cofer, n., *coffer, chest,* 1428; *ship,
ark,* 310, 339, 492: pl. -es, 1428.
OF. cofre.

cofly, adv., *quickly,* 1428.

coker, n., *stocking, legging:* pl.
cokrez, 40. OE. cocer, *quiver.*

colde, adj., *cold,* 60, 1591. OE.
ceald, cāld.

cole, n., *coal,* 456. OE. col.

coler, n., *collar,* 1569, 1744. AN.
coler, OF. -ier.

color, v. tr.: pp. 456. OF. colorer.

coltor, n., *colter of plough,* 1547.
OE. culter.

colwarde, adj., *villainous, treacherous,* 181. Cf. OF. colvert.

com, v. intr., *come:* inf. com, 54,
61, 70, 191, 1110, 1366, 1368;
come, 467, *703; 3 pl. com, 1326;
comen, 1680; pret. 2 sg. 878;
3 sg. 361, 1088, 1089, 1339, 1621,
1702; pret. 3 pl. 85, 89; comen,
946, 1093, 1316, 1574; pret. subj.

3 sg. com, 36; imper. pl. comez,
60, 801. OE. cuman.

comaund, v. tr., *command:* pres.
3 sg. -es, 1428; pret. 3 sg. 624,
1741; 3 pl. 898. OF. comander.

combraunce, n., *trouble,* 4.

combre, v. tr., *overwhelm, destroy:*
3 sg. -z, 1024; pp. 901, 920. Cf.
OF. encombrer, acombrer.

come, n., *coming,* 1706. Cf. OE.
cyme.

comende, v. tr., *commend:* inf. 1.
Lat. commendāre.

comfort, n., *comfort, relief,* 492,
1809; *encouragement,* 512; *satisfaction, joy,* 459. OF. confort.

comly, adj., *fair,* 54, 334, 508, 512,
1070: comlych, 546. Cf. OE.
cymlic.

comly, adv., *fairly,* 312.

comparisun, v. tr., *compare:* pres.
3 sg. -ez, 161. Cf. OF. compareson, n.

compas, n., in phrase 'in þe compas of,' *in the space or limits
of, in,* 319, 1057. OF. compas.

compas, v. tr., *plan, devise:* inf.
1455; pret. 1 sg. compast, 697.
OF. compasser.

compaynye, n., *company,* 119. OF.
compaignie.

comynes, n. (in pl. only), *common
people,* 1747. OF. comun.

con, v., pret. pres., *know, be able:*
1 sg. con, 1056; 3 pl. con, 1561;
pret. 3 sg. cowþe, 1, 381, 1100,
1287, 1700; couþe, 531, 813, 1555;
3 pl. cowþe, 1578, couþe, 1576.
OE. cunnan.

con, aux v., *did:* 3 sg., 301, 344,
768, 1362; 3 pl. 363, 945. ME.
variant of gan, pret. sg. of OE.
ginnan.

**concubine,** n.: pl. -s, 1353, 1519; concubynes, 1400. OF. concubine.

**conforme,** v. refl., *conform, make like:* imper. sg. conforme, 1067. OF. conformer.

**connyng,** *n., learning, (magic) art,* 1611, 1625: pl. coninges, 1611. Cf. OE. cunnan, *know.*

**conquer,** v. tr., *win,* 1431; *attain to, succeed in learning,* 1632; pres. subj. 2 sg. conquere, 1632; pret. 3 sg. conquerd, 1431. OF. conquerre.

**conqueror,** n. 1322. OF. conquerour.

**conquest,** v. tr., *conquer:* pp. conquest, 1305. OF. conquester.

**consayve,** v. intr., *conceive:* inf. 649. OF. conceiv–, from concevoir.

**conterfete,** v. tr., *feign:* pres. subj. 3 pl. conterfete, 13. OF. contrefait, pp. of contrefaire.

**contrare,** adj., *unnatural,* 266; as noun, 4; in contrary of, *opposite,* 1532: contrary, 1532. AN. contrarie.

**contre,** n., *country,* 281, 1679; cuntre, 1362, 1612. AN. cuntre, OF. contre.

**controeve,** v. tr., *contrive:* pret. 3 pl. 266. OF. contreuv–, from controver.

**conveye,** v. tr., *conduct,* 678; fig. *accompany,* 768: inf. 678; conveyen, 768. OF. conveier.

**coperoun,** n., *top:* pl. -es, 1461. AN. cuperun, OF. couperon.

**corage,** n., *heart,* 1806. OF. corage.

**corbyal,** n., *raven,* 456. The form *corbyal,* with inserted y(i), is

not found elsewhere, and may possibly be corrupt; cf. *corbel, Gaw.* 1355. OF. corbel.

**coroun,** n., *crown,* 1444: crowne, 1275. AN. corune, OF. corone.

**cors,** see **course.**

**corse,** n., *body,* 1072; pers. pron., 683 (see note). OF. cors.

**corse,** v. tr., *curse,* 1033; *swear at,* 1583; part. as adj., 1800: pret. 3 sg. 1583; pp. 1033, 1800. OE. cursian.

**corsye,** n., *corrosive:* pl. -s, 1034. OF. corosif.

**cort,** n., *court:* cort, 191, 1109, 1368, 1374, 1530, 1562, 1751; corte, 17, 60, 70, 89, 546, 1054. OF. cort.

**cortays,** adj., *gracious, fair,* 512, 1089; as noun, 1097: cortayse, 1097. OF. corteis.

**cortaysly,** adv., *graciously,* 564, 1435.

**cortaysye,** n., *goodness,* 13. OF. cortesie.

**cortyn,** n., *curtain (of bed),* 1789. OF. cortine.

**coruppte,** adj., *corrupt,* 281. OF. corupt, or Lat. corruptus.

**corven,** see **kerve.**

**cost**[1]**,** n., *contrivance,* 1478; *property:* pl. -ez, 1024. ON. kostr.

**cost**[2]**,** n., *coast; region, country,* 85. 1322: coste, 478; koste, 912; pl. costez, 1024, coostez, 1033; costese, 460. OF. coste.

**costoum,** n., *custom,* 851. OF. custume.

**couhouse,** n., *cow-shed,* 629. OE. cū + hūs.

**counsayl,** n., *counsel,* 1056, 1201, 1426, 1605, 1619; *purpose,* 683: conseyl, 1056, 1619. AN. cunseil, OF. conseil.

count, v. tr., *count,* 1731; reflex., *consider,* 1685: 3 sg. -es, 1685; pp. 1731. AN. cunter, OF. conter.

countenaunce, n., *expression,* 792. OF. countenance.

course, n., 264; *course at dinner,* 1418: cors, 264: pl. course, 1418. OF. cours, cors.

cout, v. intr., *cut:* inf. 1104. Etym. doubtful.

couþe, part, adj., *known,* 1054. See con, pret. pres.

*covacle, n., *cover:* pl. -s, 1461 (see note), -z, 1515. OF. covescle.

covenaunde, n., *covenant,* 564. OF. covenant.

cover, v. tr.: pret. 3 sg. 1440; pp. 1458 (as adj.), 1707. OF. covrir.

covetyse, n., *covetousness,* 181. OF. coveitise.

coveyte, v. tr., *desire:* 2 sg. -s, 1054. OF. coveiter.

cowpe, see cuppe.

cowwardely, adv., *miserably,* 1631. Cf. OF. coart.

coyntyse, n., *wisdom, skill,* 1287, 1632, 1809; *fine dress,* 54: coyntyse, 1287, 1809; quayntyse, 1632; quoyntis, 54. OF. cointise, queintise.

crafte, n., *power, skill, wisdom,* 13, 549, 1100, 1452; *way,* custom, 697, 865; pl. -z, *works, deed,* 549. OE. cræft.

crag, n.: pl. -ez, 449. Cf. Welsh craig.

crak, n., *blast,* 1210: pl. krakkes, 1403. Cf. OE. cracian, *resound, 'crack.'*

crave, v. tr., *beg:* 1 sg. 801. OE. crafian.

Creator, n., 394, 917: gen. sg. -es, 191. OF. creator.

crepe, v. intr., *creep:* inf. 917. OE. crēopan.

croked, adj., *crooked,* 1697; *wicked,* 181. Cf. ON. krōkr, *hook, crook.*

crone, n., *crane:* pl. -z, 58. OE. cran.

crouk, v. intr., *croak:* 3 sg. -ez, 459. Prob. echoic; cf. OE. crācettan.

crowne, see coroun.

cruppel, n., *cripple:* pl. -ez, 103. OE. crypel.

cry, n., *cry,* 1564; *proclamation,* 1574. OF. cri.

crye, v. tr. and intr., *cry, call out; weep;* 153, 393, 394, 770, 1080, 1508, 1582; *resound,* 1210; *proclaim,* 1361, 1751: inf. 1361; 3 sg. -s, 1508, 1582; pret. 3 sg. 153, 770, 1210; 3 pl. 393, 394; pp. 1080, 1751. OF. crier.

crysolyte, n., *chrysolite:* pl. -s, 1471. OF. crisolite.

cubit, n., 319; pl. -es, 405; cupy- dez, 315. Lat. cubitum.

cuntre, see contre.

cupborde, n., *sideboard,* 1440.

cuppe, n., *cup,* 1461, 1520: pl. cowpes, 1458; kowpes, 1510. OE. cuppa, OF. coupe.

cupple, n., *pair,* 333. OF. cuple.

cupydez, see cubit.

curious, adj., *curious,* *1483; *skil- ful,* 1452; *exquisite,* 1353; see note for 1109: kyryous, 1109. OF. curius.

## D.

daȝe, v. intr., *dawn:* pret. 3 sg. 1755. OE. dagian.

**dale,** n., 384. OE. dæl.

**dalt,** see **dele.**

**dam,** n., *water, ocean,* 416. OE. *damm; cf. OFris. dam.

**damp,** v. tr., *damn, doom:* pp. dampped, 989. OF. damner, dampner.

**Danyel,** prop. n., *Daniel,* 1157, 1611, 1641, 1743, 1753, 1756: Daniel, 1302, 1325. Lat., OE. Daniel.

**Daryus,** prop. n., *Darius,* 1771: Daryous, 1794. Lat. Darius.

**dasande,** part. adj., *dazing,* 1538. ON. *dasa.

**date,** n., 425. OF. date.

**daube,** v. tr., *plaster:* imper. sg. 313. OF. dauber.

**daunger,** n., *refusal,* 71; *danger,* 342, 416. OF. dang(i)er.

**day,** n., 361, 427, 445, 476, 481, 494, 526, 659, 1188, 1364, 1753, 1755, 1791, 1794; in pl., *duration,* 520; dayez of ende, *last days, the Judgment,* 1032; upon dayez, 578: pl. -ez, 295, 353, 369, 403, 429, 442, 520, 578; -es, 1032, 1594; gen. pl. -ez, 224. OE. dæg.

**daynty,** n., *delicacy:* pl. -s, 38; -ez, 1046. OF. daint(i)e.

**day-rawe,** n., *dawn, first streak of day,* 893. Cf. (?) OE. rāw.

**debonere,** adj., *gracious, courteous,* 830. OF. debonaire.

**dece,** n., *dais:* dece, 38, 1399, 1517; dese, 115; des, 1394. OF. deis.

**declar,** v. tr., *interpret:* inf. 1618. OF. declarer.

**decre,** n., *decree,* 1745. OF. decret.

**ded,** adj., *dead,* 289, 1016; as pl. noun, dede, 1096: dede, 1020. OE. dēad.

**dedayn,** n., *indignation, anger,* 74. OF. dedeyn.

**dede,** n., *deed, performance, act,* 74, 110, 588: pl. -z, 181, 265, 541, 591, 597, 1021, 1801; -s, 1061, 1136, 1360, 1659. OE. dǣd, dēd.

**defence,** n., *prohibition,* 243, 245. OF. defense.

**defowle,** v. tr., *defile, pollute:* inf. 1147; pp. 1129, 1798. OF. defouler.

**degre,** n., *rank, condition,* 92. OF. degre.

**deȝt(t)er,** see **doȝter.**

**deken,** n., *deacon;* pl. -es, 1266. OE. dēacon.

**dele,** v. tr., *deliver,* 1756; *utter, deliver,* 344, 1641; *exchange,* 1118; intr. *associate,* 137; dele wyth, *deal with,* 1561; in phrase 'dele drwry wyth,' *have love of,* 1065: 3 sg. -s, 1641; pp. dalt, 1756. OE. dǣlan.

**delful,** adj., *doleful, sorrowful,* 400. Cf. OF. doel, deol, *grief.*

**delyver,** adj., *delivered (of child),* 1084. OF. delivre.

**delyver,** v. tr., *deliver,* 500; *make away with, destroy,* 286: inf. 286, 500. OF. delivrer.

**deme,** v. tr., *decree,* 110, 1745; *judge, consider,* 1118; *name, call,* 1020, 1611: pp. (all cases). OE. dēman.

**demerlayk,** n., *magic, magic art,* 1561; pl. demorlaykes, 1578. OE. dwimer + ON. leikr.

**demm,** v. intr., *dam up, fill up:* pret. 3 sg. 384. OE. *demman.

**denounce,** v. tr., *?declare* (see note): pp. 106. OF. denonc(i)er.

**depart,** v. tr., *divide,* 1738; intr.
*separate,* 1074; *go away, leave,*
396, 1677: pret. 3 sg. 396, 1677;
3 pl. 1074; pp. 1738. OF. de-
partir.

**depe,** adj., *deep,* 374, 384, 416, 852;
*profound,* 1609; *great,* 1425.
OE. dēop.

**depe,** adv., *far down,* 158. OE.
dēope.

**depryve,** v. tr., *dispossess, divest,*
1227, 1738; *take away,* 185: pp.
1227, 1738. OF. depriver.

**dere,** adj., *worthy, noble,* 92, 115,
1302, 1306, 1367, 1771, 1794, 1806;
as n., sg. 1399; pl. 1394; *beloved,* 52, 814; *costly, valuable,*
1118, 1279, 1743, 1792; in less
precise senses, often w. meaning
hardly determinable: *precious,
important, excellent, worthy,*
683, 698, 1604, 1609: superl. derrest, 115, 1118, 1306. OE. dēor.

**dere,** adj., *harsh, severe,* 214. OE.
dēor.

**dere,** v. tr., *harm:* imper. pl. -z,
862. OE. derian.

**derelych,** adv., *excellently, beautifully,* 270. OE. dēorlīce.

**derf,** adj., *bold, dreadful,* 862. ON.
djarfr.

**derfly,** adv., *boldly,* 1641; *quickly,*
632: dervely, 632.

**derk,** adj., *dark,* 1020; as noun,
*night,* 1755. OE. deorc.

**derne,** adj., *secret, hidden,* 588;
*profound,* 1611. OE. dierne,
derne.

**derne,** adv., *secretly,* 697.

**dervely,** see **derfly.**

**dese,** see **dece.**

**desyre,** v., *desire:* 2 sg. -s, 545;
pres. subj. 3 sg. dezyre, 1648.
OF. desirer.

**deþe,** n., *death:* deþe, 246, 1021,
1249, 1266, 1787; deth, 372, 374,
1648; dethe, 1032. OE. dēað.

**devel,** n., *(the) Devil,* 1500; gen.
sg. -ez, 180. OE. dēofol.

**device,** see **devyse.**

**devine,** n., *diviner, prophet,* 1302.
OF. devin.

**devine,** v. tr., *interpret:* inf. 1561.
OF. deviner.

**devinor,** n., *diviner, soothsayer:*
pl. -es, 1578. OF. devinour.

**devoutly,** adv., 814. Cf. OF. de-
vot(e), adj.

**devoyde,** v. tr., *cast out, destroy:*
inf. 908. OF. devoidier.

**devoydynge,** vbl. n., *destroying,*
544.

**devyse,** v. tr., *order, appoint,* 110,
238; *contrive, design,* 1100,
1288; *conceive,* 1046; *set forth,*
1157, 1325, 1756; *expound,* 1604:
inf. 1100; device, 1046; pret.
3 sg. 1157, 1604, 1756; devised,
1288; pp. devised, 110, 238, 1325.
OF. deviser.

**dew,** n., 1688. OE. dēaw.

**deystyne,** n., *fate,* 400. OF. des-
tinee.

**dialok,** n., *discourse:* pl. -ez, 1157.
OF. dialoge.

**ding,** v. tr., w. down, *knock down,
strike down:* pret. 3 pl. dungen,
1266. OSw. diunga, ODan.
dinge.

**disches,** see **dysche.**

**display,** v. tr., *exhibit, reveal:* 3 sg.
displayes, 1542; pp. 1107. OF.
despleyer.

**displese,** v. tr., *displease,* 196, 1136; intr., *be displeased,* 1494: 2 sg. dyspleses, 1136; pret. 3 sg. 1494; pp. 196. OF. desplaisir.

**dispyse,** v. tr., *treat with contempt, abuse:* pp. 1790. OF. despis–, from despire.

**disserve,** v. tr., *deserve:* pret. 3 sg. 613. OF. deservir.

**disstrye,** v. tr., *destroy:* inf. 907; dysstrye, 520; pp. 1160. OF. destruire.

**distres,** n., *sorrow, anguish,* 307 (see note) ; in phrase 'wyth distres,' *by force, with violence,* 1160: distresse, 307. OF. destresse.

**distres,** v. tr., *press hard, put to sore straits:* pret. 3 pl. distresed, 880. OF. destresser.

**dittez,** see **dutte.**

**divinite,** n., *learning in divine things,* 1609. OF. devinite.

**do,** v. tr., *put,* 1224; done down of, *put down from,* 1801; *do,* 110, 341, 342, 692, 1647; *make,* 320; *ruin, destroy,* 989; do away, *put an end to, destroy,* 286, 862: inf. 286, 342, 1647; 3 sg. dos, 341; pret. 1 pl. diden, 110; imp. pl. dotz, 862; pp. don, 320, 692, 989, 1224; done, 1801. OE. dōn.

**dobler,** n., *a large plate,* 1146: pl. dubleres, 1279. AN. dobler, dubler ; OF. doblier.

**doel,** n., *sorrow, grief,* 158, 852, 1329. OF. doel.

**dogge,** n., *dog,* 1792. OE. docga.

**doȝter,** n., *daughter:* pl. -ez, 814; deȝter, 270, 866, 939, 977, 993; deȝtters, 899; deȝteres, 933. OE. dohtor.

**doȝty,** adj., *brave, valiant. bold,* 1182, 1791: superl. doȝtyest, 1306. OE. dohtig.

**dom,** n., *decree (of punishment), judgment,* 214, 219, 246, 597, 717, 1756; *command,* 632; *influence, power,* 1325; *mind,* 1046: dome, 219, 597, 632, 1325, 1756: pl. -ez, 717. OE. dōm.

**dool,** n., *part,* 216; *intercourse,* 699: doole, 699. OE. dāl.

**dor,** n.. *door,* 320, 500, 653; *gate,* 1182. OE. dor.

**dorst,** see **durre.**

**dotage,** n., *folly, madness,* 1425.

**dote,** v. intr., *do folly,* 286; *act foolishly,* 1500; *be dazed, astonished,* 852; 3 sg. -es, 1500; 3 pl. -en, 286; pret. 3 sg. 852. Cf. MDu. doten.

**dotel,** n., *fool,* 1517.

**doun,** adv., *down,* 150, 1266, 1292, 1590, 1801; w. ellipsis of verb, 289. OE. ādūne.

**doungoun,** n., *dungeon,* 158, 1224. OF. donjon.

**douþe,** coll., n., *men,* 270, 597; *army, nobility,* 1196, 1367: douthe, 1196; duthe, 1367. OE. duguþ.

**dow,** v. intr., *avail:* pret. 3 sg. 374. OE. dūgan.

**dowve,** n., *dove,* \*481, 485: douve, \*469 (see note). OE. dūfe– (in cpd.).

**dowelle(d),** see **dwell.**

**dowrie,** n., *dower, inheritance,* 185. OF. douaire.

**draȝt,** n., *mark, character:* pl. -es, 1557. ?OE. \*draht.

**drawe,** v. tr., *bring,* 1160; intr., *move, come go,* 500, 599 (see note), 1329, 1394; refl., drawe adreȝ, *draw back, decline, re-*

*fuse* (see note), 71: inf. 500,
draw, 599; 3 sg. 1329; pret.
3 pl. droȝ, 71; droȝen, 1394; pp.
drawen, 1160. OE. dragan.

drede, n., *dread, fear*, 295, 390, 990,
1538, 1543: dred, 342. Cf. OE.
ondrǣdan, v.

dreȝe, see dryȝe.

dreȝly, see dryȝly.

dreme, n., *dream:* pl. -s, 1578, 1604.
?OE. *drēam.

drepe, v. tr., *kill, destroy:* 3 sg. -z,
246, 599; pret. 3 sg. 1648; pp.
1306. OE. drepan.

dress, v. tr., *prepare*, 92; *array,
place*, 1399, 1477; *?portion out*,
1518 (see note): pp. 92, 1399,
1518; dresset, 1477. OF.
dresser.

drink, n., *drink, drinking*, 123:
drynk, 182; pl. -ez, 1518. OE.
drinc.

drink, v. tr., 1517; intr., 1791: pret.
3 sg. drank, 1517, 1791. OE.
drincan.

droȝ, droȝen, see drawe.

droȝþe, n., *drought*, 524. OE.
drūgað.

dronkken, part. adj., *drunk*, 1500.
OE. druncen.

drovy, adj., *turbid*, 1016. Cf. OE.
drōf, *troubled, turbid*.

drown, v., intr.: pret. 3 pl. 372;
pp. 989. Prob. OScand. *druȝna.

druye, see drye, adj.

drwry, n., *love*, 699: drwrye, 1065.
OF. druerie.

drye, adj., *dry*, 385, 412, 460; as
noun, *dry land*, 472; physio-
logical, referring to people,
1096; drye, 460, 1096; druye,
412, 472; dryȝe, 385. OE. drȳge,

drye, v. tr., *dry:* pp. 496. OE.
drȳg(e)an.

dryȝ, adj., *heavy, great*, 342. OE.
*drēog; cf. ON. drjūgr.

dryȝa, see drye.

dryȝe, v. tr., *suffer*, 372, 400, 1032,
1224; *endure*, 599; intr., *be suffered*, 491: inf. 372, 599, 1032;
dryȝ, 400; dreȝe, 1224; pret.
3 sg. 491. OE. drēogan.

dryȝly, adv., *angrily*, 74, 344; *continuously, without stopping*, 476:
dreȝly, 476.

Dryȝtyn, n., *the Lord*, 214, 243, 295,
669, 997, 1007, 1065, 1136, 1139,
1146, 1314, 1491, 1652, 1661,
*1711; dryȝttyn, ' 344; gen.
dryȝtynez, 219. OE. dryhten.

drynk, see drink.

dryve, v. tr., *drive, send*, 214, 289,
313, 433, 692; intr., *be driven,
move swiftly, rush*, 219, 416,
1425, 1760; *fly*, 472: 3 sg. -z,
433, 692; -s, 1760; pret. 3 sg.
drof, 214, 219, 416, 1425; imper.
sg. dryf, 472; pp. dryven, 289,
313. OE. drīfan.

dubbe, v. tr., *dress, array:* pp. 115,
1688, 1743. OE. dubbian.

dubleres, see dobler.

duk, n., *duke, leader*, 38, 1182, etc.;
*king*, 1745: duk, 1182, 1367,
1745, 1771; duc, 1235; pl. -ez,
38, 1518. OF. duc.

dungen, see ding.

dunt, n., *blow*, 1196. OE. dynt.

dure, v. intr., *last:* 3 pl. -n, 1021;
pret. 3 sg. 1757. OF. durer.

durre, pret. pres., *dare:* pret. ind.,
3 sg. dorst, 476; 3 sg. durst, 342;
3 pl. dorstan, 976; pret. subj.
1 sg. durst, 615. OE. durran.

**dusch,** v. intr., *rush:* pret. 3 sg. 1538. Echoic.

**duthe,** see **douþe.**

**dutte,** v. tr., *close up, shut,* 588, 1182; intr., 320: 3 sg. dittez, 588; pret. 3 sg. dutte, 1182; pres. part. dutande, 320. OE. dyttan.

**dwell,** v. intr.: inf. dowelle, 1674; 3 sg. -ez, 158; pret. 3 sg. dowelled, 376, 1196, 1770. OE. dwellan.

**dych,** n., *ditch,* 1792: pl. diches, 1251. OE. dīc.

**dyȝe,** v. intr., *die:* inf. 1329; dyȝen, 400. ON. deyja.

**dyȝt,** v. tr., *ordain,* 243, 699; *place,* 1794; dyȝt to deþe, *put to death,* 1266; *clothe, dress,* 1688, 1753; *prepare* 632, 818, 1794: inf. dyȝt, 818; pret. 3 sg., dyȝt, 632, 699; 3 pl. diȝten, 1266; pp. dyȝt, 243, 1688, 1753, 1794. OE. dihtan.

**dym,** adj., *dark* (of water), 1016: dymme, 472. OE. dimm.

**dyn,** n., *din, noise,* 692, 862: dyne, 692. OE. dyne.

**dyngnete,** n., *high place,* 1801. OF. dignete.

**dyspleses,** see **displese.**

**dyspyt,** n., *defiance, anger,* 821. OF. despit.

**dysche,** n., *dish,* 1146: pl. disches, 1279. OE. disc.

**dyscover,** v. tr., *reveal:* pret. subj. 1 sg. 683. OF. descovrir.

**dysheriete,** v. tr., *disinherit:* inf. 185. OF. desheriter.

**dysstrye,** see **disstrye.**

### E.

**Ebru,** adj., *Hebrew (language),* 448. OF. Ebreu.

**efte,** adv., *again, a second time,* 481, 482, 647; *likewise,* 562; *afterwards,* 248, 1073, 1141, 1144. OE. eft.

**egge,** n., *edge (of blade),* 1104; *sword,* 1246; *brink,* 383, 451: pl. -z, 383, 451. OE. ecg.

**eggyng,** vbl. n., *egging, instigation,* 241. ON. eggja.

**elde,** n., *age,* 657. OE. ieldu, eldu.

**ellez,** conj., *provided that,* 466, 705. OE. elles, adv.

*****em,** n., *uncle,* 924. OE. ēam.

**emperor,** n., 1323. OF. emperour.

**empyre,** n., *empire,* 540, 1349; *imperial power,* 1332: empire, 1332. OF. empire.

**enaumayl,** v. tr., *inlay:* pp. enaumayld, 1411; enaumaylde, 1457. OF. enamailler.

**enbaned,** part. adj., 1459 (see note).

**enclose,** v. tr., *shut in:* imper. sg. enclose, 334. OF. enclos-, from enclore.

**enclyne,** v. tr., *incline:* pp. 518. OF. encliner.

**ende,** n., *end,* 303, 1732; *conclusion* (= *what followed*), 608; worlde withouten ende, 712; dayes of ende, *last days,* 1032; on ende, *upright,* 423, upon ende, 1329. OE. ende.

**ende,** v. intr., *die:* inf. 402. OE. endian.

**endentur,** n., '*jointing by means of notches'—NED.,* 313. OF. endent(e)ure.

**enfaminie,** v. intr., *famish, starve:* pret. 3 pl. 1194. Cf. OF. famine, n.

enforse, v. tr., *drive:* pret. 3 pl. 938. OF. enforcier.

engender, v. tr., *beget:* pret. 3 pl. 272. OF. engendrer.

enherite, v. tr., *inherit, receive:* inf. 240. OF. enheriter.

enmie, n., *enemy:* pl. -s, 1204. OF. enemi.

enorl, v. tr., *surround:* pp. 19. Cf. OF. ourler.

enpoysen, v. tr., *poison:* pret. 3 sg. 242. OF. empoisonner.

enprysonment, n., *imprisonment,* 46. OF. emprisonnement.

enter, v. intr.: inf. 329; 3 sg. -es, 1240; pret. 3 pl. entred, 842; imper. sg. enter, 349. OF. entrer.

entre, n., *entrance,* 1779. OF. entree.

entyse, v. tr., *provoke:* 2 sg. -s, 1137; 3 sg., 1808. OF. enticier.

er, adv., *before,* 491. OE. ǣr.

er, conj., *before* (after neg. often *until*), 60, 360, 383, 590, 616, 648, 901, 932, 1203, 1204, 1234, 1262, 1503, 1756, 1778, 1785; w. ever, 834; w. redundant 'ne,' 225 (see note), 1205. OE. ǣr.

er,· prep., *before,* 946, 1088, 1312, 1339, 1670. OE. ǣr.

erbe, n., *herb:* pl. -s, 1675, 1684; -z, 532. OF. erbe.

erde, n., *land, region; dwelling;* 596, 601, 1006: erd, 892. OE. eard.

ere, n., *ear:* pl. -z, 689, 874, 879; -s, 585, 1670. OE. ēare.

erigaut, n., *a kind of cloak,* 148. OF. herigaut.

erly, adv., *early,* 895, 946, 1001. OE. ǣrlīce.

erne-hwed, adj., *having the color of an eagle,* 1698. OE. earn + hīw.

ernestly, adv., *?quickly,* 277; *?wrathfully,* 1240. OE. eornost-līce.

erþe, n., *ground,* 150, 452, 520, 533, 1027, 1160, 1332, 1591, 1693; (*the*) *earth, world,* 273, 277, 289, 303, 326, 368, 406, 528, 648, 734, 925, 1006, 1323, 1336, 1593; *mould, dust* (Lat. pulvis), 747: erþe, 277, 289, etc., 18 times; urþe, 150, 273, 303, 326, 368, 1593, 1693. OE. eorðe.

ese, n., *ease,* at ese, 124. OF. eise.

ete, v. intr., *eat:* pret. 3 sg. ete, 241, 1684. OE. etan.

eþe, adj., *easy,* 608. OE. ēaðe.

Eve, prop. n., 241. OE., OF. Eve.

evel, adj., *evil,* 747; as n. 573: pl. -ez, 277. OE. yfel, Kentish efel.

even, adv., *even, just,* 317, 510, 602, 1654. OE. efne.

eventyde, n., *evening,* 479, 485, 782. OE. ǣfentīd.

ever, adv., *always, at all times,* 158, 328, 455, 474, 527, 812, 1006, 1068, 1594; *ever, at any time,* 164, 198, 254, 255, 285, 290, 291, 432, 558, 613, 717, 1137, 1147; for emphasis after 'er,' 834; for ever, 402, 1802. OE. ǣfre.

evermore, adv., *ever, for all time,* 1020, 1031, 1273, 1523.

everuch, adj., *every,* in phrase 'everuch one,' 1221. OE. ǣfre ylc.

ewer, n., *pitcher used to carry water for washing the hands:* pl. -es, 1457. AN. ewer, OF. aiguiere.

**excuse,** v. tr., 70; refl., 62: pret.
3 pl. 62; imper. sg. excuse, 70.
OF. escuser, excuser.

**exorsism,** n., = *exorcist:* pl. -us,
1579. Late Lat. exorcismus.

**expoune,** v. tr., *expound, set forth,
explain:* inf. expowne, 1729;
3 sg. -z, 1058; pret. 3 sg. expouned, 1492; expowned, 1606.
OF. espondre, expondre.

**expouning,** vbl. n., *expounding,*
1565.

**expresse,** adv., *plainly,* 1158. OF.
expres, -se, adj.


# F.

**face,** n., *face, countenance,* 253, 304,
585, 595, 903, 978. 1055, 1539,
1810. OE. face.

**fader,** n., *father,* 112, 684, 1155,
1338, 1429, 1601, 1610, 1624,
1644; of the Lord, 542, 680, 729,
919, 1051, 1175, 1229, 1721, 1726.
OE. fæder.

**falce,** adj., *false;* as pl. noun, 1168:
falce, 205, 1167, 1168, 1522;
false, 474; fals, 188, 1341. OF.
fals.

**falewe,** v. intr., *become pale:* pret.
3 sg. 1539. OE. feal(u)wian.

**falle,** v. intr., *fall, sink,* 221, 271,
399, 450, 559, 1684; *perish,* 725;
*befall, happen, come,* 22, 494,
567; falle on, 462; falle to,
*betake oneself to,* 837; falle
fro, *spring from,* 685; has fallen
forþ (Lat. venit, see note),
304: inf. 22, 567, 685, 725; 3 sg.
-ez, 462, 494; 3 pl. -en, ?271, 837;
pret. 3 sg. fel, 450; pret. 3 pl.
fellen, 221, 399; pp. fallen, 304,
559, 1684. OE. feallan, fallan.

**fals(e),** see **falce.**

**famacion,** n., *report, defamation:*
pl. -s, 188: Cf. OF. diffamation.

**fame,** v. tr., *report:* pp. *reputed,*
275. OF. famer.

**fande,** see **fynde.**

**fanne,** v. intr., *flap, flutter:* 3 sg.
-s, 457. Cf. OE. fann, n.

**fantum,** n., *phantom, illusion:* pl.
fantummes, 1341. OF. fantosme.

**farande,** adj., *handsome,* 607;
*pleasant, joyous,* 1758: farand,
1758. ON. farandi.

**fare,** v. intr., *go, pass,* 100, 618;
fare forth, 621, 929, 1683; (of
time) *pass,* 403; *fare,* 466, 1106:
inf. 618; 3 sg. fares, 1683; 3 pl.
fare, 466; pres. subj. 3 sg. fare,
100; pret. 3 sg. ferde, 1106
(from OE. fēran, wk. v.); imper. sg. fare, 621, 929; pp. faren,
403. OE. faran.

**fare,** n., *behavior,* 861. OE. faru.

**fast,** adv., *firmly,* 1147; *earnestly,*
936; *fast, quickly,* 380, 440, etc.:
fast, 440, 618, 897, 936, 942, 944,
1147, 1648, 1751, 1762; faste,
380, 631, 903, 905, 1194, 1420.
OE. fæste.

**fat,** n., 627. OE. fætt.

**fatte,** v. tr., *fatten:* pp. 56. OE.
fættian.

**fatte,** n., *vat, tub,* 802. OE. fæt.

**faþme,** v. tr., *clasp, embrace:* pp.
399. OE. fæðmian.

**faure,** adj., *four,* 958, 1015, 1683;
on alle faure, 1683: fawre, 938,
950; fowre, 540; fourre, 1244.
OE. fēower.

**faurty,** see **forty.**

**faute,** n., *fault, misdeed, transgression:* faute, 571, 680, 725; faut,

236, 1122; pl. fautez, 177, 694;
fautes, 996; fawtes, 1736. OF.
faute.

**fautlez,** adj., *faultless,* 794.

**fauty,** adj., *guilty,* 741.

**fax,** n., *hair,* 790: faxe, 1689. OE.
feax.

**fayle,** v. intr., *fail,* 236, 548, 658,
1194, 1631; w. 'of,' *be wanting,*
737; w. 'of,' *miss, fail to obtain,* 889; of sun, *set,* 1758;
of face, *blanch,* 1539; tr. *lack,*
1535: pres. subj. 3 sg., fayly,
548; 3 pl. -n. 737; pret. 3 sg.
236, 1194, 1539, 1758; pres. part.
faylande, 1535; pp. 658, 889,
1631. OF. faillir.

**fayn,** adj., *glad, well-pleased,* 642,
962, 1752: superl., faynest, 1219.
OE. fæg(e)n.

**fayn,** adv., *gladly,* 1629.

**fayned,** part. adj., *false,* 188. OF.
feindre.

**fayre,** adj., *fair,* 3, 174, 217, 270,
493, 593, 607, 729, 866, 1042, 1106,
1279: fayr, 174, 493, 1014;
superl. fayrest, 207, 253, 1043,
1378. OE. fæger.

**fayre,** adv., *fitly, well,* 27, 316, 506,
1486; *kindly, courteously,* 89,
639; *justly,* 294; superl. fayrest,
115. OE. fægre.

**fayth,** n., *belief,* 1161, 1165: faythe,
1168; in fayth, *truly,* 1732. Cf.
OF. fei; perhaps NF. feid (=
feið).

**faythful,** adj., 1167.

**fayth-dede,** n., *deed of faith:* pl.
-s, 1735.

**feble,** adj., *poor, mean,* 47, 101:
febele, 145. OF. feble.

**fech,** v. tr., *fetch:* inf. fech, 1429;
pret. 3 sg. 1155; imper. sg. fech,

621; pl. -ez, 98, 100. OE.
fecc(e)an.

**fedde,** part. adj., *fed,* 56. OE.
fēdde.

**fee,** n., *city:* pl. -s, 960. AN. fee,
OF. fe, fié.

**fe3t,** v. intr., *fight,* 1191; of waves,
404: 3 pl. 1191; pres. part.
fe3tande, 404. OE. feohtan,
fehtan.

**fe3t,** n., *fighting,* 275. OE. feoht.

**fel,** adv., *cruelly,* 1040. See **felle,**
adj.

**fela3schyp,** n., *intercourse,* 271;
coll., *company,* 1764. LOE.
fēolagscipe.

**felde,** n., *field, country,* 98, 370,
1750; *field of battle,* 1767: pl.
-z, 370. OE. feld.

**fele¹,** v. tr., *smell,* 1019; *taste,* 107:
inf. 107, 1019. OE. fēlan.

**fele²,** v. refl., *hide:* pres. subj. 1 sg.
fele, 914. ON. fela.

**fele,** adj., *many,* 177, 1417, 1529,
1579; absol. as pron., 88, 162.
OE. feola. feolo.

**fele-kyn,** adj., *of many kinds,
various,* 1483.

**felle,** adj., *stern, cruel; dreadful;*
139, 156, 283, 421, 954, 1737. OF.
fel.

**felly,** adv., *fiercely, cruelly,* 559, 571.

**felonye,** n., *crime, sin,* 205. OF.
felonie.

**feloun,** n., *evil-doer, wretch,* 217.
AN. felun, OF. felon.

**felt,** n., *matted hair,* 1689. OE.
felt.

**femmale,** n., *female:* gen. sg., -z,
696. OF. femelle.

**fende,** n., *fiend, devil,* 205: pl. -z,
221; -s, 1341; fende, 269. OE.
fēond.

**fende**, v. intr., w. 'of,' *fend off, ward off:* 3 pl. fende, 1191.

**fenden**, adj., *fiendish*, 224.

**feng**, see **fonge**.

**fenny**, adj., *dirty, vile*, 1113. OE. fennig.

**fer**, adv., *far*, 31, 1680. Comp., fyrre, 131, 766, 1732, 1764, 1780; ferre, 97. OE. feor. See also **ferre**, adj., **fyr**, adj.

**ferde**, part. adj., *frightened*, 975: ferd, 897. OE. fǣran, fēran.

**ferde**, n., *fear*, 386.

**ferde**, see **fare**.

**fere**¹, n., *company*, in phrase 'in fere,' *together*, 399, 696. OE. gefēr.

**fere**², n., *companion*, 1062. ONth. īœra, OE. gefēra.

**ferk**, v. intr., *move quickly, walk*, 133; w. 'up,' *start up*, 897: 3 sg. -ez, 897; pret. 3 sg. 133. OE. fercian.

**ferly**, adj., *wonderful*, 1460; as noun, *marvel*, 1529, 1563, 1629: *ferlyche, 1460. OE. fǣrlic, fērlic.

**ferly**, adv., *dreadfully, terribly*, 269, 960, 975.

**ferlyly**, adv., *wonderfully*, 962.

**fers**, adj., *fierce, proud, high-spirited*, 101, 217. OF. fers.

**ferre**, adv., *far*, 98. OE. feorran. See also **fer**.

**fery**, v. tr., *carry:* pp. 1790. OE. ferian.

**fest**, n., *feast*, 81, 164, 642, 1364, 1758: feste, 54, 162, 1393. OF. feste.

**festen**, v. tr., *fasten*, 156, 1255; *establish*, 327: 1 sg. festen, 327; imper. pl. -ez, 156; pp. festned, 1255. OE. fæstnian.

**fester**, v. tr.: 3 sg. *festres, 1040. Cf. OF. festrir.

**festival**, adj., *befitting a feast*, 136. OF. festival.

**fete**, n., *fact*, in phrase 'in fete,' *in fact, indeed*, 1106. OF. fait, fet.

**fetly**, adv., *fitly, neatly*, 585.

**fette**, v. tr., *fetch:* inf. 802; 1 sg. fete, 627. OE. fetian.

**fetter**, n.: pl. -ez, 156; fettres, 1255. OE. feter.

**fettle**, v. tr., *make (ready), provide:* pret. 3 sg. 585; pp. 343. ?Cf. OE. fetel, *belt.*

**feture**, n., *features, part of body:* pl. -z, 794. OF. feture.

**fetyse**, adj., *well-proportioned*, 174; as noun, *skill*, 1103: fetys, 1103. OF. fetis.

**fetysely**, adv., *skilfully, beautifully*, 1462.

**fewe**, adj., *few*, 1735. OE. fēawe.

**flake**, n.: pl. -s, 954. Cf. ON. flak.

**flaker**, v. intr., *flutter:* pres. part. flakerande, 1410. Cf. OE. flacor, *flying (of arrows)*, and flicorian, *flutter.*

**flaumbeande**, part. adj., *glowing, flashing*, 1468. OF. flamber.

**flaunk**, n., *flake, spark:* pl. -es, 954. Cf. Sw. flanka, *flake.*

**flay**, v. tr., *terrify:* pret. 3 sg. 960, 1723. OE. (Merc.) flēgan.

**fle**, v. intr., *flee:* inf. 377, 914; pret. 3 pl. flowen, 945, 975. OE. flēon.

**fleez**, n., *fleece* (used figuratively of ornamentation), 1476. OE. flēos.

**fleme**, v., *drive (out), banish:* inf. 287; 3 sg. -z, 596; flemus, 31. OE. flīeman, flēman.

**flesch,** n., *flesh, life* (translating
Vulg. caro) ; 202, 269, 287, 303,
356, 403, 462, 547, 560, 694, 975,
1040: flesche, 1553. OE. flǣsc.

**fleschlych,** adj., *sensual,* 265. OE.
flǣsclic.

**flete,** v. intr., *float,* 387, 432, 1025;
*drift,* 421; tr. *flood, fill,* 685:
inf. 685; 3 sg. -z, 1025; pret.
3 sg. flote, 421, 432; flette, 387.
OE. flēotan.

**flod,** n., *flood,* 324, 369, 397, 404, 415,
429, 450, 531; *water,* 538: pl.
-ez, 324. OE. flōd.

**flokke,** n., *company, host:* pl. -z,
837; -s, 1767. OE. flocc.

**flokke,** v. intr., *flock:* pret. 3 sg.
386.

**flor,** n., *floor,* 133. OE. flōr.

**flor,** n., *flower:* pl. -es, 1476. OF.
flor.

**flose,** v. intr., *?be shaggy:* pret.
3 sg. 1689. Cf. ON. flosna, *to
hang in threads.*

**flot,** n., *grease, scum,* 1011. OE.
*flot (in flotsmeru), or ON. flot.

**flote,** n., *host,* 1212. OF. flote.

**flote,** v., see **flete.**

**flow,** v. intr., *flow:* pret. 3 sg. 428;
floȝed, 397. OE. flōwan.

**flowen,** see **fle** and **flyȝe.**

**flwe,** see **flyȝe.**

**flyȝe,** v. intr., *fly:* pret. 3 sg. flwe,
432; 3 pl. flowen, 1010. OE.
flēogan, flēgan.

**flyȝt,** n., *flight,* 377, 457, 530. OE.
flyht.

**flyt,** n., *strife,* 421. OE. flīt.

**flyte,** v. intr., *strive, chide:* pres.
part. flytande, 950. OE. flītan.

**fo,** n., *foe,* 1219; pl. foes, 1767.
OE. fā(h), adj.

**fode,** n., *food,* 339, 1194; *person:*
pl. -z, *people,* 466. OE. fōda.

**fogge,** n., *grass (of second
growth),* 1683. Etym. unknown.

**fol,** n., *fool,* 750, 996: pl. -es, 202.
OF. fol.

**fol,** adv., see **ful.**

**folde,** n., *earth, land,* 257, 287, 477,
540, 950, 1014, 1665; in phrase
'(up)on folde,' often merely
expletive: 251, 356, 403, 1043,
1147, 1175, 1644. OE. folde.

**folde,** v. tr., *lay:* imper. sg. folde,
1026. OE. fealdan, fāldan.

**fole,** n., *foal:* as gen. pl. fole, 1255.
OE. fola.

**fole,** v. intr., *become mad, foolish:*
3 sg. -s, 1422. Cf. OF. folier.

**foler,** n., *foliation,* 1410 (see note).

**foles,** see **fowle.**

**folȝe,** v. tr., *follow,* 677, 918, 978,
1062, 1165, 1212; w. prepositions,
6, 1752; intr., 429, 974, 1736:
3 sg. -s, 6, 1736; -z, 677, 918;
pret. 3 sg. 1752; 3 pl. 974, 978,
1165; imper. sg. folȝ, 1062;
pres. part. folȝande, 1212; folwande, 429. OE. folgian.

**folk,** n., *folk, people,* 100, 224, 251,
685, 730, 837, 960, 1014, 1096,
1129, 1529, 1665, 1752: folke,
386, 542, 1161; gen. pl. folken,
271. OE. folc.

**folmarde,** n., *polecat,* 534. OE.
*fūl mearð.

**folyly,** adv., *unchastely,* 696.

**folwand,** see **folȝe.**

**foman,** n., *foe,* 1175. OE. fāhman.

**fon,** see **fyne.**

**fonde,** v. intr., *try:* pret. 3 sg. 1103.
OE. fandian.

**fonge,** v. tr., *take,* 540; intr., 377,
457: 3 sg. -z, 457; 3 pl. 540;

pret. 3 sg. feng, 377. OE. fangen,
pp. of fōn.

**font,** n., 164. OE. font.

**for,** prep., 134, 142, 166, 232, etc.;
*on account of, because of,* 47,
177, 178, 179, etc.; *for the sake
of,* 729, 754, 757; *as,* 275, 655,
1087, 1163, 1368; *to,* 75, 143; *in
spite of,* 867, 1332, 1550; *against,*
1143; *from,* 740 (see note); *in
exchange for,* 1118; *for to,*
with inf., 91, 336, 373, 402, etc.;
for þy sake, 922; for noȝt, 888;
for ever, 402, 1802. OE. for.

**for,** conj., 5, 28, 31, 35, 55, etc.; *because,* 67, 559, 735; for þat, 279.

**forbede,** v. tr., *forbid:* pres. 3 sg.
-s, 1147; pp. forboden, 45, 826,
998. OE. forbēodan.

**forfare,** v. intr., *perish,* 560, 571;
tr. *destroy,* 1051, 1168: inf. 1168;
pret. 3 sg. forferde, 560, 571,
1051. OE. forfaran.

**forfete,** v. tr., *forfeit,* 177; 743 (see
note); inf. 177; pres. subj. 3 pl.
forfete, 743. OF. forfait, pp. of
forfaire.

**forgar,** v. tr., *lose, forfeit:* pret.
3 pl. forgart, 240. Cf. ON.
fyrirgöra.

**forge,** v. tr., *make, construct:* pp.
343. OF. forgier.

**forgyve,** v. tr., *forgive:* inf. 731.
OE. forgiefan, -gefan.

**forȝe,** n., *furrow:* pl. -s, 1547. OE.
furh.

**forȝete,** v. tr., *forget,* 463, 739, 1528,
1660; *abandon, forsake,* 203:
inf. 739; 3 sg. -s, 1660; 3 pl. -en,
1528; pret. 3 sg. forȝet, 203;
forȝete, 463. OE. forgietan,
-getan.

**forjust,** n., *overthrow in jousting:*
pp. 1216. Cf. OF. juster.

**forknow,** v. tr., *recognize, perceive:*
pp. forknowen, 119. Cf. OE.
cnāwan.

**forlote,** v. tr., *omit:* imper. pl. -z,
101. Cf. ON. lāta.

**forloyne,** v. tr., *forsake,* 1165;
*stray, err,* 282, 750; forloyne,
*astray, in error,* 750, 1155: 3 pl.
forloyne, 1165; pp. 282; forloyne, 750, 1155. OF. for-
loignier.

**formast,** superl. adj., *first (in
time),* 494. OE. formest, infl.
by mǣst, māst.

**forme,** n., *form, shape; way;* 3,
174, 253, 1468, 1535: pl. -z, 3;
-s, 1468. OF. forme.

**forme,** v. tr., *make, fashion; create:*
imper. sg. forme, 316; pp. 560,
1341, 1462, 1665. OF. former.

**forme-foster,** n., *first offspring,*
257. OE. forma + fōstor.

**fornes,** n., *boiler, cauldron,* 1011.
OF. fornais.

**forray,** v. tr., *pillage:* inf. 1200.
Cf. OF. forrer.

**forredles,** adj., *without counsel, in
dismay,* 1595. See **redles.**

**forsake,** v. tr., *renounce,* 210; absol.
*decline, refuse,* 75: pret. 3 sg.
forsoke, 210; pp. forsaken, 75.
OE. forsacan.

**forselet,** n., *fortress,* 1200. AN.
forcelet.

**forset,** v. tr., *beset:* imper. pl. forsettez, 78. OE. forsettan.

**forsoþe,** adv., *truly,* 1737. OE.
forsōð.

**forst,** n., *frost,* 524. OE. forst.

**forth,** adv., 77, etc.; in phrase 'at
forþ naȝtes,' *late at night,* 1764:

forth, 77, 465, 521, 667, 677, 854,
929, 938, 1683; forthe, 421, 621,
857; forþ, 304; forþe, 1429.
OE. forð.

forty, adj., 224, 369, 403; pron.
faurty, 741, 743. OE. fēowertig.

forþer, v. tr., *hasten:* inf. 304. OE.
fyrðrian.

*forþering, vbl. n., *aiding, for-
warding,* 3.

forþikke, adv., *very thick,* 226. See
þikke.

forþrast, v. tr., *shatter, destroy:* pp.
forþrast, 249. OE. forþræstan.

forþy, conj., *therefore, for that
reason,* 33, 233, 262, 519, 545,
1020, 1105, 1245: forþi, 1175.
OE. forþȳ.

forþynk, v. impers., *regret, repent,*
285; tr., 557: 3 sg. forþynkez,
285; pret. 3 sg. forþoȝt, 557.
Cf. OE. forþencan and þyncan.

forward, n., *agreement, promise,*
1742: forwarde, 327. OE. fore-
weard.

foschip, n., *enmity, hatred,* 919:
fooschip, 918.

fote, n., *foot,* 174, 477; of measure-
ment, 1200; (up)on fote, 79, 88,
432, 914: pl. fete, 156, 255, 397,
903, 1255, 1790; fette, 618, 802;
fet, 1062. OE. fōt.

found, v. intr., *set out, depart:* 3 sg.
-ez, 1764; imper. pl. -ez, 903.
OE. fundian.

founder, v. t.·., *send to the bottom,
cause to be engulfed:* pret. 3 sg.
1014. OF. fondrer.

founs, n., *bottom,* 1026. AN. founz,
OF. fonz.

four(r)e, see faure.

fowle, n, *fowl, bird,* 474, 530, 538:

pl. foulez, 56; foles, 1410. OE.
fugol.

fowle, adj., *foul,* 140: foule, 462.
OE. fūl.

fowle, adv., *shamefully,* 1790.

fowle, v. tr., *defile:* pret. 3 pl. 269;
pp. fouled, 1495.

fox, n., 534. OE. fox.

fraunchyse, n, *liberality,* 750. OF.
franchise.

fray, v. tr., *frighten:* 3 sg. -es, 1553.
Cf. affray.

frayst, v. tr., *examine, test:* inf.
1736. ON. freista.

fre, adj., *free;* as pl. noun, *free-
men,* 88; *noble, fair,* 203, 275,
607, 1062; as noun, 929; as
mere conventional epithet, 861;
*righteous,* 741; contrasted w.
false, 474. OE. frēo.

freke, n., *man,* 6, 139, 177, 236,
245, 282, 593, 897, 1219, 1780,
1798; of angels, 621, 919: pl.
-z, 79, 540, 621, 725; -s, 1680.
OE. freca.

frelych, adj., *noble,* 162; *beautiful,
fair,* 173: frely, 173. OE.
frēolic.

frelych, adv., *fairly:* comp. freloker, 1106.

frende, n., *friend,* 139, 642, 1229;
used loosely, 'fyn frendez'
(Vulg. justi), 721: pl. -z, 399,
721, 861. OE. frēond.

fresch, adj., *bright, unsullied,* 173.
OE. fersc, perhaps infl. by OF.
freis, fresche.

frete, v. tr., *eat, gnaw,* 1040; *de-
vour,* 404: 3 sg. -s, 1040; pp.
freten, 404. OE. fretan.

frette, v. tr., *ornament,* 1476; *furnish,* 339: imper. sg. frette, 339;
pp. 1476. OF. freter.

**fro**, adv., 685. ON. frā.

**fro**, prep., *from,* 31, 129, 221, 282. etc.; fro . . . to, 132, 227, 288; fro þat, as conj., *from the time that,* 1198; fro fyrst þat, 1069; fro, elliptically, as conj., *after,* 353, 833, 1325. ON. frā.

**frok**, n., *dress, garment,* 136: pl. frokkes, 1742. OF. froc.

**froþande**, part. adj., *frothing* (= *vile*), 1721. Cf. ON. froða, n., freyða, v., *froth.*

**fryst**, v. intr., *delay:* 1 sg., fryst, 743. OE. frystan, or ON. fresta.

**fryt**, n., *fruit,* 245, 1043, 1044: fruyt, 1468. OF. fruit.

**fryth**, n., *wood, wooded country,* 534, 1680. ?OE. frið.

**ful**, adv., as intensive, *full, very,* 20, 26, 27, 43, etc.: fol, 1754; foul, 1458. OE. ful.

**ful**, adj., *full,* 83, 364, 1011, 1599, 1626. OE. ful(l).

**fulfylle**, v. tr., *carry out,* 264; *finish, bring to an end,* 1732: inf. 264; pp. 1732. OE. full-fyllan.

**fulȝe**, v. tr., *baptize:* pp. 164. OE. fulli(g)an.

**fulle**, n., in phrase 'to þe fulle,' *to satiety,* 120; *completely,* 343.

**funde**, see **fynde**.

**fust**, see **fyste**.

**fyftene**, adj., *fifteen,* 405. OE. fīftēne.

**fyfty**, adj., 721; hundreth and fyfte, 442; absol. 316, 429, 729, 737, 739. OE. fīftig.

**fygure**, n., *figure,* 1460; (*written*) *character,* 1726: pl. -s, 1460. OF. figure.

**fyle¹**, v. tr., *soil:* pp. 136. OE. *fȳlan.

**fyle²**, v. tr., *cut, form by filing;* pp. 1460. Cf. OM. fil, WS. fēol, *file.*

**fylle**, v. tr., *fill:* 3 sg. -z, 462; 3 pl. -n, 111; imper. pl. -s, 1433; pp. 104, 1008. OE. fyllan.

**fylsen**, v. tr., *support, aid:* pret. 3 sg. 1167, 1644. Cf. OE. fylstan.

**fylter**, v. intr., *become tangled,* 1689; *huddle together,* 224; *join,* 696; *join in battle,* 1191: 3 pl. fylter, *224, 696, 1191; pret. 3 sg. 1689. ?Cf. OF. feltrer.

**fylþe**, n., *filth,* 6, 31, 202, 251, 265, 355, 547, 559, 574, 680, 730, 845, 923, 1051, 1122, 1721, 1798: pl. -z, 14. OE. fȳlð.

**fylyole**, n., *?column, turret:* pl. -s, 1462. OF. fillole.

**fyn**, adj., *fine,* 794, 1742; *choice,* 1122; *good, righteous,* 721. OE. fin.

**fynde**, v. tr., *find, discover,* 3, etc., absol., 203, 1726; *perceive,* 133, 593: inf. 3, 887, 1554; 1 sg. 203, 1726, 1737; 2 sg. -z, 472, 587; 3 sg. -z, 459, 477, 593, *1295; pres. subj. 2 sg. fynde, 902; 3 sg. fynde, 466; pret. 3 sg. fande, 133; 3 pl. founden, 265; fonde, 1212; pp. founden, 547, 694, 730, 1161; founde, 339, 721, 996; fonden, 356; fonde, 173; funde, 1735. OE. findan.

**fyne**, v. intr., *cease,* 369, 450; *stop,* 929: pret. 3 sg. fyned, 450; fon, 369; imper. sg. fyne, 929. OF. finer.

**fynger**, n.: pl. -es, 1103, 1723; fyngres, 1533, 1553. OE. finger.

**fynne**, n., *fin,* 531. OE. finn.

**fyole,** n., *cup:* pl. -s, 1476. OF.
fiole.

**fyr,** adj., *far, distant,* 1680. OE.
feor.

**fyr,** n., *fire,* 627, 954, 1011; *fever,*
1095: pl. -es, 1095. OE. fŷr.

**fyrmament,** n., 221. Lat. firma-
mentum.

**fyrre,** see **fer.**

**fyrst,** adj., 222, 493, 494: fyrste,
205; as noun in adverbial
phrases: fro fryst, 1069, of
fyrst, 1714, *from the beginning.*
OE. fyrst.

**fyrst,** adv., 377, 1530, 1634, 1718.
OE. fyrst.

**fysch,** n., *fish,* 531: pl. -ez, 288.
OE. fisc.

**fyste,** n., *fist, hand,* 1723: fust,
1535. OE. fŷst.

**fyþel,** n., *violin,* 1082. OE. *fiðele.

**fyþer,** n., *feather,* 1026: pl. -ez, 530,
1484. OE. fiðer.

**fyve,** adj., 940; as noun, 737, 739.
OE. fif.

## G.

**galle,** n., *gall,* 1022. OE. gealla,
galla.

**gar,** v. tr., *make, cause,* 896, 1361,
1645; *drive,* 690: 3 sg. -ez, 690;
pret. 3 sg. gart, 1361, 1645; 3 pl.
896. ON. gör(v)a; cf. OE.
gearwian.

**garnade,** in phrase 'apple garnade,'
*pomegranate,* 1044. OF. (pome)
garnade.

**garnyst,** part. adj., *ornamented,*
1277. OF. garniss-, from garnir.

**gate,** n., *way,* 676, 767, 931. ON.
gata.

**gaule,** n., *vile person, wretch:* pl.
-z, 1525. The word is used in the

sense of *filth, Pearl* 1059 and
*Pat.* 285. Cf. the similar use of
'filth' as a term of abuse in *Wm.
of Palerne,* 2542, 'þat foule
felþe' = 'wretch.' OE. gealla,
galla, *sore on a horse,* perhaps
same word as gealla, *gall* (see
galle).

**gay,** adj., *merry,* 830; *bright,* 1315,
1444, 1811. OF. gai.

**gaye,** adv., *brightly, gorgeously,*
1568.

**gayn,** adj., *profitable, good,* 259,
749. ON. gegn.

**gayn,** v. intr., *avail:* 3 pl. -es, 1608.
ON. gegna.

**gaynly,** adj., *gracious,* 728.

**gazafylace,** n., 'the box in which
offerings to the Temple were
received,'—NED., 1283. OF.
gazophilace<Late Lat. gazo-
phylacium.

**geder,** v. refl., *gather:* inf. 1363.
OE. gaderian.

**gef,** see **give.**

**gemme,** n.: pl. -s, 1441, 1468. OF.
gemme.

**gender,** v. tr., *beget:* pp. 300. OF.
gendrer.

**gendre,** n., *kind:* pl. -z, 434. OF.
gendre.

**gent,** adj., *fair, exquisite,* 1495.
OF. gent.

**gentryse,** n., *nobility,* 1159. OF.
genterise.

**gentyle,** adj., *noble,* 1235, 1257;
*fair,* 1309; absol. as pl. n., gentyle, *nobles,* 1216: superl. gentylest, 1180. OF. gentil.

**gentyle,** adj., *heathen, pagan,* 76
(see note), 1432: gentyl, 76.
OF. gentil.

**gentylman,** n.: pl. gentylmen, 864.

**gere,** n., *apparel,* 1811; *apparatus*
(of vessels of temple), 1505; as
coll., *affairs,* 16: guere, 1505.
ON. görvi; OE. gearwe.

**gere,** v. tr., *clothe, attire,* 1568;
*adorn,* 1344; *array, set up,* 1444:
pp. 1344, 1444, 1568. See **gere,**
n., and **gar.**

**gest,** n., *guest,* 641: pl. -es, 830, 862,
872; -ez, 98. OE. gest; infl. by
ON. gestr.

**get,** v. tr.: imper. sg. ʒete, 842 (see
note); pp. geten, 1505; ?ʒat, 66
(see note). OE. -gietan, -getan,
ON. geta.

**gette,** n., *device, fashion:* pl. -s,
1354. OF. jet.

**gilde,** v. tr., *gild:* pp. gilde, 1344.
OE. gyldan.

**give,** v. tr., *give,* 259, etc.; *make
known, show,* 1326: 3 sg. gives,
1528; pret. 3 sg. gef, 753, 1326;
pp. geven, 259, 1627. ON. gefa;
OE. giefan, gefan.

**glad,** adj., *happy, merry,* 123, 641,
830, 1077. OE. glæd.

**glade,** v. tr., *make glad,* 1083: pret.
3 sg. 499. OE. gladian.

**glam,** n., *noise,* 849; *speech,* 830;
*message,* 499. ON. glamm.

**glede,** n., *kite,* 1696. OE. glida.

**glem,** n., *radiance,* 218. OE. glæm.

**glent,** v. intr., *shine:* pret. 3 sg.
glent, 218. Cf. Sw. dial. glänta.

**glette,** n., *filth, sin,* 306, 573. OF.
glette.

**glod,** see **glyde.**

**glope,** v. intr., *stare in fright, be
amazed:* pret. 3 sg. 849. Cf.
Norw. dial. glopa.

**glopnedly,** adv., *fearfully, in a state
of alarm,* 896. Cf. ON. glūpna,
and ME. glope, above.

**glori,** n., 1337. OF. glorie.

**glorious,** adj., 218. OF. glorious.

**glory,** v. intr., *exult:* pret. 3 pl.
1522. OF. glorier.

**glotoun,** n., *glutton:* pl. -es, 1505.
AN. glutun, OF. gluton.

**glyde,** v. intr., *go (quietly), walk,
come:* 3 sg. -z, 325, 677, 767;
-s, 1590; pret. 3 sg. glod, 499;
pres. part. glydande, 296. OE.
glīdan.

**glyffe,** v. intr., *stare in amazement,
become frightened:* pret. 3 sg.
glyfte, 849. Cf. Scotch gliff.

**\* gnede,** adv., *in a niggardly, beg-
garly manner,* 146. OE. (Merc.)
\*gnēde.

**go,** v. intr., *go, walk;* w. forth, 77:
inf. 810; 3 sg. gotz, 325, 341;
gos, 611, 1590; pres. subj. 1 pl.
gon, 1811; pret. 3 sg. ʒede, 432,
973; imper, pl. gotz, 77; pres.
part. goande, 931. OE. gān.

**goblot,** n., *goblet:* pl. -es, 1277;
gobelotes, 1475. OF. gobelet.

**God** (god), n., *god,* 1324, 1663; pl.
goddez, 1608, 1719; goddes,
1165, 1343, 1522, 1525; *God (of
Israel),* 16, 231, 259, 296, 301,
411, 508, 591, 611, 641, 677, 728,
739, 749, 753, 765, 947, 1102, 1162,
1326, 1528, 1598; *God (the Son),*
1072; under God, 1077: Godde,
767; Gode, 1730; gen. Godez,
341, 499, 896; Goddes, 1627, 1662;
Goddez, 1799. OE. god.

**god,** adj., *good,* 123, 137, 341, 639,
641, 677, 849: gode, 1619; good,
611; goud, 1102, 1447; goude,
1525; comp. better, 704, 865, 870;
absol. þe better and þe wers, 80;
þe luþer and þe better, 163;
superl. best, 276; absol., 114, 130,

913, 1202, 1242; of þe best(e), 170, 1179. OE. gōd.

**god,** see also **goud,** n.

**godlych,** adj., *gracious, benevolent,* 753: superl. godelest, 1608. OE. gōdlic.

**golde,** n., 1271, 1276, 1279, 1283, 1344, 1408, 1444, 1456, 1475, 1476, 1481, 1488, 1569, 1638, 1744: gold, 1404. OE. gold.

**golden,** adj., 1525.

**gome,** n., *man,* 137, 145, 1337; *servant,* 77: pl. -z, 77, 99; -s, 1315. OE. guma.

**Gomorre,** prop. n., *Gomorrah,* 690, 722, 911: Gomorra, 957. OF. Gomorre, OE. Gomorra.

**gorde,** v. intr., *rush,* 911: pret. 3 sg. gorde, 957. Etym. uncertain.

**gore,** n., *filth,* 306. OE. gor.

**gorst,** n., *gorse, heath covered with gorse:* pl. -ez, 99, 535. OE. gorst.

**gost,** n., *spirit,* 325, 1627: goste, 728; pl. gostes, 1598. OE. gāst.

**gote,** n., *stream:* pl. -z, 413. Cf. MLG. gote.

**goud,** n., *good thing, benefit,* 1048, 1326, 1528; as coll., *wealth,* 1315; in pl., *goods, property,* 1200, 1282: goud, 1048; god, 1315; pl. goudes, 1200, 1326, 1528; godes, 1282. OE. gōd, neut. See also **god,** adj.

**goun,** n., *garment,* 145: pl. -es, 1568. OF. goune.

**governor,** n., *ruler:* pl. -es, 1645. OF. governour.

**grace,** n., *favor (of God), grace, mercy,* 731, 758, 1097, 1522, 1811; *the divine influence in man,* 296; *favor asked, prayer,* 1347. OF. grace.

**gracyously,** adv., *in a pleasing manner,* 488. Cf. OF. gracious, adj.

**grattest,** see **grete.**

**graunt,** v. tr., *grant, consent,* 810; absol. 765: 1 sg. graunt, 765; pret. 3 pl. 810. OF. granter.

**graunt mercy,** an expression of thanks, 765. OF. grant merci.

**grave,** v. tr., *bury,* 1332; *ornament by engraving,* 1475; *engrave, write,* 1324, 1544: pp. graven (all cases). OE. grafan.

**gray,** adj., 1696: graye, 430. OE. grǣg.

**graýþe,** v. tr., *prepare, equip,* 343; *array,* 1485: pp. 343, 1485. ON. greiða.

**graýþely,** adv., *promptly, readily,* 341. ON. greiðliga.

**grece,** n., *steps,* 1590. OF. grez, pl. of gre.

**gredirne,** n., *gridiron,* 1277. Pop. etym.<gredire, variant of gredile (AN. gredil, OF. greïl).

**greme,** n., *wrath,* 16, 947. ON. gremi.

**gremen,** v. tr., *anger, vex,* 1347; intr., *become angry,* 138: inf. 1347; pret. 3 sg. 138. OE. gremian.

**grene,** adj., *green,* 488, 602, 767; as noun, (*green*) *grass,* 634; *anything green, verdure,* 1028. OE. grēne.

**gresse,** n., *grass,* 1028. OE. græs.

**grete,** adj., *great,* 138, 689, 765, 837, 947, 963, 964, 969, 1037, 1380, 1767, 1782; grete streete, *highway* (cf. F. grande route), 77; as pl. noun, 1363: gret. 12, 1283, 1321, 1348, 1534; superl. grattest, 1645. OE. grēat.

**gretyng,** vbl. n., *weeping,* 159. OE.
grētan.

**greve,** n., *thicket, grove:* pl. -s, 99.
OE. grǣfa.

**greve,** v. tr., *vex, anger,* 302, 306,
774; *harm, punish,* 138: inf.
138; pp. 302, 306, 774. OF.
grever.

**greving,** vbl. n., *grieving,* 159.

**grone,** v. intr., *groan:* inf. 1077.
OE. grānian.

**gropande,** part. adj., *searching,
testing,* 591. OE. grāpian.

**gropyng,** vbl. n., *touch, handling,*
1102.

**grounde,** n., *ground, earth,* 445, 798,
910, 957, 1214, 1234, 1307, 1330;
*earth as opposed to heaven,* 1324,
1663; *foundation,* 911; fig. (of
God), 591; *upon grounde,* 1363.
OE. grund.

**growe,** v. intr., *grow,* 1028, 1043;
*increase,* 277: inf. 1028, 1043;
pret. 3 pl. grewen, 277. OE.
grōwan.

**gruche,** v. tr., *be unwilling to grant,*
1347; absol., 810: pres. subj.
3 pl. gruchen, 1347; pret. 3 pl.
gruȝt, 810. OF. grucher.

**grymly,** adv., *dreadfully,* 1534. OE.
grimlīce.

**grymme,** adj., *horrible,* 1553, 1696.
OE. grim(m).

**grysly,** adj., *horrible, ghastly,* 1534.
OE. grislic.

**gryspyng,** n., *gnashing,* 159. Contracted from OE. gristbitung.

**guere,** see gere.

**gye,** v. tr., *govern, rule:* inf. 1663;
3 sg. -s, 1598, 1627. OF. guier.

**gylt,** n., *guilt,* 731: gult, 690. OE.
gylt.

**gyn,** n., *contrivance* (= *ark,* cf. *Pat.*
285), 491. Aphetic form of OF.
engin.'

### H.

**Habraham,** see, Abraham.

**hach,** n., *hatch, deck,* in phrase 'under hatch,' 409. OE. hæc.

**hagherlych,** adv., *fitly,* 18: haȝerly,
1707. Cf. ON. hagliga, *skilfully.*

**halde,** v. tr., *hold,* 734; *possess,
maintain,* 35, 652, 1349; *take,
preserve,* 335; *adhere to, keep
to* (of promise or punishment),
244, 1636; *measure,* 315; *contain,* or perh. *extend,* 1387;
*consider,* 276, 1062, 1078, 1140;
halde utter, *keep cut,* 42; w. of,
*maintain allegiance to, be faith-
ful to,* 1162: inf. 652, 1162,
1636; 2 sg. -z, 734; -s, 1062;
3 sg. -z, 35; -s, 1140, 1349; pret.
3 sg. helde, 1387; imper. sg.
halde, 335; holde, 315; pp.
halden, 42, 244, 276, 1078. OE.
healdan, hāldan.

**hale,** v. intr., *hasten,* 380; hale of,
'take a "*pull*" at'—*NED.,* take
a drink of, 1520: pret. 3 sg.
1520; 3 pl. aled, 380. OF. haler.

**half,** n., *side, shore,* 1039; *quarter,*
950; *half, part,* 719; on Godez
halve, *in God's name,* 896: halve,
896; pl. halves, 1039; half, 950.
OE. healf, half.

**halȝe,** v. tr., *consecrate,* pret. 3 sg.
506, 1163. OE. hālgian.

**halke,** n., *recess:* pl. -z, 104, 321.
'Perhaps a diminutive of OE.
*halh, healh, corner'—NED.*

**halle,** n., *hall, room, banquet-hall,*
90, 129, 1391, 1402, 1439, 1588;
pl. -z, 321. OE. heall.

halle-dore, n., 44.
halle-flor, n., 1397.
halsed, see haylse.
halt, adj., *lame*, 102. OE. healt, halt.
halyday, n., *festival*, 134, 141, 166. OE. hāligdæg.
hamper, v. tr., *pack:* pret. 3 sg. hamppred, 1284. Prob. here from ME. hamper, n.<OF. hanaper.
hande, see honde.
hande-helme, n., *helm moved by hand*, 419. OE. hand + helma.
hapen, v. impers., *befall:* 3 sg. -ez, 27. Cf. Sw. dial. happa, and see happe, n.
happe, n., *blessing, state of blessedness:* pl. -z, 24. ON. happ.
happe, v. tr., *cover:* imper. sg. happe, 626. Etym. unknown.
harde, adj., *hard; difficult, severe;* 442, 524, 663, 714, 1150, 1342: hard, 562, 1209; comp., harder, 50. OE. heard.
harde, adv., *hard,* 159, 424; *violently,* 44; *fiercely,* 1204; *severely, harshly,* 543, 596. OE. hearde.
hardy, adj., *bold,* 143. OF. hardi.
hare, n.: pl. -z, 391, 535. OE. hara.
harlot, n., *base fellow, beggar, villain,* 34, 39, 148, 1584; of Sodomites, 860, 874: gen. sg. -ez, 874; ?harlatez, 34; pl. -ez, 860; -es, 1584. OF. harlot.
harlottrye, n., *obscenity, unchastity,* 579.
harme, n., 166. OE. hearm.
harme, v., tr.: inf. 1503. OE. hearmian.
hasp, v. tr., *fasten:* pp. 419. OE. hæpsian.

haste, n.: in hast(e), 599, 1503; upon haste, 902; wyth haste, 39: hast, 599. OF. haste.
haste, v. tr., *urge on:* pret. 3 pl. 937. OF. haster.
hastyly, adv., *hastily, quickly,* 1150: hastyfly, 200. Cf. OF. hastif.
hate, n., 915, 1138; *outburst of hate or wrath,* 714. Cf. OE. hete, infl. by ON. hatr, and OE. hatian, v.
hate, v. tr.; 3 sg. -s, 168, 577; pret. 3 sg. 396, 1090. OE. hatian.
hatel, adj., *fierce,* 227; as noun, *anger,* 200. OE. hatol.
hatere, n.: pl. -z, *clothes,* 33. OE. pl. hæteru.
hatte, n., *hat* (of knight's headgear): pl. -s, 1209. OE. hæt.
hat(t)e, see hete.
hatter, see hote, adv.
haþel, n., *man,* 27, 35, 409, 594, 895, 1330, 1597, 1762. OE. æþele, or perhaps metathesis of OE. hæleþ (Holthausen).
have, v. tr., *have,* 67, 74, 123, 164, etc.; *put,* 1443; *hold,* 941, 1704; w. on, upon, *wear,* 30, 141, 1276; as auxiliary, 66, 69, 75, 95, etc.; forms: inf. 164, 183, 260, 726, 1140; haf, 972, 1320, 1455; 1 sg. haf, 66, 67, 652, 735, etc. (9 times); have, 193, 351, 749, 1636; 2 sg. hatz, 141, 328, 346, 1595, 1597, 1625; habbez, 95; havez, 171; 3 sg. hatz, 30, 306, 517, 586 (19 times); habbez, 308, 325; habbes, 995; habes, 555; 1 pl. haf, 95; 3 pl. han, 202, 693, 694, 774, 1631; haf, 709; habbe, 105; habbez, 75; hatz, 517; pres. subj. 2 sg. haf, 616, 1115; 3 sg. have, 317, 590; 3 pl. haf, 692; pret. ind. 3 sg.

hade, 74, 461, 610, 640, etc. (34
times) ; had, 248, 424, 679; 3 pl.
hade, 831, 941, 1466, 1704, 1779;
haden, 123, 833, 1162, 1719; had,
702; pret. subj. 2 sg. hade, 1138;
3 sg. hade, 424, 1229, 1232, 1244,
1320; 3 pl. hade, 1484; imper.
sg. haf, 321, 349; pp. hade, 1443;
nade (= ne hade), 404. OE.
habban.

**havek**, n., *hawk:* pl. -ez, 537. OE.
hafoc.

**haven**, n., 420. OE. hæfen.

**haylse**, v. tr., *greet:* pret. 3 sg. 612;
halsed, 1621; 3 pl. 814. ON.
heilsa (halsed, 1621, perh. infl.
by OE. hālsian).

**hayre**, see **ayre**.

**he**, pers. pron.: masc. he, 3, 17, 21,
24, etc.; in absol. cst., 1219,
1573; hym (dat. or acc.), 6, 16,
154, 157, etc.; refl., 63, 124, 125,
294, etc.; ?attracted from nom.,
1118, see note: him, 745, 1230,
1297; hem, 889, 915. Fem. ho,
2, 475, 477, 478, etc.; hir (dat.
or acc.), 480², 482, 624. Neut.
hit, 11, 22, 23, 32, etc.; refl., 927;
redundant, 926; anticipative,
1553; with plur. verb., 112, 171,
253, 379, etc. Plural, þay, 10, 11,
12, 61, etc.; thay, 9 (*th* capital) ;
he, 62, 657, *1267; hem (dat.
or acc.), 24, 67, 68, 71, etc.; refl.
62, 170, 267, 1363: hym, 130, 820,
843; ?hom, 1715. OE. hē, hēo,
hit, etc.

**hede(s)**, see **heved**.

**he3e**, see **hy3e**.

**he3þe**, n., *height*, 317; upon hy3t,
458. OE. hēahðo, hēhðu.

**helde**, v. intr., *fall*, 1330; *proceed,
go*, 39, 678; *incline, be disposed,*

1681: 3 sg. -s, 1330; -z, 678;
pret. subj.(?) 3 sg. helded, 39;
pp. heldet, 1681. OE. hieldan,
heldan.

**helde**, see **holde**.

**hele**¹, n., *heel:* pl. -s, 1789. OE.
hēla.

**hele**², n., *health*, 1099; *welfare,
safety*, 920. OE. hǣlu.

**hele**, v. tr., *heal:* pret. 3 sg. 1098.
OE. hǣlan.

**helle**, n., *hell*, 168, 227, 577, 911, 968;
personified, 961. OE. hell.

**helle-hole**, n., *the pit of hell*, 223.
OE. hell + hol.

**help**, n., 1345. OE. help.

**helpe**, v. tr., *help:* inf. 762; pret.
3 sg. help, 1163. OE. helpan.

**hem**, see **he**.

**hemself, hemselven**, see **self**.

**hence**, adv., 944. Cf. OE. heonon.

**hende**, adj., *gracious*, 612, 1172; as
pl. noun, *pleasant things*, 1083:
hynde, 1098. Cf. OE. gehende.

**hendelayk**, n., *courtesy*, 860.

**henge**, v. tr., *hang*, 1584; intr.,
1734: inf. heng, 1734. ON.
hengja.

**hent**, v. tr., *seize, take*, 376, 883,
1150, 1179, 1209; *receive*, 151;
refl. (w. dat.), *take to oneself,
practise*, 710: 3 pl. henttez, 710;
pres. subj. 3 sg. hent, 151; pret.
3 sg. hent, 376, 1150, 1179; 3 pl.
883, 1209. OE. hentan.

**hepe**, n., *heap*, 912, 1211; *host,
great company*, 1775: pl. -s, 912,
1775. OE. hēap.

**her**, poss. pron., *their*, 24, 75, 76, 117,
etc.; here, 978; hor, 1524;
þayres, absol., 1527. See also **he**.

**her**, poss. pron., *her*, 378, 477, 980,
*981, 1085; hir, 487, 667, 985,
1072, 1119. See also **he**.

herafter, adv., 291: hereafter, 1319. OE. hēræfter.

herbisyde, adv., *near here,* 926.

here, adv., 619, 622, 842, 875, 927, 943, 1563, 1613, 1629, 1725, 1740; here away, *hither,* 647 (see note). OE. hēr.

here, n., *company,* 409, 902. OE. here.

here, see ayre, n.

here, v. tr., *hear,* 197, etc., w. 'of,' 193: inf. 1164; pret. 1 sg. herde, 197; 3 sg., 961, 973, 1586; pp. 193, 1597. OE. hīeran, hēran.

here, v. tr., *worship, glorify:* pret. 3 pl. hered, 1086; heyred, 1527. OE. herian.

hereinne, adv., 147, 1595. OE. hērinne.

herʒe, v. tr., *ravage, pillage:* 3 sg. -z, 1294; pret. 3 sg. herʒed (up), 1179; pp. heyred, 1786. OE. her(g)ian.

heritage, n., 652. OF. heritage.

herken, v. tr., *hear,* 193; *give heed to,* 980; *attend,* 1369; *seek,* 458: inf. herken, 458; herkken, 980, 1369; pp. herkned, 193. OE. hercnian.

hern, n., *eagle:* pl. -ez, 537 (see note). OE. earn.

herself, see self.

hert, n., *heart,* 27, etc.; *purpose,* 682: hert, 27, 31, 172, 204, 283, 563, 575, 592, 594, 682, 850, 897, 1002, 1083, 1240, 1347, 1420, 1425, 1434, 1538, 1625, 1653, 1655, 1681, 1711, 1723; hertte, 620; pl. herttez, 516. OE. heorte.

hert, v. tr., *hurt:* pret. 3 sg. hert, 1195. OF. hurter.

hertte, n., *hart:* pl. -z, 391; -s, 535. OE. heor(o)t.

hervest, n., *harvest,* 523. OE. hærfest.

hest, n., *command,* 94, 341; *promise,* 1636: heste, 94; pl. -es, 341. Cf. OE. hǣs.

hete, n., *heat,* 524, 604. OE. hǣtu.

hete, v. tr., *promise, vow,* 24, 665, 714, 1162, 1346, 1636; passive, *to be called,* 299, 448, 926, 1322: 1 sg. hyʒt, 665; 3 sg. hetes, 1346; hat, 448; hatte, 926; pret. 3 sg. hyʒt, 24, 299; pp. hyʒt, 714, 1162, 1636; hatte, 1322. OE. hātan.

heterly, adv., *cruelly,* 1222; *quickly,* 380. Cf. MLG. hetter.

heþe, n., *heath,* 535. OE. hǣð.

heþyng, n., *scorn, contempt,* 579, 710. ON. hæðing.

heved, n., *head,* 876, 1707: hede, 150; pl. hedes, 1265. OE. hēafod.

heven, v. tr., *raise, lift; exalt;* 506, 920, 1601; *extol,* 24: pret. 3 sg. 24, 506; pp. 920, 1601, 1714. OE. hafenian.

heven, n., *heaven,* 33, *50, 161, 206, 227, 389, 393, 603, 734, 808, 961, 1336, 1340, 1527, 1643, 1664, 1688, 1721, 1807. OE. heofon.

heven-glem, n., *gleam of dawn,* 946.

Heven-kyng, n., *King of heaven,* 1628. OE. heofoncyning.

heyned, see here and herʒe.

hidde, part. adj., *hidden,* 1600; as noun, *hidden thing, secret,* 1628: hide, 1600. See hyde, v.

hider, adv., *hither,* 100, 922. OE. hider.

hil, n., *hill,* 902, 927, 946: hille, 430; hylle, 406; pl. hilles, 447; hyllez, 380. OE. hyll.

hile, v. tr., *cover:* pp. 1397. ON. hylja.

hir, see he.

his, poss. pron., 3, 9, 10, 11, etc.: absol. 1140, 1163: hys, 8, 63, 467; hise, 1216. See also he.

hit, poss. pron., *its,* 264, 956, 1016, 1021, 1033. See also he.

hitself, see self.

hitte, v. intr., *come:* 3 sg. -z, 479. ON. hitta.

ho, see he.

ho-beste, n., *female animal:* pl. -z, 337.

hod, n., *hood,* 34. OE. hōd.

hodlez, n., *without a hood,* 643.

hol, adj., *whole, sound,* 102, 594. OE. hāl.

holde, n., *possession, dominion* (Dan. 5. 11, in regno tuo), 1597. OE. heald.

holde, see halde.

hole-foted, adj., *web-footed,* 538.

holʒe, adj., *hollow,* 1695. OE. holh.

holk, v. tr., *dig:* pret. 3 sg. holkked (out), 1222. Cf. MLG. holken.

holly, adv., *wholly, entirely,* 104, 1140.

holy, adj., 1602, 1625, 1799. OE. hālig.

home, n., 240, 1762. OE. hām.

homme, n., *bend of knee:* pl. -s, 1541. OE. hom(m).

honde, n., *hand:* honde, 174, 734, 740, 1106, 1412, 1510, 1544, 1704; hande, 941; hondez, 663, 883; hondes, 1445, 1718; handez, 34, 155; handes, 1341. OE. hand, hond.

hondel, v. tr., *handle:* 3 pl. hondel, 11. OE. handlian.

hondelyng, vbl. n., *handling, touch,* 1101.

hondewhyle, n., *moment,* 1786. OE. handhwīl.

honest, adj., *virtuous, pure,* 14, 18, 594; *seemly, fair,* 166, 638; *clean* (of animals), 505: honeste, 18. OF. honeste.

honestly, adv., *chastely,* 705; *in a seemly manner, fittingly,* 134, 1083.

honor, n., 35. OF. (h)onor.

honor, v. tr.: inf. 1714; 3 sg. -ez, 594; pret. 3 sg. 1340. OF. (h)onorer.

honyse, v. tr., *ruin, destroy:* 3 sg. -z, 596. OF. honiss–, from honir.

hope, n., *expectation,* 714; *belief,* 1653. OE. hopa.

hope, v. intr., *hope, expect,* 860; tr., *think, suppose,* 148, 663, 1681: 2 sg. -z, 148; 3 sg. 663; pret. 3 sg. 860, 1681. OE. hopian.

hore, n., *hair:* pl. in phrase 'camp hores,' 1695. ON. hár.

hors, n., *horse,* on hors, 79, 1209: horce, 1684. OE. hors.

hortyng, vbl. n., *harming,* 740. OF. hurter.

horwed, part. adj., *unclean,* 335. OE. *horgian.

horye, v. tr., *hurry:* pret. 3 pl. 883. Etym. obscure.

hote, adj., *hot,* 626; *angry, wrathful,* 200, 1602; *biting,* 1195: hot, 200. OE. hāt.

hote, adv., *hotly,* 707: comp. hatter, 1138. OE. hāte.

hound, n.: pl. -ez, 961. OE. hund.

hous, n., 104, 143, 376, 623, 808, 836, 1786; (of the temple), 1284, 1290, 1714, 1799: hows, 1714; pl. houses, 1391; howsez, 553, 805. OE. hūs.

hous-dore, n., 602.

housholde, n., 18.

hove¹, v. tr., *lift, raise,* 206, etc.;
refl., 927: 3 sg. -z, 927; pp.
hoven, 206, 413, 1451; hofen,
1711. Cf. ME. hoven, pp. of
heve<OE. hebban.

hove², v. intr., *soar,* 458; *?come
flying, hover,* 485: 3 sg. -z, *458,
485. Etym. unknown.

how, adv., 140, etc.; *how is it that,
why,* 143; *how so, howsoever,*
1753; how, 143, 209, 270, 464,
466, 496, 682, 738, 1070, 1112,
1753; hou, 140, 915, 1110, 1150,
1154, 1159. OE. hū.

hue, see hwe.

huge, adj., *great,* 4, 1659; quasi-
adv., 1311. Aphetic from OF.
ahuge.

hundreth, n., hundreth and fyfte,
442: pl. hundred, 315; hundreth,
426. OE. hundred, ON. hun-
draðˀ.

hunger, n., 1195, 1243. OE. hungor.

hurkle, v. intr., *crouch, rest,* 406;
*cower, bend,* 150: 3 sg. hurkelez,
150; pret. 3 sg. 406. Cf. MLG.
hurken.

hurl, v. intr., *rush,* 376, 413, 874,
1204, 1211; tr., *hurl,* 44, 223:
3 pl. -es, 1204; pret. 3 sg. 376,
874; pres. part. hurlande, 413,
1211; pp. 44, 223. ?Imitative;
cf. LG. hurreln.

hurrok, n., *?'the part of a boat between the sternmost seat and the
stern'—NED.,* 419. Etym. uncertain; Ekwall (*Engl. Stud.* 44.
169) suggested OE. þurruc, by
subtraction of þ mistaken for
the article.

hwe, n., *form, aspect,* 1707; *hue,
color:* pl. -s, 1119, hues, 1483.
OE. hīw.

hwed, part. adj., *colored,* 1045.

hyde, n., *hide,* 630. OE. hȳd.

hyde, v. tr., *hide:* inf. hyde, 682;
huyde, 915. OE. hȳdan. See
also hidde.

hyȝe, adj., *high, lofty,* 115, 379, 380,
406, 451, 535, 537, 1391, 1664;
*exalted, great,* 35, 193, 1330, 1332,
1749; (esp. of God), 50, 542,
1162, 1653, 1660, 1711; *intense,*
604; *fast,* 976; *advanced,* 656;
*loud,* 1564; on hyȝe, 413; as
noun, *high region,* 391; superl.
as noun (of God), 1653: hyȝe,
50, 193, etc. (14 times); hiȝe,
1332, 1564; heȝe, 1391; hyȝ, 35,
379; superl. hyȝest, 406, 451,
1653; heȝest, 1749. OE. hēah,
hēh.

hyȝe, adv., *high,* 206, 458, 552, 1166,
1381, 1498; *loud,* 1206, 1783:
hiȝe, 1206, 1381. OE. hēah, hēh.

hyȝe, n., *servant:* pl. -z, 67. OE.
hīga.

hyȝe, v. intr., *hasten:* 3 sg. -z, 538,
610; -s, 1762; pret. 3 sg. 623;
heȝed, 1584; 3 pl. 392; imper.
sg. hyȝ, 33. OE. hīgian.

hyȝly, adv., *745, 1527: hiȝly, 920.
OE. hēahlice, hēhlice.

hyȝt, n., see heȝþe.

hyȝt, v., see hete.

hyȝtle, v. tr., *adorn, ornament:* pret.
3 sg. 1290. Etym. unknown; cf.
ME. hyȝt.

hylle(z), see hil.

hynde, see hende.

hyne, n., *stripling, fellow:* pl. hyne,
822. OE. hīna, gen. pl. of hīwa.
See also hyȝe, n.

hyrn, n., *corner:* pl. hyrne, 1294.
OE. hyrne.

**hyve,** n., 223. OE. hȳf.

**hymself, himself, -selven,** see **self.**

## I.

**I,** pers. pron.: 64, 66, 67, 69, etc.;
me (dat. or acc.), 25, 68, 70, 105,
etc.; refl., 553, 914, 915; pl.:
we, 95, 622, 670, 843, etc.; uus
(dat. or acc.), 246, 471, 473, 842,
etc. OE. ic.

**ibrad,** see **ibrede.**

**ibrede,** v. tr., *overspread, cover:*
pret. 3 sg. ibrad, 1693. OE. ge-
brǣdan.

**idolatrye,** n., 1173. OF. idolatrye.

**if,** conj., 12, 13, 36, 49, 99, 165, 291,
472, 550, 586, 752², 763, 771, 841,
928, 1029, 1053, 1063, 1065, 1125,
1129, 1133, 1632, 1633; *even if,*
*though,* 914; *granted that,* 1665;
*whether,* 607, 692; what if, 737,
741, 751; *but if, unless,* 1110,
1360; if þat, 759: ȝif, 584, 613,
615, 736, 750, 758, 775, 1089, 1122,
1153. OE. gif.

**ilk,** adj., *same, very,* 105, 195, 571,
573, 782, 1755, 1756; pron., 511,
930: ilke, 511, 569, 628, 675,
1233, 1669. OE. ilca, n.

**ille,** adj., *evil,* 272, 864; as noun,
*harm,* 735; *evil,* 577: pl. -z, 577.
ON. illr.

**ille,** adv., *ill,* 73, 693, 955, 1141. ON.
illa.

**ilyche,** adv., *in the same manner,*
*equally,* 228, 1386, 1477; *at the*
*same pace,* 975: ilych, 1386;
aliche, 1477. OE. gelīce; cf.
ON. ālīka.

**image,** n., 983. OF. image.

**in,** adv., 679, 1240, 1782. OE. in.

**in,** prep., *in,* 3, 4, 6, 17, etc.: *into,*
98, 559, 689, 725, 1581; *among,*

730; *within* (temporal), 1620;
*during,* 173, 369; *at,* 781; expressing manner, 301, 328, 612,
639, 827; *by means of, through,*
249, 1095, 1667; *in respect to,*
19, 236, 276; *in* phrases: in
armes, 1306; in asent, 788; in
blande, 885; in bour, 1126; in
compaynye, 119; in daunger,
416; in felaȝschyp, 271; in erde,
601; in fere, 399, 696; in fete,
1106; in hast, 599; in honde,
1704; in hit kynde, 1016; in
londe, 122; in lykyng, 239; in
þe myddes, 1388; in þe plow, 68;
in sete, 557, 1055; in space, 1606;
in stoundes, 1603; in talle, in
tuch, 48; in twynne, 966; in
þronge, 504, 754; in þrynne,
1727: inne (at end of clause),
169, 290, 1092. OE. in.

**inde,** see **ynde.**

**inhelde,** v. tr., used absol., *pour in:*
pp. inhelde, 1520. See **helde,** v.

**inmong,** prep., *among,* 1485. Ana-
lytical variant of ME. imong,
from OE. gemang.

**inmongez,** prep., *among,* 278.

**inmydde,** prep., *in the midst of,*
1677. Variant of ME. onmidde,
amidde, OE. on midde.

**inmyddez,** prep., *in the midst of,*
125. See also **myddes.**

**innoghe,** adj., *enough,* 1303, 1359;
absol., 1671; as exclam., 669: innoȝe, 808, 1671; inogh, 116. OE.
genōh.

**innoghe,** adv., *enough,* 297. OE.
genōh.

**inobedyent,** adj., 237. OF. in-
obedient, or Late Lat. inobedient-
em.

**inspryng**, v. tr., *leap into:* pret. 3 sg. inspranc, 408. Cf. OE. springan.

**instrument**, n.: pl. -es, 1081. OF. instrument.

**insy3t**, n., *regard, opinion,* 1659.

**into**, prep., 129, 140, 180, 223, 234, etc.; *up to* (temporal), 660. OE. intō.

**inwith**, adv., *within,* 14.

**ire**, n., 572. OF. ire.

**Israel**, n., 1179, 1294: gen. sg. Israel, 1314. Lat. Israel.

**iwysse**, adv., *certainly,* 84. OE. gewiss, adj.

### J.

**jape**, n., (*evil*) *trick, device* (of carnal intercourse): pl. -z, 272, 864, 877. OF. *jape.

**Japheth**, prop. n., 300. OE. Jafeð, OF. Japhet.

**javel**, n., *low fellow:* pl. -es, 1495. Etym. obscure.

**Jerico**, prop. n., *Jericho,* 1216. OF. Jerico.

**jeaunt**, n., *giant:* pl. -ez, 272. OF. jeaunt, geaunt.

**Jerusalem**, prop. n., abbreviated jrlem, 1180, 1235, 1432; jrhlem, 1159; jsrlem, 1441. OF. Jerusalem.

**jolef**, adj., *fair, noble,* 300; *worthy, true,* 864: jolyf, 864. OF. jolif.

**jostyse**, n., *judge,* 877. OF. justise.

**joy**, n., 491, 1309: joye, 128, 1304. OF. joye.

**joyne**[1], v. tr., *join, mix,* 434 (see note); intr., *be joined, be added,* 726: inf. 726; pp. 434. OF. joign–, from joindre.

**joyne**[2], v. tr., *enjoin, order:* pret. 3 sg. 877, 1235. Aphetic for ajoyne (OF. enjoign–, from enjoindre).

**joynt**, n.: pl. -es, 1540. OF. joint.

**joyst**, part. adj., *lodged,* 434 (possibly *glad,* see note). ?Cf. ME. (a)gist, OF. agister.

**Ju**, n., *Jew:* pl. -es, 1236, 1612; Juise, 1159; gen. pl. Juyne, 1170. OF. Giu.

**Juda**, prop. n., *Judah,* 1170. Lat. Juda(s).

**Jude**, prop. n., *Judea,* 1432: Judee, 1180. OF. Judee.

**juel**, n., *jewel:* pl. -es, 1441, 1495. AN. juel, OF. joel.

**juelrye**, n., *jewelry,* 1309. OF. juelerye.

**juggement**, n., *judgment,* 726. OF. jugement.

**juise**, n., *judgment, doom,* 726. OF. juise.

**Juise**, see **Ju**.

**jumpred**, n., *?confusion, grief,* 491. Etym. unknown; perh. related to ME. jumpre, jompre, v., *jumble.*

**justise**, v. tr., *govern, rule:* pret. 3 pl. 1170. OF. justic(i)er.

**Juyne**, see **Ju**.

### K.

**kable**, n., *cable,* 418. OF. cable.

**kaiser**, see **cayser**.

**ka3t**, see **cache**.

**kake**, n., *cake:* pl. -z, 625, 635. ON. kaka.

**kare**, see **care**.

**kark**, n., *trouble, labor,* 4. AN. kark(e).

**karle**, n., *churl, base fellow,* 208: carle, 876. ON. karl.

**kart**, n., *cart,* 1259. ON. kartr; cf. OE. cræt.

**kayren**, see **cayre**.

**kayser**, see **cayser**.

**kene**, adj., *wise,* 1575; *mighty, great,* 1339, 1374, 1593; *sharp,*

839, 1253, 1697: superl. kennest,
1575. OE. cēne.

**kenely,** adv., *hastily,* 945. OE.
cēnlīce.

**kenne,** v. tr.; *make known, teach,*
697, 865; *know,* 1702: inf. 865,
pret. 1 sg. kende, 697; 3 sg.
kenned, 1702. OE. cennan, ON.
kenna.

**kepe,** v. tr., *regard,* 508; *take notice
of, mark,* 292; *hold,* 264; *obey,*
979; *preserve, maintain,* 1229;
*entertain,* 89; intr., *behave,* 234:
inf. 264, 292; 3 sg. -s, 234; -z,
508; pret. 3 sg. keped, 979, 1229;
pp. keppte, 89. OE. cēpan.

**kerve,** v. tr., *carve,* 1108, 1382, 1407,
1452; *cleave,* 1547; *tear,* 1582;
intr., 1104; inf. 1104, 1108; 3 sg.
-s, 1582; cerves, 1547; pp.
corven, 1382, 1407, 1452. OE.
ceorfan.

**kest,** v. tr., *cast, throw,* 234, 414, 634,
1515, 1712, 1744; *devise,* 1455;
kest up, 460, 951 (of clouds):
inf. 1455; 3 sg. -ez, 634; pret.
3 pl. -en, 951, 1515; pp. kest,
234, 414, 1712, 1744; kast, 460.
ON. kasta.

**kest,** n., *glance,* 768; *device, contrivance,* 1070: cast, 768.

**kever,** v. tr., *cure,* 1605; *restore,*
1700: inf. 1700; pret. 3 sg. 1605.
OF. cuevre, from couvrer, but
with meaning of recouvrer.

**keye,** n., *key:* pl. -s, 1438. OE.
cǣg.

**klubbe,** n., *club,* 1348: pl. clobbez,
839. ON. klubba.

**knave,** n., *servant,* 801; *knave,
wicked person,* 855: gen. sg. -z,
801; pl. -z, 855. OE. cnafa.

**knawe,** v. tr., *know,* 61, 297, 851,
917, 1435, 1575; *perceive,* 281,
373, 827, 1530; *recognize,* 231,
1087; *make known,* 1751: inf.
231, 1435; know, 917; pret. 3 sg.
knew, 281, 851, 1530; pret. 3 pl.
knewe, 1087; knewen, 61, 827;
pp. knawen, 297, 1751; knauen,
1575; cnowen, 373. OE. cnāwan.

**knawlach,** n., *knowledge,* in phrase
'com to knawlach,' *recovered
his mind,* 1702. Cf. OE. *(ge)-
cnāwlǣcan, v.

**kne,** n, *knee,* 40: pl. cnes, 1541.
OE. cnēo(w).

**knele,** v. intr., *kneel:* 3 sg. -s, 1345,
1591. OE. cnēowlian.

**knokke,** v. tr., *knock:* 3 sg. -s,
1348. LOE. cnocian.

**know,** see **knawe.**

**knyf,** n., *knife,* 1104. OE. cnīf.

**knyƷt,** n., *knight:* pl. -es, 1397, 1431,
1519. OE. cniht.

**knyt,** v. tr., *make binding, establish:* pret. 3 sg. knyt, 564. OE.
cnyttan.

**koste,** see **cost(e).**

**kote,** n., *cottage,* 801. OE. cote.

**kow,** n., *cow,* 1685: kuy, 1259. OE.
cū.

**kowpe,** see **cuppe.**

**koynt,** see **quoynt.**

**krakkes,** see **crak.**

**Kryst,** prop. n., *Christ,* 23, 161, 972,
1067. OE. Crīst.

**kydde,** see **kyþe.**

**kylle,** v. tr., *strike,* 876, 1267; *kill,*
1252: 1 pl. kylle, 876; 3 pl.
*kyllen, 1267; pp. kylde, 1252.
?OE. *cyllan.

**kyndam,** n., *kingdom,* 1700, 1731:
kyndom, 161. OE. cynedōm.

**kynde,** adj., *natural, lawful,* 697.
OE. (ge)cynde.

**kynde,** n., *kind, species,* 334, 336,
505, 507, 1483; *nature,* 263;
agayn kynde, *unnaturally,* 266;
by (of) kynde, *by nature, naturally,* 865, 1024, 1033, 1128; in
hit kynde, 1016: pl. -z, 336; -s,
1483. OE. (ge)cynd.

**kyndly,** adv., *fittingly,* 1; *exactly,*
319: kyndely, 319. Cf. OE. ge-
cyndelīce.

**kyng,** n., 1201, 1215, 1296, 1305, 1339,
1366, 1530, 1564, 1582, 1590, 1593,
1621, 1642, 1685, 1741, 1747, 1789;
(of the Lord) 17, 50, 393, 546,
1087: kynge, 1550; gen. sg. -es,
1221; pl. -es, 1170, 1374; -ez,
1510. OE. cyning.

**kynne,** v. tr., *conceive,* 1072; *engender, arouse,* 915: pp. 915,
1072. OE. cennan.

**kyppe,** v. tr., *seize:* 3 pl. kyppe,
1510. ON. kippa.

**kyryous,** see **curious.**

**kyrk,** n., *church* (of the Temple),
1431: kyrke, 1270. ON. kirkja;
cf. OE. cyrice.

**kyst,** n., *chest, coffer,* 1438; of the
ark, 346, 449, 464, 478: kyste,
449; pl. -es, 1438. ON. kista.

**kyte,** n., *kite:* gen. kyte, 1697. OE.
cȳta.

**kyth,** n., *country, region:* kyth, 571,
912, 1110, 1201, 1305, 1316;
kythe, 901; pl. -ez, 414; -es,
1231; gen. pl. -yn, 1366. OE.
cȳðð.

**kyþe,** v. tr., *make known, show,* 23,
208, 1435; *acknowledge,* 1368;
*practise,* 851: inf. 1368, 1435;
pret. 3 sg. kydde, 23, 208; 3 pl.
kyþed, 851. OE. cȳðan.

**L.**

**lache,** v. tr., *receive:* pres. subj.
2 sg. lache, 166; pp. 1186. OE.
læcc(e)an.

**ladde,** n., *fellow,* 36. Etym. uncertain.

**laddre,** n., *ladder:* pl. -s, 1777. OE.
hlǣder.

**lady,** n., 1059, 1589; my Lady,
*Virgin,* 1084: pl. ladis, 1352,
1370; ladies, 1375; ladyes, 1434.
OE. hlǣfdīge.

**lafte,** see **leve**[1], v.

**laȝe,** v. intr., *laugh:* 3 sg. -s, 661;
pret. 2 sg. laȝed, 670; 3 sg. 653,
668; 3 pl. loȝen, 495. OE. hlieh-
han, hlæhhan.

**lake,** n., 1023: llak, 438. OF. lac;
Lat. lacus.

**lake-ryfte,** n., *cavernous den:* pl. -s,
536. Lat. lacus (of Vulgate);
see **rifte.**

**lakke,** v. tr., *offend against:* pret.
3 pl. 723. Cf. MDu. laken.

**lale,** v. tr., *speak:* pret. 3 sg. 153,
913. Cf. Dan. lalle.

**lamp,** n., 1273: pl. -es, 1485. OF.
lampe.

**langage,** n., *language,* 1556. OF.
langage.

**lanse,** v. intr., *spring forth,* 966; tr.
*utter, speak,* 668; *split open,* 957,
1428: inf. lance, 1428; 3 pl.
lance, 966; pret. 3 sg. 957; 3 pl.
668. OF. lanc(i)er.

**lantez,** see **lene.**

**lape,** v. intr., *drink:* inf. 1434. OE.
lapian.

**lappe,** v. tr., *enwrap, clothe:* pp. 175.
Cf. OE. læppa, *skirt of a gar-
ment.*

**large,** adj., 438, 1386, 1549, 1773;
*great,* 1658; as noun, *breadth,*
314. OF. large.

lasche, v. intr., *blaze, burn:* pret.
3 sg. 707. Prob. onomatopoetic.
lasne, v. intr., *subside, fall:* pret.
3 sg. 438, 441. Cf. OE. læs, *less.*
lasse, see lyttel.
last, n., *sin, vice:* pl. -es, 1141. ON.
lǫstr, gen. lastar.
laste, adj., 608; as noun, at þe
last(e), *at last, finally,* 446, 888,
1096, 1193; bi þe laste, *at last,*
1327: last, 608, 888. OE. latost,
superl. of læt.
laste, v. intr., *last, endure:* inf. last,
894; 3 sg. -z, 568; lasttes, 1124;
pres. subj. 3 sg. laste, 1594; pret.
3 sg. laste, 227, 1298. OE.
læstan.
lat, adj., *remiss, unmindful,* 1172.
OE. læt.
late, adv., 1804: comp. in phrase,
'never þe later,' *nevertheless,*
1352. OE. late.
laþe, v. tr., *invite, urge:* 1 pl. laþe,
900; pret. 3 sg. 809, 936; imper.
pl. -z, 81; pp. 163. OE. laðian.
lauce, v. tr., *solve, do away with,*
1589; intr., *loosen,* 957: inf.
1589; pret. 3 sg. laused, 957. Cf.
ON. lauss, *loose;* leysa, *loosen.*
*launce, *branch:* pl. -s, 1485 (see
note). OF. lance.
launde, n., *open space in woods,
pasture;* (up)on launde, 1000,
1207. OF. launde.
lavande, part. adj., *pouring, flowing,* 366. OE. lafian.
lawe¹, n., *law,* 1167, 1174, 1307: law,
263; laue, 723; pl. -z, 188. LOE.
lagu.
lawe², n., *hill,* 992. OE. hlāw.
lay, v. tr., *lay low, put down,* 1307,
1650; *place,* 1025; *set, assign,*
425; *impose,* 263: inf. 425, 1650;

imper. sg. lay, 1025; pp. layd,
263, 1307. OE. lecgan.
lay(e), see lyʒe.
layk, n., *amusement,* 122; *device*
(in evil sense), 274; *behavior,*
1053, 1064: pl. -ez, 122, 274. ON.
leikr.
layke, v. intr., *play:* imper. pl. -z,
872. ON. leika.
layte, v. tr., *seek,* 1768; intr., 97:
imper. pl. -z, 97; pp. 1768. ON.
leita.
lazar, n., *diseased beggar:* pl. -es,
1093. Late Lat. lazarus.
leaute, n., *fidelity,* 1172. OF. leaute.
lebard, n., *leopard:* pl. -ez, 536.
OF. leopard, lebard.
lecherye, n., 1350. OF. lecherie.
led, n., *lead,* 1025. OE. lēad.
lede, n., coll. *people, nation,* 691,
740, 772; *man, person,* 347, 609,
1093, 1419, 1768; *servant,* 614;
pl. *men, people,* 97, etc.: led,
691; leede, 772; pl. -z, 97, 116,
256, 308, 412, 495, 836, 909, 990,
993; -s, 1051, 1193, 1293, 1596,
1773. OE. lēod, f., and lēod, m.
leder, n., *leader:* pl. -es, 1307. Cf.
OE. lǣdan, v.
ledisch, adv., *of the people, national,*
1556: ludych, 73; ludisch, 1375.
lef, adj., *dear, precious,* 772, 939;
absol, as noun, 1066: leef, 1066;
leve, 1622. OE. lēof.
lefly, adj., *dear, lovely,* 977. OE.
lēoflic.
lege, adj., *pertaining to feudal allegiance, requiring allegiance,*
94; *owing allegiance,* 1174; as
noun, *sovereign, lord,* 1368. OF.
li(e)ge.
legioun, n., *armed host,* 1773: pl.
-es, 1293. AN. legiun, OF.
legion.

leȝen, see lyȝe.

lel, adj., *fair*, 1069; *true*, 425. OF. leel.

lelly, adv., *loyally, faithfully*, 1066.

leme, v. tr., *shine, gleam*: pret. 3 sg. 1273, 1486. Cf. OE. lēoma, n.

lemman, n., *mistress*, 1352: pl. lemanes, 1370. OE. lēofman.

lende, v. intr., *remain, tarry*: pp. lent (= *tarrying, abiding*), 1084. OE. lendan.

lene¹, v. tr., *give, grant*: pret. 2 sg. lantez, 348: pp. lent, 256. OE. lǣnan.

lene², v. refl., *lean*: pret. 3 sg. 784. OE. hleonian.

lenge, v. intr., *remain, abide, dwell*: inf. 81, 800, 803, 807, 1023; 3 sg. -z, 772, 779; pret. 3 sg. 497, 960, 994; 3 pl. 412, 891, 1419; imper. sg. lenge, 614. OE. lengan.

lenger, -est, see longe.

lenþe, n., (of space) 314, 315, 1383, 1594; on lenþe, *along the length* (of the table), 116; (of time) 224, 239, 425, 568: lencþe, 224. OE. lengðu.

lepe, v. intr., *run, rush*, 990; *leap, spring*, 1209; *crack, 'fly,'* 966: 3 sg. -s, 966; 3 pl. -s, 1209; pp. lopen, 990. OE. hlēapan.

lepre, adj., *leprous*, 1094. OF. lepre.

ler, n.: pl. -s, *features*, 1542. OE. hlēor.

lere, v. tr., *teach*: inf. 843. OE. lǣran.

lerne, v. tr., *learn*: pp. 693. OE. leornian.

lese, adj., *false*, 1719. OE. lēas.

lese, v. tr., *destroy*, 932; *fail*, 887: pret. 3 pl. lest, 887; pp. lorne, 932. OE. lēosan.

lest, conj.: 151, 166, 943. OE. (þȳ) lǣs þe.

let, v. tr., *let, permit*, 732, 1434; in phrase 'let one,' *let alone*, 670, 872; *think, regard*, in phrase 'let lyȝt,' 1174, 1320: inf. 732; pres. subj. 1 pl. let, 670; pret. 3 sg. lette, 1174; imper. sg. let, 1434; pl. -ez, 872; pp. let, 1320. OE. lǣtan, lētan.

lette, v. tr., *hinder, deprive*: pp. 1803. OE. lettan.

letter, n., *letter* (*of alphabet*), 1536, etc.; *inscription, writing*, 1580; pl. *learning*, 1561: pl. lettres, 1536, 1549, 1565, 1596, 1634. OF. lettre.

leþe, v. intr., *soften, be merciful* (w. dat.), 752; *cease*, 648: inf. 752; pres. subj. 3 sg. leþe, 648. Etym. uncertain.

leþer, n., *leather*, 1581. OE. leðer.

leve, adj., see lef.

leve¹, n., *leaf*, 488, etc.; (of book), 966: pl. -z, 488, 605, 609, 966; -s, 1464, 1485. OE. lēaf, n.

leve², n., *leave, permission*, in phrase 'wyth yor (þy) leve,' 94, 347, 715; take leve, *depart*, 401. OE. lēaf, f.

leve¹, v. tr., *leave* (*behind*), 378, 1004, 1678; (as inheritance), 1337; *give up, abandon*, 1233: inf. 1233; 3 sg. -s, 1678; 3 pl. -z, 378; pret. 3 sg. lafte, 1337; pp. lafte, 1004. OE. lǣfan.

leve², v. tr., *believe*, 608, 1493; intr. 752; *have faith*, 1703: inf. 608, 752; pret. 3 sg. 1703; imper. sg. leve, 1493. OE. līefan, lēfan.

lewed, adj., *ignorant*, 1580, 1596. OE. lǣwede.

leyen, see lyȝe.

**lik,** v. tr., *lick,* 1000; *drink, sip,*
1521: inf. 1000; 3 pl. likked,
1521. OE. liccian.

**likkes,** see **lyke.**

**limpe,** impers. v., *befall, happen:*
pp. lumpen, 424, 1320. OE.
limpan.

**llak,** see **lake.**

**lo,** interj., 94, 541. OE. lā.

**lodezmon,** n., *guide,* 424. Cf. OE.
lādmann.

**lodly,** adv., *in a loathsome manner,*
1093; *with abhorrence or loathing,* 1090. OE. lāðlīce.

**lodlych,** adj., *hateful, vile,* 274:
loþelych, 1350. OE. lāðlic.

**lof,** see **luf,** n.

**lofly,** see **luflych.**

**lofte,** n., in phrase '(up)on lofte,'
*aloft, on high, above; on top*
(1025): 206, 318, 692, 808, 947,
1004, 1210, 1273, 1342, 1407, 1444,
1649, 1777, 1803; loft, 1025.
LOE.. loft, ON. lopt. See **aloft.**

**loge,** n., *small house, dwelling,* 800;
*arbor* (of decoration), 1407: pl.
logges, 1407. OF. loge.

**loge-dor,** n., 784.

**logge,** v. intr., *pass the night:* inf.
807. OF. log(i)er.

**logging,** n., *dwelling,* 887.

**loȝ,** n., *sea, (the) deep,* 441: loȝe,
1031; loghe, 366. ?ONth. luh.

**loȝ,** adj., *low,* 1761. ON. lāgr.

**loȝe,** adv., *low,* 798.

**loȝe,** v. tr., *abase, humble:* pp.
1650.

**loȝen,** see **laȝe.**

**loȝly,** adv., *humbly,* 614, 745.

**loke,** v. intr., *look, see,* 269, 495, 691,
769, 817, 903, 1069, 1581; w. 'on,'
28, 1370, 1580, 1804; w. 'to,'
263, 401, 1059; *take care, see to
it,* 317, 905, 944: inf. 28, 263, 691,

1370, 1804; 3 sg. -z, 401, 817;
pret. 3 sg. 269, 769; 3 pl. 495,
1580; imper. sg. loke, 317, 1059,
1069; pl. -s, 903; loke, 905, 944;
pp. 1581. OE. lōcian.

**lome,** n., *vessel* (of ark), 314, 412,
443, 495. Cf. OE. gelōma.

**lome,** adj., *lame,* 1094. OE. lama.

**lomerande,** part. adj., *stumbling,
hobbling,* 1094. Prob. based on
ME. lome.

**londe,** n., *land, country,* 308, 909,
932, 1797; *world,* 568; in formal
phrase 'in londe,' 122: pl. -s,
1293, 1768. OE. land, lond.

**longe,** adj., (of space), 1386, 1462,
1777; (of time), 256, 807;
absol. as noun, upon longe, *at
length,* 1193: long, 807; superl.
lengest, 256. OE. lang, long.

**longe,** adv., *for a long time,* 809,
1768; fol. by 'er,' 932: long,
1521; comp. in phrase 'no
lenger,' 810, 982. OE. lange,
longe.

**longe,** v. intr., *pertain, belong:*
pret. 3 sg. 1090; 3 pl. 1747. Cf.
OE. gelang, adj.

**longing,** vbl. n., *anxiety, solicitude,*
1003: longyng, 779. OE.
langung.

**lopen,** see **lepe.**

**lorde,** n., *lord, ruler, noble,* 73, 94,
97, 122, 153, 1418, 1589, 1797;
*husband,* 656; (the) *Lord,* 28,
212, 345, 347, 410, 424, 435, 489,
497, 612, 675, 714, 717, 752, 761,
769, 828, 913, 925, 986, 1004, 1053,
1066, 1172, 1228, 1356, 1448, 1454,
1493, 1642, 1703, 1804, 1807: lord,
138; gen. sg. lordes, 1797; pl.
-s, 1367, 1375, 1521, -z, 1571. OE.
hlāford.

lordeschyp, n., 1658. OE. hlāford-
scipe.

lore, n., *learning*, 1556. OE. lār.

lorne, see lese.

los, n., *uncertainty, quandary*, 1589.
OE. los.

lose, v. tr., *destroy*, 909; *lose*, 586,
1141, 1797: 3 sg. -s, 1141; 1 pl.
-n, 909; pp. losed, 586; lost,
1797. OE. losian.

losyng, vbl. n., *perdition*, 1031. OE.
losing.

lot, n., *sound, speech*, 668. ON. lāt.

Loth, prop. n., *Lot*, 772, 798, 809,
817, 841, 853, 900, 913, 925, 936,
939, 977, 993, 1003: Loot, 784;
gen. sg. Lothez, 836; Lothes,
981; Lotez, 887. Lat. Loth.

loþe, v. tr., *hate*: pres. 3 pl. loþe,
16. OE. lāðian.

loþelych, see lodlych.

loud, adj., 390: loude, 1207. OE.
hlūd.

loude, adv., 153, 950. OE. hlūde.

louflych, see luflych.

loute, v. intr., *bow*: 3 sg. -z, 798.
OE. lūtan.

love, n., *palm*: pl. -z, 987. ON. lōfi.

love¹, v. tr.: inf. lovy, 1066; 1 sg.
luf, 1434; 2 sg. lovyez, 841; 3 sg.
Iovyes, 1053, 1060, 1809; lovies,
1052; 3 pl. lovez, 823; pret. ind.
3 sg. loved, 275; 3 pl. 723; pret.
subj. 3 sg. lovied, 21; pp. loved,
1059. OE. lufian.

love², v. tr., *praise, glorify*: inf.
1289; pret. 3 sg. 275, 497, *1703;
3 pl. 987; pres. part. lovande,
1719; pp. 925. OE. lofian.

love, see luf, n.

lovyng, vbl. n., *praising*, 1448.

lowke, v. intr., only in pres. part.
lowkande, *closing, forming a
mass*, 441. OE. lūcan.

ludych, ludisch, see ledisch.

luf, n., *love*, 843; *beloved person*,
401²; coll. *mistresses*, 1419: lof,
843; love, 1419. OE. lufu.

luf-lowe, *flame of love*, 707. Cf.
ON. logi.

luflych, adj., *lovely, fair*, 939, 1486;
*dear*, 1804; *courteous*, 809: luflych, 809; luflyche, 939; louflych,
1486; lofly, 1804. OE. luflic.

luflyly, adv., *courteously*, 163.

lug, v., *move heavily, be dragged*:
pret. 3 sg. 443. ON. lugga.

lult, v. tr., *sound*: pp. 1207. Perh.
imitative; cf. Norw. lilla.

luly-whit, adj., *lily-white*, 977. OE.
lilie + hwīt.

lump, n., 1025. Cf. Norw. and Sw.
dial. lump.

lumpen, see limpe.

lust, n., 1350. OE. lust.

lusty, adj., *fair* (as formal epithet),
981.

luþer, adj., *wicked*, 163; absol. as
noun, *evil*, 1090. OE. lȳðre.

lyf, n., *life*, 256, etc.; on lyve, *alive*,
293, 356, 1321: lyf, 256, 308, 325,
333, 425, 841, 900, 1023, 1594,
1658, 1719; gen. sg. lyvez, 648;
lyve, 173, 293, 356, 1321. OE.
līf.

lyflode, n., *means of living*, 561.
OE. līflād.

lyft, adj., *left*, 1581: lyfte, 981. OE.
lyft.

lyftande, part. adj., *heaving*, 443.

lyfte, v. tr., *raise*, 1649, 1777; *set
up, decree*, 717; *?excite* (or
perh. *surpass*, in phrase 'lyftez
mervayle,' *is more than strange*),
586: inf. 717; lyft, 1649; 3 sg.
-z, 586, pret. 3 pl. lyfte, 1777.
ON. lypta.

lyfte, part. adj., *raised*, 1407.

**lyfte,** n., *sky, heavens,* 366, 435, 1356, 1448, 1493, 1761 : lyft, 212. OE. lyft.

**ly3e,** v. intr., *lie:* 3 sg. lygges, 1126, 1792; 3 pl. lyggez, 99; pret. 3 sg. lay, 460; laye, 609; ly3e, 172; 3 pl. le3en, 936; pp. leyen, 1003. OE. licgan.

**ly3t,** adj., *pure,* 987. OE. lēoht, lēht.

**ly3t,** adj., *light,* 1026; absol. in phrase 'let ly3t of,' *disregard, treat with disrespect,* 1174, 1320. OE. lēoht, lēht, līht.

**ly3t,** n., *light,* 1272, 1486; *spark* in phrase 'lyves ly3t,' 648 : pl. ly3t, 1486. OE. lēoht, lēht.

**ly3t,** v. intr., *alight,* 476; *descend,* 691 ; (of the Incarnation), 1069; *stop, turn aside* (Vulg. *declinate*), 800; *fall* (*upon*), 213, 235 : inf. 476, 691, 800; pret. 3 sg. ly3t, 213, 235, 1069. OE. līhtan.

**ly3tly,** adv., *quickly,* 817, 853. OE. lēohtlic.

**lyke,** adj., *like,* 212, 790 : lyk, 1436; superl. lykkest, 261. Adv. like, *as if,* 1008. Cf. OE. gelīc.

**lyke,** v. intr., and impers., *like, please:* inf. 36, 1064; 3 sg. -z, 539, 693; -s, 1646, 1663, 1726; 3 pl. likkes, 1141; pres. subj. 3 sg. lyke, 717; pret. 3 sg. 73, 411, 435, 1649, 1650, 1700; pret. subj. 3 sg. 771. OE. līcian.

**lyken,** v. intr., *be like, resemble:* 3 sg. lyknes, 1064.

**lykor,** n., *liquor:* pl. -es, 1521. OF. licor.

**lykyng,** vbl. n., *pleasure,* 239, 1803; *wish, inclination,* 172 : pl. -es, 1803. OE. līcung.

**lym,** n., *limb:* pl. -ez, 175. OE. lim.

**lyoun,** n., *lion:* pl. -ez, 536. AN. liun, OF. lion.

**lyre,** n., *flesh,* 1687. OE. līra.

**lysoun,** n., *?glimpse, trace,* 887. ?OF. luision.

**lyst¹,** n., *boundary, region,* 1761. OE. līste.

**lyst²,** n., *pleasure,* 693, 843. OE. lust.

**lyste,** v. impers., *be pleasing;* me lyst, *I please, like:* 3 sg. lyst, 872, 1000; pret. 3 sg. lyste, 415; lyst, 1766; liste, 1356. OE. lystan.

**lysten,** n., *sense of hearing,* 586. Cf. ONth. lysna, *listen.*

**lyte,** adj., *few,* 119. OE. lȳt.

**lyttel,** adj., *little,* 233, 736, 965, 990; as noun, a lyttel, 451, 617; at lyttel, 1710; of time, *a little while,* 614: little, 1232; comp. lasse, in 'never þe lasse,' 215; as n. in 'no lasse,' 1640. OE. lȳtel.

**lyttel,** adv., *little,* 465, 935. OE. lȳtel.

**lyþerly,** adv., *meanly, wretchedly,* 36. Cf. luþer.

**lyve,** v. intr., *live;* 239, etc.; ?quasi-tr., *practise,* 172 : inf. 239, 1031; lyvy, 558; 2 sg. lyvyes, 1114; pres. subj. 2 sg. lyvie, 581; pret. 3 pl. 261; ?pp. 172. OE. lifian.

**lyve,** n., see lyf.

### M.

**ma,** see make.

**mach,** n., *mate,* 695; *companion,* 124. OE. gemæcca.

**machche,** v. intr., *be joined* (= *attend,* i. e. for service) : pres. 3 sg. -s, 1512.

**mad,** see make.

**madde,** adj., *foolish,* 654. Cf. OE. gemæd.

**maȝty,** adj., *mighty,* 273, 279. OE. mihtig, mæhtig (Angl.). See also **myȝty.**

**maȝtyly,** adv., *fiercely,* 1267.

**make,** n., *equal, peer,* 248; *wife,* 703, 994: pl. -z, 331, 334. Cf. OE. gemaca.

**make,** v. tr., 52, etc.; make god chere, 641; moon, 373; joye, 1304; prisoner, 1308: inf. 373, 628, 1202, 1238, 1286, 1365, ?1566, 1668; 3 sg. -s, 1304, 1795; pres. subj. 2 pl. make, 819; matz, 695; pret. 1 sg. made, 285, 291, 664, 701, 1662; 3 sg. 52, 124, 198, 212, 542, 1662; mad, 641; 3 pl. *mad, 1391; imper. sg. ma. 625; make, 309, 314, 1067; pp. maked, 254, 1071, 1308, 1799; made, 1720; mad, 91, 247. OE. macian.

**male,** n., 695, 703; pl. -z, 337. OF. ma(s)le.

**malscrande,** part. adj., *bewildering,* 991. OE. *malscrian.

**malte,** v. intr., *melt, soften,* 776; *filter in,* 1566: inf. malt, 1566. OE. meltan.

**malyce,** n., *wickedness,* 518; *anger,* 250: malys, 250. OF. malice.

**Mambre,** prop. n., *Mamre,* 674, 778. OE. Mambre.

**man,** n., *man, person,* 51, 124, 341, etc.; *servant,* 1512; indef., *one,* 180, 183, 189; in general sense, referring to whole species, 285, 332, 514, 518, etc.: man, 51, 180, 189, 341, etc. (12 times); mon, 124, 183, 285, 436, etc. (11 times); gen. sg. mannez, 514, 515, 575; manez, 520; monnez, 332; monnes, 1673; pl. men,

119, 137, 644, 652, etc. OE. mann, monn.

**mancioun,** n., *dwelling* (of Ark), 309. AN. mansiun, OF. mansion.

**Mane,** n., *Mene,* 1727, 1730. Vulg. Mane.

**maner,** n., *mode,* 701. AN. manere, OF. maniere.

**manerly,** adj., *properly, becomingly,* 91.

**mangerye,** n., *banquet, feast,* 52: mangerie, 1365. OF. mangerie.

**mankynde,** n., 278: monkynde, 564.

**manne,** v. tr., (of sexual intercourse): inf. 869. OE. mannian.

**mansed,** part. adj., *cursed,* 774. Cf. OE. āmānsod.

**Mararach,** prop. n., *Ararat,* 447 (see note). OF. Ararach.

**margerye-perle,** n., *pearl,* 556. OF. margerie + perle.

**marie,** v. tr., *give in marriage, marry:* inf. 52: as adj. maryed, 815. OF. marier.

**marre,** v. tr., *corrupt,* 279; *destroy,* 991: 3 pl. marre, 279; pp. ,991. OE. merran.

**marryng,** vbl. n., *ruining, spoiling,* 186.

**marschal,** n., 118, 1427: marchal, 91. OF. mareschal.

**maryage,** n.: pl. -z, 186. OF. mariage.

**mase,** n., ?*confusion,* 395. ?OE. *mase.

**maskle,** n., *spot,* 556. OF. mascle.

**masse,** n., *mass* (= *gospel*), 51 (see note). OE. mæsse.

**mast,** n., 417. OE. mæst.

**mater,** n., *matter, subject, substance,* 1566, 1617, 1635. AN. matere, OF. matiere.

Maþew, prop. n., *Matthew*, 25, 51. OF. Mathiu.

mawgre, n., *displeasure*, 250. OF. maugre.

may, pret. pres., *can, may* (pret. often has pres. force) : 1 sg. may, 70, 291, 750, 1567; 2 sg. 176, 655, 1115; 3 sg. 32, 104, 177, 183, 189, 339, 551, 599, 663, 776, 1023, 1027, 1043, 1052, 1119, 1131; 1 pl. 843, 1112, 1812; 2 pl. 1319; pret. 1 sg. moȝt, 914; myȝt, 682; 2 sg. moȝtez, 655; 3 sg. moȝt, 22, 62, 704, 890, 894, 1320, 1668; myȝt, 3, 225, 260, 377, 567, 921, 1046, 1392, 1517, 1550; 3 pl. moȝt, 372, 705, 708, 1083, 1108, 1205, 1720; myȝt, 530, 835, 1199, 1252, 1785. OE. mæg–(meahte) mihte.

mayden, n., of the Virgin, 248, 1069: pl. -ez, 815, 867, 934; -es, 1267, 1299. OE. mægden.

maynful, adj., *mighty*, 1730. Cf. OE. mægen, n.

maynly, adv., *loudly*, 1427.

mayntnaunce, n., *maintaining, support*, 186. OF. maintenaunce.

mayny, see meyny.

mayster, n., *lord, ruler*, 125, 1237, 1427, 1512, 1793; of God, 748, 771, 1113: pl. -z, 252; -es, 1740. OF. maistre.

maysterful, adj., *despotic*, 1328.

maysterry, n., *force*, 1241. OF. maistrie.

mede, n., *reward*, 12, 1632: pl. -z, 24. OE. mēd.

Mede, prop. n., *Mede*, pl. -s, 1740, 1771, 1793. OE. pl. Mēdas.

medo, n., *meadow:* pl. -es, 1761. OE. mǣd, gen. mǣdwe.

megre, adj., *lean, thin*, 1198. OF. megre.

meke, adj., *gentle*, 815; *merciful*, 771; as noun, = *meek servant*, 776. ON. miūkr.

mekely, adv., 783.

meken, v. tr., *humble, soften:* pret. 3 sg. mekned, 1328.

mele, n., *meal*, 226, 625. OE. melo.

mele, v. intr., and tr., *speak, tell:* inf. 748; pres. 1 sg. mele, 736; 3 sg. -z, 51; pret. 3 sg. 859. OE. mǣlan.

menddyng, vbl. n., 764. Cf. OF. amender.

mene, adj., *inferior, small*, 1241. Cf. OE. gemǣne.

mene, v. tr., *mean, signify*, 1567, 1730, 1733; *tell, explain*, 1635: 3 sg. -s, 1567, 1730, 1733; imper. sg. mene, 1635. OE. mǣnan.

meng, v. tr., *mix*, 625; *join*, 337: imper. sg. meng, 337; menge, 625. OE. mengan.

men-sclaȝt, n., *manslaughter*, 182. Cf. OE. monnslieht, -slæht (Angl.).

menske, n., *honor, dignity*, 121, 522, 1740: mensk, 646. ON. mennska.

menske, v. tr., *honor:* 3 sg. -z, 141; pp. 118.

mercy, n., 395: mersy, 776. OF. merci.

mercyable, adj., *merciful*, 1113. OF. merciable.

mercyles, adj., 250.

mere, n., *sea*, 991. OE. mere.

mere, n., *boundary*, 778. OE. (ge)-mǣre.

merit, n., *reward*, 613. OF. merite.

merk, adj., *obscure*, 1617. OE. mirce.

merk, n., *darkness*, 894. OE. mirce.

merk, v. tr., *set, place*, 558, 637, 1487; *write*, 1617, 1727: 3 sg. merkkez, 637; pret. 3 sg. 558; pp. 1617, 1727; merkked, 1487. OE. mearcian.

merþe, see myrþe.

mervayl, n., *marvel, wonder*, 22, 1164: mervayle, 586. OF. merveille.

mery, see myry.

meschef, n., *misfortune, trouble*, 708, 1164; *evil plight*, 373: pl. -ez, 708; -es, 1164. OF. meschef.

mese, v. tr., *moderate:* inf. 764. Cf. OF. amesir.

message, n., *messenger*, 454. OF. message.

messe, n., *portion:* pl. -z, 637. OF. mes.

mester, n., *need*, 67. AN. mester, OF. mestier.

mesurable, adj., *temperate, mild*, 859. OF. mesurable.

mesure, n., *moderation*, 215, 247, 565. OF. mesure.

metalle, n.: pl. -s, 1513. OF. metal.

mete, adj., *proper, fitting*, 337, 637; *equal*, 1662. Cf. OE. gemǣte.

mete, n., *food*, 121, 466, 644, 646, 818, 1198, 1354, 1683; *feast, dinner*, 118, 125: pl. -s, 1354. OE. mete.

mete, v. tr., *meet*, 86, 797; intr., 1394; mete wyth, 371: inf. 797, pret. 3 sg. mette, 371; 3 pl. metten, 86, 1394. OE. mētan.

mett, n., *measure:* pl. -ez, 625. OE. (ge)met.

metz, n., *?pity*, 215. Cf. mese, v., and see note.

meþe, n., *moderation, mildness, mercy*, 247, 565; meth, 436. OE. mǣþ.

meþelez, adj., *extraordinary*, 273. OE. mǣþlēas.

meve, v. intr., *move*, 303; *proceed, walk*, 783: 3 sg. -z, 303; pres. part. mevande, 783. OF. muev-, from movoir.

meyny, n., *household, company*, 331, 454; *multitude*, 514: mayny, 514. OF. meyne.

misschapen, part. adj., *monstrous, wicked*, 1355. Cf. OE. scapen, pp. of scieppan.

mistrauþe, n., *unfaithfulness*, 996. Cf. OE. trēowð.

Mizael, prop. n., *Mishael*, 1301 (Dan. 1. 6). Lat., OE. Misael.

mo, see much.

mode, n., *mood*, 713; *anger*, 215, 565, 764; *thought, idea*, 1635: mod, 713. OE. mōd.

moder, n., *mother:* gen. sg. in phrase 'moder chylde,' 1303. OE. mōdor.

modey, adj., *brave, proud*, 1303. OE. mōdig.

molde, n., *earth*, in phrase '(up)on (þis) molde,' *on earth, in the world*, 279, 286, 514, 522, 558, 613, 708, 1114, 1656; in pl. = *lands*, 454: mold, 708; pl. moldez, 454. OE. molde.

mon, see man.

monsworne, part. n., *perjury*, 182. Cf. OE. mānswerian, v.

mony, adj., *many*, w. sg. noun and indef. article, 659, 1286, 1298, 1303, 1352, 1372, 1440, 1488, 1773; without article, 43, 1299, 1439, 1602; pl. 96, 193, 321, 367, etc.: absol. as pron., 521, 572, 1194, 1479, 1692, 1784: moni, 1298, 1299, 1303; monye, 521, 1093; monie, 1194. OE. manig, monig.

monyfolde, adv., *many times, greatly,* 278. OE. manigfeald, -fáld, adj.

monyth, n, *month,* 427, 493, 1030. OE. mōnaδ.

moon, n., *moan,* 373. OE. *mān.

mor, n., *moor,* 1673; *earth,* 385. OE. mōr.

morken, v. intr., *grow dark:* 3 sg. -es, 1760. Cf. merk.

morkne, v. intr., *rot:* inf. 407. ON. morkna.

morne, n., *morning,* 493; *next day, morrow,* 1001, 1793: morn, 493. OE. morgen.

morne, v. intr., *mourn:* pres. part. *mornande, 778. OE. murnan.

mornyng, n., *morning,* 804. See morne.

morsel, n., 620. OF. morsel.

morter, n., *candlestick with a wide bowl to catch grease:* pl. -es, 1487. AN. morter, OF. mortier.

mot, pret. pres., *may,* 580; pret., *must,* generally w. present meaning: 3 sg. mot, 580; 2 sg. most, 1673; pret. 3 sg. most, 407, 1031; moste, 1331. OE. mōt–mōste.

mote, n., *spot, blemish,* 556. OE. mot.

mount, n., 994: *mounte,* 447. OE. munt.

mountayn, n.: pl. -ez, 385. AN. muntayne, OF. montagne.

mowþe, n., *mouth,* 1669. OE. mūδ.

much, adj., 22, 182, 190, 250, etc.; als much as, 1730; comp. more (of quantity), 96, 296, 1725; absol. 736; mo, *more* (of numbers), 96, 674; absol. 940, 1303; superl. most, *largest,* 254: moste, 385. OE. mycel. See also mukel.

much, adv., 189, 285, 774, 1072, 1494; comp. more, 76, 168, 1107, 1137, 1154, 1453; no more, 385, 513, 759, 762, 894, 1135; never more, 48, 191. OE. mycel.

mudde, n., 407. Cf. MLG. mudde.

mukel, adj., *large, great,* 52, 366, 514, 1164. OE. mycel. See also much.

mul, n., *dust,* 736. OE. myl.

multyplye, v. intr.: pret. 3 pl. 278; imper. pl. -z, 522. OF. multiplier.

munster, n., *church, temple,* 1267. OE. mynster.

my, poss. pron., 55, 56, 57, 60, etc.: myn, 682, 688, 689, 698, 1667; absol. 1668. OE. mīn.

myddes, n., *midst,* in phrase 'in þe myddes,' 1388. See also inmyddez.

mydnyȝt, n., *midnight,* 894. OE. midniht.

myȝt, n., *might, power,* 1656, 1662, 1668: pl. -es, 644, 1699; -ez, 748. OE. miht.

myȝty, adj., *mighty,* 1237. OE. mihtig. See also maȝty.

myke, n., *"crutch"* or *forked support on which a mast rests when lowered,* 417. ?MDu. micke.

mylde, n., *merciful,* 728. OE. milde.

myle, n.: pl. -z, 674; myle, 1387. OE. mīl.

mylke, n., *milk,* 637. OE. meolc, milc.

mylke, v. tr., *milk:* inf. 1259. OE. milcian.

mynde, n., *mind, heart,* 518, 852, 1328, 1421, 1566; *thought,* 1355; *purpose,* 1502. Cf. OE. gemynd.

mynne, v. impers., *think,* 25; tr. and intr. w. 'on,' *remember,* 436

(see note), 771: inf. 436, 771;
3 sg. mynez, 25. ON. minna.

**mynstrasy,** n., *minstrelsy,* 121. OF.
menestralsie.

**mynt,** v. tr., *purpose:* 3 sg. -es,
1628. OE. myntan.

**mynystre,** v. tr., *serve:* pret. 3 sg.
644. OF. ministrer.

**myre,** n., *mire,* 1114. ON. mȳrr.

**myrþe,** n., *mirth, joy, pleasure,* 132,
189: merþe, 703, 1519. OE.
myr(i)gð.

**myry,** adj., *pleasing,* 701; *merry
pleasant* (sometimes as mere epithet), 130, 254, 331, 417, 783, 934,
1760; of the weather, *fine,* 804,
1760: myri, 934; mery, 1760;
superl. myriest, 254, 701. Quasi-
adv. myry, *merrily,* 1516. OE.
myr(i)ge.

**myryly,** adv., *happily, cheerfully,*
493.

**myself, myselven.** see self.

**mysse,** v. tr., *fail to obtain, miss,*
189; (intr.) w. 'of,' 551; *lack,*
1198; in passive, *to be absent,
missing,* 994: inf. 189, 551; pp.
myst, 994, 1198. OE. missan.

**mysseleve,** n., *misbelief,* 1230. Cf.
OE. lēafa.

**myst,** n., 1760. OE. mist.

## N.

**Nabugo,** prop. n., shortened form
of Nabugodenozar, 1226, 1233.

**Nabugodenozar,** prop. n., *Nebuchadnezzar* (written Nabugo de
Nozar), 1304, 1312, 1331, 1338,
1430, 1603, 1651, 1671: Nabigodenozar, 1176, 1218. OF. Nabugodenozar.

**Nabuzardan,** prop. n., *Nebuzaradan,*
1236, 1261, 1281, 1291, 1613;
Nabizardan, 1245. Lat. Nabuzardan.

**nade,** see **have.**

**naȝt,** see **nyȝt.**

**naker,** n., *kettle-drum:* gen. pl. -yn,
1413. OF. nacre.

**name,** n., 410, 1236, 1324, 1610:
nome, 297. OE. nama.

**nas,** see **be.**

**nature,** n.: 1087; natwre, 709. OF.
nature.

**nauþer,** conj., *neither;* correl. with
ne, 1104, 1336; reinforcing ne,
1028, 1226, 1556: nawþer, 1028.
OE. nāhwæðer, nauðer.

**nay,** adv., 729, 743, 758. ON. nei.

**nay,** v. tr., *deny,* 805; intr., *refuse,*
65; 3 sg. nay, 805; pret. 3 sg. 65.
OF. neier.

**nayte,** v. tr., *use:* inf. 531. ON.
neyta.

**naytly,** adv., *properly,* 480. Cf. ON.
neytr, *good, fit for use.*

**ne,** adv., *not,* 152, 178, *550, etc.;
þat . . . ne, *without,* 983;
redundant after er, 225 (see
note), 1205, and usually in combinations: nel, 513; nyl, 1261;
nolde, 805, etc.; nas, 727, etc.;
nere, 21; nif, 21. Conj. *nor,* 34,
48, 108, 136, etc. OE. ne.

**nede,** n., *need,* 1163. OF. nīed, nēd.

**nede,** adv., *of adversity,* 407. OE.
nīede, nēde.

**nedes,** adv., *of necessity,* 1331. OE.
nīedes, nēdes.

**nedlez,** adj., *useless,* 381.

**neȝe,** adv., *nigh, nearly,* 484, 704,
1422; as prep., *near,* 803: neȝe,
803, 1422; nyȝe, 484, 704. OE.
nēah, nēh.

neȝe, v. tr., *come to, approach:* inf.
neȝe, 143, 1017; neȝ, 805; ?neȝen,
32 (see note); pret. 3 sg. 1754.

nekke, n., *neck,* 1638. OE. hnecca.

nel, see wyl.

nem, see nym.

ner, adv., *nearly,* 1558, 1585; as
prep., *near,* 414: nere, 414. ON.
nǽr; OE. nēar, nēr, comp. of
nēah.

nere, see be.

neve, n., *(clenched) hand,* 1537.
ON. hnefi.

neven, v. tr., *name:* inf. 1376; 3 pl.
-en, 1525; pret. 3 sg. 410. ON.
nefna.

never, adv., *never, at no time,* 29,
45, 48, 107, etc.; emphatic neg.,
*by no means, not at all,* 587, 615,
668, 1103, 1555; never . . . er,
359, 381, 1312; never more, 191;
never þe + compar., 215, 1352;
never so, 1330. OE. nǽfre.

newe, adj., 526: nwe, 1354. OE.
nēowe, nēwe.

next, adv., w. 'after,' *immediately
after,* 261. OE. nēahst, nēhst,
superl. of nēah.

nice, adj., *wanton, lascivious,* 1354,
1359; *fastidious, dainty,* 824:
nyse, 824. OF. nice.

nif, conj., ne + ȝif, *if not, unless,*
21: nyf, 424.

niye, see nye.

no, adj., 136, 141, 142, 197, etc.; no
mon, 514, 1656; with comparatives: better, lasse, lenger,
mo(re), 234, 385, 513, etc. OE.
nān. See also non.

noble, adj., 121, 167, 1218, 1281,
1302, 1338, 1372, 1430; as pl.
noun, 1226. OF. noble.

nobleye, n., *nobility,* 1091. OF.
nobleye.

no-bot, adv., *only,* 1127.

Noe, prop. n., *Noah,* 297, 301, 345,
*359, 410, 480, 481, 484, 505, 513,
gen. Noe, 425. Lat. Noe, OE.
Nōe.

noȝt, pron., *nothing,* 106, 209, 374,
992, 1023, 1245; for noȝt, *in
vain,* 888. OE. nōwiht.

noȝty, adj., *wicked, bad,* 1359.

nold, see wyl.

nome, see name.

nome(n), see nym.

non, adj. pron., 21, 426. 735, 795, 868,
1056; absol. 72, 101, 578, 1088,
1399; pl. none, 262; non oþer,
342, 508, 742, 1681, 1704: none,
101, 426. OE. nān.

norne, see nurne.

norture, n., *nurture, upbringing,*
1091. OF. norture.

not, adv.: 22, 32, 33, 70, etc.; noȝt,
84. See noȝt.

note¹, n., *work, occupation,* 1233;
*practice, custom,* 727; *trouble,
pains,* 381; *position, power,*
1651. OE. notu.

note², n., *note (of music):* pl. -s,
1413. OF. note.

noted, part, adj., *famed, renowned,*
1651.

notyng, vbl. n., *using,* 1354. OE.
notian.

noumbre, n., *number,* 737, 1376;
*count,* 1731; *quantity,* 1283.
AN. numbre, OF. nombre.

now, adv., *now, at this time, forthwith,* 64, 944, 1008, 1015, etc.;
now at þis tyme, 106; ryȝt now,
1754; w. imperative, or introducing clause, temporal meaning
being weakened or effaced: 75,

125, 301, 345, \*359, 513, 521, 545,
669, 709, 746, 761, 921, 1225; as
conj., *seeing that,* 1111; *suppose
that, if,* 721: now, 64, 75, 125,
301, etc. (33 times); nou, 921,
1008, 1015, 1111, 1305, 1505. OE.
nū.

**noye,** see **nuye.**

**noyse,** n., *clamor, din,* 849, 873; of
music, 1413, 1415. OF. noise.

**nummen,** see **nym.**

**nurne,** v. tr., *say, declare,* 65, 669;
*entreat, urge,* 803: 1 sg. norne,
803; pret. 3 sg. 65, 669. Etym.
obscure. The word is peculiar
to the Gawain-poet.

**nuye,** v. tr., *trouble, vex,* 306, 578,
1603; *harass,* 1176, 1236: inf.
noye, 1236; 3 sg. nuyez, 578;
pret. 3 sg. 1176; pp. nwyed, 306;
nyed, 1603. Cf. OF. anuier,
anoier.

**nye,** n., *trouble,* 1376; *anxiety,*
1002; *woe, trouble, vexation,
anger,* 301: nye, 1376, niye, 1002;
nwy, 301; pl. nyes, 1754. Cf.
OF. anuy.

**nyf,** see **nif.**

**ny3e,** see **ne3e.**

**ny3t,** n., *night,* 359, etc.; at forþ
na3tes, *late at night,* 1764: ny3t,
\*359, 526, 779, 803, 888, 1203,
1754, \*1779; na3t, 484, 578, 807,
1002; na3tes, 1764. OE. niht,
neaht (Angl. næht).

**nyl,** see **wyl.**

**nym,** v. r., *take;* 480, etc.; *have,
feel,* \*1002 (see note): 3 sg.
nymmes, 480; nymmez, 481;
pret. 3 sg. nem, 505; nome, 1613;
pp. nomen, \*1002, 1281; \*nummen, 1291. OE. niman.

**nyse,** see **nice.**

**nytel,** v. intr., *?struggle:* pret. 3 sg.
888. Etym. obscure.

## O.

**Oo,** interj., 861.

**obeche,** v. refl., *do obeisance to:*
pret. 3 sg. 745. OF. obeïss–,
from obeïr.

**odde,** adj., *odd,* 426; abs. 505. ON.
odda–.

**oddely,** adv., *singly, solely,* 923;
*singularly,* 698.

**of,** prep., *of,* 7, 74, 111, 149, etc.;
*from,* 596, 855, 892, 901, etc.;
with 'out,' 287, 289, 1316, 1441,
1575; *by* (agent), 243; *with, by
means of,* 1253, 1277, 1404, 1408,
1433; denoting material, 1271,
1276, 1279, etc.; with 'out,' 1342,
1408; *because of,* 848, 1019, 1706,
1728; *in respect to,* 27, 92, 253,
314, etc.; *concerning,* 26, 51, 425,
843, etc.; in partitive sense, 42,
88, 170, 207, etc.; *out of, among,*
923; in various idiomatic combinations: because of, 1519; in
contrary of, 1532; on payne of,
46; of armes, 1773; of kynde,
1033. OE. of.

**of,** adv., *off,* 630, 876, 1191, 1265.
OE. of.

**ofte,** adv., *often,* 410, 423, 952, 1274,
1328, 1584, 1597, 1601. OE. oft.

**o3e,** pret. pres. v.: pret. 3 sg. a3t,
*ought,* 122. OE. āgan.

**o3t,** pron., *anything,* 663, 1092. OE.
āwiht.

**oke,** n., *oak,* 602. OE. āc.

**olde,** adj., 601, 1123, 1263: superl.
aldest, 1333. OE. eald, āld.

**olipraunce,** n., *vanity, ostentation,*
1349. Etym. obscure.

olyve, n., 487. OF. olive.

on, adv., 30, 477, 1661. OE. on.

on, prep., *on, upon, in,* 78, 198, 213, 228, etc.; expressing time, 445, 479, 481, 485, etc.; manner, 1775, 1782, esp. on . . . wyse, 271, 327, 696, 1063, 1171, 1187; *of* (with verbs of thinking), 25, 436, 771, 819; *in,* in phrase 'on Ebru,' 448; in phrases: on alle faure, 1683; on benche, 1499; on dece, 38; on ende, 423; on erd, 892; on folde, 403; on fote, 79, on Godez, halve, 896; on honde, 1412; on hors, 79; on hyʒe, 413; on launde, 1000; on lenþe, 116; on molde, 279; on mor, 385; on naʒt, 578; on payne of, 46; on ryʒt, 1513; on urþe, 273; on þe waye, 606; on wyde, *about,* 1423. OE. on.

on, num. and pron., *a single,* 108, 112, 152, 551, 803, 1244, 1555; *one and the same,* 716, 718; *alone,* 670, 731, 872, 927; absol., 25, 63, 178, 299, 997, 999, 1555; w. superl., 892; ani on, 42; uch on, 71, 267, 394, 497, 825, 890, 1024, 1111; everuch one, 1221, þyn one, 923 (see note): one, 25, 178, 670, 731, 825, 872, 927, 1024, 1111, 1221. OE. ān.

onelych, adv., *only,* 1749. Cf. OE. ānlic, adj., ǣnlīce, adv.

onez, adv., *once,* 23, etc.; at onez, *at one time, together,* 402, 519, 566, 672, 732, 909, 963, 1086; at þis onez, *for this one time,* 624, 801: onez, 23, 402, 566, 600, 601, 624, 672, 732, 761, 801, 909, 963, 1146; ones, 519, 982, 1086, 1144, 1357, 1672.

onhede, n., *unity, concord,* 612. on + hede.

onsware, n., *answer,* 753. OE. ondswaru.

on-yʒed, adj., *one-eyed,* 102.

open, v. tr.: inf. 1600. OE. openian.

ordaynt, part. adj., *ordained,* 237. AN. ordeiner, OF. ordener.

ordenaunce, n., 698. OF. ordenance.

ordure, n., *filth,* 1092, 1101. OF. ordure.

orenge, n., *orange,* 1044. OF. orenge.

organe, n., *a wind instrument:* pl. -s, 1081. OF. organe.

ornement, n., *ornament, furnishing:* pl. -es, 1799; urnmentes, 1284. OF. o(u)rnement.

orppedly, adv., *quickly,* 623. OE. orpedlīce.

oste, n., *host,* 1204. OF. oste.

oþer, adj., 84, 149, 175, 235, etc.; absol. as pron. sg., 267, 268, 299, 765, 999, 1227; pl. oþer, 25, 279, 332, 340, 596, 741, 937, 1389, 1511; non oþer, 342, 508, 742, 1704; *nothing else,* 1681; ayþer oþer, 338, 705; redundant after superlatives, 256, 701, 1749. OE. ōðer.

oþer, conj., *or,* 42, 417, 418, 419, etc.; wheþer . . . oþer, 113. OE. ōðer.

oþerwayez, adv., *otherwise,* 448.

oure, poss. pron., 28, 345, 410, 424, etc.: our, 986. OE. ūre.

oure, n., *hour,* 1779. OF. (h)oure, hore.

out, adv., 98, 353, 364, 475, 505, 842, 941, 990, 1046, 1203, 1222, 1462, 1790, 1802; *protruding,* 41; be out, *pass,* 442; w. of, 287, 289,

923, 1316, 1342, 1408, 1441, 1460,
1516, 1575, 1654, 1783; out of
age, *advanced in age*, 656: oute,
41, 1046. OE. ūt.

**outberst**, v. intr., *burst out:* pret.
3 pl. outborst, 1251.

**outcomlyng**, n., *stranger*, 876. Cf.
OE. pp. ūtancumen.

**outkast**, v. tr., *cast out:* pp. outkast, 1679.

**outtaken**, pp., as prep., *except*, 357,
1573.

**ouþer**, pron., *either*, 795. OE.
āwðer<āhwæðer.

**over**, prep., *over, across*, 133, 406,
472, 482, 981, 1293, 1776; *above*,
1314. OE. ofer.

**overbrawden**, part. adj., *covered
over*, 1698. OE. oferbrǣdan.

**overgo**, v. intr., *pass:* pret. 3 sg.
overȝede, 1753. OE. ofergān.

**overseye**, v. intr., *pass by:* pp. 1686.

**overtake**, v. tr.: pret. 3 pl. overtok,
1213.

**overtorne**, v. intr., *go round, pass
by:* pret. 3 pl. 1192.

**overþwert**, adj., *placed crosswise*,
1384. Cf. ON. þvert, neut. of
þverr.

**overþwert**, adv., *crosswise*, 316.

**overwalte**, v. tr., *overflow:* 3 sg.
-z, 370.

**overȝede**, see **overgo**.

**owne**, see **aune**.

**ox**, n., 1086: oxe, 1682; pl. -en, 66.
OE. oxa.

## P.

**pakke**, v. tr., *pack:* pret. 3 sg. 1282.
MLG. pakken.

**Palastyn**, prop. n., *Palestine*, 1177.
Lat. Palæstīna.

**palays**, n., *palace*, 83, 111, 1531,
1781:, palayce, 1389. OF. palais.

**palle**[1], n., *fine cloth*, 1637. OE.
pæll.

**palle**[2], n., *paling, fence of stakes*,
1384. OF. pal.

**papejaye**, n., *parrot:* pl. -s, 1465.
AN. papejaye, OF. papegai.

**paper**, n., 1408. AN. papir, OF.
papier.

**paradys**, n., *paradise, garden of
Eden*, 238, 1007; *heaven*, 195;
*supreme bliss*, 704: paradis,
1007. OF. paradis.

**parage**, n., *lineage*, 167. OF.
parage.

**paramorez**, n., *love*, 700. OF. par
amour(s).

**parchmen**, n., *parchment*, 1134.
OF. parchemin.

**pare**, v. tr., *cut*, 1408; *mark*, 1536:
pret. 3 sg. 1536; pp. 1408. OF.
parer.

**parforme**, v. tr., *bring to pass:*
pret. 3 sg. 542. OF. parformer.

**parget**, n., *plaster spread on a wall*,
1536. Cf. OF. pargeter, v.

**paflatyk**, adj., *paralytic*, 1095. OF.
paralytique.

**part**, v. tr., *divide*, 1107; *descend*,
242: pret. 3 pl. 242. OF. partir.

**partryke**, n., *partridge:* pl. -z, 57.
OF. perdriz, pertriz.

**passe**, v. intr., *go, pass*, 72, etc.;
*surpass*, 1389; passe out of, *come
from*, 1654: inf. 942; pres. 3 pl.
-n, 844, 1780; pret. 3 sg. passed,
72, 769, 856; past, 1654; imper.
sg. passe, 615; pres. part. passande, 1389; pp. passed, 395,
past, 1672. OF. passer.

**pau**, n., *claw:* pl. ?paune, 1697.
OF. powe, poue.

paume, n., *palm, hand,* 1533: pl. -s, 1542. OF. paume.

payne, n., *penalty,* 46, 244, 716; *pain, suffering* (inflicted as punishment), 190: pl. -s, 1227. OF. peine.

payre, n., *pair,* 335, 338². OF. paire.

payre, v. intr., *deteriorate,* 3 sg. -s, 1124. Aphetic form of ME. apayre (OF. empeirier).

pece, n., *piece:* pl. -s, 1348. OF. pece, piece.

pen, n.: pl. -ez, 322. OE. penn.

penaunce, n., 1116, 1131. OF. penance.

peni, n., *penny:* pl. -es, *money,* 1118. OF. pening, penig.

penitot, n., *peridot, chrysolite:* pl. -es, 1472. OF. peritot.

penne, n., *pen,* 1546, 1724. OF. penne.

penne-fed, part. adj., *fed in a pen,* 57.

pent, v. intr., *belong, pertain:* pret. 3 sg. 1270. Cf. OF. apendre.

peple, n., *people,* 111, 396, 651, 885: pl. peplez, 242. OF. poeple.

per, n., *peer, equal,* 1336; *rival,* 1214: pere, 1336. OF. per.

peraunter, adv., *perchance,* 43. OF. par aventure.

Perce, prop. n., *Persia,* 1772. OF. Perce.

peril, n.: *856; perile, 942. OF. peril.

perle, n., *pearl,* 1068, 1116, 1117, 1124: pl. -s, 1132, 1467, 1472. OF. perle.

perre, coll. n., *jewelry, precious stones,* 1117. OF. perrerie, perrie.

Perse, prop. n., *Persian:* pl. Perses, 1739. OF. Perse.

pertly, adv., *openly, plainly,* 244. Cf. OF. apert.

Phares, n., *Upharsin,* 1727, 1736, 1737. Vulg. Phares.

pich, n., *pitch,* 1008. OE. pic.

pik, v. intr., *pick, peck:* pp. 1466. OE. pīcan.

pinacle, n.: pl. -s, 1463. OF. pinacle.

pipe, n.: pl. pipes, 1413; pypes, 1081. OE. pīpe.

pit, n., 1008. OE. pytt.

place, n., *72, 146, 238, 785, 1282, 1317, 1443; *palace, residence,* 1385: pl. -s, 1013. OF. place.

planed, part. adj., 310. OF. planer.

plant, v. tr.: pret. 3 sg. plantted, 1007. OE. plantian.

plaster, n., 1549. OF. plastre.

plat, adj., *flat,* 1379. OF. plat.

plat, adv., *entirely,* 83.

plat, v. tr., *strike:* pret. 3 pl. plat, 1265. OE. plættan.

plater, n., *platter,* 638. AN. plater.

plattyng, vbl. n., *striking,* 1542.

play, n., *reveling,* 1494, 1502; *intercourse,* 700. OE. plega.

play, v. intr., *bestir oneself, be busy:* pret. 3 pl. 787. OE. plegan.

playn, adj., *plain, smooth,* 1068, 1134, 1531. OF. plain.

playn, n., *plain,* 1379: pl. -es, 1216. OF. plain.

plek, n., *piece of ground, spot,* 1379. OE. *plecce; cf. MDu. plecke.

plese, v. tr., *please:* inf. 338. OF. plaisir.

plow, n., 68. OE. plōh.

plunge, v. tr.: pp. 1008. AN. plunger, OF. plongier.

plye, v. intr., *incline, tend,* 196; tr. *cover,* 1385: 3 sg. -s, 196; pret. 3 sg. plyed, 1385. OF. plier.

**plyt¹**, n., *sin, guilt*, 1494. OE. pliht.

**plyt²**, n., *condition:* pl. -ez, 111. AN. plit, OF. *pleit, ploit.

**polle**, n., *head*, 1265. Cf. Du. polle.

**polment**, n., *a kind of pottage*, 628, 638. Lat. pulmentum.

**polyce**, v. tr., *polish:* inf. 1131; pp. 1068; polysed, 1134. OF. poliss–, from polir.

**polyle**, n., *poultry*, 57. OF. polaille.

**pomgarnade**, n., *pomegranate:* pl. -s, 1466. OF. pome garnade.

**porche**, n., 785. OF. porche.

**porpre**, n., *purple*, 1568, 1743; adj. 1637; porpor, 1743. OE. purpure, and OF. purpre, porpre.

**Porros**, prop. n., *Porus*, 1772. Lat. Porus.

**port**, n., *gate*, 856. OF. porte.

**portraye**, v. tr., *draw, carve; fashion, form;* 1271, 1465, 1536; *devise*, 700: pret. 1 sg. 700; 3 sg. purtrayed, 1536; pp. portrayd, 1271, purtrayed, 1465. OF. pourtraire.

**porvaye**, v. tr., *arrange beforehand, settle on:* 3 sg. -s, 1502. AN. porveier; OF. porveeir, porveoir.

**post**, n., *pillar:* pl. -es, 1278. OE. post.

**potage**, n., *pottage*, 638. OF. potage.

**pover**, adj., *poor*, 773, 1074; as noun, 127; *poor servant*, 615: pover, 1074; povere, 615, 773; pl. poveren, 127. OF. povre.

**pover**, adv., *poorly*, 146.

**power**, n., 1660: pouer, 1654. AN. poer, pouair; OF. poeir, pooir.

**poynt**, n., *moment*, 628; *height*, 1502, 1677; uch a poynt, *every-*thing, 196: poynte, 628. OF. point.

**poynted**, part. adj., 1408. OF. pointer.

**poyntel**, n., *a pointed instrument for writing*, 1533. OF. pointel.

**poysened**, part. adj., 1095. OF. poisonner.

**pray**, n., *that which is taken in war, prey:* in pray, as prey, 1297. OF. preie.

**pray**, v. tr., *plunder:* pret. 3 sg. 1624. OF. pre(i)er.

**pray**, v. tr., *beseech, ask:* inf. 232, 615; pp. 72. OF. preier.

**prayse**, v. tr., *value*, 146; *praise*, 148, etc.; *glorify*, 1313: inf. 148, 189 (ger.); pret. 2 sg. 146; 3 sg. 642, 1313; 3 pl. 1479; pp. 1117. OF. preisier.

**prece**, n., *press, throng*, 880. OF. presse.

**preche**, v. tr., *proclaim, declare:* pres. part. prechande, 942. OF. prechier.

**precious**, adj., 1282: presyous, 1496. OF. precious.

**prelate**, n.: pl. -s, 1249. OF. prelat.

**prese**, v. tr., *press* in phrase 'prese to deþe,' 1249: pret. 3 pl. 1249. OF. presser.

**presens**, n., *presence*, 8, 147, 1496. OF. presence.

**present**, v. tr.: pret. 3 sg. 1297; pp. 1217. OF. presenter.

**presoner**, n., *prisoner:* pl. -es, 1217, 1297; -s, 1308. AN. prisoner, OF. prisonier.

**prest**, n., *priest*, 1131: pl. -es, 1249, 1265; -ez, 8. OE. prēost.

**prest**, adj., *ready, eager*, 147. OF. prest.

**prestly**, adv., *quickly*, 628.

**preve**, see **prove**.

**profecie,** n., *prophecy,* 1158; *company of prophets,* 1308: pl. -s, 1158. OF. profecie.

**profer,** v. intr., *project:* pret. 3 pl. profert, 1463. OF. proferer.

**proper,** adj., *excellent,* 195. OF. propre.

**prophete,** n., 1614; profete, 1624; pl. -s, 1300, 1492. OF. prophete.

**proud,** adj., 232: proude, 1177; prowde, 1772; superl. pruddest, 1300. LOE. prūd, ON. prūðr.

**prove,** v. tr., *prove, show, find* (*to be*), 1158, 1496, 1748; intr. *prove,* 704: inf. preve, 704; pp. proved, 1158, 1496; preved, 1748. OF. prover (pruev–).

**province,** n., 1300, 1614: provynce, 1624. OF. province.

**prudly,** adv., *proudly,* 1379, 1466. Cf. LOE. prūtlīce.

**pryce,** adj., *chief, most eminent,* 1614, absol. 1308; almost adv., *as most worthy, choice, above all,* 1117: prys, 1117. OF. pris.

**pryde,** n.: 179, 1227, 1349, 1389, 1450, 1657, 1677. LOE. prȳto, prȳdo.

**prymate,** n., *chief, head,* 1570. OF. primat.

**prynce,** n., 49, 167, 195, 1214, 1217, 1570, 1654, 1660, 1748, 1772; pl. prynces, 1215, 1518. OF. prince.

**pryncipal,** adj., *princely, royal,* 1781: pryncipale, 1531. OF. principal.

**pryncipalte,** n., *dominion, sovereignty,* 1672, 1738. OF. principalte.

**prys,** see **pryce,** adj.

**pryvvy,** adj., *intimate, 'close':* superl. pryvyest, 1748. OF. prive.

**pryvyly,** adv., *privately, in a place apart,* 238; *skilfully,* 1107: pryvely, 238.

**pulle,** v. tr., 1265; intr., 68: inf. 68; pret. 3 pl. pulden, 1265. OE. pullian.

**pure,** adj., *pure, unalloyed,* 1271; *true, very* (= *itself*); 704, 1570. OF. pur.

**pure,** v. tr., *purify:* inf. 1116. OF. purer.

**purely,** adv., *entirely, completely,* 1660.

**pursaunt,** n., *space, enclosed ground,* 1385. AN. purceynt, OF. porceint.

**pursue,** v. tr., used absol.: pret. 3 sg. 1177. AN. pursuer, OF. porsievre, porsuire.

**puryte,** n., 1074. OF. purite.

**put,** v. tr.: pp. put, 244, 1214. LOE. putian.

**puttyng,** vbl. n., 46.

**pyche,** v. tr., *place, set,* 477, 785, 1463; *array,* 83: inf. 477; pp. pyȝt, 83, 785, 1463. ?OE. *piccean.

**pye,** n., *magpie:* pl. -s, 1465. OF. pie.

**pyese,** n., in phrase 'in pyese,' perhaps for 'in pryse,' 1124 (see note).

**pyȝt,** see **pyche.**

**pyle,** v. tr., *pillage, rob:* pret. 3 pl. 1270; pp. 1282. OE. pylian.

**pylere,** n., *pillar:* pl. -s, 1271, 1479. OF. piler.

**pyned,** part. adj., *wasted, consumed,* 1095. OE. pīnian.

**pynkardine,** n., *some precious stone:* pl. -s, 1472 (see note).

**pypes,** see **pipe.**

**pyte,** n., *pity,* 396: pite, 232.

## Q.

quat, see who, interr. pron.

quavende, part. adj., *causing things to quake, overwhelming,* 324. OE. *cwafian, parallel formation to cwacian.

quayntyse, see coyntyse.

qued, n., *evil,* 567. OE. cwēad.

quelle, v. tr., *kill, destroy:* inf. 324, 567. OE. cwellan.

quen, see when.

quene, n., *queen,* 1351, 1586, 1593, 1619. OE. cwēn.

queþe, v. tr., *say* (only in pret.) : 3 sg. quod, 139, 345, 349, 729, 733, 739, 757, 761, 765, 925, 929, 1593; 3 pl. 621, OE. cweðan.

quite, see whyte.

quo, see who, rel. pron.

quod, see queþe.

quos, see who, rel. pron.

quoynt, adj., *skilfully made, beautiful,* 1382, 1459; *well-dressed,* 160; *dainty,* 871: koynt, 1382. OF. coint.

quoyntis, see coyntyse.

quyk, adj., *living,* 324; as pl. noun, quykez, 567; *prompt,* 624; quik, 324. OE. cwicu.

quyle, conj., *while,* 1686: quyl, 627. OE. hwīl, n.

quyte, v. tr., *repay:* 1 sg. quyte, 1632. OF. quiter.

## R.

rac, n., *driving clouds, storm,* 433. Cf. Norw. and Sw. dial. rak.

rachche, see reche.

rad, adj., *frightened,* 1543. ON. hrǣddr.

radly, adv., *quickly, promptly,* 671, 797. OE. hrædlīce.

rafte, see reve.

raȝt, see reche.

rank, see ronk.

rankor, n., *wrath,* 756. OF. rancor.

rape, n., *blow,* 233. Prob. echoic.

raspe, v. tr., *scratch:* pret. 3 sg. 1545, 1724. OF. rasper.

rasse, n., *?top,* 446 (see note). Etym. unknown.

ratted, part. adj., *ragged, torn,* 144. Cf. ME. rat, *rag;* etym. obscure.

raven, n., 455, 465. OE. hræfn.

raw, adj., (of silk) 790. OE. hrēaw.

rawþe, n., *pity,* 972; *remorse,* 233. Cf. OE. hrēow.

rayke, v. intr., *go,* 671; *flow,* 382; refl. *betake oneself,* 465: inf. 671; 3 sg. -z, 465; pres. part. raykande, 382. ON. reika.

rayn, n., 440, 953, 959. OE. regn.

rayne, v. intr.: inf. 354; pres. part. raynande, 382. OE. regnian.

rayn-ryfte, n., *break in the clouds through which rain pours,* 368. Cf. ON. ript.

reame, see reme.

rebaud, n., *dissolute man:* pl. -ez, 873. OF. rebaud.

rebel, adj., *disobedient, rebellious,* 455. OF. rebelle.

rebounde, v. intr., *be driven back:* pret. 3 sg. rebounde, 422. AN. rebundir, OF. rebondir.

reche, n., *smoke,* 1009. OE. rēc.

reche¹, v. intr., *care:* 3 sg. reches, 465. OE. rēc(e)an, recc(e)an.

reche², v. tr., *grant, give,* 561, 1739; *yield, render,* 1369; *reach,* 890; *touch,* 10; intr. *arrive, come, go,* 619, 766, 906, 1766; *extend,* 1691: inf. 890, 1369; rachche, 619; 2 pl. reche, 906; 3 pl. -en, 10; pres. subj. 3 sg. reche, 1766;

**pret.** 3 sg. raȝt, 561, 766, 1691; pp. raȝt, 1739. OE. ræc(e)an.

**recorde,** v. tr.: 3 sg. -z, 25. OF. recorder.

**recoverer,** n., *recovery, safety,* 394. AN. recoverer, OF. recovrier.

**red,** adj., 1045. OE. rēad.

**rede,** v. tr., *guide, protect,* 1642; *counsel,* 1346; *interpret,* 1578; *read,* 194, 1555, 1596, 1633; absol., 7: inf. 1555, 1578, 1596; 2 sg. -s, 1633; 3 pl. -n, 7; pres. subj. 3 sg. rede, 1642; 3 pl. reden, 1346; pp. red, 194. OE. rǣdan, rēdan.

**redles,** adj., *without counsel, in dismay,* 1197: rydelles, 969. OE. rǣdlēas, rēdlēas.

**redy,** adj., *ready,* 345, 724, 869; in pregnant sense, *prompt (to obey),* 294. Cf. OE. rǣde.

**reflayr,** n., *odor, scent,* 1079. OF. *reflair.

**refrayne,** v. tr., *restrain:* inf. 756. OF. refrener.

**regioun,** n., 760, 964. AN. regiun.

**reȝtful,** n., *righteous,* 724. OE. rihtful.

**rehayte,** v. tr., *cheer:* inf. 127. OF. rehaiter.

**reken,** adj., *righteous, pious,* 10, 738, 756; *merry,* 1082. OE. recen.

**rekenly,** adv., *properly, piously,* 1318; *courteously,* 127. OE. recenlīce.

**rekken,** v. tr., *enumerate, relate,* w. up: inf. 2. OE. recenian.

**relece,** v. tr., *release, deliver:* 1 sg. 760. OF. relesser.

**relygioun,** n., *state of being bound by monastic vows,* 7; *?religious house,* 1156. AN. religiun, OF. religion.

**relyk,** n.: pl. -es, 1156, 1269. OF. relique.

**reme,** n., *realm,* 1572: pl. reames, 1316. OF. reaume.

**remnaunt,** n., *rest, remainder,* 433, 738. OF. remenant.

**remue,** v. tr., *remove, take away:* pp. 646, 1673. OF. remuer.

**renaye,** v. tr., *refuse:* pp. 105. OF. reneier.

**rend,** v. tr.: pp. 1595. OE. rendan. See also **rent.**

**rengne,** n., *reign, dominion, kingdom,* 1334, 1642, 1652, 1734, 1739. OF. regne.

**rengne,** v. intr., *reign, rule:* pret. 3 sg. 1169, 1321; imper. pl. -z, 527; pp. 328. OF. regner.

**renk,** n., *man,* 766, etc.; renk of relygioun, *man belonging to a monastic order,* 7; ring, 592; gen. sg. renkes, 786; pl. renkez, 7, 96, 105; renkkes, 969, 1514. OE. rinc, ON. rekkr.

**renischche,** *adj., strange,* 96; *mysterious,* 1545: runisch, 1545. Etym. obscure.

**renne,** v. intr., *run,* 391, etc.; *continue,* 527: inf. 527, 1392; 3 pl. -n, 1514; pret. 3 sg. ran, 797; 3 pl. runnen, 391; ran, 1208, 1269, 1782. ON. renna, OE. rinnan.

**rent,** part. adj., *torn,* 40, 144.

**renyschly,** adv., *?strangely,* 1724.

**rere,** v. tr., *raise,* 873; intr. *rise (up),* 366, 423, 1461: 3 pl. -s, 1461; pret. 3 sg. 366, 423; 3 pl. rerd, 873. OE. rǣran.

**res,** n., *rush, run,* 1782. OE. rǣs.

**reset,** n., *refuge, shelter,* 906. OF. recet.

resoun, n., *statement,* 194; *words, talk,* 184; *sense,* 1633; *commendation,* 2; *wisdom,* 328: reysoun, 328; pl. -ez, 184, 194; -z, 2. OF. reison, resoun.

resounable, adj., *sensible, wise,* 724. OF. reisonable.

rest, n., *repose,* 1208. OE. rest.

rest, n., *remainder, rest,* 890, 1766. OF. reste.

reste, v. intr., *rest, stay, remain,* 446, 616, 619, 906; *stand,* 738: 3 sg. -s, 738; pret. 3 sg. rest, 446; imper. pl. rest, 906; pl. resttez, 619; pp. restted, 616. OE. restan.

restlez, adj., *unceasing,* 527. OE. restlēas.

restore, v. tr.: pp. 1705. OF. restorer.

reve, v. tr., *rob, take away:* pret. 3 sg. rafte, 1431; pp. 1142, 1739. OE. rēafian.

revel, n., 1369. OF. revel.

reverence, n., 10; reverens, 1318, 1369. OF. reverence.

reward(e), n., *reward, recompense, return,* 208, 1346. NF. reward, OF. regard.

rewle, v. refl., *conduct oneself:* pret. 3 sg. 294. OF. reuler.

reynyez, n. pl., *reins (as seat of feelings),* 592. OF. reins.

rialte, n., *royalty,* 1321: rialty, 1371. OF. rialte, realte.

riboudrye, n., *debauchery, lechery,* 184. OF. ribauderie.

ridle, v. intr., *fall (as from a sieve), sift:* pres. part. ridlande, 953. Cf. LOE. hriddel, n.

rifte, n., *fissure, cleft:* pl. -s, 964. Cf. OIcel. ript; Dan. and Norw. rift.

ring, see renk.

robbe, v. tr., *rob, steal:* pret. 3 sg. 1156; pp. 1142. OF. rob(b)er.

robbor, n.: pl. -s, 1269. OF. rob(b)ere.

robe, n., 144, 1595. OF. robe.

roborrye, n., *robbery,* 184. OF. roberie.

roche, n., *rock, cliff:* pl. -z, 537. OF. roche.

roȝ, adj., *rough,* 1545, 1724: roȝe, 382. OE. rūh.

roȝly, adj., *?rough,* 433 (see note).

rok, n., *rock,* 446; *palace,* 1514 (see note). OF. roke.

role, v. intr., *roll:* pret. 3 sg. 423. OF. roler.

rollande, part. adj., *waving, curly,* 790.

romye, v. intr., *roar, cry:* 3 sg. -s, 1543. OF. rumier (see note).

ronk, adj., *violent, severe,* 233; *full-grown,* 869; *vile, bad,* 455, 760, 873: rank, 233. OE. ranc, ronc.

rore, v. intr., *roar:* 3 sg. -z, 1543; pret. 3 pl. 390. OE. rārian.

ros, see ryse.

rose, n., 1079; *Roman de la Rose,* 1057. OF. rose.

rose, v. tr., *praise:* inf. 1371. ON. hrōsa.

roste, v. tr., *roast:* pret. 3 sg. rostted, 959; pp. 59. OF. rostir.

rote[1], n., *root,* 619. LOE. rōt<ON. rōt.

rote[2], n., *decay,* 1079. Cf. OE. rotian, v., and Norw. and Icel. rot, n.

rote[3], n., *musical instrument, probably a kind of violin,* 1079. OF. rote.

roþele, (see note on 59), v. intr., *?huddle,* 890; tr. *?bring to-*

*gether, ?prepare,* 59: pret. 3 sg. 890; pp. 59. ?Cf. ON. hroða.

roþer, n., *rudder,* 419. OE. rōðer.

roþun, n., 1009, perhaps for *rotun, rotten,* used as noun. ?ON. rotinn.

roum, n., *room,* 96. OE. rūm.

rounde, adj., 927, 1121; *on rounde, around,* 423. AN. rund, OF. rond.

rowtande, part. adj., *rushing,* 354. OE. hrūtan.

rowte, n., *company, band:* pl. -s, 969, 1197, 1782. OF. route.

royl, adj., *?royal, splendid,* 790. OF. roial. (*NED.* s. v. royl, gives only this instance, defined as *?rich, luxuriant,* and relates to *roil,* v., *roll, flow.*) See also ryal.

rubie, n.: pl. -s, 1471. OF. rubi.

ruddon, n., *redness,* 893. Cf. ON. roðna, *redden,* and OE. rudu, *redness.*

ruele, v. intr., *fall:* pret. 3 sg. 953. Perh. OF. rueler, rouler, *roll.*

runisch, see renische.

rurd, n., *cry,* 390. OE. reord.

rusche, v. intr.: pret. 3 sg. 368. AN. russher, OF. reusser, ruser.

ruþe, v. tr., *arouse:* 3 pl. -n, 895; pp. 1208. Etym. unknown.

rwe, v. impers., *repent:* 3 sg. -z, 290; pret. 3 sg. 561. OE. hrēowan.

rwly, adv., *pitifully,* 390. OE. hrēowlīce.

ryal, adj., *royal, splendid,* 786: rial, 1082. OF. rial. See also royl.

ryally, adv., *royally,* 812.

ryche, adj., of wide application, often a formal epithet: *mighty, great, noble, wealthy, splendid,*

*costly,* 37, etc.; as noun, *great man,* sg. 1321; as pl. 1208: 37, 51, 176, 216, 571, 786, 812, 878, 1053, 1073, 1159, 1197, 1208, 1223, 1276, 1309, 1321, 1506, 1513, 1514, 1642, 1658, 1685; rych, 1299, 1371; riche, 127; superl. rychest, 1217, 1572. OE. rīce.

ryche, adv., *richly,* 1411. OE. rīce.

rychely, adv., *splendidly, brightly,* 1045. OE. rīclīce.

ryde, v. intr.: inf., 1572; 3 sg. -s, 1293. OE. rīdan.

rydelles, see redles.

ryg, n., *storm, tempest,* 382: ryge, 354. ?ON. hregg.

ryȝt, adj., *right,* 282. OE. ryht.

ryȝt, adv., *correctly,* 1346; *just, right* (as intensive), 59, 1061, 1754. OE. ryhte.

ryȝt, n., *right* (as distinguished from wrong), 194; in phrases, have ryȝt, *be right (in doing),* 1318; by ryȝt, *correctly, truthfully,* 1633; *rightfully, with justice,* 2; on ryȝt, *truly,* 1513: riȝt, 2. OE. riht, ryht.

ryȝtez, adv., *precisely,* 427. OE. ryhtes, gen. sg. of ryht.

ryhtwys, adj., *righteous,* 294, 328. OE. ryhtwīs.

ryngande, part. adj., *resounding,* 1082. OE. hringan.

rynging, vbl. n., 1513.

rype, adj., *ripe,* 1045; *mature,* 869: ripe, 1045. OE. rīpe.

rype, v. tr., *search into, scrutinize:* pres. part. rypande, 592. OE. rȳpan.

ryse, v. intr., *rise,* w. up, 671, 797: inf. 363; 3 sg. -s, 369, 1793; -z, 853; pret. subj. 3 sg. rise, 932; pret. 3 sg. ros, 797, 893, 1009,

1766; rysed, 509, 838, 971, 1203, 1778; 3 pl. ros, 671. OE. rīsan.

**ryth**, n., *bull*, 1543. OE. *hrīð.

## S.

**sacrafyse**, n., *sacrifice:* 510; sacrafyce, 1497; sacrefyce, 1447; sakerfyse, 507. OF. sacrifice.

**sadde**, adj., *solemn*, 595; *dignified*, 640; *sorrowful*, 525; *long*, 1286, *great*, 657: sad, 595. OE. sæd.

**sadel**, n., *saddle:* pl. -es, 1213. OE. sadol.

**saf**, see **save**.

**safyre**, n., *sapphire:* pl. -s, 1469. OF. safir.

**sage**, adj., *wise*, 1576. OF. sage.

**saȝe**, see **sawe**.

**saȝtle**, v. intr., *become reconciled*, 230, 1139; *settle* (by confusion w. ME. satle), 445: pret. 3 sg. 230, 445; pp. 1139. OE. sahtlian.

**saȝtlyng**, vbl. n., *reconciliation*, 490; *peace*, 1795.

**sake**, n., 922. OE. sacu.

**saklez**, adj., *innocent*, 716. LOE. sacléas.

**sakre**, tr. v., *dedicate:* pp. 1139. OF. sacrer.

**Salamon**, prop. n., *Solomon*, 1453: Salomon, 1286; gen. sg. Salamones, 1171. Lat. Salomon, OF. Salamon.

**sale**, n., *hall, main room of a palace:* 107, 120, 1260, 1417, 1442, 1577, 1722, 1757. OE. sæl.

**salt**, adj.: 984, 995. OE. sealt, salt.

**salt**, n., 820, 823, 825, 997, 999. OE. sealt, salt.

**same**, adj., 660. ON. samr.

**samen**, v. tr., *assemble*, 53, 126, 361; intr. *consort with*, 870: inf. 870;

samne, 53; pp. samned, 126, 361. OE. samnian.

**samen**, adv., *together*, 400, 468, 645, 1291, 1363. OE. samen, ON. saman.

**samenfere**, n., *fellow-traveller:* pl. -s, 985.

**sample**, n., *illustrative story:* pl. -s, 1326. OF. essample.

**sancta sanctorum**, n., 1274, 1491.

**sapyence**, n., *wisdom*, 1626. OF. sapience.

**sardiner**, n., *precious stone* (mentioned in Rev. 4. 3), 1469. Late Lat. sardīnus.

**Sare**, prop., n., *Sarah:* 623, 649, 654, 660, 661, 666, 667. Lat. Sarai.

**sarre(st)**, see **sore**.

**sat**, see **sytte**.

**Satanas**, prop. n., *Satan*, 1449. Lat. Satanas.

**sathrapa**, n., *satrap, governor:* pl. -s, 1576. Lat. satrapa.

**sauce**, n., 823. OF. sauce.

**saudan**, n., *sultan*, 1323: gen. sg. -s, 1364, 1388. OF. soudan.

**saule**, see **sawle**.

**saundyver**, n., *sandiver, glass-gall*, 1036. OF. suin de verre.

**\*sauteray**, n., *psaltery, mediæval stringed instrument*, 1516. OF. sauterie.

**save**, prep., *except*, 409: saf, 1749. OF. sauf.

**save**, v. tr.; inf. 332, 358, 388, 922, 988; pp. 992. OF. sauver.

**savement**, n., *safety*, 940. OF. sauvement.

**Savior**, n.: 176, 746: saveour, 576. OF. sauveour.

**savor**, n., *taste*, 995; *smell*, 510, 1447. OF. savour.

**savor**, v. tr., *flavor*, 825; *know, apprehend*, 581 (see note) : pres. 3 sg. saverez, 825; imper. sg. *savor, 581. OF. savorer.

**savyte**, n., *safety*, 489. OF. sauvete.

**sawe**, n., *saying, word, speech*, 1545, 1599, 1609, 1737; *command, decree*, 109, 1670: sawe, 109; saȝe, 1670; pl. saȝes, 1599, 1737; sawes, 1609; sauez, 1545. OE. sagu.

**sawle**, n., *soul:* 1130, 1599, 1626; saule, 290, 575, 1135; sawele, 1139; pl. saulez, 332. OE. sāw(e)l.

**say**, v. tr.: inf. 53, 1112, 1552; 2 sg. seggez, 621; 3 sg. saytz, 29, 75; says, 657; pres. subj. 1 sg. say, 868; pret. 3 sg. sayde, 63, 97, 470, 612, 631, 654, 661, 681, 715, 822, 919, 1622; sade, 210; 3 pl. sayden, 645, 647; imper. sg. say, 139. OE. secgan.

**sayl**, n., 420. OE. seg(e)l.

**sayne**, v. tr., *bless:* pret. 3 pl. 986; pp. 746. OE. segnian.

**scale**, v. tr.: pret. 3 pl. *1776. OF. escaler.

**scape**, v. intr., *escape:* inf. 62, 928; pret. 3 pl. 529. Cf. NF. escaper. See **ascape**.

**scarre**, v. tr., *frighten, alarm*, 838; *scatter*, 598 (see note); intr., *?spread, ?rise*, 1784; 3 sg. -z, 598; pret. 3 sg. 1784; pp. 838. Cf. ON. skirra.

**scaþe**, n., *harm, injury*, 151, 1186; w. emphasis on evil bringing 'harm' about, *wrong, sin*, 21, 196, 569, 598, 1148; *dire punishment*, 600; skaþe, 151, 598, 1186. ON. skaði.

**scelt**, see **skelt**.

**schadow**, n., *shade*, 605. OE. sceadu.

**schad**, see **schede**.

**schal**, v., 28, etc.; *ought* (past tense), 61, 152, 1077; *to be (about)* to, 249: 1 sg. schal, 211, 286, 292, 307, etc.; 2 sg. schal, 329, 1640; schalt, 742; 3 sg. schal, 28, 29, 47, 289, etc.; 1 pl. schal, 907; 3 pl. schal, 170, 523, 716, 718, 725, 1740; schul, 107; schin, 1435; schyn, 1810; pres. subj. 1 sg. schale, 553; 3 pl. schal, 712; pret. 1 sg. schulde, 915; 2 sg. 1110; 3 sg. 42, 152, 566, etc.; schuld, 249, 1365; 1 pl. schulde, 112; 3 pl. 53, 61, 671, 934, 1363; pret. subj. 3 pl. 108. OE. sculan.

**schalke**, n., *man*, 1029: pl. schalkez, 762. OE. sc(e)alc.

**schame**, n., 597, 850: schome, 1115. OE. sc(e)amu.

**schame**, v. intr., *feel shame:* 3 sg. -z, 580. OE. sc(e)amian.

**schap**, n., *shape, form*, 1121: pl. schappes, 1460. OE. gesc(e)ap.

**schape**, v. intr., *endeavor*, 762; tr. *decree*, 742. Cf. OE. scieppan, pp. sc(e)apen.

**scharp**, adj., *keen, intense*, 850; *great*, 1310; *penetrating*, 840; *swift*, 475: scharpe, 475, 850. OE. sc(e)arp.

**schaven**, part. adj., *scraped*, 1134. OE. sc(e)afan, v.

**schawe**, see **schewe**.

**schede**, v. intr., *fall:* pret. 3 sg. schad, 1690. OE. scēadan.

**schelde**, n., *shield* or *flank (of a boar)*: pl. -z, 58. OE. sceld.

**schende**, v. tr., *confound, disgrace*, 47, 580; *destroy, ruin*, 742, 1029;

absol., 519: inf. 519, 742; pp.
schent, 47, 580, 1029. OE.
scendan.

schene, adj., *beautiful, fair,* 170,
1076, 1310. OE. scīene, scēne.

schepon, n., *cattle-shed,* 1076. OE.
scypen.

*schere-wyke, n.: pl. -s, *groin,* 1690
(see note).

schewe, v. tr., *exhibit, display,* 1117,
1310; *display, show* (malice,
etc.), 250, 919; *offer,* 122; *prove,*
600, 1805; *expound, set forth,*
662, 1599, 1626; *speak, utter,*
840; refl., *appear,* 170; intr., *appear,* 553; *be seen,* 791: inf.
schewe, 122, 170, 553; schawe,
1599, 1626; 3 pl. schewe, 840;
pret. 1 sg. 662; 3 sg. *791; pp.
600, 919, 1117, 1310, 1805;
scheued, 250. OE. scēawian.

schin, see schal.

schome, see schame.

schonie, v. tr., *shun:* pret. 3 sg.
1101. OE. scunian.

schor, n., *shower,* 227. OE. scūr.

schortly, adv., *quickly, hastily,* 519,
600, 742. OE. sc(e)ortlīce.

schote, v. intr., *rush:* pret. 3 sg.
schot, 850. OE. scēotan, str. v.;
scotian, wk. v.

schout, n., *shout,* 840. Cf. ON.
skūta, *taunt.*

schowve, v. tr., *thrust violently,
cast,* 44, 1029; *eject,* 1740: pp.
44, 1029, 1740. OE. scūfan.

schrank, see schrynke.

schrewe, n., *wicked person:* pl. -z,
186. OE. scrēawa.

schrewedschyp, n., *wickedness,* 580.

schroude-hous, n., *dwelling which
affords shelter,* 1076.

schrowde, n., *garment, clothes,* 47,
170. OE. scrūd.

schryfte, n., *shrift, sacrament of
penance,* 1115, 1130, 1133. OE.
scrift.

schrylle, adj., *shrill,* 840. Cf. LG.
schrell.

schrynke, v. intr., *shrink:* pret.
3 sg. schrank, 850. OE. scrincan.

schulder, n., *shoulder,* 981: pl. -es,
1690. OE. sculdor.

schunt, v. intr., *go aside:* pp.
schunt, 605. Etym. obscure,
perh. derivative of OE. scunian
(see schonie).

schyn, see schal.

schyne, v. intr., *shine:* inf. 1115;
3 sg. -s, 1121; pret. 3 sg. schyned,
1532. OE. scīnan.

schyre, adj., *bright, shining,* 553,
605, 1278; quasi-adv., 1121:
schyr, 1121. OE. scīr.

scla3t, n., *slaughter,* 56. OE. slieht,
slæht.

scole, n., *drinking-cup,* 1145. ON.
skāl.

scolere, n., *scholar:* pl. -s, 1554.
OE. scolere.

scomfyte, v. tr., *discomfit, throw
into confusion:* pret. 3 sg. 1784;
pp. scoumfit, 151. Aphetic from
OF. desconfit, pp. of desconfire.

scorne, n., 827. OF. escarn.

scorne, v. tr.: pp. 709. Cf. OF.
escarnir.

scowte-wach, n., *sentinel, guard*
(here prob. collective), 838. OF.
escoute + OE. wæcca.

scoymus, adj., *having repugnance
or abhorrence, particular,* 21,
1148: skoymos, 598. AN. es-
coymous.

**scrape,** v. tr.: pp. 1546. OE.
scrapian, ON. skrapa.

**\*scrof,** adj., *?rough*, 1546. ?Cf. OE.
scruf, *scurf.*

**scrypture,** n., *inscription, writing*,
1546. Lat. scrīptūra.

**scylful,** adj., *righteous*, 1148. See
**skyl.**

**se,** v. intr., *look*, 661, 1225; tr. *see*,
68, etc.; *perceive*, 398, 515: inf.
se, 126, 176, 595, 1055, 1112, 1810;
see, 68, 192, 262, 988; 1 sg. se,
515; pres. subj. 3 sg. se, 178;
see, 576; pret. 2 sg. seȝ, 1710;
3 sg. 209, 398; syȝe, 788; 3 pl.
syȝe, 985; seȝen, 1529; imper.
sg. se, 661, 1225; pp. sen, 1169.
OE. sēon.

**seche,** v. tr., *seek, try to find*, 454,
469, 471, 482, 484, 478, 1559, 1615;
*try, endeavor* (w. inf.), 201,
1286; intr., w. after, 420; *go,
come*, 29, 510, 563, 940, 1130,
1371: inf. 29, 420, 454, 471, 482,
1559, 1615; 3 sg. -z, 469, 478,
484; pres. subj. 3 sg. seche,
1130; pret. 3 sg. soȝt, 201, 510,
563, 940, 1286; 3 pl. soȝtten,
1371. OE. sēc(e)an.

**secounde,** adj., 427. OF. second.

**sede,** n., *seed*, 336, 523; offspring,
660: sed, 358. OE. sǣd, sēd.

**see,** n., *sea:* 1015, 1020; se, 984;
gen. sg. se, 1039. OE. sǣ.

**seete,** see **sete,** n.

**sege,** n., *siege*, 1185. OF. sege,
siege.

**segge,** n., *man:* 117, 398, 549, 973;
segg, 681; pl. -z, 93, 833, 844;
-s, 1401, 1559, 1785. OE. secg.

**Segor,** prop. n., *Zoar:* 926, 973, 986,
992. Lat. Segor.

**seȝ(en),** see **se.**

**seknesse,** n., *sickness*, 1078. OE.
sēocness.

**selcouth,** n., *marvel, wonder*, 1274.
OE. sel(d)cūð.

**self,** intens. pron., *very, same*, 243,
etc.; as noun, 579, 786: self,
1418, 1769; selve, 660; selven,
243, 579, 786, 1068, 1399, 1745.
In cpd. pronouns, often w. no
intensive force and equivalent to
simple pronouns: myself, 291;
myselven, 194, 691, 700, 1572;
þyself, 581, 582 (refl.); yorselven, 863; yowself, 340; hymself, 23, 209, 490, 584; himself,
924, himselfe, 1498; hymselven,
9, 219, 284, 435, 695, 1426, 1448,
1591, 1656, 1702; himselven,
1237; hirself (refl.), 654, 822;
hitselven, 281; hemself, 15, 388
(refl.), hemselven (refl.), 702.
OE. self.

**selle,** v. tr.: 3 pl. -n, 1038. OE.
sellan.

**sely,** adj., *harmless, helpless*, 490.
OE. sǣlig, sēlig.

**Sem,** prop. n., *Shem*, 299, 555. Lat.
Sem.

**semblaunt,** n., *demeanor*, 640;
*friendly welcome*, 131. OF. semblant.

**semble,** n., *assembly, throng*, 126.
OF. assemblee, AN. semble(e).

**sem,** n., *seam, blemish*, 555. OE.
sēam.

**seme,** adj., *seemly*, 1810; *pleasing,
seemingly good*, 549. ON. sœmr.

**seme,** v. impers., *become*, 793; intr.
*seem*, 117, 416: pret. 3 sg. 117,
416, 793. ON. sœma.

**semely,** adv., *in a pleasing manner*,
1442. ON. sœmiliga.

**semly**, adj,, *seemly, fair,* 209, 262, 816, 1299; as noun, 870, 1055 (of Lord): semely, 1469; semlych, 1247; superl. semloker, 868. ON. sœmiligr.

**sende**, v. tr., 53, etc.; absol., 780; w. out, 353: inf. 666; 1 sg. sende, 353; 3 sg. -z, 595; pres. subj. 3 sg. sende, 1811; pret. 3 sg. sende, 53, 489, 780, 1005, 1454; imper. sg. sende, 1615; pp. sende, 781, 922, 1705, 1722. OE. sendan.

**ser**, adj., *single, separate,* 507; *various,* 336, 358, 1418: sere, 1418. ON. sēr.

**sergaunt**, n., *servant:* pl. -ez, 109. OF. serjant.

**serge**, n., *wax candle:* pl. -s, 1489. OF. cerge.

**servage**, n., *servitude, bondage,* 1257. OF. servage.

**servaunt**, n.: 631, 773; pl. -es, 988. OF. servant.

**serve**, v. intr., 530, 1264, ?1417, 1812; tr., 18, etc.: inf. 530, 724, 750, 1449, 1505, 1510, 1812; pret. 3 sg. 639, 997, 1146; 3 pl. 1264, *1406; imper. pl. -z, 820; pp. 18, 38, 120, 829, 1115, 1417. OF. servir.

**servyse**, n., *service,* 1152; (at table), 1401. OF. servise.

**sese**[1], v. tr., *seize, take possession of:* 3 sg. -s, 1795; pret. 3 sg. 1313. OF. saisir, seisir.

**sese**[2], v. intr., *cease, fail:* inf. 523. OF. cesser.

**sesoun**, n., *season:* pl. -ez, 523. AN. se(i)sun, OF. se(i)son.

**set**, part. adj., *appointed,* 1364.

**sete**[1], n., in phrase 'to þe sete,' 59 (see note). 'Related to *sit*— NED.

**sete**[2], n., *seat, throne; abode:* 37, 176, 557, 1055, 1388, 1395, 1705; seete, 92. ON. sǣti.

**sete**, see **sette**, **sytte**.

**seten**, see **sytte**.

**sette**, v. tr., *set, place, put, seat,* 37, etc.; *bring about,* 1225; sette sege, 1185; sette on, *decide on, choose,* 469; sette at lyttel, *disregard,* 1710; sette syȝt toward, *turn toward,* 672; *sit* (by confusion with str. verb), 1395; refl., *apply oneself,* 1453: inf. sete, 1395; 3 sg. settez, 469, 636; pret. 1 sg. sette, 290; 2 sg. set, 1710; 3 sg. sette, 507; sete, 1453; 3 pl. setten, 672; pp. sette, 37, 673, 986, 1185, 1388, 1449; set, 1015, 1225, 1401. OE. settan.

**seþe**, v. tr., *cook:* pres. subj. 3 sg. seþe, 631. OE. sēoðan.

**seue**, n., *pottage,* 108: pl. -z, 825. OE. sēaw.

**seven**, adj.: 334, 353, 1188, 1380, 1387, *1453, 1686. OE. seofon.

**sevenþe**, adj., 361, 427. OE. seofoða.

**sewer**, n., *servant charged with the service of the table,* 639. Cf. OF. asseour.

**sex**, adj., *six,* 426. OE. sex.

**seye**, v. intr., *pass:* pp. 353. OE. sīgan.

**sideborde**, n., *side-table:* pl. -s, 1398. OE. sīd + bord.

**sir**, n., 715, 900, 1622. Reduced form of **syre**.

**sitte**, see **sytte**.

**sive**, n., *sieve,* 226. OE. sife.

**skarmoch**, n., *skirmish, encounter,* 1186. OF. escarmoche.

**skaþe**, see **scaþe**.

**skele**, n., *platter:* pl. -s, 1405. ?OF. escuele.

skelt, v. intr., *?apply oneself*, 1554;
tr. *spread*, 1186, 1206; *?serve*,
827: pret. 3 sg. scelt, 827; pret.
3 pl. skelten, 1554; pp. skelt,
1186, 1206. Etym. obscure.

skete, adj., *swift, lively*, 1186. ON.
skjōtr.

skowte, v. intr., *scout, search:* 3 sg.
-z, 483. OF. escouter.

skoymos, see scoymos.

skwe, n., *sky, cloud:* skwe, 483;
scue, 1784; pl. -s, 1759; skewes,
1206. 'Prob. of Scand. origin
and related to *sky'*—NED.

skyg, adj., *fastidious*, 21. Cf.
Norw. and Sw. dial. skygg.

skyft, v. tr., *change* (= *disobey*):
pp. 709. ON. skipta.

skyl, n., *reason*, 151; *sense*, 823;
*significance*, 1554; *mind*, 827;
*ordinance, decree*, 569, 709:
scylle, 151. ON. skil.

skyly, n., *?separation, ?purpose*, 529
(see note); *excuse*, 62: skylly,
529.

skyre, adj., *clear*, 1776. ON. skīrr.

skyrme, v. intr., *fly swiftly, dart
about:* 3 sg. -z, 483. OF. es-
kirmir.

skyvalde, see note on 529.

slauþe, n., *sloth*, 178. 'Formed directly on slaw, slow, in place of
OE. slǣwð'—NED.

slaye, v. tr., *slay:* pret. 3 sg. slow,
1221; 3 pl. slowen, 1247; slouen,
1264; pp. slayne, 55, 1785. OE.
slēan.

sleke, v. tr., *quench*, 708. Cf. OE.
sleccan.

slepe, v. intr., *sleep:* pres. part.
slepande, 1785. OE. slēpan.

sly3t, n., *skill*, 1289. ON. slǣgð.

slyp, n., *stroke, blow*, 1264.

slyppe, v. intr., *escape*, 1785; w.
by, *slip, pass*, 985: inf. 1785;
pret. 3 pl. 985. MLG. slippen.

smach, n., *scent, smell*, 461, 1019.
Cf. OE. smæc (infl. by verb?).

smache, v. intr., *smell:* pres. part.
smachande, 955. OE. smæc-
c(e)an.

smal, adj., 226. OE. smæl.

smart, adj., *bitter*, 1019. OE.
smeart.

smartly, adv., *sharply, severely*, 711.

smelle, n., 461, *1019. ?OE. *smel.

smod, n., *filth*, 711. Cf. LG. smad-
dern, v.

smoke, n., 955. OE. smoca.

smoke, v. intr.: 3 sg. -z, 226. OE.
smocian.

smolderande, part. adj., *suffocating*,
955. ME. smolder, n. prob. a
variant of ME. smorðer (based
on OE. smorian).

smolt, v. intr., *go, start off*, 461;
*escape* (perh. *be at peace*), 732:
inf. 732: 3 sg. -es, 461. Etym.
obscure.

smoþely, adv., *quietly, peaceably*,
732. Cf. OE. smōð, adj.

smylt, part. adj., *strained*, 226 (see
note).

smyte, v. tr., *smite:* inf. 566, 711.
OE. smītan.

snaw, n., *snow*, 222. OE. snāw.

so, adv., 17, 140, 147, 151, etc.; w.
indef. article, 144, 728, 1014, 1075,
1339; *thus*, 29, 69, 118, 661, 984,
988, 1129, 1225, 1257, 1331; *accordingly*, 685; *true* (after 'is'),
669; as intensive, often meaningless, 218, 434, 455, 552, etc.;
*soever*, 100, 422, 819, 1648; correl. w. 'as,' 198, 200, 201, 227,
519, 1045, 1076; so . . . to,

904; so þat, 83. OE. swā. For
'who so,' etc., see **who**, rel.

**so**, conj., *as*, 786: sone so, *as soon
as*, 1550; introd. parenthesis,
232, 1148. OE. swā.

**soberly**, adv., *solemnly*, 1497;
*humbly*, 799. OF. sobre.

**Sodamas**, prop. n., *Sodom:* 672,
679, 689, 722, 780, 781, 868, 956;
Sodomas, 844, 910, 1005; Sodomis, 773. Lat. Sodoma.

**sodenly**, adv., *suddenly*, 201, 910,
1769. Cf. OF. soudain.

**soerly**, adj., *filthy, base*, 117 (see
note). ON. saurligr.

**softe**, adj., *fair, wild*, 445. OE.
sōfte.

**softely**, adv., 822.

**soȝt**, see **seche**.

**solace**, n., *pleasure, joy:* 870, 1080,
1418, 1678, 1757, 1812. OF. solas.

**solase**, v. tr., *entertain, cheer:* pret.
3 sg. 131. OF. solasier.

**solemne**, adj., 1171: solempne, 1447.
OF. solem(p)ne.

**solemnete**, n., *solemnity, 'high
estate,'* 1678; wyth solemnete,
*ceremoniously*, 1313; *festival*,
1757: solempnete, 1678, 1757.
OF. solempnete.

**solempnely**, adv., *ceremoniously*, 37.

**solie**, n., *seat, throne*, 1171: soly,
1678. Lat. solium.

**somer**, n., *summer*, 525: pl. -es,
1686. OE. sumor.

**somones**, n., *summons*, 1498. OF.
somo(u)nes.

**sonde**, n., *messenger*, 53: pl. -s,
781. OE. sand, sond. ˙

**sondezmon**, n., *messenger*, 469.

**sone**, adv., *quickly, without delay*.
*soon*, 361, 461, 463, 501, 1059,
1150, 1435, 1437, 1478, 1649, 1705,

1743; as sone as, 219; sone so,
1550. OE. sōna.

**sonet**, n., *music*, 1516; *?musical
instrument*, 1415: pl. -ez, 1415.
OF. sonet.

**songe**, n., 1080. OE. sang, song.

**songe(n)**, see **synge**.

**sonne**, see **sunne**.

**sope**, n., *sup, draught*, 108. OE.
sopa.

**soper**, n., *supper*, 107, 829, 997, 1763.
OF. soper.

**sore**, adj., *painful*, 1078; *suffering,
sore*, 1111: superl. sarrest, 1078.
OE. sār.

**sore**, adv., *sorely, deeply*, 290, 557,
1136; *grievously*, 1195: comp.
sarre, 1195. OE. sāre.

**sorȝe**[1], n., *sorrow*, 75, 563, *778;
sorȝ, 1080. OE. sorg.

**sorȝe**[2], n., *filth*, 846 (see note).
Cf. ON. saurr, *filth;* ON. sori,
and Sw. sörja, *mud*, and ON.
saurgan, *pollution*.

**sorser**, n., *sorcerer:* pl. -s, 1579.
AN. sorcer, OF. sorcier.

**sorsory**, n., *sorcery*, 1576. OF.
sorcerie.

**soth**, adj., *true*, 1643: sothe, 515.
OE. sōð.

**sotte**, n., *fool*, 581. OF. sot, adj.

**soþe**, n., *truth:* pl. -s, 1598, 1626.
OE. sōð.

**soþefast**, adj., *true, very*, 1491. OE.
sōðfæst.

**soþely**, adv., *truly:* 657; sothely,
666; soþly, 299; sothly, 654.
OE. sōðlice.

**soufre**, n., *sulphur*, 954, 1036. OF
soufre.

**souly**, adj., *vile*, 1111. Cf. **sowle**.

**soun**, n., *sound*, 973; *noise, clamor*
(Vulg. clamor), 689. AN. soun,
OF. son.

**soun,** see **sun.**

**sounde,** adj., *sound, well,* 1078; *perfect,* 555; quasi-adv., *safe,* 1795. Cf. OE. gesund.

**soune,** v. intr., *sound:* pret. 3 sg. 1670. OF. suner.

**soupe,** v. intr., *eat supper:* pp. 833. OF. souper.

**sour,** adj., *sour, bitter,* 1036; as noun, 820. OE. sūr.

**sour,** adj., *base, vile,* 192. Cf. ON. saurr, and see note on 117.

**soverayn,** n., *sovereign,* 93, 178, 210, 552, 557, 780, 1152, *1225, 1289, 1313, 1643; as adj., 1454, 1670 (perh. gen.). OF. soverain.

**sowle,** adj., *unclean, foul,* 168. Cf. WFlem. sowelen, v.

**soyle,** n., *earth ground,* 1387. AN. soyl.

**space,** n., *time, opportunity,* 1774; *?course, custom,* 755; in space, *shortly, soon,* 1606. OF. espace.

**spakly,** adv., *promptly,* perh. *certainly,* 755. ON. spakliga.

**spare,** v. tr., 776, 1245; intr., 755: inf., 755, 776, 1245. OE. sparian.

**spec,** n., *speck,* 551. OE. specca.

**speche,** n., *speech, discourse, words:* 3, 26, 729, 761, 874, 1058, 1098, 1492, 1565, 1592, 1602, 1729. OE. spǣc, spēc.

**special,** adj., *specially chosen,* 1492. OF. especial.

**sped,** n., *aid,* 1607; as adj., in 'sped whyle,' *short time,* 1285. OE. spēd.

**spede,** v. intr., *succeed,* 1058; tr. *prosper,* 511; *cause,* 551: inf. 551, 1058; 3 sg. -z, 511. OE. spēdan.

**spedly,** adv., *quickly,* 1729. OE. spēdlīce.

**speke,** v. intr., *speak:* inf. 301; 3 sg. -s, 511; pret. 3 sg. speke, 1220; 3 pl. speken, 646, 845; pp. spoken, 1671. OE. sp(r)ecan.

**spere,** n., *spear:* pl. spere, 1383. OE. spere.

**spitous,** adj., *abominable,* 845. Aphetic from AN. despitous.

**spitously,** adv., *shamefully, in contempt,* 1220, 1285.

**spote,** n., *stain,* 551. OE. spot.

**spoyle,** v. tr., *plunder,* 1774; *seize as booty,* 1285: inf. 1774; pret. 3 sg. 1285. OF. espoillier.

**sprad,** see **sprede.**

**sprawlyng,** vbl. n., 408. OE. sprēawlian.

**sprede,** v. intr., *be spread out,* 1565; *be diffused, be present,* 1607: 3 sg. -s, 1565; pret. 3 sg. sprad, 1607. OE. sprǣdan.

**spryng,** v. intr., *go forth, spread:* inf. 1362. OE. springan.

**\*spumande,** part. adj., *spuming, foaming,* 1038. OF. espumer.

**spure,** v. tr., *ask:* pret. 3 sg. 1606. OE. spyrian.

**spute,** v. intr., *utter:* pret. 3 pl. sputen, 845. Aphetic from OF. desputer.

**spye,** v. tr., *spy, discover,* 1774; intr., 780: inf. 780; pp. 1774. OF. espier.

**spylle,** v. tr., *destroy, kill,* 511, 1220: *scatter,* 1248: 3 sg. -z, 511; pret. 3 sg. spylt, 1220; 3 pl. spylled, 1248. OE. spillan.

**spyrakle,** n., *breath* (spiraculum vitæ, Vulg. Gen. 7. 22), 408. OF. spiracle.

**spyryt,** n., 1607. AN. spirit, OF. esperit.

**spyrytually,** adv. (abbrev. spūally), 1492. Cf. OF. spiritual, adj.

spyser, n., *dealer, apothecary:* pl.
-ez, 1038. OF. espicier.

spyt, n., *wrath,* 755. Aphetic from
OF. despit.

stable, v. tr., *establish,* 1334, 1652;
*set,* 1667: pret. 3 sg. 1334; pp.
1652, 1667. OF. establir.

stac, see steke.

stad(de), see stede.

stal, n., *place, room,* 1506. OE.
steall, stall.

stalle, v. tr., *place,* 1378; *en-
throne,* 1334; *bring to a stand,
stop,* 1184: inf. 1184; pp. 1334,
1378. OE. *steallian; perh. also
OF. estaler.

stalworth, adj., *mighty,* 255; *strong,*
884; *immovable,* 983: superl.
stalworþest, 255. OE. stǽl-
wierðe.

stamyn, n., *prow,* 486. ON. stamn.

stanc, n., *pool,* 1018: pl. stangez,
439. OF. estanc.

stande, v. intr.: inf. stonde, 1490;
3 sg. -z, 984; -s, 999; pres. subj.
3 sg. stande, 1618; pret. 3 sg.
stod, 486; 3 pl. stod, 255. OE.
standan.

stang, see stanc.

stare, n., *power of sight,* 583.

stare, v. intr., *gaze, look,* 389, 787;
*shine,* 1396, 1506: pret. 3 sg. 787,
1506; 3 pl. 389; stayred, 1396.
OE. starian.

state, n., 1708. OF. estat.

statue, n., 995. OF. statue.

staue, v. tr., *stow, lodge, place:* 3 sg.
-z, 480; pp. 352, 357; stawed,
360; stowed, 113. OE. stōwigan.

stede, v. tr., only in pp., *placed,
fixed:* stad, 90, 1506; stadde,
806, 983. ON. steðja, pp. staddr.

steke, v. tr., *shut up, enclose,* 157,
352, 360; *fasten, lock,* 884, 1524;

*close, stop,* 439 (w. up), 754;
intr., *be shut in* (infl. in meaning by wk. stykke q. v.), 1199:
inf. 754; pret. 3 sg. stac, 439;
3 pl. steken, 884; stoken, 1199;
imper. pl. stekez, 157, 352; pp.
stoken, 360, 1524. OE. *stecan.

stele, v. tr., *capture by surprise,*
1778; intr. (w. oute), *slip, steal,*
1203: pret. 3 pl. stel, 1203;
stelen, 1778; see also stollen.
OE. stelan.

stemme, v. intr., *stop, delay:* pres.
subj. 2 pl. stemme, 905. ON.
stemma.

stepe, n., *step,* 905. OE. stæpe,
stepe.

stepe, adv., *brightly,* 1396.

steppe, adj., *bright, brilliant,* 583.
OE. stēap.

sterre, n., *star:* pl. -z, 1378. OE.
steorra.

steven¹, n., *voice,* 770; *sound, noise,
outcry,* 1203, 1402, 1524, 1778.
OE. stefn, fem.

steven², n., *appointed time, assigna-
tion,* 706. OE. stefn, masc.

steven³, n., *command, bidding,* 360,
463. ON. stefna, LOE. stefn.

stewarde, n., 90. OE. stīweard.

stiffe, adj., *rigid,* 983; *stout, stal-
wart,* 255: superl. styfest, 255.
OE. stīf.

stifly, adv., *firmly, fast,* 157: styfly,
352, 1652.

stik, see stykke.

stod, see stande.

stoffe, v. tr., *fill, crowd:* pp. 1184.
OF. estoffer.

stoken, see steke.

stokke, n., (only in plural), *wooden
block,* i. e. *lifeless image* in
phrase 'stokkes and stones,' 1343,
1523, 1720; *frame of timber for*

*confining and punishing crimi-
nals, stocks,* 46, 157 : -s, 1343,
1523, 1720; -z, 46; stokez, 157.
OE. stocc.

**stollen,** part. adj., *stolen, secret,* 706.
See **stele.**

**ston,** n., *stone, rock,* 983, 999, 1343,
1523, 1667, 1720; *precious stone,*
1120, 1280, 1396, 1470: pl. -es,
1120, 1280, 1343, 1396, 1470, 1523 :
-ez, 1720. OE. stān.

**stonde,** n., *blow,* 1540. Cf. OE.
stunian, *strike, dash against.*

**stonde,** see **stande.**

**stonen,** adj., *made of stone,* 995.

**ston-harde,** adv., *firmly,* 884.

**stop,** v. tr., *close up:* pret. 3 sg. 439.
OE. *stoppian.

**storme,** n., 225. OE. storm, ON.
stormr.

**stound,** n., *time, moment,* 1716; in
stoundes, *at (different) times,*
1603. OE. stund.

**stout,** adj., *strong, bold,* 787, 1184;
w. vaguer meaning, *great,
mighty,* 1343, 1396: stoute, 1343,
1396. OF. estout.

**stowed,** see **staue.**

**strange,** adj., *foreign,* 875; *odd,
singular,* 409; *unheard of, monstrous,* 861: straunge, 409. OF.
estrange.

**stray,** v. intr.: inf. 1199. OF.
estraier.

**strayne,** v. tr., *weaken:* pret. 3 sg.
1540. OF. estraindre.

**strayt,** adv., *closely, hard,* 880, 1199.
OF. estreit, *close.*

**streche,** v. intr., *walk, hasten:* imper. pl. -z, 905. OE. strecc(e)an.

**streme,** n., *stream, current:* pl. -z,
364, 374. OE. strēam.

**strenkle,** v. tr., *scatter, dispel:* inf.
307 (see note). Etym. uncertain.

**strenkþe,** n., *force, violence,* 880,
1155; *might,* 1430, 1667: strenþe,
1155, 1430. OE. strengðu.

**strete,** n., *street,* 787, 806; *highway,*
77: pl. streetez, 77. OE. strǣt,
strēt.

**strok,** n., 1540. OE. strāc.

**stronge,** adj., *strong, mighty,* 835,
1181, 1652; *powerful,* 1034;
*severe,* 1227, 1540; *great,* 1494:
strong, 1034; comp. as n.
stronger, 835. OE. strang,
strong.

**strye,** v. tr., *destroy:* inf. 307, 1768;
pret. 3 sg. 1018; stryede, 375.
Aphetic from OF. destruire.

**stryke,** v. tr., *strike up, sound:*
pret. 3 pl. strake, 1402. OE.
strīcan.

**stud,** n., *place,* 1334, 1378; *high
place,* 389. OE. stede, styde.

**sturne,** adj., *loud:* pl. sturnen,
1402. OE. styrne.

**styfest,** see **stiffe.**

**styfly,** see **stifly.**

**styȝe,** v. intr., *climb, mount:* pret.
3 pl. styȝe, 389. OE. stīgan.

**styȝtle,** v. tr., *arrange, take charge
of:* pp. 90. Cf. OE. stihtan.

**stykke,** v. tr., *fasten,* 157; *set, fix,*
583: imper. stik, 157; pret. 3 sg.
583. OE. stician.

**stylle,** adj., *quiet,* 589, 1203; *dumb,*
1523: stille, 1523. OE. stille.

**stylle,** adv., *still, quietly:* 486, 497,
706, 936, 1781. OE. stille.

**stylly,** adv., *quietly,* 806; *stealthily,*
1778. OE. stillīce.

**styngande,** part. adj., *stinging,* 225.
OE. stingan.

stynke, v. intr.: pres. 3 sg. stynkkez, 577; 3 pl. stynkes, 847; pres. part. stynkande, 1018. OE. stincan.

stynt, v. intr., *cease, stop:* inf. 225, 381, 1261; 3 sg. *styntez (MS. stystez), 359. OE. stintan.

styry, v. intr., *stir:* inf. 1720; pret. 3 sg. 403. OE. styrian.

such, adj., 190, 192, 658, 703, etc.; as pron., 1039, 1061; such a, 354, 748, 873, 971, etc.; such anoþer, 1668; oþer such, 1036; such . . . as, 640: suche, 541, 1009, 1039, 1588. OE. swylc.

sue, v. intr., *follow:* pret. 3 sg. 681; 3 pl. swyed, 87. AN. suer, suir(e), OF. sivre.

suffer, v. tr., 716, etc.; ?intr., *?be suffered,* 892: inf. 716, 718, 1256; pret. 3 sg. suffred, 892; pp. soffered, 1701. OF. suffrir, soffrir.

sulp, v. tr., *defile, pollute:* imper. sg. sulp, 1135; pp. 15, 550, 1130. ?Cf. Mod. Germ. dial. sölpern, *to soil.*

sum, adj., *some,* 628; absol. as pron. in pl.: pl. summe, 388, 389, 1094², 1497. OE. sum.

sumquat, adv., *a little,* 627.

sumtyme, adv., *once, formerly,* 1152, 1157, 1257, 1260; *sometime,* 582.

sumwhyle, adv., *formerly,* 1496.

sun, n., *son,* 649: soun, 666, 1299; pl. -ez, 112, 258, 298, 331, 350; -es, 1673; sunnes, 1221. OE. sunu.

sunne, n., *sun,* 932, 1758; in phrase 'under sunne,' 549: sonne, 932. OE. sunne.

suppe, v. tr., *sup, take (liquid food):* inf. 108. OE. sūpan, *suppan.

surely, adv., 1643. Cf. OF. sur, adj.

sustnaunce, n., *sustenaunce,* 340. AN. sustenaunce, OF. sostenance.

sute, n., *sort, kind,* in phrase 'of sute,' *to match,* 1457. AN. siwte, sute, OF. sieute.

swan, n.: pl. -ez, 58. OE. swan.

swap, n., *blow,* 222. Imitative; cf. Mod. Germ. dial., schwappen.

sware, adj., *square,* 319, 1386. OF. esquarré.

sware, v. tr., *answer:* 3 pl. sware, 1415. ON. svara.

swarme, v. intr.: 3 sg. -z, 223. Cf. OE. swierman, v., and swearm, n.

swayf, n., *swinging blow,* 1268. ON. sveif.

swayn, n., *servant:* pl. -es, 1509. LOE. swein<ON. sveinn.

swe, see swey.

sweande, part. adj., *swelling, 'flowing,'* 420. See swey.

swelt, v. intr., *perish,* 108; tr. *destroy,* 332: inf. 108, 332. OE. sweltan, ON. svelta.

swemande, part. adj., *afflicting, grievous,* 563. Cf. OE. āswǣman.

swenge, v. intr., *rush, run:* 3 pl. -n, 109; pret. 3 sg. 667. OE. swengan.

swepe, v. intr., *hasten:* 3 pl. -n, 1509. OE. *swǣpan; cf. ON. sveipa.

swere, v. tr., *swear:* pret. 3 sg. swer, 667. OE. swerian.

swete, adj., *sweet, fair,* 640, 788, 816, 1055, 1521, 1810: superl. swettest, 1006, 1247. OE. swēte.

swetnesse, n., *sweetness,* 525. OE. swētness.

*sweve, v. intr., *whirl:* pret. 3 pl. 222. ON. *sveifa.

**swey,** v. intr., *come, walk,* 788; *rush,* 956: inf. 788; pret. 3 sg. swe, 956. ON. sveigja, or perh. OE. *swēgan. See also **sweande,**

**swolȝe,** v. tr., *kill:* pret. 3 sg. 1268. Based on OE. swelgan.

**sworde,** n., 1253, 1268. OE. sweord.

**swyed,** see sue.

**swyer,** n., *squire:* pl. -ez, 87. OF. esquier.

**swyfte,** adj., 1509. OE. swift.

**swyftly,** adv., 87. OE. swiftlīce.

**swymme,** v. intr., *swim:* pret. 3 pl. 388. OE. swimman.

**swyn,** pl. n., *swine,* 58. OE. swīn.

**swyppe,** v. intr., *slip away, escape:* pret. 3 pl. 1253. OE. swipian.

**swyre,** n., *neck,* 1744. OE. swīra.

**swyþe,** adv., *quickly, swiftly,* 1176, *1211, 1509, 1619; greatly,* 354, 987; *very,* 816, 1283, 1299. OE. swīðe.

**Syboym,** prop. n., *Sidon,* 958. Lat. Seboim (Vulg.), OF. Sidoyne.

**syde,** n., *side,* 78, 228, 320, 555, 1380, 1387, 1442; pl. *outskirts, surroundings,* 956, 968: pl. -z, 144, 956; -s, 968. OE. sīde.

**syence,** n., *skill, wisdom,* 1454, 1599; in pl. *different kinds of knowledge,* 1289: pl. ciences, 1289. OF. science.

**syȝe,** see **se.**

**syȝt,** n., *vision, sight,* 29, 552, 595, 1722; *appearance,* 1406; *glimpse,* 610; *view,* 1548, and in phrase in . . . syȝt, 1221, 1812; *look, glance,* 672, 1005; *(eye) sight,* (often pleonastic), 192, 576, 706, 1710: syȝte, 552; syȝtes, 1722. OE. (ge) sihð, gesiht.

**syke,** v. intr., *sigh:* pres. part. sykande, 715. OE. sīcan.

**syle,** v. intr., *go, pass:* pret. 3 sg. 131. ?Cf. Norw. and Sw. dial. sila, *to flow.*

**sylk,** n., 790. OE. sioloc.

**sylver,** n., 1277, 1344. OE. siolfor.

**sylveren,** adj., *silvery,* 1406. OE. seolfren, silfren.

**symbal,** n., *cymbal:* pl. -es, 1415. OF. cimbale.

**symple,** adj., *free from guile, open,* 746; *humble,* 120: superl. symplest, 120. OF. simple.

**synful,** adv., 15, 716, 1111. OE. synfull.

**synge,** v. intr.: 3 pl. -n, 7; pret. 3 sg. songe, 1516; 3 pl. songen, 1763. OE. singan.

**syngne,** n., *sign,* 489: pl. -s, 1710. OF. signe.

**synk,** v. intr., 398, etc.; tr., 1014: inf. 398, 910; 3 sg. synkkes, 689; synkkez, 1026; pret. 3 pl. sunkken, 968; pres. part. synkande, 445; pp. sonkken, 1014. OE. sincan.

**synne,** n., *sin:* 199, 550, 1018, 1135, 1797; pl. -z, 514. OE. synn.

**synne,** v. intr.: pp. 679. Cf. OE. syngian.

**syre,** n., *lord:* 661, 1112; gen. 'syre soun,' 1299; pl. -z, 799; -s, 1260. OF. sire.

**syt,** n., *sorrow,* 1257; *vexation,* 566: syte, 1257. ON. *sȳt, var. of sūt.

**sytte,** v. intr., *sit,* 91, etc.; *be,* 550: inf. sitte, 91, 107; 3 sg. -z, 550, 552, 601, 773, 796; -s, 1498, 1500; sittez, 479; 3 pl. sytte, 1257; pret. 3 sg. sat, 992; sete, 661, 1171; 3 pl. sete, 645, 1260; seten, 829, 1482, 1763; pp. seten, 833. OE. sittan.

syþe, n., *time, period,* 1169, 1453;
in pl. (denoting frequency),
1188, 1417, 1686: pl. syþe, 1188,
1417; -z, 1686. OE. sīð.

syþen, adv., *then, afterwards,* 387,
557, 638, 799, 1292, 1635; *next,*
116, 175, 998; *since,* 262. OE.
siððan.

syþen, conj., *since, seeing that,* 684.
OE. siððan.

**T.**

tabarde, n., *upper garment,* 41. OF.
tabart.

table, n., 39, 132², 832, 1419. OF.
table.

taborn, n., *tabor, small drum:* pl.
-es, 1414. Late Lat. tabornus;
cf. OF. tabor.

take, v. tr., *seize, capture,* 154, 836,
1192, 1232, 1297; *catch, find,* 763,
943; *take, receive,* 330, 1131; *regard,* 735, 935; in idiomatic
phrases: t. counsayl, 1201; t. to
. . . ille, 735; t. leve, 401; t.
waye, 804; inf. 804, 836, 1232;
3 sg. -z, 401; -s, 1201; pret. 3 pl.
token, 935, 1297; tok, 1192; imper. sg. take, 330; pl. -z, 154;
tatz, 735; pp. taken, 943, 1131;
tan, 763. LOE. tacan, ON. taka.

tale, n., *statement, words; story;*
48 (see note), 587, 662, 676, 1437,
1557: talle, 48. OE. talu.

talke, n., *discourse,* 735.

talke, v. intr., *talk,* 132; *say,* 154:
3 sg. -z, 154; pret. 3 sg. talkede,
132. Frequentative formation on
OE. talian.

talle, see tale.

tame, adj.: 311, 362. OE. tam.

tan, see take.

tatz, see take.

tayt, n., *pleasure,* 889; *sport, play,*
*935 (see note). ON. teiti.

tayt, adj., *lively, agreeable,* 871.
ON. teitr.

Techal, prop. n., *Tekel,* 1727, 1733.
Vulg. Thecel.

teche, n., *sin, vice,* 943, 1230; *sign,*
1049: pl. -s, 1049. OF. teche.

teche, v. tr., *show,* 676; *teach,* 160,
1733: inf. (all cases). OE.
tǣc(e)an.

tede, see tyȝe.

tee, v. intr., *proceed, go:* 3 pl. -n,
9; subj. 3 sg. tee, 1262. OE.
tēon.

telde, n., *dwelling, house,* 866. OE.
teld.

telde, v. tr., *raise* w. up: inf. 211;
3 sg. -s, *1808; pp. 1342. OE.
teldan.

telle, v. tr., *tell:* inf. 687, 1153;
imper. sg. telle, 1634; pp. tolde,
1623. OE. tellan.

teme, v. intr., *conceive,* 655; *attach
oneself, turn to,* 9: inf. *655;
3 pl. -n, 9. OE. tīeman, tēman.

temple, n., 1151, 1490: temmple, 9,
1262. OE. templ, and OF.
temple.

tempre, v. tr., *restrain, moderate:*
imper. sg. tempre, 775. OE.
temprian.

temptande, part. adj., *afflicting, dis-
tressing,* 283. OF. tempter.

ten, adj., 763. OE. tīen, tēn.

tender, adj., 630. OF. tendre.

tene, adj., *angry,* 1808.

tene, n., *anger, vexation,* 283, 687,
1137; *?pains, trouble,* 1232. OE.
tēona.

tene, v. tr., *afflict:* 1 sg. 759. OE.
tēonian.

**tenfully,** adv., *sorrowfully, bitterly,*
160. Cf. OE. tēonful, adj.

**tent,** v. tr., *heed, pay attention to,*
935; *attend,* 676: inf. 676; pret.
3 pl. 935. ME. tent, n., aphetic
from OF. attent; cf. OF. at-
tendre.

**tere,** v. tr., *tear:* pp. torne, 1234.
OE. teran.

**terme,** n., *period,* 239, 568; *date,*
*appointed time,* 1393; *word, ex-*
*pression,* 1733. OF. terme.

**terne,** n., *lake,* 1041. ON. *tarnu.

**teþe,** see **toþ.**

**tevel,** v. intr., *strive, struggle:* pret.
3 pl. 1189. Etym. obscure.

**Thanes,** prop. n., *Thamanin,* 448
(see note). OF. Thanez (Mandeville).

**the,** v., *grow:* pret. 3 pl. ?thyȝe,
1687 (see note). OE. þēon.

**the,** see **þou.**

**then,** see **þen.**

**throne,** n.: 1112, 1396: trone, 211,
1794. OF. trone, throne.

**thus,** see **þus.**

**thyȝe,** see **the,** v.

**tid,** see **tyd.**

**to,** adv., *to,* 162, 662, 1551. OE. tō.

**to,** prep., 8, 9, 16, 29, etc.; *up to,*
383, 397; *down to,* 798; *till,*
1032; *for,* 204, 309, 340, 808; *of,*
1391; *toward,* 1172, 1230; *in re-*
*spect to,* 174, 315, 844, 1659; *ac-*
*cording to,* ?59, 1604; after
adjectives, 49, 212, 261, 608, 790,
1139, 1162; bef. infin. (and ge-
rund), 45, 53, 54, 64, etc.; *for*
*to,* 91, 336, 373, 402, etc.; *fro . . .*
*to,* 132, 227, 288; *so . . . to,* 904;
in phrases: to deþe, 1266; to þe
fulle, 120; to grounde, 445; to
non ille, 735; to peces, 1348.
OE. tō.

**to,** adv., *too,* 22, 182, 861, 1376. OE.
tō.

**to,** n., *toe:* pl. -s, 1691. OE. tā.

**tocleve,** v. intr., *be cleft asunder:*
3 sg. -s, 1806. OE. tōclēofan.

**togeder,** adv., *together:* 160, 307,
399, 441, 702, 783, 949, 1191, 1284,
1692; togedere, 1290. OE. tōgædere.

**toȝe,** adj., *tough,* 630. OE. tōh.

**token,** n.: pl. -es, 1049. OE. tācen.

**token,** v. tr., *signify, denote:* pret.
3 pl. 1557. OE. tācnian.

**token,** see **take.**

**tokerve,** v. tr., *cut up,* 1250; *divide,*
1700: inf. 1700; pret. 3 pl. tocorven, 1250. OE. tōceorfan.

**tolke,** n., *man,* 498, 757, 889: tolk,
687; pl. tulkkes, 1189, 1262;
tulkes, 1623. ON. tūlkr.

**Tolowse,** prop. n., 1108.    OF.
Tolouse.

**tom,** n., *time, opportunity,* 1153.
ON. tōm.

**tomarred,** part. adj., *ruined,* 1114.

**tonge,** n., 1524. OE. tunge.

**tool,** n., 1342: pl. toles, 1108. OE.
tōl.

**topace,** n., *topaz,* 1469. OF. topace.

**torende,** v. intr., *burst apart:* pret.
3 sg. torent, 368. OE. tōrendan.

**torive,** v. tr., *cleave, asunder:* pret.
3 sg. torof, 964. Cf. ON. rīfa.

**Torkye,** prop. n., *Turkey,* 1232.
OF. Turquie.

**tormenttor,** n.: pl. -ez, 154.   OF.
tormentour.

**torne,** n., *deed:* pl. -z, 192. AN.
tourn, OF. tor, tour.

**torne,** v. intr., *turn around,* 976;
*go, proceed,* 64; t. to hele, *be-*
*come sound, be cured,* 1099: inf.
976; 1 sg. *turne (MS. tne), 64;
pret. 3 sg. 1099. OE. turnian.

**torres,** see **tour.**

**tote,** n., *?elbow* (see note): pl. -z, 41.

**totorne,** part. adj., *torn, ragged,* 33, 41. OE. tōteran.

**toþ,** n., *tooth:* pl. teþe, 160. OE. tōð.

**toun,** n., *town, city:* 64, 775, 907, 990, 1234, 1778; toune, 721, 763; pl. -ez, 751. OE. tūn.

**tour,** n., *tower,* 1189, 1383; applied to heaven (cf. *Pearl* 965), 216; *tower-shaped cumulus,* 951: pl. -es, 1189, 1383; torres, 951. OE. torr, LOE. tūr; OF. tor, tour.

**tow,** see **two.**

**towalten,** v. intr., *burst forth, overflow:* pret. 3 pl. towalten, 428. See **walte.**

**toward,** prep., 672, 1005, 1373: towarde, 679, 778. OE. tōweard.

**towche,** v. tr., *touch,* 283, 1091, 1099, 1657; *taste,* 245; *reach,* 1393; *tell,* 1437: inf. 1091; pret. 3 sg. 245, 283, 1099, 1657; pp. 1393, 1437. OF. toucher.

**tramountayne,** n., *pole-star,* 211. OF. tramontaine.

**trasch,** n., *?rag:* pl. -ez, 40 (see note). Cf. Sw. trasa, *rag.*

**traw,** v. tr., *believe,* 587, 655, 662; *hope,* 388; intr. w. upon, *believe,* 1049; *think,* 1335, and in phrase 'I trawe,' 1686, 1803: inf. 655; trow, 1049; 1 sg. trawe, 1686; trowe, 1803; pret. 3 sg. trawed 1335; 3 pl. 388; pres. part. trawande, 662; imper. sg. traue, 587. OE. trēow(i)an.

**trawþe,** n., *faithfulness, loyalty,* 236; in phrase 'by hys (hir) trawþe,' 63, 667; *truth,* 1490, 1604, 1703, 1736; *righteousness,*

723; trauþe, 723, 1490. OE. trēowð.

**trayled,** part. adj., *decorated with a trailing pattern,* 1473. NF. trailler.

**traysoun,** n., *treason,* 187. AN. treysoun, OF. traison.

**traytor,** n.: pl. -es, 1041. OF. traitor, acc. of traitre.

**trayþely,** adv., *?quickly,* 907: trayþly, 1137. Etym. unknown.

**tre,** n., *tree,* 622, 1342: pl. -s, 310, 1041. OE. trēo(w).

**tresor¹,** n., *treasure,* 866. OF. tresor.

**tresor²,** n., *treasurer,* 1437. OF. tresor = tresorer (Godefroy, date 1360).

**tresorye,** n., *treasury,* 1317. OF. tresorie.

**trespas,** v. intr., *transgress, sin:* pres. subj. 3 sg. trespas, 48; pp. trespast, 1230. OF. trespasser.

**treste,** n., *trestle, support for boards which formed table:* pl. -s, 832. OF. treste, orig. trestre.

**trichcherye,** n., *treachery,* 187. OF. tricherie.

**troched,** adj., *provided with pinnacles,* 1383 (see note).

**tron,** see **tryne.**

**trone,** see **throne.**

**trot,** n., 976. OF. trot.

**trow,** see **traw.**

**trumpe,** n., *trumpet:* pl. -n, 1402. OF. trumpe.

**trusse,** v. tr., *stow away:* pret. 3 sg. 1317. OF. trusser.

**trwe,** adj., *true, faithful, virtuous,* 682, 759, 1189, 1623: as noun, 702; *right,* 1168: true, 702. OE. trēowe.

**trwly,** adv., *faithfully,* 1490. OE. trēowlīce.

**tryed,** part. adj., *chosen,* 1317. OF. trier.

**tryfled,** part. adj., *ornamented with trefoils,* 1473. Cf. OF. trefle, trifoil, n.

**tryne,** v. intr., *go, ste; :* pret. 3 sg. tron, 132; pres. part. trynande, 976. Cf. OSw. trina.

**trysty,** adj., *faithful,* 763. Cf. ME. trust, v., ON. treysta (see *NED.*).

**tuch,** n., *?deed,* 48 (see note). OF. touche.

**tulk(k)es,** see **tolke.**

**tulke,** v. intr., *sound:* pret. 3 pl. tulket, 1414. ?ON. tūlka (see note).

**tult,** see **tylt.**

**tuyred,** pp. ?error for tyrved, *over-turned, destroyed,* 1234. (See *NED.* s. tirve, v.²). ?OE. *tierfian.

**twenty,** adj., 1383; n. 757, 759. OE. twentig.

**twentyfolde,** adv., *twenty times,* 1691. OE. twentigfeald.

**tweyne,** adj., *two,* 674, 782, 788; n. 1749. OE. twēgen, masc.

**two,** adj., 155, 702, 814, 866, 934, 977, 996, 1192; noun, 871, 1573: tow, 866. OE. twā, fem., and tū, neut. See **twayne.**

**twyne,** v. intr., *twine:* pres. part. twynande, 1691. Cf. OE. twīn, n., and WFris. twine, v.

**twynne,** n., in phrases: on twynne, 1047, *in two;* in twynne, 966, *apart.* OE. (ge)twinn.

**twynne,** v. intr., *part:* inf. 402.

**tyd,** adv., *quickly,* 901; a(1)s (also) tyd, *as soon as possible, at once, immediately,* 64, 1099, 1213: tid, 901. ON. tītt, neut. of tīðr,

**tyde,** n., *time,* 1393. OE. tīd.

**ty3e,** v. refl., *tie, bind;* 702, pp. as adj., *joined together,* 1634 (see note): pp. ty3ed, 702; tede, 1634. OE. tīgan, *tēgan.

**ty3t¹,** v. refl., *?betake oneself:* pret. 3 sg. ty3t, 889. OE. tyhtan.

**ty3t²,** v. tr., *set, give,* 1153; intr., *endeavor, succeed,* 1108: inf. 1108, 1153. Etym. obscure.

**tykle,** adj., *uncertain,* 655. ?Cf. OE. tinclian, *tickle.*

**tylle,** prep. (always postpositive), *to,* 882, 1064, 1174, 1752. ON. til.

**tyl,** conj.: *until,* 484, 498, 548, 831, etc. (10 times); til, 906, 1192, 1356, 1544, 1657, 1699.

**tylt,** v. tr., *throw, push,* 832, 1213: pret. 3 pl. tult, 1213; pp. tylt, 832. OE. *tyltan.

**tymbre,** n., *timbrel, tambourine:* pl. -s, 1414. OF. timbre.

**tyme,** n., *time:* 106, 660, 781, 1149, 1657, 1769. OE. tīma.

**tyne¹,** v. tr., *enclose:* pret. 3 sg. 498. OE. tӯnan.

**tyne²,** v. tr., *lose,* 216; *destroy, ruin,* 775, 907: inf. 907; pres. 2 sg. -z, 775; pret. 3 sg. tynt, 216. ON. tӯna.

**tyraunt,** n., general term of abuse, *vile sinner, villain:* pl. -ez, 943. OF. tyrant.

**tyrauntyre,** n., *tyranny,* 187. Cf. OF. tirannerie.

**tyrve,** v. tr., *strip,* w. of: inf. 630. Etym. uncertain.

**tyþe,** adj., *tenth,* 216. OE. tēogoða, tēgoða.

**tyþyng,** n., *tidings, information:* 498, 1557; pl. -ez, 458. LOE. tīdung; ON. tīðendi, pl.

**tyxte,** n., *text,* 1634. NF. tyxte, OF. texte.

### Þ.

**þaȝ,** conj., *though,* 48, 72, 103, 217, etc. OE. þēah.

**þare,** see þer.

**þat,** conj., *that,* 53, 126, 195, 198, etc.; *so that,* 72, 178, 395, 433; etc.; *so* . . . þat, 152, 269, 280, 590; *in order that,* 104, 173, 914, 1811, 1812; after 'so,' 83; after various conjs., bot þat, *if not,* 881; if þat, 759; when þat, 961, 1537: that, 433. OE. þæt.

**þat,** dem. pron., *that,* 29, 32, 45, 51, etc.; absol., 251, 309, 600, 796, 1144; w. on, other, 149, 235, 299, 765; pl. þo, 97, 490, 553, 635, etc.; absol, 939, 1243; þose, 509, 842, 848, 851, etc.; w. oþer, 332, 340; absol. 261, 273, 1810; (þo, 24 times; þose, 17 times); bi þat, *by that time,* 397, 967, 1211, 1687; with þat, *thereupon,* 671; for þat, 279. OE. þæt. See also þe, adv.

**þat,** rel. pron., indecl., *that, who, which,* 2, 5, 6, 7, etc.; *that which,* 652, 898, 1098, 1517; *those that,* 286, 376; w. redundant pers. pron., *(who, which),* 274, 448, 926; þat . . . his, *whose,* 32, 1109. OE. þæt, dem.

**þayres,** poss. pron., see her, poss. pron., *their.* Cf. ON. gen. pl. þeira.

**þe,** adv., *the,* w. comp., 296. OE. þē, instr. of þæt.

**þeder,** see þider.

**þede,** n., *vessel,* properly *brewer's strainer,* 1717. Etym. uncertain.

**þefte,** n., *theft,* 183. OE. þīefð, þēofð.

**þen,** conj., *than,* 76, 168, 674, 1100, 1128, 1132, 1137, 1138, 1155, 1196, 1303, 1704: þenne, 1108. OE. þænne, þanne.

**þenk(kez),** see þynke.[1]

**þenne,** adv., *then, at that time; next, besides,* 53, etc.; unemphatic introductory part., *then, now,* 178, 926, 929; parenthetical or resumptive, 176, 349, 1054, 1065, 1143; introducing apodosis, 15, 39, 1067; correl. w. when, 529, 1401; as n. preceded by prep., by þenne, 989; er þenne, 1088, 1312, 1339; er þenne, conj., *before,* 1670: þenne, 77, 93, 169, 240, etc. (74 times); þen, 15, 39, 53, 85, etc. (27 times); þenn, 344, 349, 929, 1333, thenne (th apparently used as capital for þ), 73, 109, 361, 1357. OE. þænne, þanne.

**þer,** adv., *there,* 11, 70, 126, 239, etc.; introducing vb., 100, 250, 263, 373, etc.; *on that occasion, then,* 203, 216, 1319: as conj., *where,* 158, 238, 379, 412, etc.; *wherever,* 1117; *when,* 1004; þer as, *where, when,* 24, 769: þere, 70, 126, 564, 593, etc. (12 times, þer, 54 times); þare, 1076. OE. þǣr, þēr.

**þeraboute,** adv., *thereabout,* 1796. OE. þǣrābūtan.

**þerafter,** adv., *afterwards:* 93, 157, 1089, 1135, 1220, 1635, 1763, 1766. OE. þǣræfter.

**þeratte,** adv., *thereat,* 1554. OE. þǣræt.

**þerby,** adv., *beside* or *near that, near by,* 1034: þerbi, 1404. OE. þǣrbi.

**þerbysyde,** adv., *near there,* 673.

þerinne, adv., *therein, in it:* 311, 321, 351, 352, 372, 498, 527, 698, 800, 1029, 1072, 1264, 1667, 1715, 1800; þerin, 993. OE. þǣrinne, þǣrin.

þerof, adv., *thereof, of it,* 306, 604, 1499, 1507, 1752; *because of that,* 972. OE. þǣrof.

þeron, adv., *thereon,* 244, 386, 388, 507, 635, 1025, 1026, 1028, 1482, 1719. OE. þǣron.

þeroute, adv., *without, outside, out of that place,* '44, 109, 220, 453, 495, 502, 807, 881, 1184, 1196. OE. þǣrūt(e).

þerover, adv., *above,* 1407. OE. þǣrofer.

þerto, adv., *thither,* 1394; *for that purpose,* 701. OE. þǣrtō.

þertylle, adv., *thither,* 1509. See tylle.

þerupone, adv., *thereon,* 1665.

þerve, adj., *unleavened, unsoured,* 635. OE. þeorf.

þerwyth, adv., *thereat, thereupon,* 138, 528, 1501; *with that (them),* 1406. OE. þǣrwiþ.

þese, see þis.

þester, n., *darkness,* 1775. OE. þēostru.

þewe, n., *thief:* pl. -s, 1142. OE. þēof.

þewe, n., *ordinance,* 544; *custom, manner of action,* 203; *gracious deed, courtesy,* ?755, 1436: pl. -z, 203, 544, 755; -s, 1436. OE. þēaw.

þewed, adj., *gracious,* 733.

þi, see þy.

þider, adv., *thither,* 45, 61, 1366, 1478; þeder, 64, 461, 1775. OE. þider.

þikke, adj., *thick, dense,* 220, 222; as n. 1687 (see note); *frequent, occurring in quick succession,* 952: þik, 952, 1687. ON. þykkr; cf. OE. þicce.

þikke, adv., *thickly, closely,* 504, 953; *fast,* 1416: þykke, 504; comp. þiker, ?*very thickly,* 1384.

þink(ez), see þyng.

þirle, v., *pierce:* pret. 3 sg. 952. OE. þyrlian.

þis, dem. pron., *this,* 65, 106, 140, 143, etc.; absol. 42, 229, 1013, 1049, 1751: þys, 1751; gen. sg. þyse, 1802: pl. þise, 84, 279, 596, etc. (15 times); þyse, 105, 207, 210, etc. (14 times); þese, 1710; þis, 822. OE. þis, neut.

þole, v. tr., *suffer:* inf. 190. OE. þolian.

þoȝt, n., *thought,* 516. OE. þōht.

þoȝt, see þynke[1] and þynke.[2]

þonkke, v. tr., *thank:* 3 sg. -s, 745. OE. þancian, þoncian.

þor, see þer.

þorȝ, see þurȝ.

þorp, n., *hamlet, town:* pl. -es, 1178. OE. þrop, þorp.

þose, see þat.

þou, per. pron., *thou:* þou (abbrev. þu), 95, 140, 141, 142, etc.; þow, 145, 733, 742, 930; þo, 173; þe (dat. or acc.), 327, 330, 349, 545, etc.; refl., 169, 333, 921, 1067, etc.; plur. 3e, 352, 527, 800, 819, etc.; yow (dat. or acc.), 357, 523, 617, 799, etc.; refl. 352, 522; ethical dat. 904. OE. þū.

þowsand, n., *thousand:* pl. -ez, 220. OE. þūsend.

þrad, pp., ?*afflicted, punished,* 751. OE. þrēad, pp. of þrēan.

þral, n., *serf, fellow,* 135. OE.
þræl.

þrawen, -ez, see þrowe, v., and
þrowen, part. adj.

þre, adj., *three,* 298², 315, 350², 625,
635, 993, 1728. OE. þrēo.

þrefte, adj., *unleavened,* 819 (see
note). See also þerve.

þrenge, see þrynge.

þrep, n., *contradiction,* 350. Cf. OE.
þrēapian, *rebuke.*

þrepyng, vbl. n., *strife, quarreling,*
183.

þrete, v. tr., *urge on,* 937; *foretell
threateningly,* 680, 1728: 3 sg. -s,
680, 1728; pret. 3 pl. þratten, 937.
OE. þrēatian.

þretty, adj., *thirty,* 751; n. 317, 754:
þrette, 317. OE. þrītig, þrittig.

þrevenest, see þryven.

þro, n., *anger,* 754. ON. þrā, neut.

þro¹, adv., *thoroughly,* 1805. OE.
þurh.

þro², adv., *violently,* 220; *quickly,*
*590 (see note). ON. þrār, adj.

þroble, v. intr., *crowd, press:* pret.
3 pl. 879; pres. part. þrublande,
504 (see note).

þroly, adv., *violently, fiercely,* 180,
504. See þro, adv.²

þrong, n., *throng, crowd,* 135, 754:
þronge, 504. Cf. OE. geþrang.

þrong(en), see þrynge.

þrote, n., *throat:* 180, 1569. OE.
þrote.

þrowe, v. tr., *throw,* 635, 1384,
*?cover; turn, incline,* 516; intr.,
*rush,* 590; *fall w. violence, be
flung,* 220; *crowd, press,* 879
(cf. þrowen, part. adj., and
note on 504) : 3 sg. þrawez, 590;
pret. 3 sg. þrwe, 635, 879; 3 pl.
þrwen, 220; pp. þrowen, 1384,

þrawen, 516. OE. þrāwan. See
also þrowen, part. adj.

þrowen, part. adj., *crowded, close,*
504 (see note) : þrawen, 1775.
See þrowe.

þrwe(n), see þrowe.

þryche, v. tr., *crowd:* pp. þry3t,
135. OE. þrycc(e)an. See also
þry3t, part. adj.

þryd, adj., *third,* 1639; n.: þryd,
69, 249, 300; þrydde, 1571, 1573,
1748. OE. þridda.

þryez, adv., *thrice,* 429. Cf. OE.
þrīwa.

þryftyly, adv., *in a becoming manner,* 635. See þryve.

þry3t, part. adj., *?crowded, thick,*
1687 (see note). See þryche.

þrynge, v. intr., *press, crowd
around,* 879, 930, 1639; *press on,*
1775; *rush,* 180: 3 sg. -z, 180;
-s, 1639; pres. subj. 3 sg. þrenge,
930; pret. 3 pl. þrongen, 1775;
þrong, 879. OE. þringan.

þrynne, adj., *three,* 606, 1805; absol.
645; in þrynne, 1727. LOE.
þrinna<ON. þrinnr.

þryvande, part. adj., *worthy,* 751.

þryve, v. intr., *thrive, flourish:*
inf. 249. ON. þrīva-sk. See
also þryven, þryvande.

þryven, part. adj., *grown up,* 298;
*noble, honorable,* 1571, 1639:
superl. þryvenest, 1639; þrevenest, 1571.

þunder-þrast, n., *thunderbolt,* 952.
OE. þunor; cf. OE. þræstan, *to
force.*

þur3, prep., *through,* 1204, 1761;
*throughout,* 1361, 1362; *by means
of,* 731, 1115, 1607; *because of,
in consequence of,* 236, 241, 1325,
1498: þor3, 1761. OE. þurh.

þur3out, prep., *throughout,* 1559.
OE. þurhūt.

þus, adv., *thus,* 26, 47, 71, 314, 681,
1109, 1349, 1685, 1733, 1797, 1805:
thus, 161. OE. þus.

þy, poss. pron., 165, 169, 171, etc.
(16 times); þi, 95, 148, 348, etc.
(9 times); þyn, 143, 172, 175,
etc.; þyn one, 923 (see note).
OE. þīn.

þyng, n., *thing, matter,* 1600: pl.
-es, 1281, 1627; þinges, 5, 1355;
þynk, 819; þink, 1359; þinkez,
916. OE. þing.

þynke¹, v. tr., *think, conceive,* 590;
*intend, purpose,* 304, 711, 1729;
*determine,* 138; *consider,* 749;
intr. w. on, *remember, bear in
mind,* 819: 1 sg. þenk, 304, 711,
1729; 3 sg. þynkez, 749; pret.
3 sg. þo3t, 138; imper. pl. þenkkez, 819; pp. þo3t, 590. OE.
þenc(e)an.

þynke², v. impers., *seems:* pres.
subj. 3 sg. þynk, 744; pret. 3 sg.
þo3t, 562, 1504. OE. þync(e)an.

þyse, see þis,

þyself, see self.

# U.

uche, adj., *each,* 31, 124, 333, 334,
etc.; with indef. art. 'uch(e) a,'
78, 196, 368, 370, etc. (23 times);
in phrase uch on(e), 71, 267, 394,
497, etc.: uche, 78, 370, 384, etc.
(35 times); uch, 31, 124, 196,
etc. (30 times; so always when
fol. by on); uuche 378. OE.
(Merc.) ylc.

ugly, adj., *horrible, frightful:*
superl. uglokest, 892. ON.
uggligr.

u3ten, n., *early morning,* 893. OE.
ūhta.

umbe, prep., *about, around,* 879,
1569, 1687, 1689, 1744. OE. ymbe.

umbe, adv., 1384, 1474. OE. ymbe.

umbebrayde, v. tr., *accost:* pret.
3 sg. umbebrayde, 1622. Cf. OE.
bregdan.

umbegrouen, part. adj., *overgrown,
covered,* 488.

umbekest, v. tr., *circle about:* 3 sg.
-ez, 478.

umbely3e, v. tr., *surround,* 836.
OE. ymblicgan.

umbesweyed, part. adj., *encircled,*
1380.

umbeþor, adv., *thereabout,* 1384.

umbewalt, v. tr., *surround:* pret.
3 sg. umbewalt, 1181.

umbre, n., *shade,* 524 (see note).
AN. umbre, OF. ombre.

unblyþe, adj., *dismal,* 1017. OE.
unblīðe.

unbrosten, part. adj., *unbroken, not
burst,* 365. See berste.

uncheryst, adj., *uncared for,* 1125.

unclannes, n., *uncleanness, impurity,* 1800, 1806: unclannesse, 30.
OE. unclǣnness.

unclene, adj., *unclean, evil,* 550, 710,
1144, 1713. OE. unclǣne.

unclose, v. tr., *disclose,* 26: *unlock,*
1438: 3 sg. -z, 26; -s, 1438.

uncouþe, adj., *foreign, strange,* 414:
uncowþe, 1600, 1722. OE. uncūð.

under, prep., *under, beneath,* 226,
483, 602, 605, 616, 626, 1246, 1255,
1459, 1695; in phrases: under
god, 1077, under hach, 409; under sunne, 549. OE. under.

undergo, v. tr., *understand, perceive:* pret. 3 sg. under3ede, 796
(see note).

underȝede, see undergo.

undo, v. tr., *destroy:* pret. 3 sg. undyd, 562. OE. undōn.

unfayre, adj., *unseemly, disgraceful,* 1801.

unfolde, v. tr., *make known, disclose,* 1563; intr., *unfold, open up,* 962: pret. 3 sg. 962; imper. sg. unfolde, 1563. OE. unfealdan, -fāldan.

unfre, adj., *base, shameful,* 1129.

ungarnyst, part. adj., *not properly adorned or dressed,* 137.

ungoderly, adj., *vile, base,* 145, 1092. ?Extension of ME. ungodly (see note).

unhap, n., *misfortune,* 143, 1150; *calamity,* 892. Cf. ON. ūhapp.

unhappen, adj., *wicked, vile,* 573. Cf. ON. heppinn.

unhaspe, v. tr., *reveal:* inf. 688. See haspe.

unhole, adv., *unsoundly, insanely,* 1682. Cf. OE. unhāl, adj.

unhonest, n., *impure, vile,* 579.

unhyle, v. tr., *uncover:* 2 sg. -s, 1628; pp. unhuled, 451. Cf. OE. hulu, *husk.*

unknawen, adj., *unknown,* 1679.

unkyndely, adv., *ungratefully,* 208.

unmard, adj., *undefiled, virgin,* 867.

unnevened, adj., *unmentioned,* i. e., *unthought of, impossible,* 727. See neven.

unryȝt, n., *wrong,* 1142. OE. unriht.

*unsavere, adj., *disagreeable,* 822.

unsmyten, adj., *unharmed,* 732.

unsounde, adj., *corrupt, wicked,* 575.

unsoundely, adv., *harshly, fatally,* 201.

unstered, adj., *undirected,* 706. Cf. OE. stēoran.

unswolȝed, adj., *unharmed,* 1253. See swolȝe.

unto, prep., 9, 1235. Cf. OS. untō.

untrwe, adj., *untrue, false,* 184, 456, 587, 1161.

untwyne, v. tr., *?separate:* 2 sg. -z, 757.

unþewe, n., *fault, vice:* pl. -z, 190. OE. unþēaw.

unþonk, n., *harm,* 183. OE. unþanc.

unþryvandely, adv., *unworthily, poorly,* 135.

unþryfte, n., *wickedness, folly,* 516, 1728.

unþryftyly, adv., *basely, vilely,* 267.

unwaschen, adj., *unwashed,* 34.

unwelcum, adj., 49.

unworþelych, adj., *unworthy, shameful,* 305.

up, adv., 2, 211, 323, 439, 460, 506, 671, 897, 963, 1179, 1263, 1480, 1808; *aroused,* 834; *up* (from bed), 1001: upe, 1010; uppe, 1421. OE. ūp.

upbrayde, v. tr., *raise:* 3 pl. -z, 848. Cf. OE. bregdan.

upcaste, v. tr., *proclaim:* pp. upcaste, 1574.

upfolden, part. adj., *folded,* 643.

uplyfte, part. adj., *uplifted,* 987.

upon, prep., *upon, on,* 416, 719, 925, 1451, etc.; expressing manner, 902, 912, upon . . . wyse, 268, 1728, 1805; in phrases: upon bench, 1395; upon borde, 470; upon dayez, 578; upon dece, 1399; upon ende, *finally,* 1329; upon folde, 251, etc.; upon fote, 88; upon grounde, 1363; upon haste, 902; upon hyȝt, 458; upon launde, 1207; upon lofte, 206;

upon longe, *at length,* 1193; upon
molde, 558; upon soyle, 1387;
upon throne, 1112; upon urþe,
326; upon uȝten, 893. Adv. 141,
1049, 1276, 1427. OE. upon.

**upon,** adj., *open,* 318, 453, 501, 882.
OE. open.

**uprere,** v. tr., *rear up:* pret. 3 sg.
uprerde, 561.

**upryse,** v. intr., *arise:* inf. 896.

**upwafte,** v. intr., *rise up:* pret. 3 pl.
upwafte, 949.

**urnment,** see **ornement.**

**urþe,** see **erþe.**

**urþly,** adj., *earthly,* 35. OE. eorþlic.

**usage,** n., *custom,* 710. OF. usage.

**use,** v. tr., *use,* 11; *practise,* 202,
251, 1173, 1359; *spend,* 295, refl.
(of sexual intercourse), 267:
inf. 1359; 3 sg. -z, 295; 3 pl. -n,
11; pret. 3 sg. 251, 1173; 3 pl.
267; pp. 202. OF. user.

**usle,** n., *ashes,* 747: pl. usellez, 1010.
OE. ysel.

**utter,** adv., *outside, without,* 42, 927.
OE. ūtor, uttor.

**utwyth,** adv., *outwardly,* 14.


## V.

**vale,** n., 673. OF. val.

**vanysche,** v. intr.: pret. 3 sg. vanist, 1548. Aphetic from OF.
evaniss-, from evanir.

**vanyte,** n., 1713. OF. vanite.

**vayle,** v., *be of service,* 1151; *be
worth,* 1311: pret. 3 pl. 1151,
1131. OF. vaill-, fr. valoir.

**\*vayneglorie,** n., 1358. OF. vayneglorie.

**vengaunce,** n., \*247, 744, 1013. OF.
vengeance.

**venge,** v. intr., *take vengeance:* inf.
\*wenge, 201; pret. 3 sg. 199, 559.
OF. venger.

**venkquysche,** v. tr., *vanquish,
destroy:* pret. 3 sg. venkquyst,
544; pp. venkkyst, 1071. OF.
vainquiss-, from vainquir.

**venym,** n., *evil,* 574. OF. venim.

**verayly,** adv., *verily, truly,* 664,
1548. Cf. OF. verai, adj.

**vergynyte,** n., 1071. OF. virginite.

**vertuous,** adj., *precious,* 1280. OF.
vertuous.

**vessel,** n., as collective, 1311, 1429,
1451, 1791: vessayl, 1791; pl.
vesselles, 1151, 1315; vessayles,
1713. OF. vessel.

**vesselment,** coll. n., *vessels:* 1280,
1288. OF. vesselement.

**vesture,** n.: pl. -s, 1288. OF.
vesture.

**vice,** n., 199. OF. vice.

**vilte,** n., *vileness,* 199. OF. vilte.

**violent,** adj., 1013. OF. violent.

**vouche,** v. intr., *resolve:* inf. 1358.
OF. voucher.

**voyde,** v. tr., w. *away, do away
with,* 744: *lay waste,* 1013; intr.,
*disappear,* 1548: inf. 744; pret.
3 sg. 1013, 1548. OF. voider.

**vycios,** adj., *vicious,* 574. OF.
vicious.

**vyl,** adj., *vile,* 744. OF. vil.

**vylanye,** n., *sin, shameful wickedness,* 544, 574: vylaynye, 863.
OF. vilanie.

**vyle,** v. refl., *defile:* 3 pl. -n, 863.
OF. viler.

**vyole,** n., *vial, small vessel:* pl. -s,
1280. Southern form of ME.
fiole (OF. fiole).

**vyolence,** n., 1071. OF. violence.

# W.

**wach,** n., *state of wakefulness,* 1003; *guard, sentry,* 1205: wache, 1003. OE. wæcce.

**waft,** see **weve.**

**wage,** v. tr., *wave:* pp. 1484. Cf. Sw. vagga.

**wake,** v. tr., *guard, watch:* pret. 3 pl. 85. OE. wacian.

**waken,** v. tr., *arouse, awaken; rouse up, raise:* inf. 323; wakan, 948; pret. 3 sg. wakened, 437, 933; wakned, 1166, 1175; pp. wakned, 891. OE. wæcnan.

**wakker,** see **wok,** adj.

**wale,** adj., *choice,* 1716; *noble,* 1734. Cf. ON. val, *choice.*

**wale,** v. tr., *choose,* 921; *?adjudge,* 1734: imper. sg. wale, 921; pp. walt, 1734. Cf. ON. val, *choice;* velja, *choose.*

**walk,** v. intr.: inf. 1674; 3 pl. -ez, 503. OE. wealcan.

**walkyrie,** n., *witch, sorceress:* pl. -s, 1577. OE. wælcyrie.

**walle,** n.: 1381, 1390; pl. -s, 1181, 1190, 1776. OE. weall, wall.

**walt,** see **wale.**

**walte,** v. intr., *burst forth, overflow* (Vulg. rupti sunt), 364; *?burst,* 501; *bubble forth,* 1037: 3 sg. -z, 1037; -s, 364; pret. 3 sg. walt, 501. Cf. ONth. wæltan, *roll,* appar. infl. in meaning by OE. weallan, *bubble forth.*

**walter,** v. intr., *roll;* inf. 1027; pret. 3 sg. 415. Frequentative from OE. wæltan.

**wan,** see **wynne.**

**wappe,** v. tr., w. upon, *fling open:* pret. 3 pl. 882. ?ON. vappa.

**war,** adj., *watchful, cautious,* 292, 589; *aware,* 606, 970; in phrase 'be by hem war,' *take warning by them,* 712. OE. (ge)wær.

**war,** v. intr., only imper. phrase, 'war þe,' *see to it, be careful, beware:* 165, 545, 1133, 1143. OE. warian.

**warisch,** v. tr., *protect:* inf. 921. NF. wariss-, from warir, OF. guarir.

**warlaȝe,** n., *wizard:* pl. -s, 1560. OE. wærloga.

**warme,** v. tr.: pret. 3 sg. 1420. OE. wearmian.

**warnyng,** n., 1504. OE. wearnung.

**warp,** v. tr., *hurl,* 444; *utter,* 152, 213; intr. *rush,* 284: inf. 152; pret. 3 sg. warp, 213; werp, 284, 3 pl. warpen, 444. ON. varpa.

**wary,** v. tr., *curse, condemn:* inf. 513. OE. wiergan, wærgan.

**waryed,** part. adj., *cursed,* 1716.

**wasch,** v. tr., *wash,* 323, etc.; intr. 1138: inf. 323, 355; wasche, 548, 802; imper. sg. wasch, 1127; pp. waschen, 831, 1133, 1138; waschene, 618. OE. wascan.

**wassayl,** interj. *'your health!'* 1508. AN. wassail.

**wast,** v. tr., *destroy,* 326, 431, 1178; *waste,* 1489: inf. 326, 1489; pret. 3 sg. wast, 1178; pp. wasted, 431. NF. waster, OF. guaster.

**wasturne,** n., *wilderness,* 1674. Variant of ME. wastine from NF. wastine.

**water,** n., *water, flood,* 323, 371, 375, 387, 422, 428, 437, 472, 496, 548, 617, 1027, 1037, 1133; *stream,* 1380, 1776: pl. watterez, 437, 496; watteres, 1776; wateres, 1380. OE. wæter.

**wawe,** n., *wave:* pl. -z, 382; waȝez, 404. ON. vāgr.

**wax,** n., 1487. OE. weax.

**wax,** v. intr., *increase,* 375, 397, 521;
*grow, become,* 204, 1123, 1198;
*befall,* 235: pres. subj. 3 sg.
wax, 1123; pret. 3 sg. wex, 204,
235; wax, 375; 3 pl. wexen,
1198; waxed, 397; imper. pl.
waxez, 521. OE. weaxan.

**waxloke,** n., *waxen lump:* pl. -s,
1037. ?OE. locc.

**way,** n.: 777; on þe waye, 606; by
þe way, 974: waye, 804: pl.
wayez, 282, 767. OE. weg.

**wayferande,** part. adj., *wayfaring,*
79. OE. weg fērende.

**waykne,** v. intr., *weaken:* pret.
3 sg. 1422. Cf. ON. veikr, *weak.*

**wayne,** v. tr., *?give, ?obtain,* 1616;
*send,* 1504; refl. *recover,* 1701:
inf. 1616; pret. 3 sg. 1504, 1701.
For etym., see note on 1616.

**wayte,** v. intr., *be careful,* 292:
*look,* 1423; tr. *search,* 99; *ex-*
*amine,* 1552: 3 sg. -z, 1423;
imper. pl. -z, 99. NF. waiter,
OF. gaiter.

**wedde,** v. tr.: inf. 934; pp. 69.
OE. weddian.

**wedded,** part. adj., 330.

**wede,** n., *dress,* 793; in pl. *clothes,*
*garments,* -z, 20, 117, 140, 142,
165, 169, 217, 1353; -s, 1208, 1582.
OE. wǣde, wēde.

**wede,** v., *go mad:* pret. 3 sg. wed,
1585. OE. wēdan.

**weder,** n., *storm, wind; air;* 444,
475, 847, 948; *weather,* 1760: pl.
-ez, 948. OE. weder.

**weȝe,** v. tr., *bear, bring,* 1420, 1508;
w. upon, *bear heavily upon, op-*
*press,* 719: inf. weye, 719; pret.
3 pl. 1420; imper. sg. weȝe, 1508.
OE. wegan.

**weȝt,** n.: pl. -es, *scales, balance,*
1734. Cf. OE. gewiht.

**wekked,** see **wykked.**

**wel,** adv., *well,* 113, 165, 320, 322,
etc.; *very* in 'wel nyȝe,' 704:
comp. better, 234: superl. best.
275, 539, 913, 1060. OE. wel.

**welawynnely,** adv., *very joyfully,*
831. Cf. OE. wynn, *joy.*

**welcom,** adj., 813. Cf. OE. wil-
cuma, n.

**welde,** v. tr., *rule, govern,* 17, 195,
644, 1646, 1664; *use, possess,*
705, 835, 1351: inf. 705, 835, 1351,
1646; 3 sg. -z, 17, 195, 644; -s,
1664. OE. wieldan, weldan.

**wele,** n., *prosperity,* 651. OE. wela.

**welgest,** see **wely.**

**welkyn,** n., *sky,* 371. Cf. OE.
wolcen.

**welle,** n., *spring, fountain:* pl. -z,
439. OE. wielle, welle.

**welle-hede,** n., *well-head, spring,*
*364: pl. -z, 428.

**wely,** adj., *mighty, strong:* superl.
welgest, 1244. OE. welig.

**wen,** see **when.**

**wench,** n., *girl,* 974, 1250; *con-*
*cubine,* 1423, 1716: pl. -es, 974,
1250, 1423, 1716. Shortened
form of ME. wenchel (OE.
wencel).

**wende,** v. intr., *go:* 3 sg. -z, 675,
777; pret. 3 sg. went, 415, 857;
3 pl. went, 501; imper. sg.
wende, 471; pl. -z, 521. OE.
wendan.

**wene,** v. tr., *think:* 1 sg. wene, 821.
OE. wēnan.

**wenge,** see **venge.**

**wepe,** v. intr., *weep:* pres. part.
wepande, 777. OE. wēpan.

**weppen,** n., *weapon,* 835. OE.
wǣpen, wēpen.

**were,** v. tr., *near,* 287; refl. *defend
oneself* (= *excuse oneself*), 69:
3 sg. -z, 287; pret. 3 sg. wer,
69. OE. werian.

**werk,** n., *labor,* 136, 1258; *action,
deed, doing,* 171, 266, 305, 355,
589, 658, 760, 763, 1050, 1328,
1350; *creation,* 198; *structure,*
1480; *construction,* 1390; *ado,*
1725: pl. -ez, 171, 266, 355, -es,
1480; werkkez, 136, 760, 763;
werkkes, 1258, 1328, 1350. OE.
weorc.

**werre,** n., *war,* 1178. NF. werre,
OF. guerre.

**wers,** comp. adj., *worse,* 113; as n.,
80; *smaller,* 719: worre, 719;
worse, 1320; superl. werst, 694.
OE. wierse, werse; cf. ON.
verri.

**weryng,** vbl. n., *wearing, use,* 1123.

**wete,** v. tr., *wet:* inf. 1027. OE.
wǣtan, wētan.

**weþer,** see **wheþer.**

**weve,** v. tr., *fling, push,* 453; *shut,*
857; *rush,* 422: pret. 3 sg. wafte,
422, 453; waft, 857. OE. wǣfan
(infl. by ON. viefa).

**weye,** see **weȝe.**

**wex(en),** see **wax.**

**what-kyn,** adj., *what kind of,* 100.

**what,** see **who.**

**wheder,** conj., *whither,* 917. OE.
hwæðer.

**wheder,** adv., *nevertheless,* 570.
OE. hwæð(e)re, hweðre.

**whederwarde,** adv., *whithersoever,*
422.

**when,** conj., 37, etc.; *whenever,*
1047, 1700; *at which time,* 361;
when þat, 961, 1537; correl. with

'then,' 343, 529: when, 37, 61,
89, 281, etc. (32 times); quen,
435, 529, 560, 563, 1047, 1084,
1514; wen, 343. OE. hwanne,
hwænne.

**where,** conj., 444, 491, 1079; where
so, for simple *where,* 675; *wherever,* 791; wher, 1080. OE.
hwǣr, hwēr.

**wheþer,** interr. conj., 717; introd.
indir. questions, 583, 918; correl. w. oþer, 113: weþer, 717.
OE. hwæðer, hweðer.

**whichche,** n., *chest* (= *ark*), 362.
OE. hwicce.

**who,** interr. pron., 877; introd. indir. question, 1699. Neut. what,
35, 752, 757, 913; introd. indir.
question, 152, 1119, 1556, 1557,
1567, 1587; what if, 737, 741,
751; exclam. 487, 845, 846, 855,
1241, 1583: quat, 741, 1119:
whatt, 845. OE. hwā.

**who,** rel. pron., who so, *whoever,*
1, 1647, 1649; quo so, 1650;
quos . . . so, *whosoever,* 1648;
dat. wham, 259. Neut. what so,
*whatever,* 819, 1099. OE. hwā.

**why,** interr. adv., 828, 1595. OE.
hwȳ.

**whyl,** conj., *while,* 206, 568, 780,
1114; whyle, 1124, 1655; whil,
1298. OE. hwīl, n.

**whyle,** n., *while, time,* 743, 833,
1285; *short time,* 1620. OE.
hwīl.

**whyte,** adj., *white,* 793, 1440;
*bright,* 1120: whit, 793; quite,
1440. OE. hwīt.

**wich,** see **wych.**

**wittnesse,** v. tr.: inf. 1050. Cf.
OE. witnes, n.

**wlate,** impers. v., *cause loathing,* 305; pers., *be disgusted, feel horror,* 1501: 3 sg. -s, 1501, -z, 305. OE. wlātian.

**wlatsum,** adj., *abominable, detestable,* 541.

**wlonk,** adj., *fair, fine,* 606, 793, 831, 899, 933; as noun, *fair, pure,* 1052: wlonc, 899. OE. wlanc, wlonc.

**wo,** n., *woe,* 284, 1701; *affliction, calamity,* 541. OE. wā.

**wod,** adj., *mad,* 828, 1558; *angry,* 204; *raging,* 364: wode, 364, 1558. OE. wōd.

**wod,** n., *wood,* 370, 1028: wode, 387. OE. wudu.

**woȝe,** n., *wall:* 832, 1545, 1724; wowe, 1531, 1630; pl. woȝes, 1424; wowez, 839, wowes, 1403. OE. wāg.

**wok,** adj., *weak:* comp. as noun, wakker, 835. OE. wāc.

**wolf,** n.: pl. -es, 1676. OE. wulf.

**wombe,** n., *belly,* 462: pl. -s, 1250, 1255. OE. wamb, wāmb.

**won¹,** n., *dwelling, house; palace;* 140, etc.; *stalls* (Vulg. mansiunculas) 311; *city,* 928; won, 140, 533, 891, 928, 1508, 1770; wone, 1489; pl. -es, 779, 841, 1178, 1197; -ez, 311, 375, 471. Cf. OE. gewuna.

**won²,** n., *custom,* 720. OE. wuna.

**won,** v. intr., *dwell:* inf. 1676; 2 sg. -ez, 875; pres. 3 sg. wonyes, 1807; wonies, 1340; wons, 326; pret. 3 sg. wonyed, 431, 675; 3 pl. wonyed, 252; woned, 362; pres. part. wonyande, 293. OE. wunian.

**wonde,** v. tr., *fear:* pret. 3 sg. 855. OE. wandian.

**wonder,** n., 584, 1310, 1504: wunder, 1390. OE. wundor.

**wonder,** adv., *wonderfully, exceedingly, very,* 5, 153, 880, 1381.

**wonderly,** adv., *extraordinarily, greatly,* 570. OE. wundorlīce.

**wone,** v. intr., *decrease:* pp. 496. OE. wanian, wonian.

**wonen,** see **wynne.**

**wonnyng,** n., *dwelling,* 921. OE. wunung.

**wont,** v. tr., *lack,* 13; intr. w. of, *be wanting,* 739: pres. subj. 3 sg. wont, 739; 3 pl. wont, 13. ON. vanta.

**wonte,** part. adj., *accustomed, used,* 1489. Cf. OE. wunian.

**wonye,** see **won,** v.

**worcher,** n., *creator,* 1501. Cf. OE. wyrcean, v.

**worde,** n., *word,* 152, 213, 348, 1555, etc.; *command,* 348: pl. -z, 149, 210, 302, 344, 512, 756, 809, 848, 859; -s, 1592, 1641, 1662, 1725; worde, 840. OE. word.

***wordlych,** n., *earthly,* 49 (see note). OE. woroldlic.

**work,** see **wyrke.**

**worlde,** n., *world,* 228, 252, 293, 323, 355, 371, 431, 496, 548, 685, 847, 1123, 1360, 1501, 1614, 1646; *reign, power,* 1298; worldez goud, 1048; worlde wythouten ende, 712; gen. -z, 1048; -s, 1802. OE. weorold, worold.

**worm,** n., *serpent:* pl. -ez, 533. OE. wyrm.

**worre,** see **wers.**

**worschyp,** n., *honor, dignity:* worschyp, 545, 651, 1120; worchyp, 1127, 1592, 1616, 1802. OE. weorðscipe.

**worse,** see **wers.**

wórþe, adj., *worth,* 1244. OE.
weorð.

worþe, v. intr., *become, be:* inf. 580,
686, 1066; 2 sg. -s, 1738; pres.
subj. 2 sg. worþe, 901, 1056,
1116; 3 sg. worþe, 60, 727, 925,
1125; imper. pl. -z, 521. OE.
weorðan.

worþly, adj., *worthy, good,* 471,
651; *honorable, illustrious,* 1298,
1351: worþely, 651, worþelych,
471, 1351. OE. weorðlic.

worþy, adj., *worthy,* 84, 113; as n.,
718; *honored,* 231.

wost, see wyt.

woþe, n., *danger, harm,* 855, 988.
ON. váði.

wowe(z), see woʒe.

wrak, see wreke.

wrake, n., *vengeance, (God's) punishment,* 213, 235, 386, 718, 970,
1050, 1143, 1225, 1808: wrache,
204, 229. OE. wracu, partly confused w. OE. wræc.

wrakful, adj., *angry, bitter,* 302.

wrange, adj., *wrong,* 268; quasi-
adv. wrank, *?violently, ?sud-
denly,* 891. ON. (v)rangr.

wrange, n., *wrong,* 76.

wrappe, v. refl., *wrap oneself, clothe
oneself:* 2 sg. -z, 169. Etym.
uncertain.

wrast, v. tr., *thrust, throw,* 1802;
*raise,* 1166; *blow,* 1403; pret.
3 sg. wrast, 1166; 3 pl. wrasten,
1403; pp. wrast, 1802. OE.
wræstan.

wrastle, v. intr., *struggle:* pret.
3 pl. 949. OE. wræstlian.

wrath, n.: 204, 326, 690, 746, 1143,
1166. ONth. wræððo.

wrathe, v. tr., *anger,* 719, 828; intr.,
*become angry,* 230: pret. 3 sg.
230, 719, 828. OE. wráþian.

wrech, n., *wretch,* 230, 828: pl. -ez,
84, 851. OE. wrecca.

wreke, v. intr., *w. on, take
vengeance:* pret. 3 sg. wrek, 198;
wrak, 570. OE. wrecan.

wrench, n., *trick, deceitful deed:*
pl. -ez, 292. OE. wrenc.

wroʒt, see wyrke.

wroth, adj., *angry,* 5; *fierce,* 1676:
wroþe, 1676. OE. wráþ.

wroth, see wyrke.

wroþly, adv., *angrily, fiercely,* 280:
wroþely, 949. OE. wráþlíce.

wruxeled, part. adj., *arrayed,
adorned,* 1381 (cf. Gaw. 2191 for
meaning). OE. wrixlian.

wryste, n., *wrist,* 1535. OE. wrist.

wryt, n., *writing,* 1552, 1567, 1630;
*Scripture,* 657. OE. (ge)writ.

wryte, v. tr., *write:* 3 sg. -s, 1534;
pp. wryten, 1725. OE. wrítan.

wryþe, v. intr., *writhe, wriggle:*
3 pl. -z, 533. OE. wríþan.

wunder, see wonder.

wunnen, see wynne.

wych, indef. interr., *which, what,*
1060, 1074: wich, 169, 1060. OE.
hwilc.

wych, n, *wizard:* pl. -ez, 1577.
OE. wicca.

wychecrafte, n., *witchcraft,* 1560.
OE. wiccecræft.

wyd, adv., *wide,* 318. OE. wíde.

wyde, adj., *wide, broad,* 370; on
wyde, *around,* 1423. OE. wid.

wydo, n., *widow:* pl. -ez, 185. OE.
widwe.

wyf, n., *wife, woman,* 69, 330, 349,
658, 813, 821, 899, 933, 981, 1244,

1351: pl. wyves, 1250; wyvez, 112, 298, 350, 503. OE. wīf.

**wyȝe,** n., *man, person, one:* wyȝe, 280, 284, 293, 545, 589, 658, 875, 933, 970, 1052, 1298, 1585, 1770; wyȝ, 5, 230, 675; pl. -z, 235, 606, 712, 813, 899, 908; -s, 1181, 1587. OE. wiga.

**wyȝt,** n., *creature,* 471. OE. wyht.

**wyȝt,** adv., *quickly,* 617. ON. vīgt, neut. of vīgr.

**wyȝtly,** adv., *quickly,* 908.

**wyk,** adj., *wicked, evil,* 1063; wykke, 908. Cf. OE. wicca, *wizard.*

**wyket,** n., *wicket, gate, door,* 857, 882: wykket, 501. NF. wiket, OF. guichet.

**wykked,** adj., *wicked,* 570, 718, 1050, 1360: wekked, 855. Based on wyk(ke), q. v.

**wyl,** v., *will, wish, be willing,* 360, etc.; as auxiliary, 358, 444, 513, 517, etc.; used elliptically, *mean, signify,* 1552; pret. in apodosis of condition, 36, 1153; pret. w. pres. meaning, *would like to,* 928, 1058, 1140, 1629: 1 sg. wyl, 358; 2 sg. wylt, 165, 764, 930; 3 sg. wyl, 517; pres. subj. 2 sg. wyl, 1065; pret. 1 sg. wolde, 928, 1153, 1629; 3 sg. 36, 126, 231, etc.; 2 pl. 800, 1153; 3 pl. 444, 807. Combined w. ne, pres. 1 sg. nel, 513; 3 sg. nyl, 1261; pret. 3 sg. nolde, 1091, 1154, 1233, 1245; 3 pl. 805. OE. willan.

**wylde,** adj., *wild,* 58, 302, 415, 533, 948, 1269, 1676; as noun, *wild animals,* 311, 362, 387, 503, 529, 1674. OE. wilde.

**\*wylfulnes,** n., *wilfulness, obstinacy,* 231. Cf. OE. \*wilfull.

**wylger,** adj., *?wild,* 375 (see note). Etym. uncertain.

**wylle,** n., *will, purpose; heart, mind;* 200, 232, 302, 309, 565, 687, 738, 928, 1646; *rage,* 76 (see note). OE. willa.

**wylsfully,** adv., *wilfully,* 268. Cf. OE. willes ful.

**wyly,** adv., *cunningly,* 1452. Cf. OE. wīl, wile.

**wynde,** n., *wind,* 437, 444, 1484; wynd, 847; pl. -z, 421, 457, 948. OE. wind.

**wynde,** v. intr., *turn, take one's way:* 3 pl. -z, 534. OE. windan.

**wyndow,** n., 318: wyndowe, 453. ON. vindauga.

**wyndowande,** part. adj., *scattering in the wind,* 1048. OE. wyndwian.

**wyne,** n., *wine,* 1420, 1716: wyn, 1127, 1508. OE. wīn.

**wynge,** n., *wing,* 1484: pl. -z, 475. ON. vængr.

**wynne,** v. tr., *obtain, get, win,* 617, 650, 1120, 1305, 1550, 1777; *prevail on, induce,* 1616; *beget,* 112; intr., *make (force) one's way,* 140, 882, 1004, 1374, 1577; *issue,* 1669: inf. 617, 650, 1550; 3 sg. -s, 1120; pret. 2 sg. wan, 140; pret. 3 pl. wonnen, 882, 1374, 1577; wonen, 1777; imper. sg. wynne, 1616; pp. wonnen, 1004, 1669; wonen, 112; wunnen, 1305. OE. winnan.

**wynnelych,** adj., *gracious,* 1807. OE. wynlic.

**wynter,** n., 525. OE. winter.

**wyrde,** n., *fate, destiny:* pl. wyrdes, 1224, 1605. OE. wyrd.

**wyrke,** v. tr., *do, make; create; construct;* 5, 171, 205, 280, etc.; *provoke,* 821; intr., *act,* 1063,

1319: inf. wyrke, 1287; work,
663; 2 sg. wyrkkes, 1063; pret.
2 sg. wro3tez, 720; pret. 3 sg.
wro3t, 5, 205, 280, 1319, 1699;
wroth, 821; pret. 3 pl. wro3t,
725; imper. sg. wyrk, 311; pp.
wro3t, 171, 318, 348, 1381, 1455.
OE. wyrcan.

**wyrle,** v. tr., *whirl:* ?pret. 3 sg.
wyrle, 475. ON. hvirfla.

**wyse,** adj., *wise,* 1555, 1560; as n.,
1319, 1741: wys, 1592. OE. wīs.

**wyse,** n., *manner, way,* only in
phrase, (up)on . . . wyse,
268, 271, 327, 696, 1063, 1171,
1187, 1432: pl. -s, 1805, wyse,
1728. OE. wīse.

**wyse,** v. tr., *send,* 453; *instruct,*
1564: 3 sg. wysses, 1564; pret.
3 sg. 453. OE. wīsian, wissian.

**wyst(e),** see w, v.

**wyt,** n., *wisdom,* 348, *reason,
senses,* 1422, 1701; *mind,* 515;
*meaning,* 1630: *wytte,* 1630; pl.
wyttez, 515. OE. wit.

**wyt,** pret. pres., *know, perceive, understand:* inf. 1052, 1319, 1567,
1630; 2 sg. wost, 875; pres.
subj. 3 sg. wyt; pret. 3 sg. wyst,
152, 1699, 1770; 3 pl. wyste. OE.
witan–wiste.

**wyte,** v. tr., *blame:* inf. 76. OE.
wītan.

**wyter,** adv., *clearly,* 1552. ON. vitr,
*wise.*

**wyter,** v. tr., *inform:* pp. 1587.

**wyterly,** adv., *clearly, surely,* 171,
1567.

**wyth,** prep., *in company with, along
with,* 86, 118, 124, etc.; *together
with,* 58, 339, 468, etc.; *against,
for,* 56; denoting means, 19, 111,
112, etc.; manner, 10, 43, 71, 139,
etc.; agent, 90, 91, 1142, 1495;

cause, 516; with various verbs
and nouns denoting combination,
agreement, etc., 137, 327, 337,
etc.; *at* (temporal), 213, 671; in
phrases: wyth yor leve, 94; with
sy3t, 192; with þat, 671: with,
19, 43, 118, 121, etc. (in less than
one-third of the cases). OE.
wið.

**wythal,** adv., *in addition,* 636.

**wyþerly,** adv., *fiercely,* 198. Cf.
OE. wiðer, *against.*

**wythhalde,** v. tr., *withhold:* inf.
740.

**wythinne,** adv.: 20, 305, *312, 434,
593, 883, 969, 1182, 1184, 1193,
1195, 1385, 1391, 1465. Prep.:
284, 431, 1048, 1069, 1566, 1607;
of time, 1779, 1786: withinne,
284, 1465. OE. wiðinnan.

**wytles,** adj., *distracted,* 1585. OE.
witlēas.

**wythouten,** adv., *without,* 20, 313,
1205, 1487. Prep. 252, 350, 417,
556, 660, 712, 931, 1105, 1122:
wythoute, 1205, 1487, 1725;
withouten, 417. OE. wiðūtan.

# Y.

**ydropike,** adj., *dropsical,* 1096. OF.
ydropike.

**y3e,** n., *eye,* 133, 583, 768: pl. -n,
576, 588, 792, 978, 1005, 1222,
1695. OE. ēage, ēge.

**Ynde,** prop. n., *India:* 1231, 1772.
OF. Inde.

**ynde,** n., *deep blue,* 1411. OF.
inde.

**yor,** poss. pron., *your:* 94, 618, 620,
801, etc. OE. ēower.

**yorself,** see **self.**

**yow,** see þou.

**yowself,** see **self.**

**yre,** n., *ire,* 775, 1240, 1503. OF. ire.

**yþe,** n., *wave:* pl. *yþez, 430. OE. ȳþ.

## 3.

**3ark,** v. tr., *prepare, make ready,* 652; *set up,* 1708; *grant,* 758: 1 sg. 3ark, 758; pp. *652, 1708. OE. gearcian.

**3arm,** n., *outcry,* 971. Cf. ON. jarmr.

**3at,** see **get.**

**3ate,** n., *gate, entrance,* 796: pl. -s, 785, 854, 884, 1188, 1263; -z, 837, 938, 941. OE. geat, gæt.

**3ederly,** adv., *entirely,* 463. Cf. OE. *geǣdre.

**3e,** adv., *yea, yes,* 347. OE. gēa.

**3e,** see **þou.**

**3ede,** see **go.**

**3e3e,** v. intr., *cry:* pret. 3 pl. 846. Cf. ON. geyja.

**3elde,** v. tr., *give,* 665; *restore,* 1708; inf. pp. 3olden, 1708. OE. gieldan, geldan.

**3ellyng,** vbl. n., *yelling,* 971. OE. giellan, gellan.

**3elpe,** v. intr., *boast:* pret. 3 pl. 3olped, 846. OE. gielpan, gelpan.

**3eme,** v. tr., *guard, rule over:* 3 sg. -s, 1493; pret. 3 sg. 464, 1242. OE. gīeman, gēman.

**3ender,** adv., *yonder,* 1617. OE. geon + suffix -der; cf. Goth. jaindre.

**3epe,** adj., *alert, prompt, bold,* 881; as n. 3ep, 796. OE. gēap, gēp.

**3eply,** adv., *quickly, soon,* 665, 1708. OE. gēaplīce.

**3er,** n., *year:* 494, 1286; pl. -ez, 426, 526; 3er, 1192; 3ere, 1453. OE. gēar, gēr.

**3erne¹,** v. tr., *desire:* 2 sg. -z, 758; pp. 66. OE. giernan, gernan.

**3erne²,** v. intr., *run:* pret. 3 sg. 3ornen, 881. OE. geiernan.

**3estande,** part. adj., *frothing,* 846. Cf. OE. gist, *yeast.*

**3et,** adv., *yet, hitherto,* 197, 815, 867, 1312; w. future, 517, 648; *still,* 847, 984, 1021, 1049, 1158; *further, besides,* 1232, 1525, 1803; *even, even now,* 754, 758; w. comparatives, 50, 96, 97; *nevertheless,* 120, 230, 450, 664, etc. (14 times): 3ette, 867. OE. gīet, gēt.

**3ete,** see **get.**

**3if,** see **if.**

**3is,** adv., *yes, truly,* 1113. OE. gīse.

**3isterday,** n., *yesterday,* as gen., 463. OE. gistrandæg.

**3okke,** n., *yoke:* pl. -z, 66. OE. geoc.

**3olden,** see **3elde.**

**3olped,** see **3elpe.**

**3omerly,** adj., *lamentable,* 971. OE. gēomerlic.

**3on,** adj., *yon,* 751, 772. OE. geon.

**3onde,** adj., *yon,* 721. Cf. OE. geond, adv.

**3onge,** adj., *young,* 783, 881; 3ong, 842. OE. geong.

**3ore-whyle,** adv., *a short time ago,* 842. OE. gēara + hwīl.

**3ornen,** see **3erne².**

## Z.

**\*Zedechyas,** prop. n., *Zedekiah,* 1169. Lat. Sedecias.

# BIBLIOGRAPHY

This bibliography is select, containing only the more important works on each subject.

## I. EDITIONS

Early English Alliterative Poems, in the West-Midland Dialect of the Fourteenth Century. Edited by Richard Morris (Early English Text Society, Vol. 1). London, 1864; revised edition, 1869. Cited as M.

Selections from Purity, comprising lines 235-544, 947-72, 1009-51, in Morris's Specimens of Early English. Oxford, 1867, and in Morris and Skeat's Specimens of Early English, Part II, Oxford, 1872, revised 1884, 1894

## II. TRANSLATIONS

I. GOLLANCZ, edition of Pearl (see below under VIII), pp. xxviii-xxx. Paraphrases of Purity, lines 361-70, 381-3, 414-24, 551-6, 1110-32.

JESSIE L. WESTON, Romance, Vision, and Satire, pp. 153-70. Boston, 1912. Poetic rendering of lines 1357-1812 (Belshazzar's Feast).

## III. DATE, AUTHORSHIP, AND RELATIONSHIP TO OTHER POEMS

MORRIS, Preface to Early English Alliterative Poems (see above under I).

M. TRAUTMANN, Über Verfasser und Entstehungszeit einiger Alliterierender Gedichte des Altenglischen. Halle, 1876. Also published with sub-title Habilitationsschrift, by which name it is often cited.

M. TRAUTMANN, Der Dichter Huchown und seine Werke (Anglia I. 109-49).

TEN BRINK (see below under VII).

M. C. THOMAS, Sir Gawayne and the Green Knight. A Comparison with the French Perceval, preceded by an Investigation of the Author's Other Works. Zürich, 1883.

KNIGGE (see below under V), pp. 1-10.

HENRY BRADLEY, Academy, Jan. 14, 1888.

J. B. HENNEMAN, Untersuchungen über das Mittelenglische Gedicht 'Wars of Alexander,' pp. 30-5. Berlin, 1889.

GOLLANCZ, Introduction to edition of Pearl (see below under VIII).

G. NEILSON, 'Huchown of the Awle Ryale,' the Alliterative Poet. A Historical Criticism of Fourteenth Century Poems ascribed to Sir Hew of Eglintoun. Glasgow, 1902.

J. T. T. Brown, Huchown of the Awle Ryale and his Poems, examined in the Light of Recent Criticism. Glasgow, 1902.

C. F. Brown, The Author of the Pearl, considered in the Light of Theological Opinions (Publications of the Modern Language Association 19. 146-8).

C. G. Osgood, Introduction to edition of Pearl (see below under VIII).

C. Reicke, Untersuchungen über den Stil der Mittelenglischen Alliterierenden Gedichte Morte Arthure, The Destruction of Troy, The Wars of Alexander, The Siege of Jerusalem, Sir Gawayn and the Green Knight: ein Beitrag zur Lösung der Huchown-Frage. Königsberg i. Pr., 1906.

H. N. MacCracken, Concerning Huchown (Publications of the Modern Language Association 25. 507-34).

H. Bateson, Introduction to edition of Patience (see below under VIII).

J. E. Wells' Manual of the Writings of Middle English 1050-1400, New Haven, 1916, should be consulted for further bibliography of the Huchown question and of the separate alliterative poems.

## IV. SOURCES

C. F. Brown, Note on the Dependence of 'Cleanness' on the 'Book of Mandeville' (Publications of the Modern Language Association 19. 149-53).

O. F. Emerson, A Parallel between the Middle English Poem Patience and an Early Latin Poem attributed to Tertullian (Publications of the Modern Language Association 10. 242-8).

O. F. Emerson, A Note on the M. E. 'Cleanness' (Modern Language Review 10. 373-5).

S. B. Liljegren, Has the Poet of 'Patience' read 'De Jona'? (Englische Studien 48. 337-41).

## V. METRE AND ALLITERATION

F. Rosenthal, Die Alliterierende Englische Langzeile im 14. Jahrhundert (Anglia 1. 414-59).

J. Schipper, Englische Metrik 1. 195-212. Bonn, 1881.

J. Fuhrmann, Die Alliterierenden Sprachformelm in Morris' Early English Alliterative Poems und in Sir Gawayne and the Green Knight. Hamburg, 1886.

K. Luick, Die Englische Stabreimzeile im XIV., XV., und XVI. Jahrhundert (Anglia 11. 392-443, 553-618; esp. 572-85).

Max Kaluza, Strophische Gliederung in der Mittelenglischen rein Alliterirenden Dichtung (Englische Studien 16. 169-80).

J. Lawrence, Chapters on Alliterative Verse, pp. 89-99. London, 1893.

M. Trautmann, Zur Kenntniss und Geschichte der Mittelenglischen Stabzeile (Anglia 18. 83-100).

B. Kuhnke, Die alliterierenden Langzeile in der Mittelenglischen Romanze Sir Gawayn and the Green Knight (Studien zum Germanischen Alliterationsvers, Vol. 4). Berlin, 1900. Reviewed by Fischer, Anglia Beiblatt 12. 65-76, and Luick, ibid. pp. 33 ff.

J. Fischer, Die Stabende Langzeile in den Werken des Gawaindichters (Bonner Beiträge zur Anglistik 11. 1-64). Bonn, 1901. Reviewed by Luick, Anglia Beiblatt 12. 33-49. Compare further Fischer and Mennicken, Zur Mittelenglischen Stabzeile (a reply to Luick), pp. 139-54 of Bonner Beiträge 11.

M. Deutschbein, Zur Entwicklung des Englischen Alliterationsverses. Halle, 1902.

K. Luick, in Paul's Grundriss der Germanischen Philologie, 2d ed., 2. 2. 160-8. Strassburg, 1905.

J. Thomas, Die Alliterierende Langzeile des Gawayn-Dichters. Coburg, 1908.

K. Schumacher, Studien über den Stabreim in der Mittelenglischen Alliterationsdichtung (Bonner Studien zur Englischen Philologie, Vol. 11). Bonn, 1914.

## VI. LANGUAGE

Morris, Preface to Early English Alliterative Poems (see above under I), pp. xxi-xl.

F. Schwahn, Die Conjugation in Sir Gawayn and the Green Knight und den Sogenannten Early English Alliterative Poems. Strassburg, 1884.

W. Fick, Zum Mittelenglischen Gedicht von der Perle: eine Lautuntersuchung. Kiel, 1885.

F. Knigge, Die Sprache des Dichters von Sir Gawain and the Green Knight, der Sogenannten Early English Alliterative Poems, und De Erkenwalde. Marburg, 1885.

J. Fischer, Die Stabende Langzeile (see above under V), pp. 48-61.

M. Kullnick, Studien über den Wortschatz in Sir Gawayne and the Grene Knyʒt. Berlin, 1902.

K. Schmittbetz, Das Adjektiv in 'Sir Gawayn and the Grene Knyʒt' (Anglia 32. 1-60, 163-89, 359-83).

H. Bateson, Introduction to Patience (see below under VIII), pp. xxxii-vii.

H. Bateson, The Text of Cleanness (Modern Language Review 13. 377-86).

I. Gollancz, The Text of Cleanness (ibid. 14. 152-62).

O. F. EMERSON, Middle English Clannesse (Publications of the Modern Language Association 34. 494-522).

MABEL DAY, The Weak Verb in the Works of the Gawain-Poet (Modern Language Review 14. 413-5).

## VII. GENERAL

TEN BRINK, Early English Literature (translated by Kennedy) 1. 337-51. New York, 1883.

I. GOLLANCZ, Introduction to Pearl (see below under VIII).

A. BRANDL, in Paul's Grundriss der Germanischen Philologie, 1st ed., 2. 661-3. Strassburg, 1893.

C. B. BROWN, The Author of the Pearl, considered in the Light of his Theological Opinions (Publications of the Modern Language Association 19. 115-53).

W. H. SCHOFIELD, The Nature and Fabric of The Pearl. Ibid. 19. 154-203.

W. H. SCHOFIELD, Symbolism, Allegory, and Autobiography in The Pearl (ibid. 24. 585-675).

C. G. OSGOOD, Introduction to Pearl (see below under VIII).

I. GOLLANCZ, Cambridge History of English Literature. Vol. I, chapter 15. London and New York, 1907.

C. WEICHARDT, Die Entwicklung des Naturgefühls in der Mittelenglischen Dichtung vor Chaucer (einschliesslich des Gawain-Dichters), pp. 79-92. Kiel, 1900.

F. W. MOORMAN, The Interpretation of Nature in English Poetry from Beowulf to Shakespeare (Quellen und Forschungen, Vol. 95). Chapter 7. Strassburg, 1905.


## VIII. EDITIONS OF WORKS BY THE AUTHOR OF PURITY AND OTHER ALLITERATIVE POEMS FREQUENTLY CITED

Sir Gawayne, a Collection of Ancient Romance-Poems. Edited by Sir Frederic Madden. London, 1839.

Sir Gawayne and The Green Knight. Edited by Richard Morris (Early English Text Society, Vol. 4). London, 1864. Revised by I. Gollancz in 1897, and further in 1912. (Edition cited.)

Pearl and Patience (see Early Engl. Allit. Poems under I).

Pearl, an English Poem of the Fourteenth Century. Edited with a Modern Rendering by I. Gollancz. London, 1891.

The Pearl, a Middle English Poem. Edited by Charles G. Osgood. Boston and London, 1906. (Edition cited.)

Patience, a West Midland Poem of the Fourteenth Century. Edited by Hartley Bateson. Manchester, 1912. Reviewed by Emerson, Mod.

Lang. Notes 28. 171-80; Ekwall, Angl. Beiblatt 24. 33-6; Macaulay, Mod. Lang. Rev. 8. 396-8; Brandl, Archiv für die Neueren Sprachen 129. 516; Athenaeum, Oct. 26, 1912; Liljegren, Engl. Stud. 49. 142-3. 2d ed., recast and partly rewritten, Manchester, 1918. (Edition cited.)

Patience, an Alliterative Version of 'Jonah,' by the Poet of Pearl. Edited by I. Gollancz. London, 1913. Reviewed by Ekwall, Engl. Stud. 49. 144-6.

De Erkenwalde, in Horstmann's Altenglischen Legenden, Neue Folge, pp. 265-74. Heilbronn, 1881. (Erken.)

The Wars of Alexander, an Alliterative Romance. Re-edited by W. W. Skeat (Early English Text Society, Extra Series, Vol. 47). London, 1886. (Alex. C.)

The Vision of William concerning Piers Plowman. . . . Ed. by W. W. Skeat (Early English Text Society, Vols. 28, 38, 54, 81). London, 1867-1884.

The Parlement of the Thre Ages, and Wynnere and Wastoure. Edited for the Roxburghe Club by I. Gollancz. London, 1897.

The Parlement of the Thre Ages, an Alliterative Poem on the Nine Worthies and the Heroes of Romance. Edited by I. Gollancz. London, 1915.

The Romance of William of Palerne (otherwise known as the Romance of William and the Werwolf). Re-edited by W. W. Skeat (Early English Text Society, Extra Series, Vol. 1). London, 1867.

The Gest Hystoriale of the Destruction of Troy. Edited by G. A. Panton and D. Donaldson (Early English Text Society, Vols. 39, 56). London, 1869, 1874. (Destr. Troy.)

Death and Life, with Introduction by W. W. Skeat, in Bishop Percy's Folio Manuscript, edited by Hales and Furnivall, 3. 49-75. London, 1868.

Death and Liffe, an Alliterative Poem. Edited by James H. Hanford and John M. Steadman, Jr. (North Carolina Studies in Philology, Vol. 15, No. 3). Chapel Hill, N. C., 1918.

Scottish Alliterative Poems. Edited by F. J. Amours. 2 vols. (Scottish Text Society, 1897). Includes the texts Golagros and Gawayne, Awntyrs off Arthure (Awnt. Arth.), Pistill of Susan, Buke of the Howlat.

Sege of Jerusalem. Herausgegeben von G. Steffler. Marburg, 1891.

Morte Arthur. Herausgegeben von E. Björkman. Heidelberg, 1915.

# APPENDIX

THE FLOOD

**Gen. 6. 1-8.** Cumque coepissent homines multiplicari super terram et filias procreassent, videntes filii Dei filias hominum, quod essent pulchrae, acceperunt sibi uxores ex omnibus, quas elegerant. . . . Gigantes autem erant super terram in diebus illis. Postquam enim ingressi sunt filii Dei ad filias hominum illaeque genuerunt, isti sunt potentes a saeculo viri famosi. Videns autem Deus, quod multa malitia hominum esset in terra, et cuncta cogitatio cordis intenta esset ad malum omni tempore, poenituit eum quod hominem fecisset in terra. Et tactus dolore cordis intrinsecus: Delebo, inquit, hominem, quem creavi, a facie terrae, ab homine usque ad animantia, a reptili usque ad volucres caeli; poenitet enim me fecisse eos. Neo vero invenit gratiam coram Domino.

**6. 9-22.** Hae sunt generationes Noe: Noe vir justus atque perfectus fuit in generationibus suis, cum Deo ambulavit. Et genuit tres filios, Sem, Cham et Japheth. Corrupta est autem terra coram Deo, et repleta est iniquitate. Cumque vidisset Deus terram esse corruptam, (omnis quippe caro corruperat viam suam super terram) dixit ad Noe: Finis universae carnis venit coram me: repleta est terra iniquitate a facie eorum, et ego disperdam eos cum terra. Fac tibi arcam de lignis laevigatis; mansiunculas in arca facies et bitumine linies intrinsecus et extrinsecus. Et sic facies eam: trecentorum cubitorum erit longitudo arcae, quinquaginta cubitorum latitudo, et triginta cubitorum altitudo illius. Fenestram in arca facies, et in cubito consummabis summitatem ejus; ostium autem arcae pones ex latere; deorsum, cœnacula, et tristega facies in ea. Ecce ego adducam aquas diluvii super terram, ut interficiam omnem carnem, in qua spiritus vitae est subter caelum. Universae quae in terra sunt, consumentur. Ponamque foedus meum tecum, et ingredieris arcam tu et filii tui, uxor tua, et uxores filiorum tuorum tecum. Et ex cunctis animantibus universae carnis bina induces in arcam, ut vivant tecum: masculini sexus et feminini. De volucribus juxta genus suum, et de jumentis in genere suo, ét ex omni reptili terrae secundum genus suum, bina

---

* Only the longer narrative passages paraphrased by the poet are here given. Single verses quoted or alluded to will be found in the notes.

de omnibus ingredientur tecum, ut possint vivere. Tolles igitur tecum ex omnibus escis, quae mandi possunt, et comportabis apud te; et erunt tam tibi, quam illis in cibum. Fecit igitur Noe omnia, quae praeceperat illi Deus.

**7. 1-11.** Dixitque Dominus ad eum: Ingredere tu et omnis domus tua in arcam; te enim vidi justum coram me in generatione hac. Ex omnibus animantibus mundis tolle septena et septena, masculum et feminam; de animantibus vero immundis duo et duo, masculum et feminam. . . . Adhuc enim et post dies septem ego pluam super terram, . . . et delebo omnem substantiam, quam feci, de superficie terrae. Fecit ergo Noe omnia, quae mandaverat ei Dominus. . . . Cumque transissent septem dies, aquae diluvii inundaverunt super terram. Anno sexcentesimo vitae Noe, mense secundo, septimodecimo die mensis, rupti sunt omnes fontes abyssi magnae, et cataractae caeli apertae sunt.

**7. 17-24.** Factumque est diluvium quadraginta diebus super terram: et multiplicatae sunt aquae, et elevaverunt arcam in sublime a terra. Vehementer enim inundaverunt et omnia repleverunt in superficie terrae; porro arca ferebatur super aquas. Et aquae praevaluerunt nimis super terram, opertique sunt omnes montes excelsi sub universo caelo. Quindecim cubitus altior fuit aqua super montes, quos operuerat. Consumptaque est omnis caro quae movebatur super terram, volucrum, animantium, bestiarum, omniumque reptilium quae reptant super terram; universi homines et cuncta, in quibus spiraculum vitae est in terra, mortua sunt. Et delevit omnem substantiam, quae erat super terram, ab homine usque ad pecus, tam reptile quam volucres caeli; et deleta sunt de terra; remansit autem solus Noe et qui cum eo erant in arca. Obtinueruntque aquae terram centum quinquaginta diebus.

**8. 1-22.** Recordatus autem Deus Noe . . . adduxit spiritum super terram, et imminutae sunt aquae. Et clausi sunt fontes abyssi, et cataractae caeli: et prohibitae sunt pluviae de caelo. Reversaeque sunt aquae de terra euntes et redeuntes et coeperunt minui post centum quinquaginta dies. Requievitque arca mense septimo, vigesimo septimo die mensis, super montes Armeniae. At vero aquae ibant et decrescebant usque ad decimum mensem. Decimo enim mense, prima die mensis, apparuerunt cacumina montium. Cumque transissent quadraginta dies, aperiens Noe fenestram arcae, quam fecerat, dimisit corvum, qui egradiebatur, et non revertebatur, donec siccarentur aquae super terram. Emisit quoque columbam post eum, ut videret si jam cessassent aquae super faciem terrae. Quae cum non invenisset ubi requiesceret pes ejus, reversa est ad eum in arcam . . . extenditque manum, et apprehensam intulit in arcam. . . . Rursum dimisit columbam ex arca. At illa venit ad eum ad vesperam portans ramum olivae virentibus foliis in ore suo, intellexit ergo Noe quod cessassent aquae super terram. . . . Igitur sexcentesimo primo anno, primo mense, prima die mensis, imminutae sunt aquae super terram, et aperiens Noe tectum arcae, aspexit, viditque quod exsiccata esset superficies terrae. . . . Locutus est autem Deus ad Noe, dicens: Egredere de arca . . . et ingredimini super terram: crescite et multiplicamini super eam. Egressus est ergo Noe, et filii ejus, uxor illius, et uxores filiorum ejus cum eo. Sed et omnia animantia, jumenta, et reptilia quae reptant super terram secundum genus suum, egressa sunt de arca. Aedificavit autem Noe altare Domino, et tollens de cunctis pecoribus et volucribus mundis, obtulit holocausta super altare. Odoratusque est Dominus odorem suavitatis, et ait: Nequaquam ultra maledicam terrae propter homines. Sensus enim et cogitatio humani cordis in malum prona sunt ab adolescentia sua; non igitur ultra percutiam omnem animam viventem sicut feci. Cunctis diebus terrae, sementis et messis, frigus et aestus, aestas et hiems, nox et dies, non requiescent.

### Abraham and Lot

**Gen. 18. 1-15.** Apparuit autem ei Dominus in convalle Mambre sedenti in ostio tabernaculi sui in ipso fervore diei. Cumque elevasset oculos, apparuerunt ei tres viri stantes prope eum; quos cum vidisset, cucurrit in occursum eorum de ostio tabernaculi, et adoravit in terram. Et dixit: Domine, si inveni gratian in oculis tuis, ne transeas servum tuum! Sed afferam pauxillum aquae, et lavate pedes vestros [variant reading: laventur pedes vestri (see note on l. 618)] et requiescite sub arbore; ponamque buccellam panis, et confortate cor vestrum, postea transibitis: id circo enim declinastis ad servum vestrum. Qui dixerunt: fac ut locutus es! Festinavit Abraham in tabernaculum ad Saram, dixitque ei: Accelera, tria sata similae commisce et fac subcinericios panes. Ipse vero ad armentum cucurrit, et tulit inde vitulum tenerrimum et optimum, deditque puero; qui festinavit et coxit illum. Tulit quoque butyrum et lac, et vitulum quem coxerat, et posuit coram eis; ipse vero stabat juxta eos sub arbore. Cumque comedissent, dixerunt ad eum . . . Cui dixit: Revertens veniam ad te tempore isto, vita comite, et habebit filium Sara uxor tua. Quo audito Sara risit post ostium tabernaculi. Erant autem ambo senes, provectaeque aetatis, et desierant Sarae fieri muliebria. Quae risit occulte, dicens: Postquam consenui, et dominus meus vetulus est, voluptati operam dabo? Dixit autem Dominus ad Abraham: Quare risit Sara, dicens: Num vere paritura sum anus? Numquid Deo quidquam est difficile? juxta condictum revertar ad te hoc eodem tempore, vita comite, et habebit Sara filium. Negavit Sara dicens, Non risi, timore perterrita; Dominus autem: Non est, inquit, ita, sed risisti.

**18. 16-23.** Cum ergo surrexissent inde viri, direxerunt oculos contra Sodomam; et Abraham simul gradiebatur, deducens eos. Dixitque Dominus: Num celare potero Abraham quae gesturus sum? Cum futurus sit in gentem magnam, ac robustissimam, et benedicendae sint in illo omnes nationes terrae? Scio enim quod praecepturus sit filiis suis, et domui suae post se ut custodiant viam Domini, et faciant judicium et justitiam, ut adducat Dominus propter Abraham omnia quae locutus est ad eum. Dixit itaque Dominus: Clamor Sodomorum et Gomorrhae multiplicatus est, et peccatum eorum aggravatum est nimis. Descendam et videbo utrum clamorem qui venit ad me opere compleverint; an non est ita, ut sciam. . . . Converteruntque se inde, et abierunt Sodomam. Abraham vero adhuc stabat coram Domino. Et appropinquans ait: Numquid perdes justum cum impio? Si fuerint quinquaginta justi in civitate, peribunt simul, et non parces loco illi propter quinquaginta justos, si fuerint in eo? Absit a te, ut rem hanc facias, et occidas justum cum impio, fiatque justus sicut impius, non est hoc tuum, qui judicas omnem terram, nequaquam facies judicium hoc. Dixitque Dominus ad eum: Si invenero Sodomis quinquaginta justos in medio civitatis, dimittam omni loco propter eos. Respondensque Abraham, ait: Quia semel cœpi, loquar ad Dominum meum, cum sim pulvis et cinis. Quid si minus quinquaginta justis quinque fuerint? delebis, propter quadraginta quinque, universam urbem? Et ait: Non delebo, si invenero ibi quadraginta quinque. Rursumque locutus est as eum: Sin autem quadraginta ibi inventi fuerint, quid facies? Ait: Non percutiam propter quadraginta. Ne quaeso, inquit, indigneris Domine, si loquar: Quid si ibi inventi triginta? Respondit: Non faciam, si invenero ibi triginta. Quia semel, ait, cœpi, loquar ad Dominum meum: Quid si ibi inventi fuerint viginti? Ait: Non interficiam propter viginti. Obsecro, inquit, ne irascaris, Domine, si loquar adhuc semel: Quid si inventi fuerint ibi decem? Et dixit: Non delebo propter decem. Abiitque Dominus, postquam cessavit loqui ad Abraham: et ille reversus est in locum suum.

**19. 1-22.** Veneruntque duo Angeli Sodomam vespere, et sedente Lot in foribus civitatis. Qui cum vidisset eos, surrexit, et ivit obviam eis, adoravitque pronus in terram et dixit: Obsecro, Domini, declinate in domum pueri vestri et manere ibi: lavate pedes vestros, et mane proficiscemini in viam vestram. Qui dixerunt: Minime, sed in platea manebimus. Compulit illos oppido, ut diverterent ad eum; ingressisque domum illius fecit convivium, et coxit azyma, et comederunt. Prius autem quam irent cubitum, viri civitatis vallaverunt domum, a puero usque ad senem, omnis populus simul. Vocaveruntque Lot, et dixerunt ei: Ubi sunt viri qui introierunt ad te nocte? educ illos huc, ut cognoscamus eos. Egressus ad eos Lot, post tergum occludens ostium, ait: Nolite, quaeso, fratres mei, nolite malum hoc facere. Habeo duas filias, quae necdum cognoverunt virum; educam eas ad vos, et abutimini eis sicut vobis placuerit, dummodo viris istis nihil mali faciatis, quia ingressi sunt sub umbra culminis mei. At illi dixerunt: . . . Ingressus es, inquiunt, ut advena; numquid ut judices? te ergo ipsum magis quam hos affligemus. Vimque faciebant Lot vehementissime, jamque prope erat ut effringerent fores. Et ecce miserunt manum viri, et introduxerunt ad se Lot, clauseruntque ostium: Et eos, qui foris erant, percusserunt caecitate a minimo usque ad maximum, ita ut ostium invenire non possent. Dixerunt autem ad Lot: Habes hic quempiam tuorum? generum, aut filios, aut filias? Omnes, qui tui sunt, educ de urbe hac! Delebimus enim locum istum, eo quod increverit clamor eorum coram Domino, qui misit nos, ut perdamus illos. Egressus itaque Lot, locutus est ad generos suos qui accepturi erant filias ejus, et dixit: Surgite egredimini de loco isto, quia delebit Dominus civitatem hanc. Et visus est eis quasi ludens loqui. Cumque esset mane, cogebant eum Angeli, dicentes: Surge, tolle uxorem tuam, et duas filias quas habes; ne et tu pariter pereas in scelere civitatis. Dissimulante illo apprehenderunt manum ejus, et manum uxoris ac duarum filiarum ejus, eo quod parceret Dominus illi. Eduxeruntque eum, et posuerunt extra civitatem; ibique locuti sunt ad eum, dicentes: Salva animam tuam; noli respicere post tergum, nec stes in omni circa regione, sed in monte salvum te fac ne et tu simul pereas. Dixitque Lot ad eos . . . ne forte apprehendat me malum, et moriar. Est civitas haec juxta, ad quam possum fugere, parva, et salvabor in ea; numquid non modica est, et vivet anima mea? Dixitque ad eum: Ecce, etiam in hoc suscepi preces tuas, ut non subvertam urbem pro qua locutus es. Festina et salvare ibi.

**19. 23-28.** Sol egressus est super terram, et Lot ingressus est Segor. Igitur Dominus pluit super Sodoman et Gomorrham sulphur et ignem a Domino de cælo, et subvertit civitates has, et omnem circa regionem, universos habitatores urbium, et cuncta terrae virentia. Respiciensque uxor ejus post se, versa est in statuam salis. Abraham autem consurgens mane, ubi steterat prius eum Domino, intuitus est Sodomam et Gomorrham, et universam terram regionis illius: viditque ascendentem favillam de terra quasi fornacis fumum.

### Nebuchadnazzar and Belshazzar

**2 Chron. 36. 11-20.** . . . Sedecias . . . undecim annis regnavit in Jerusalem. Fecitque malum in oculis Domini Dei sui. . . . et universi principes sacerdotum, et populus, praevaricati sunt inique juxta universas abominationes Gentium, et polluerunt domum Domini, quam sanctificaverat sibi in Jerusalem. . . . Adduxit enim super eos regem Chaldaeorum, et interfecit juvenes eorum gladio in domo sanctuarii sui, non est misertus adolescentis, et virginis, et senis, nec decrepiti quidem, sed omnes tradidit in manibus ejus. . . . Si quis evaserat gladium, ductus in Babylonem servivit regi et filiis ejus.

**Jer. 52. 1-26.** . . . Sedecias . . . undecim annis regnavit in Jerusalem. . . . Et fecit malum in oculis Domini, juxta omnia quae fecerat Joakim. Quoniam furor Domini erat in Jerusalem et in Juda usquequo projiceret eos a facie sua; et recessit Sedecias a rege Babylonis. Factum est autem in anno nono regni ejus, in mense decimo, decima mensis, venit Nabuchodonosor rex Babylonis, ipse et omnis exercitus ejus adversus Jerusalem, et obsederunt eam, et aedificaverunt contra eam munitiones in circuitu. Et fuit civitas obsessa usque ad undecimum annum regis Sedeciae. Mense autem quarto, nona mensis obtinuit fames civitatem, et non erant alimenta populo terrae. Et dirupta est civitas, et omnes viri bellatores ejus fugerunt, exieruntque de civitate nocte per viam portae, quae est inter duos muros, et ducit ad hortum regis (Chaldaeis obsidentibus urbem in gyro) et abierunt per viam, quae ducit in eremum. Persecutus est autem Chaldaeorum exercitus regem, et apprehenderunt Sedeciam in deserto, quod est juxta Jericho, et omnis comitatus ejus diffugit ab eo. Cumque comprehendissent regem, adduxerunt eum ad regem Babylonis et locutus est ad eum judicia. Et jugulavit rex Babylonis filios Sedeciae in oculis ejus, sed et omnes principes Juda occidit in Reblatha. Et oculos Sedeciae eruit, et vinxit eum compedibus, et adduxit eum rex Babylonis in Babylonem, et posuit eum in domo carceris usque ad diem mortis ejus. . . . venit Nabuzardan princeps militae, qui stabat coram rege Babylonis in Jerusalem. Et incendit domum Domini, et domum regis, et omnes domos Jerusalem, et omnem domum magnam igni combussit. Et totum murum Jerusalem per circuitum destruxit, cunctus exercitus Chaldaeorum, qui erat cum magistro militiae. De pauperibus autem populi, et de reliquo vulgo quod remanserat in civitate, et de perfugis, qui transfugerant ad regem Babylonis, et ceteros de multitudine, transtulit Nabuzardan princeps militiae. . . . Columnas quoque aereas, quae erant in domo Domini, et bases, et mare aeneum, quod erat in domo Domini, confregerunt Chaldaei, et tulerunt omne aes eorum in Babylonem. Et lebetes, et creagras, et psalteria, et phialas, et mortariola, et omnia vasa aerea, quae in ministerio fuerant, tulerunt. Et hydrias, et thymiamateria, et urceos, et pelves, et candelabra, et mortaria, et cyathos: quotquot aurea, aurea et quotquot argentea, argentea tulit magister militiae; et columnas duas, et mare unum, et vitulos duodecim aereos, qui erant sub basibus, quas fecerat rex Salomon in domo Domini. Non erat pondus aeris omnium horum vasorum. De columnis autem, decem et octo cubiti altitudinis erant in columna una, et funiculus duodecim cubitorum circuibat eam, porro grossitudo ejus quattuor digitorum, et intrinsecus cava erat; et capitella super utramque aerea, altitudo capitelli unius quisque cubitorum; et retiacula, et malogranata super coronam in circuitu, omnia aerea. Similiter columnae secundae, et malogranata. Et fuerunt malogranata nonaginta sex dependentia: et omnia malogranata centum, retiaculis circumdabantur. . . . Tulit autem eos Nabuzardan magister militiae, et duxit eos ad regem Babylonis in Reblatha.

**Dan. 4. 27-33.** Responditque rex, et ait: Nonne haec est Babylon magna, quam ego aedificavi in domum regni, in robore fortitudinis meae, et in gloria decoris mei? Cumque sermo adhuc esset in ore regis, vox de caelo ruit: Tibi dicitur Nabuchodonosor rex: Regnum tuum transibit a te, et ab hominibus ejicient te, et cum bestis et feris erit habitatio tua: fœnum quasi bos comedes, et septem tempora mutabuntur super te, donec scias quod dominetur excelsus in regno hominum, et cuicumque voluerit, det illud. Eadem hora sermo completus est super Nabuchodonosor; et ex hominibus abjectus est, et fœnum ut bos comedit, et rore caeli corpus ejus infectum est, donec capilli ejus in similitudinem aquilarum crescerent, et ungues ejus quasi avium. . . . In ipso tempore sensus meus reversus est ad me, et ad honorem regni mei, decoremque perveni, et figura mea reversa est ad me; et optimates mei, et magistratus mei requisierunt me, et in regno meo restitutus sum, et magnificentia amplior addita est mihi.

**Dan. 5.** Baltassar rex fecit grande convivium optimatibus suis mille, et unusquisque secundum suam bibebat aetatem. Praecepit ergo jam temulentus ut afferrentur vasa aurea et argentea, quae asportaverat Nabuchodonosor pater ejus de templo, quod fuit in Jerusalem, ut biberent in eis rex, et optimates ejus, uxoresque ejus, et concubinae. Tunc allata sunt vasa aurea, et argentea, quae asportaverat de templo quod fuerat in Jerusalem, et biberunt in eis rex, et optimates ejus, uxores et concubinae illius. Bibebant vinum, et laudabant deos suos aureos et argenteos, aereos, ferreos ligneosque et lapideos. In eadem hora apparuerunt digiti, quasi manus hominis scribentis contra candelabrum in superficie parietis aulae regiae, et rex aspiciebat articulos manus scribentis. Tunc facies regis commutata est, et cogitationes ejus conturbabant eum, et compages renum ejus solvebantur, et genua ejus ad se invicem collidebantur. Exclamavit itaque rex fortiter ut introducerent magnos, Chaldaeos, et aruspices. Et proloquens rex ait sapientibus Babylonis: Quicumque legerit scripturam hanc, et interpretationem ejus manifestam mihi fecerit, purpura vestietur, et torquem auream habebit in collo, et tertius in regno meo erit. Tunc ingressi omnes sapientes regis non potuerunt nec scripturam legere, nec interpretationem indicare regi. Unde rex Baltassar satis conturbatus est, et vultus illius immutatus est; sed et optimates ejus turbabantur. Regina autem pro re, quae acciderat regi, et optimatibus ejus, domum convivii ingressa est, et proloquens ait: Rex in aeternum vive! non te conturbent cogitationes tuae, neque facies tua immutetur. Est vir in regno tuo, qui spiritum deorum sanctorum habet in se, et in diebus patris tui scientia et sapientia inventae sunt in eo; nam et rex Nebuchodonosar pater tuus principem magorum, incantatorum, Chaldaeorum et aruspicum constituit enim, pater, inquam, tuus, o rex! quia spiritus amplior, et prudentia, intelligentiaque et interpretatio somniorum, et ostensio secretorum, ac solutio ligatorum inventae sunt in eo: hoc est in Daniele, cui rex posuit nomen Baltassar. Nunc itaque Daniel vocetur, et interpretationem narrabit. Igitur introductus est Daniel coram rege. Ad quem praefatus rex ait: Tu es Daniel de filiis captivitatis Judae, quem adduxit pater meus rex de Judaea? Audivi de te quoniam spiritum deorum habeas, et scientia, intelligentiaque ac sapientia ampliores inventae sunt in te. Et nunc introgressi sunt in conspectu meo sapientes magi, ut scripturam hanc legerent, et interpretationem ejus indicarent mihi; et nequiverunt sensum hujus sermonis edicere. Porro ego audivi de te, quod possis obscura interpretari, et ligata dissolvere. Si ergo vales scripturam legere, et interpretationem ejus indicare mihi, purpura vestieris, et torquem auream circa collum tuum habebis, et tertius in regno meo princeps eris. Ad quae respondens Daniel, ait coram rege: Munera tua sint tibi, et dona domus tuae alteri da; scripturam autem legam tibi, rex, et interpretationem ejus ostendam tibi. O rex, Deus Altissimus regnum, et magnificentiam gloriam, et honorem dedit Nabuchodonozor patri tuo. Et propter magnificantiam, quam dederat ei, universi populi, tribus, et linguæ, tremebant, et metuebant eum. Quos volebat, interficiebat; et quos volebat, percutiebat; et quos volebat, exaltabat; et quos volebat, humiliabat. Quando autem elevatum est cor ejus, et spiritus illius obfirmatus est ad superbiam, depositus est de solio regni sui, et gloria ejus ablata est et a filiis hominum ejectus est, sed et cor ejus cum bestiis positum est, et cum onagris erat habitatio ejus, fœnum quoque ut bos comedebat, et rore caeli corpus ejus infectum est, donec cognosceret quod potestatem haberet Altissimus in regno hominum, et quemcumque voluerit suscitabit super illud. Tu quoque filius ejus, Baltassar, non humiliasti cor tuum, cum scires haec omnia; sed adversum Dominatorem cæli elevatus es, et vasa domus ejus allata sunt coram te, et tu, et optimates tui, et uxores tuae, et concubinae tuae vinum bibistis in eis; deos quoque argenteos et aureos et aereos, ferreos ligneosque et lapideos, qui non vident, neque audiunt, neque sentiunt, laudasti; porro Deum, qui habet flatum tuum in manu sua, et omnes vias tuas, non glorificasti. Idcirco ab eo missus est articulus manus, quae scripsit hoc, quod exaratum est. Haec est autem scriptura, quae digesta est: Mane, Thecel, Phares. Et haec est interpretatio sermonis; Mane: numeravit Deus regnum tuum, et complevit illud; Thecel: appensus es in statera, et inventus es minus habens; Phares: divisum est regnum tuum, et datum est Medis, et Persis. Tunc jubente rege indutus est Daniel purpura, et circumdata est torques aurea collo ejus, et praedicatum est de eo quod haberet potestatem tertius in regno suo. Eadem nocte interfectus est Baltassar rex Chaldaeus. Et Darius Medus successit in regnum annos natus sexaginta duos.

### PARABLE OF THE WEDDING FEAST

**Matt. 22. 1-14.** Et respondens Jesus, dixit iterum in parabolis eis, dicens: Simile factum est regnum cælorum homini regi, qui fecit nuptias filio suo, et misit servos suos vocare invitatos ad nuptias; et nolebant venire. Iterum misit alios servos, dicens: Dicite invitatis: Ecce prandium meum paravi, tauri mei, et altilia occisa sunt, et omnia parata; venite ad nuptias. Illi autem neglexerunt, et abierunt, alius in villam suam, alius vero ad negotiationem suam . . . Tunc ait servis suis: Nuptiae quidem paratae sunt, sed qui invitati erant, non fuerunt digni. Ite ergo ad exitus viarum, et quoscumque inveneritis, vocate ad nuptias. Et egressi servi ejus in vias, congregaverunt omnes, quos invenerunt, malos et bonos: et impletae sunt nuptiae discumbentium. Intravit autem rex ut videret discumbentes, et vidit ibi hominem non vestitum veste nuptiali. Et ait illi: Amice, quomodo huc intrasti non habens vestem nuptialem? At ille obmutuit. Tunc dixit rex ministris: Ligatis manibus, et pedibus ejus, mittite eum in tenebras exteriores; ibi erit fletus, et stridor dentium. Multi enim sunt vocati, pauci vero electi.

**Luke 14. 16-24.** . . . Homo quidam fecit cœnam magnam, et vocavit multos, et misit servum suum hora cœnae dicere invitatis ut venirent, quia jam parata sunt omnia. Et coeperunt simul omnes excusare. Primus dixit ei: Villam emi, et necesse habeo exire, et videre illam;

rogo te, habe me excusatum. Et alter dixit: Juga boum emi quinque, et eo probare illa; rogo te habe me excusatum. Et alius dixit: Uxorem duxi, et ideo non possum venire. Et reversus servus nuntiavit haec domino suo. Tunc iratus paterfamilias, dixit servo suo: Exi cito in plateas, et vicos civitatis: et pauperes, ac debiles, et claudos introduc huc. Et ait servus: Domine, factum est ut imperasti, et adhuc locus est. Et ait dominus servo: Exi in vias, et sepes: et compelle intrare, ut impleatur domus mea. Dico autem vobis quod nemo virorum illorum, qui vocati sunt, gustabit cœnam meam.